I would like to dedicate this volume to my father,
TED MACHOWSKI,
whose humility and love for Jesus stands
as a tremendous example before me and my children.
No man has had a greater impact on my life.

"There are many great devotionals out there. Most seem to fall short in two very key areas: theological richness and Christ-centeredness. This devotional will connect those who use it to both the historical biblical stories and the Jesus of the stories. Schools of all types, families, and local assemblies will do well to utilize this resource. This is both comprehensive and accessible."

Dr. Eric M. Mason, Lead Pastor, Epiphany Fellowship, Philadelphia, PA

"Marty Machowski has written the family devotional that many busy dads need—a user-friendly family worship guide. Each day provides Bible readings, food for thought, and talking points to use with the kids. This stuff is simple without being shallow. It is doctrinally sound, Christ-centered, and full of gospel grace and hope. What more could you want? Don't wait! Start using this book today!"

Dr. Tedd Tripp, Pastor; conference speaker; best-selling author of *Shepherding a Child's Heart*

"Again and again, and much to our disappointment, Luella and I would look for a solid, Scripture-centered, gospel-driven devotional to use with our children. This type of family worship resource was simply not available then. So, it is with much enthusiasm that I recommend *Long Story Short*. Through this tool your children will not only come to know the narrative of redemption, told in the pages of the Bible, but they will encounter the chief actor in that narrative, the Lord Jesus Christ. Again and again they will be confronted with their desperate need for his grace. What more could you want from a family devotional?"

Paul David Tripp, President, Paul Tripp Ministries; pastor; seminary professor; best-selling author of eleven books

"What a good idea...a family devotional book that creatively takes your kids through the Bible one step at a time. Thank you, Marty, for this terrific idea. It's a must-buy for every Christian home."

Dr. Robert Wolgemuth, Speaker; best-selling author of nineteen books

"In *Long Story Short,* Marty Machowski provides what my wife and I needed when we were struggling to find good tools to disciple our young children. We got by, but this resource would have helped us so much. I envy the parents who will have it available to them. It is simple, interactive, and faithful to Scripture. It avoids the pitfalls of moralism that is prevalent in much of the children's Bible literature today. Marty insists that you and your children meet Jesus and see the gospel of grace in every story. I can't recommend this resource enough."

Dr. Timothy S. Lane, Executive Director, Christian Counseling & Educational Foundation; coauthor of *How People Change* and *Relationships: A Mess Worth Making*

"*Long Story Short* is a wonderful concept and a practical, gospel-focused resource for family worship. It will help parents consistently give their children the Word of Life as they continually point them to the One who is Life. I also recommend it for grandparents and teachers—for all who love children and want to show them the gospel story in all of Scripture."

Susan Hunt, Author; mother; grandmother; pastor's wife; former director of Women's Ministries for the Presbyterian Church in America

"Marty has his pulse on the hectic rhythm of modern family life in this new resource for deepening a family's encounter with God through Scripture. His simple pattern of breathing in—with remembering and discovering Scripture—and breathing out, through talking about it, echoes the rich patterns of our tradition in easily accessible terms. As families disintegrate around us, this guide will help families be bound closer together through a common story and language of faith. Remember it, think about it, talk about it, and pray about it. Children will benefit from not only the content of this book, but the simple pattern of daily encounters can be a pattern for godly decision making as adults."

Dr. Philip D. Schroeder, Church Consultant; associate director of Connectional Ministries, North Georgia Conference of the UMC; author of *Children's Sermons for the Revised Common Lectionary: Using the 5 Senses to Tell God's Story*

"As a parent I have tried many different resources for devotions with my children. *Long Story Short* is by far the best material available for parents who want a brief, biblical, interesting, and gospel-centered approach to taking children through the Scriptures. The kids love it! And I love it! Marty Machowski has created a resource that will help parents fulfill the biblical obligation of Ephesians 6:4!"

Kenneth Maresco, Executive Pastor, Covenant Life Church, Gaithersburg, MD

Long Story Short

Ten-Minute Devotions
to Draw Your Family to God

Old Testament

Marty Machowski

New
Growth
Press

www.newgrowthpress.com

New Growth Press, Greensboro, NC 27429

Cover Art: A. E. O. Macha, Philadelphia, PA
Cover Design: Tandem Creative, Tom Temple, tandemcreative.net
Typesetting: Lisa Parnell, Thompson's Station, TN

ISBN-13: 978-1-935273-81-3
ISBN-10: 1-935273-81-7

                    Library of Congress Cataloging-in-Publication Data
Machowski, Martin, 1963–
    Long story short : ten-minute devotions to draw your family to God / Martin Machowski.
            p.   cm.
    ISBN-13: 978-1-935273-81-3 (alk. paper)
    ISBN-10: 1-935273-81-7 (alk. paper)
    1. Bible. O. T.—Devotional literature. 2. Families—Prayers and devotions. I. Title.

BS1151.55.M33 2010
242'.645—dc22

                                                                    2010023154

Printed in Canada

17 16 15 14 13 12 11 10   1 2 3 4 5

FSC
Mixed Sources
Product group from well-managed
forests and other controlled sources
Cert no. SW-COC-000952
www.fsc.org
© 1996 Forest Stewardship Council

Table of Contents

Foreword

By Dave Harvey

One of my kids just got home. It was an evening of pizza, with a little soul surgery on the side—compliments of one Marty Machowski, the guy who wrote this book. My wife Kimm and I discovered a long time ago that raising teens is a community project—which is what brings me back to Marty.

Marty loves my family. He's loved them since the day each of them was born. He's loved my family as their children's ministry pastor at our church, where he has labored for the past twenty-two years. He's loved my wife and kids by being a friend and counselor to me, as I led Covenant Fellowship Church for almost two decades. And he loves them now by producing this extraordinary project.

But here's the thing: he loves your family too. In fact, he values them so much that he wants to connect something he treasures to the family you love. Marty wants to take the Bible and put it in the hands of parents… so they in turn can train their kids. But I'm not talking about generic Bible stories with moral lessons attached. I'm talking about showing kids the glorious gospel from every page of the Bible. It takes a special gift to be able to do that. Just check out a few of the lessons. You'll see—Marty Machowski has that gift.

Here's why you and your kids need this material:

It's proven. In other words, Marty didn't just go away on a personal retreat and come up with these lessons. This material has been field-tested over many years, in a growing number of churches. It's been picked apart and polished; now it's being published. That's a serious gift to the next generation.

It's sound. Marty is not first a children's ministry director. He is a pastor. That means he knows the challenges of kids and their families. Marty understands that spiritual health flows from sound doctrine. So he has taken great pains to make sure that Scripture is carefully interpreted and plainly applied. But believe me, these lessons are not dry or disconnected. They follow the storyline of Scripture right to the Savior.

It's simple. Just think about it: straight-forward and relatable lessons for ten minutes a day, five days a week. Over time, that adds up. And because it's the Bible, it will be a catalyst for change in children's lives.

It was wise of you to pick up this book. Now let me encourage you to start the journey with your kids. Marty has given us the tool. Let's use it to help build the next generation!

Acknowledgments

As this devotional goes to print, I am deeply thankful to Dave Harvey for his encouragement to develop and publish this material and for his support in writing the foreword for this book. I would also like to thank the pastors of Covenant Fellowship Church for their example, which has taught me how to live out the gospel in ministry and life, and the members of our church for their encouragement.

The completion of this devotional would not have been possible if not for the faithful service of all those who participated in the editing and production of the manuscript through the years of its development. Bill Patton, Michelle Janes, Sarajane Orlando, and Janel Feldman all helped in the early editing process, while my wife Lois and Jared Mellinger read through my draft manuscript. I would also like to thank Charity Campbell for her administration and skills so helpful behind the scenes.

I am very grateful for the folks at New Growth for their investment and commitment to provide solid biblical resources for families and churches. Finally, I would like to thank Jeff Gerke for his skillful editing work to help transform deep biblical truth into easy-to-understand weekly studies.

Introduction for Parents

A few years ago, to my wife's great delight, her father gave her the family heirloom photo albums. We're not talking snapshots of Disney World held in vinyl pages. These hundred-year-old photos were carefully bound in two deeply embossed gilded leather albums. Even guests who had parted the pages of these regal books had stood in awe of the history represented in the sepia tone portraits of her great-grandfathers, aunts, and uncles. Some family heirlooms are quite valuable, like a fine antique piece of furniture, yet families wouldn't think of selling them. They safeguard them to be passed to the next generation.

In the same way, every Christian parent holds another treasure to pass along. It is the most important treasure we steward, one of surpassing value: the gospel of Jesus Christ.

The apostle Paul spoke of the treasure of the gospel when he told the Ephesians:

> And God raised us up with Christ and seated us with him in the heavenly realms in Christ Jesus, in order that in the coming ages he might show the incomparable riches of his grace, expressed in his kindness to us in Christ Jesus. (Ephesians 2:6–7 NIV)

"Incomparable riches" is the way Paul described the gospel of grace. Is there anything of greater value we have to pass along?

Like our family treasures, we can't take the gospel for granted, but need to safeguard it and deliver it unaltered to the next generation. Just think: God has entrusted us

parents with the privilege of passing this most valuable truth to the next generation! The message of salvation through faith alone, in Christ's atoning sacrifice alone, by sovereign grace alone, cannot be assumed.

A man-centered gospel is always threatening to supplant the cross-centered gospel we read in the Bible. But if we trade Jesus, who bore our sins and received the wrath of God, for a Jesus who is merely a good example, we don't have the same gospel. If we remove a call to repentance and replace it with an invitation to be God's friend, we're not passing on the treasure of the gospel in accordance with the Scriptures.

So we, as parents, must ensure that the gospel we pass on is the authentic diamond we were handed, not a pretty glass imitation. We don't want to pass on merely the worldly knowledge that will *inform* their lives; we want to pass on the biblical truth that can *transform* their lives. Though teachers in school or church can help us, passing on the truth of God's Word is our unique responsibility as parents.

Getting Started

This devotional is written to present a biblical gospel from cover to cover. It is intended to aid you in passing this treasure on to your children.

Few Christian parents would disagree with the importance of passing on the truth of the gospel to their children, yet we live in a busy world where our lives are filled with distractions. Just getting all the tasks of the day checked off our list can leave any parent exhausted. It is easy to see how, though we have a desire to pass on the truth of the gospel, we can't find the time. Schedules collide, there is homework and yard work and dishes and laundry, the car's oil should be changed, there are phone calls to make…and before you know it, everyone is getting to bed late again. On top of that, our sinful natures can think of a hundred reasons why any given time is not a good time for family Bible study.

That is where I hope *Long Story Short* will help. The Bible can seem like a long story, but when you break it down into short devotions, teaching the Bible to your family is easy to do. The goal of this devotional is to, day by day, pass on a clear gospel message showing our children how every story in the Bible points forward or back to the gospel of Jesus Christ and God's story of salvation.

You won't find a more important focus for a family devotional than a daily highlighting of the gospel of grace. Why? Simply put, the gospel "is the power of God for salvation to everyone who believes" (Romans 1:16). Clever stories and good moral lessons may entertain and even help our children, but the gospel will transform our children. The gospel is deep enough to keep the oldest and wisest parents learning and growing all their lives, yet simple enough to transform the heart of your first grader who has just begun to read.

All You Need Is Ten Minutes a Day!

If you can find ten minutes a day, you can use this tool to pass on the most valuable treasure the world has ever known. Contrary to what many believe, daily family Bible study need not take a lot of time. God can use a short, simple family devotion, consistently practiced over time, to yield more fruit in the lives of our children than we realize; and a quick daily devotion is not as easily derailed by our busy schedules. Each day, as the gospel is presented, God is at work.

Our hope in God is to see our children reading their Bibles and having devotions on their own, not because they have to, but because they want to. The truth of God's Word brings us to Christ and is effective to sustain us and help us to grow all of our days. There is simply no greater delight for Christian parents than watching the Spirit of God guiding their children through faith-filled study of God's Word. No earthly treasure compares.

God's Word, when hidden in our hearts as children, is used again and again in our lives later on. The Spirit of God will bring it back to our minds to help us in our walk with God and to enable us to encourage others we meet along the way.

Every family can find a few minutes in the daily routine. Some families gather for their devotional at the start of their day; others try the dinnertime approach. Lay the devotional book and your Bible(s) beside your plate on the dinner table. As soon as everyone is finished eating, take ten minutes for family devotions. *Long Story Short* does the work for you! All you need to do is read the passage of Scripture for the day, follow that with the short commentary, and then ask the listed questions. Finish it all up by inviting one of your children to pray.

It's Simple to Use

Long Story Short is a family devotional program designed to explain God's plan of salvation from Genesis through Revelation. Volume 1 covers the Old Testament and volume 2, the New Testament. Together, they provide three years of family devotions! For every Old Testament lesson, your family will learn the answer to the question, "How does this passage point forward to Jesus?" For every New Testament lesson, the question is, "Where is the gospel?" Since the Bible is the story of God's unfolding plan of redemption, every passage of Scripture points forward or back to Calvary.

Each week starts off with a creative activity, exercise, or bit of trivia to introduce the passage. On days one through four you review a portion of the week's Scripture passage. Special attention is given on day three to connect the current passage to the gospel. On day four we've added a question for your older children to ask you, and on day five you and your family will investigate a Bible passage from the book of Psalms or an excerpt from one of the prophets to discover how the passage points forward to Christ.

This devotional book can be used differently depending on the ages of your children. Since this program is rich in gospel truth, it works for families with children of all ages. Take a look at the following categories to find the one that best describes your family.

If Your Children Are Preschoolers

The best time to start consistent daily devotions is with children in the four-through six-year-old age group. *Long Story Short* works wonderfully with children in this age group. Don't be fooled by your five-year-old's inability to answer the listed questions. Children at this age can often understand much more than they can express. Consider some of the following techniques:

:: Feel free to skip the discussion questions and just read the answers. The questions for each of the day's devotions have answers in complete sentences. Consider using the devotional time as a familiarization of the Bible this first time through. If your child starts the program at age four, he or she will finish three years later at age seven with a tremendous foundation of gospel truth that has accumulated day by day and week by week.

:: You can also skip over the creative introductions and save them for a second time through when your children reach grade school.

:: Try rephrasing the questions to make them very simple or by making them multiple choice.

:: Another parent can be the helper, actually whispering the answers to your children. This might sound dishonest, but in reality it is the repetition that helps them remember the material.

:: You can make up simple questions for your toddlers yourself. Basic questions about the characters such as, "Who was the man who led Israel out of Egypt?" are great for younger children.

If Your Children Are in Grade School

Elementary school age is the time to call for your children to participate with you in family devotions. Some children might be reluctant at first, but persistence soon pays off. Even the most challenging child is able to handle ten minutes a day. Remember, day by day they are being exposed to the gospel truth God uses to transform lives. The creative introductions at the beginning of each week will pique the interest of your children. Read them yourself a day or so ahead to give you time to gather any objects needed for the lesson.

Start by making sure all your children have a Bible. You might have toddlers mixed in with your grade school students. That's okay. Just have them open up their toddler Bibles to the right page (that means anywhere close). Read through the passage for the day. On days when the passage is shorter, try having your older children read. (Remember, labored reading won't encourage them or the others, so wait until your children can read well before passing that responsibility to them.) If you have toddlers in the mix, let them come along for the ride but don't cater to their lower learning level. All day long they are learning by watching the older children in their daily routines. They learn about God the same way.

Read the passage, the short paragraph summary, and then move to the questions. Here are a few ideas to consider to make your discussion time work well:

:: After asking a question to your family, look back in the passage and tell them which verse to look for to find the answer.

:: Encourage all attempts to answer the question, even if they miss the answer.

:: Consider inviting children to add to their brothers' and sisters' answers. Sometimes children who are reluctant to start an answer can add to an answer to expand it.

:: Don't be afraid to call on your older children. If they seem stumped even after you tell them which verse they can find the answer in, give them clues.

Finish by asking your children to pray. Help your youngest children by having them repeat after you. As your children grow older, encourage them to pray on their own. Always help them along if they get stuck. Soon, they will be praying on their own without your help.

If Your Children Are Moving out of Grade School

The *Long Story Short* program works well with older grade school children and young teens too! They set a wonderful example for their younger brothers and sisters in answering the questions and even leading the devotions themselves.

If you have a teen who thinks the Bible studies are too easy or boring, try this exercise. Open up randomly to one of the devotions and start asking him (or her) a few questions. He is sure to find out, like we all have in our lives, that everybody needs to review.

Try some of the following ideas with your older children:

:: Use your older children to lead the creative introductions at the beginning of each week with their younger brothers and sisters.

:: Try holding your older children in reserve, allowing the younger children to answer first. Then have the older children amplify the answers their younger siblings gave.

:: Pair up a younger child with an older child and allow the older child to help give the answer to his younger brother or sister. This might sound like cheating, but the value is in hearing and remembering the details of the gospel over and over.

:: Consider where your children are in their lives on a given day. Feel the freedom to add a more subjective question to draw them out about how the passage relates to their lives personally. Questions like, "What does God want to teach you from reading this passage?" can be used for any lesson.

:: If your mix of children includes a teen, assign him (or her) to lead the devotions once a week. Encourage him to read the passage and the devotion a day in advance to become familiar with what is being asked. If you pull him aside later and offer some encouragement, he will be all the more eager to lead devotions again.

Remember, the devotional is designed to work through simple repetition over time. If you skip a day, that's okay, just pick up where you left off.

Reaping the Harvest

One day my wife, Lois, and I will hand the family photo albums we received from her father down to one of our children and, with them, pass along a portion of our family legacy. That day will be sweeter indeed if the life of the child we pass them to has been transformed by the gospel. Though we know we can't save our children, we *can* keep them soaking in the gospel. And as we do, we have this confidence: God is able and willing to save them.

As you faithfully lead your children through the devotions in this book, don't just read it as history. It is history, but it is so much more! Lead with expectation that the God of history will visit with your family. Wait and watch to see what God will do! Cling with faith to this hope, that through the gospel proclamation in your home, the Holy Spirit will regenerate the hearts of your children and lead them to faith alone, in Christ alone, by grace alone!

Week 1

God Creates the World

Pick a leaf off a plant and show it to your children. Ask them what it is and what it tells us. Draw them out for a short while. Hold the leaf in your fingers and say, "One little leaf is all we need to know that God is real. Paul tells us in the book of Romans that everyone can see God's power and knows that he is real by looking at the things God made. Every plant leaf is made up of millions of cells that use sunlight and water to make sugar for the plant to use for food! This week you will learn about God's marvelous creation."

DAY ONE

Picture It

If you brought home a goldfish, how would you set up the aquarium? What color gravel would you use for the bottom? Perhaps you would put in a few underwater plants, and stack up a larger rock or two so the goldfish had a little place to hide. You could create a world for your goldfish and set it up any way you want.

That's what God did for us when he created our world. He made mountains, rivers, trees, and everything else. The first part of the Bible tells the story of how God created the world we live in special, just for us!

 Read Genesis 1:1–2.

Think about It Some More

Who was the only one around before the world began? That's right, God was alive before the creation of the world. In fact, God has always been alive. That means God doesn't have a birthday. No matter how far back in time you go, God was there. He is the one who decided to create our world. Way back then, there was no world at all. God is so powerful that he was able to make everything we can see out of nothing at all!

Imagine what it would have been like to watch God create our earth out of nothing! God is amazing. There is only one God and nobody can do the things he can do.

Talk about It

:: What did God use to create the world? *(God didn't use anything at all. He made it out of nothing by his mighty power.)*

:: Can we make anything out of nothing? *(No, only God can create something out of nothing.)*

:: If you could make something out of nothing, what would you make? *(Help your children use their imaginations to think of something. Then explain to them that God used his imagination to make all that we see.)*

:: How can we thank God for creating our world? *(We can thank God by taking care of what he has given us, praising him for all that he made, and obeying his commands.)*

 ## Pray about It

Praise the Lord for creating such a beautiful world for us to live in.

DAY TWO

Remember It

What do you remember about yesterday's story? What do you think is going to happen today?

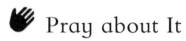 Read Genesis 1:3–25.

Think about It Some More

Did you notice that God created the stars and planets and everything in the earth and waters—just by speaking? Everything God wanted, he commanded with his voice and it appeared and came to life! When God said, "Let there be light," light suddenly appeared. That is true for everything you can see that is a part of the earth.

Nobody else can create things just by speaking. Go ahead and try if you think you can. But you will soon find that no matter how loud you shout, you won't be able to create anything the way God does.

Talk about It

:: See if you can count how many times God created things by speaking in our story. *(Parents, help your children find all the times the words "God said" occur in today's Bible passage.)*

:: What is your favorite thing God made by speaking? *(Parents, help your children look back at the passage, or list the items God made if your children are too young to read.)*

:: Did you know that God has given us the ability to create too? For instance, painters create beautiful paintings. And people can make things like houses and cars out of all that God created. But the way we create is different from how God creates. Can you tell the difference between how we make things and how God made things? *(We cannot create by speaking—we have to use our hands or some part of our body—and everything we make has to be made from something else.)*

 Pray about It

Thank God for the way he can create by the command of his voice.

DAY THREE

Connect It to Jesus

Can anyone guess how our story is about Jesus or points forward to him?

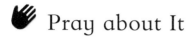 Read Colossians 1:15–17.

Think about It Some More

Although the Bible was written by men, God inspired the words they wrote. That means he was working by his Spirit while they were writing to help them know what they should write. That is how the apostle Paul could write about God creating the world even though it happened before he was born.

In today's Bible reading, Paul tells us something about God's creation that we didn't know before. He tells us that God the Son, Jesus, is the one who was doing the creating. It was Jesus who made the world we live in. Jesus created everything we see around us. Paul said it was created by him and it was all created for him.

Talk about It

:: God made so many amazing animals. Which animals do you like most?

:: If you were in charge of the creation, instead of Jesus being in charge, is there anything you would do differently? Would you put a lake right outside your home? Would you make it snow more often where you live? *(Parents, help the kids get creative here. Then remind them that God gave us creativity as one of the ways he made us like him.)*

:: Why doesn't the moon fall apart? How do the stars stay floating in the sky? Here is a hint: God gives us the answer in verse 17. Who does the Bible say is holding all the creation together? *(Verse 17 tells us that Jesus is holding the whole world together.)*

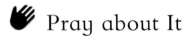 Pray about It

Thank Jesus for creating our world and holding it all together.

DAY FOUR

Remember It

What has God been teaching you this week through our Bible story?

 Read Genesis 1:26–31.

Think about It Some More

After creating our world—with all its plants and animals, the sun, the moon, and all the millions of stars—God said that everything he had made was good. But he wasn't finished yet. God saved the best part of his creating for last.

The most special part of his creation was to form man "in his own image." That means man would be able to do some of the things only God could do and be similar to God. After creating man, God put him in charge of all of God's creation and told him to rule over it. Because man was made in God's image he could do things that none of the other animals could do. He could talk with God, worship God, and have a friendship with God.

Talk about It

> ● ● KIDS, ask your parents to tell you all the ways they can think of that
> ● ● show how men and women are different from animals. See if you can
> think of some they miss.

(Man was made in God's image and is the only part of the creation that can talk with God, worship him, and have a relationship with him. Man can also create things like painting, machines, and music.)

:: Before God made man, he said that everything he had made was good. What did God say after he made man? *(Parents, if your children can't find the answer—"very good"—have them look in verse 31.)*

:: What is one very important way in which we are not like God? *(We were created; God is the creator. God has been around forever, but we have a starting point.)*

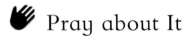 Pray about It

Thank God for making us like him so we can pray and worship him.

DAY FIVE

Discover It

Today is the day we look at a different Bible passage—from the book of Psalms or one of the prophets—to see what we can learn from it about Jesus or our salvation.

 Read Psalm 1.

Think about It Some More

At first, you might not think Psalm 1 points to Jesus, but take another look. Psalm 1 is about a man who lives for God all the time. It says this man delights in God's Word in the daytime and in the nighttime. While we all should try to live this way, there is only one man who ever lived this way every day of his whole life. That man is Jesus, the one who created our earth. Even when God changes our hearts and we try to follow God, we don't do it all the time. We fail. But Jesus never failed.

Talk about It

:: What does Psalm 1 tell us we should do all day and all night? *(We should delight in God's Word.)*

:: What does it mean to delight in God's Word? *(To help your children understand the word* delight, *ask them what they think it means to delight in ice cream. To delight in ice cream you need to eat it up, love its flavor, and wish you could have some more. That is what we do with God's Word. We read it, enjoy what it says, and we can't wait to read it some more.)*

:: Can children who can't read delight in God's Word? *(Yes, if they listen carefully when their parents read the Bible, they can delight in God's Word too.)*

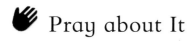 Pray about It

Ask God to help each person in your family to delight in God's Word.

Week 2

God Creates Man

Ask your children to put their fingers on their necks to feel their pulse. Ask them what they are feeling. Then ask who is causing their heart to beat. Say, "We don't have to tell our hearts to beat; they do it automatically. God created our bodies as amazing machines! But we are more than machines. God made us in his image. We can love, create, sacrifice for others, write words, and tell stories—things the animals cannot do! This week you will learn more about how God made man very special."

DAY ONE

Picture It

What if you could make something out of clay and then blow on it and it would come to life? Imagine forming a little dog, giving it two little eyes, a mouth, and a little nose. Then you form the legs, give it a tail to wag, and stand it up on its new legs. Now comes the best part: you blow right on its nose and as soon as you do, your new little pet jumps and starts barking.

What would you bring to life if you could? In today's story, we'll learn exactly how God created man! *(Optional activity: give your son or daughter a ball of modeling clay to make his or her own pet creation, then help him or her see it is hopeless to blow life into it.)*

 Read Genesis 2:4–14.

Think about It Some More

Last week we read in the first chapter of Genesis how God created man in his image. Here in chapter two it tells the story again, only this time it gives us the slow-motion, instant-replay version of how God created man.

We also learn that God made a beautiful place for man to live—a garden called Eden. Two very special trees grew in this garden. One was called "the tree of life" and the other "the tree of the knowledge of good and evil." Remember the tree of the knowledge of good and evil. Something terrible is going to happen with that tree.

Talk about It

:: Can you retell the story of how God created the man? *(Parents, have one of your children tell the story, while you or another child acts it out.)*

:: Who do you think is still missing from the creation? *(Woman is missing. God has not created her yet.)*

:: Do you know the man's name? *(The man's name is Adam. We will see that in tomorrow's Bible story. Did you know that Adam is God's word for man? They are the same word.)*

 Pray about It

Praise the Lord for how amazing he is to create a living man from dust.

DAY TWO

Remember It

What do you remember about yesterday's story? What do you think is going to happen today?

 Read Genesis 2:15–23.

Think about It Some More

God placed Adam in a wonderful garden and filled it with fruit trees. But God made a rule: Adam could not eat from one of the trees, the tree of the knowledge of good and evil. He warned Adam that if he ate from that tree he would die.

Adam was all alone in the garden, so God made animals to keep him company. When God brought the animals to Adam, Adam named each one. But none of them could talk or sing or worship God like Adam could. He still felt alone. Out of all the animals Adam couldn't find a partner to be his helper.

That was when God did something very special: he put Adam to sleep and made woman out of Adam's rib. God made the woman so she would be the perfect partner for Adam.

Talk about It

:: Do you remember how God made man? Was it different from the way he made woman? *(Adam was made from the dust, but the woman—she isn't called Eve until after the fall—was created out of Adam's rib.)*

:: Why do you think the woman would be a better helper for man than the other animals would be? *(Parents, you can get real creative here. Imagine the man dancing with an elephant or eating breakfast with a horse or having a rabbit help him plant and care for the trees in the garden.)*

:: What do we call it today when God brings a man and woman together to start a family? *(It is called marriage. When God brought Eve to Adam it was the very first marriage.)*

 Pray about It

Thank God for making the special women and girls in your life.

DAY THREE

Connect It to Jesus

Can anyone guess how our story is about Jesus or points forward to him?

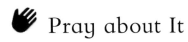 Read 1 Corinthians 15:45–49.

Think about It Some More

I'll bet you didn't know that Jesus was also called Adam. That's because Jesus came to correct the mistakes the first Adam made.

It is kind of hard to understand, but the first Adam didn't do so well. He disobeyed God and sinned. We will learn more about that next week.

Jesus came as the second Adam to give obeying God another try. If Jesus could obey God, he would be able to take away the sin that Adam brought into the world. He was kind of Adam 2.0 and this second version of Adam did a great job. Jesus lived a perfect life and didn't disobey God even once!

Talk about It

:: This Bible passage reminds us that Adam came from the dust. Where does it say Jesus, the second Adam, came from? *(Jesus came from heaven.)*

:: God created Adam and expected him to obey God's command. What was the command God gave him? *(Hint: it's in Genesis 2:16–17.)*

:: Jesus came to earth to do God's work too. What was Jesus' work? *(Jesus' work was to obey God in everything. Jesus also died on the cross to take the punishment for the sins of men.)*

 Pray about It

Thank God that he made Jesus into the second Adam. Thank him that Jesus had the same choice Adam had, but Jesus made the right choice and did not disobey.

DAY FOUR

Remember It

What has God been teaching you this week through our Bible story?

 Read Genesis 2:22–25.

Think about It Some More

When God made the woman and brought her to Adam, Adam was very excited. Finally he had found the helper he had been looking for. The moment Adam saw her, he could tell she was the perfect partner for him. Adam and the woman, whom Adam later named Eve, came together to make the very first marriage.

Did you know that God is the one who invented marriage and he did it when he created the woman and brought her to the man? Every time a man and a woman are married they are following the pattern God created all the way back in the garden of Eden.

Talk about It

> KIDS, ask your parents how excited they were on their wedding day.

(Parents, think back to what it was like to walk down the aisle or finally see your bride or groom all dressed up, and communicate that excitement to your children.)

:: What do we call it when a man and a woman promise to be together for life? *(A marriage or a wedding.)*

:: Why was the woman the perfect helper for Adam? *(She could talk with him, be his friend, help him with the work of the garden, and worship God with him.)*

> KIDS, ask your mom and dad what the perfect partner for you might be like someday.

(Everyone should look to marry someone who loves God and talks with him, just like Adam and Eve both talked with God.)

Pray about It

Thank God that he created marriage. Pray that if God calls you to marriage, he would lead you to someone who loves and worships God.

DAY FIVE

Discover It

Today we look at a passage from a psalm or one of the prophets to see what we can learn from it about Jesus.

 Read Isaiah 9:6.

Think about It Some More

Isaiah spoke of a very special child. The child would be a boy who would be in charge of the whole world. He would have some special names: Wonderful Counselor, Mighty God, Everlasting Father, and Prince of Peace.

Only one boy who was ever born was called these names—Jesus. God helped Isaiah see this long before Jesus was even born.

Talk about It

:: Can you remember why Jesus had to come and how that connects to our story about Adam? *(Parents, give them a hint that it has to do with Adam disobeying God's commands.)*

:: Do you remember the story of how Jesus was born? *(Parents, see how much your kids can remember about the birth of Christ.)*

:: Isaiah gives us several names to describe Jesus. See if you can remember some of the things Jesus did, and add another name to Isaiah's list to describe Jesus. *(Help your kids remember some of the things Jesus did. He was a healer, Savior of the world, giver of life, friend of sinners, etc. All of these can be used as names to describe Jesus.)*

Pray about It

Thank God for sending Jesus to save us from our sin so we could be adopted into God's family.

Week 3

Adam and Eve Disobey God

Ask your children for a show of hands, "Who has disobeyed at least once in their life?" Then ask them how they learned to disobey.

This is an interesting question with an amazing truth. Say, "Children don't have to be taught to disobey. They know how to do it naturally! Ever since Adam and Eve disobeyed God, all men and women and boys and girls are born sinners. This week, we will learn where our disobedience began—in the garden of Eden."

DAY ONE

Picture It

Imagine walking in a garden and noticing a snake wrapped around a tree branch. Although you might feel afraid and want to run away, you might also be very curious and want a closer look. Let's say you step closer and, when you do, the serpent starts to talk to you. This is what happened in today's Bible story.

 Read Genesis 3:1–6.

Think about It Some More

From the moment God created Adam and Eve, he blessed them with wonderful things. He placed them in a peaceful garden filled with fruit trees. He gave them to each other as the first husband and wife to share all that he created and to work the garden together.

The best part of all was that God was with Adam and Eve in the garden. But Adam and Eve sinned against God by doing the one thing God had told them not to do: they ate fruit from the forbidden tree. Instead of obeying God, they disobeyed and did what they wanted to do. That is what we call *sin*.

Talk about It

:: What is sin? *(Sin is doing what you want instead of what God tells you in the Bible to do.)*

:: Does everybody sin? *(Starting with Adam and Eve, everyone has sinned, except for Jesus.)*

:: Can you think of a way you sin? *(Encourage children to give personal examples such as, "I sometimes fight with my sister," or "I get angry and disrespectful when I have to do something I don't want to do." The point is to help them to see that we all sin against God and disobey his commands.)*

Pray about It

Take time to pray for each other, asking God to help each person in your family follow his Word.

DAY TWO

Remember It

What do you remember from our story yesterday? What do you think is going to happen today?

 Read Genesis 3:7–19.

Think about It Some More

God told Adam and Eve that if they ate the forbidden fruit they would die. But after they disobeyed, they were still alive. Although it might seem like nothing happened on the outside because they were still alive, something died on the inside. Instead of loving and enjoying God, Adam and Eve became afraid of God and hid. Their friendship with God was broken because they disobeyed. That is why they turned away from God and hid. And they did grow older and, many years later, they did die.

Talk about It

:: Why was Adam afraid? *(He heard God walking in the garden and he knew he had disobeyed God, so he hid.)*

:: Did you ever try to hide something you did wrong? *(Parents, help your children remember something from their lives or share an incident from your own life.)*

:: Why is sin so bad? *(Sin is disobeying God's command. When we sin, we are saying we don't want to do what God commands. That makes us an enemy of God.)*

Pray about It

Ask God to help you confess your sins and not try to hide them.

DAY THREE

Connect It to Jesus

Can anyone guess how our story is about Jesus or points forward to him?

 Read 1 Corinthians 15:20–22.

Think about It Some More

God was not surprised by Adam and Eve's sin. God knew all along that they would sin and even before it happened, God had a wonderful plan to make things right again. God the Father would send his only Son Jesus to earth as a baby. Jesus would grow up as a man like Adam, but instead of disobeying God, Jesus would obey him every day all the time. Because of his perfect life Jesus could take our punishment so we could be forgiven and have peace with God.

Talk about It

:: Paul wrote that death came through one man: Adam. Can you guess who the one man is who brought life and peace back with God? *(Jesus is the one who brought us life and peace.)*

:: What makes Jesus different from the other men who were born? *(Jesus wasn't just a man; he was also God. Because he was a man he could take our punishment on the cross, but because he was God and didn't sin he rose again from the grave, winning a victory over death.)*

 Pray about It

Thank God for sending his Son Jesus as a man to take our punishment on the cross.

DAY FOUR

Remember It

What has God been teaching you this week through our Bible story?

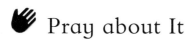 Read Genesis 3:20–24.

Think about It Some More

When God gives us something good that we don't deserve we call that *grace*. When God holds back his punishment we call that *mercy*. God showed Adam and Eve mercy and grace. They disobeyed his only rule, but instead of killing them, he killed animals and used their skins to clothe Adam and Eve.

When God killed the animals to make clothes for Adam and Eve he was pointing forward to a day when he would send Jesus to die to cover our sin so we could be forgiven.

Talk about It

:: Do you remember what grace is? *(When God gives us something good we don't deserve, that is grace.)*

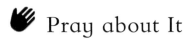 KIDS, ask your parents to tell you some ways God shows his grace to your family.

:: How is Jesus' death on the cross like the death of the animals whose skins covered Adam and Eve? *(Jesus' death covers the sins of all who trust in him. The animals point forward to what Jesus would one day do.)*

 Pray about It

Thank God for his wonderful mercy and grace.

DAY FIVE

Discover It

Today we look at a passage from a psalm or one of the prophets to see what we can learn from it about Jesus.

Read Isaiah 9:7.

Think about It Some More

This week we learned that the animal skins with which God covered Adam and Eve point forward to Jesus covering our sin by his death on the cross. In this passage, the prophet Isaiah writes about Jesus long before his birth.

When Isaiah tells us about a king who will sit on the throne of King David in righteousness forever, he is talking about Jesus. (*Righteousness* is a big word that talks about Jesus always being right and doing what is good. Jesus never sinned.) David was the man who killed the giant named Goliath and went on to become a great king—but still, David sinned. Isaiah speaks of a day when a king will rule in righteousness (without sin). Many kings reigned on the throne of David after him, but there was only one who never sinned and who lives forever. That king is Jesus!

Talk about It

Do you think you could be a king who reigns with perfect righteousness? *(Parents, help your children see that they all are sinners and even if they sinned one time they would be disqualified, if it weren't for Christ.)*

Could this passage be a prophecy about any king in the line of David other than Jesus? *(No. Every king in the line of David before Jesus died; not one of them was righteous forever.)*

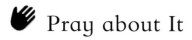 ## Pray about It

Ask God to help you live for our great king Jesus by obeying God's Word every day.

Week 4

Cain and Abel

Pull a ten-dollar bill out of your wallet or purse (any size bill will work). Ask your children what they would think if you gave it to one of them to buy a big ice cream cone, but you didn't give enough money for ice cream to everyone. (If you are leading one child, pretend she is with a group of friends.) Ask, "How would you feel if you were left out?" Tell them you are thinking of a word that begins with the letter "E." See if they can guess the word "envy" and then tell you what it means. Say, "This week you will learn what can happen when a person rejects God's grace and lives with envy in their heart."

DAY ONE

Picture It

Imagine that you and a brother or sister are both asked to clean your rooms. Your brother or sister works very hard for a whole hour. You, on the other hand, would rather be outside playing, so you pick up a few things but don't really clean your room. Later, when your parents come to check your work, they are pleased with your brother or sister's room, but they are not too happy with yours.

How would you feel if they let your brother or sister go outside and play, but they said you had to stay inside because you didn't do what they asked? Wouldn't you feel upset that you couldn't go out and a little bit sad that you didn't do a better job when you had the chance.

This is how Cain, one of Adam's sons, felt in our story today.

 Read Genesis 4:1–5.

Think about It Some More

Both Cain and Abel gave a part of what they grew or raised to God as a way to thank and worship him. When we offer back to God some of what he gave us, we call it an offering.

Did you notice that Abel brought the fat portions of his flock? That means he gave God the fattest of his animals, the best of what he raised. But it doesn't say that Cain brought the best of his crops. Nor does it say that he brought a large offering. It tells us only that he offered some of what he harvested to the Lord. So, when God looked at their offerings, he was pleased with Abel's offering but not with Cain's. That is why Cain became angry.

Talk about It

:: What kind of work did Abel do? *(Abel raised animals.)*

:: What kind of work did Cain do? *(Cain was a farmer who grew crops.)*

:: Why would they give an offering to God? *(By giving God an offering they were thanking him for providing for them. God is the one who made the crops that Cain planted grow and the one who kept Abel's flocks healthy.)*

:: What about us—do we ever bring offerings to the Lord? *(Yes, when we give our money to the church we are thanking God for helping us to earn the money we work for.)*

 Pray about It

Ask God to help you to always give him your best.

DAY TWO

Remember It

What do you remember about yesterday's story? What do you think is going to happen today?

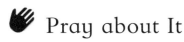 Read Genesis 4:1–8.

Think about It Some More

God could see that Cain became angry, and he warned Cain to be careful. He said that sin was crouching at his door. That meant that if Cain did not watch himself, he was going to end up doing something worse. But if Cain did what was right, God would be pleased with him. Ignoring God, Cain remained angry and did not repent, or turn away from his sin. When Cain was alone with Abel, he killed him.

There is a warning for us here: unless we turn away from our sin and turn back to God, our sin will only get worse.

Talk about It

:: What do you think Cain should have done? *(Parents, draw your children out here. Cain should have repented or turned away from his anger against his brother and asked God to forgive him.)*

:: Can you remember a time when you were angry? Did staying angry ever bring about something good? *(Parents, you might want to help your children remember when their anger led to even more problems.)*

:: How does God warn us when we sin? *(God's warnings to us are written in the Bible; for example, Galatians 6:7–8 says that we reap what we sow. That means if we sow seeds of sin we will reap bad consequences.)*

 ## Pray about It

Ask God to help you turn away from your sin and follow his Word.

DAY THREE

Connect It to Jesus

Can anyone guess how our story is about Jesus or points forward to him?

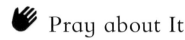 Read Genesis 4:9–12.

Think about It Some More

Adam's sin, which started when he ate the forbidden fruit, spread to his children. At first we saw how sin hurts our relationship with God, and now we can clearly see how sin also affects the people around us.

Brothers should love one another, but because of sin Cain killed Abel. From Adam's very first sin all the way through history until now, every person after Adam was born a sinner, except for one. There is only one far-off grandson of Adam who never sinned. Jesus is the only one who never ever sinned. Jesus always obeyed God, his Father, and he always loved the people around him.

Talk about It

:: How did God know what Cain did? *(God knows everything. We cannot hide our sin from God.)*

:: What are the ways we can sin so that God doesn't know what we did? *(God always knows our sin. There is no way to sin so that God cannot see.)*

:: How was Jesus different from Cain? *(Even though he was tempted, Jesus never sinned. Jesus also gave an offering—his very own life.)*

 ## Pray about It

Thank Jesus for giving the very best offering of all, his own life.

DAY FOUR

Remember It

What has God been teaching you this week through our Bible story?

 Read Genesis 4:13–16.

Think about It Some More

Did you notice that Cain didn't say he was sorry or ask for God's forgiveness for killing his brother? Cain was concerned only about himself. Even so, God was kind to Cain. He put a special mark on his forehead so that everyone would know not to hurt him. Although God could have killed Cain immediately for what he did, he let him live and allowed Cain time to turn away from his sin and turn back to God.

God often gives us time to repent. Even though we are sinners he allows us to live so that we can turn away from our sin, trust in Jesus, and turn to him for forgiveness.

Talk about It

:: Think back over our story. Make a list of the sins Cain committed. *(Cain did not give God his best in the offering. He envied his brother and became more and more angry. He didn't listen to God's warning and then killed his brother. Cain didn't say he was sorry or ask for forgiveness.)*

> KIDS, ask your mom and dad if they are sinners too.

(As parents it is important for us to be able to admit that we too sin against God. Consider sharing a way that you don't follow God's commands, to help your children see that you need Jesus too!)

:: What about you—can you make a list of the sins you have committed against God? *(Parents, help your children see that they are sinners like Cain. It is too easy to identify with Abel in this story and miss the truth that we are more like Cain than we realize.)*

:: What punishment could God have given Cain? *(Cain could have been killed by God for what he did to his brother.)*

✋ Pray about It

Thank God for not quickly punishing you so that you could believe in Jesus and ask God to forgive you for your sins.

DAY FIVE

Discover It

Today we look at a passage from a psalm or one of the prophets to see what we can learn from it about Jesus.

 Read Psalm 2:1–2.

Think about It Some More

Did you know that David, who lived one thousand years before Jesus, wrote this psalm that talks about Jesus? The only way he could write about Jesus was if God was helping him.

Peter and John, two of Jesus' disciples, later quoted from this psalm when they were speaking to the religious rulers (Acts 4:25–27). They told them that Jesus was the one David described as the Lord's anointed and that the people who plotted against him were the Jews who had killed Jesus.

Talk about It

:: How could David write about Jesus long before Jesus was even born? *(God inspired those who wrote the Bible; thus, it was God who led David to write about Jesus. If you read Acts 4:28 you will see that it tells us that even Jesus' death was planned by God.)*

:: To plot against someone means that you plan to do something bad to them. What did the religious rulers plot against Jesus? *(The religious rulers plotted to kill Jesus.)*

:: David describes people who rage or get angry and plot to kill Jesus in this psalm. How is their sin like the sin Cain committed against his brother?

Pray about It

Ask God to help you love the Lord and live for him like David did.

Week 5

God Chooses Noah

Bring an umbrella and open it up as you start today's Bible study. Wait and see what your children say. Explain to them that it is going to rain inside the house and they are going to get wet. After they stop laughing, introduce Noah and explain that people thought he was crazy too! Say, "God instructed Noah to build a ship on dry land with no water in sight. This week you will learn how God used Noah to deliver his people."

DAY ONE

Picture It

What would happen if a hunger-crazed bear broke into our home while we were away and tore through the house looking for food? Imagine him ripping open the living room sofa in his search for crumbs, and then breaking open the refrigerator and dragging a bowl of left-over spaghetti into the dining room, spilling sauce everywhere. Imagine him tracking sauce from room to room as he continues his rampage. Soon there are bear footprints—and a huge mess—in every room of the house.

When we come home we would see how the bear had ruined our home. This is like what sin did to the world God created.

 Read Genesis 6:5–8.

Think about It Some More

Although Adam sinned, he still knew God and taught his children to bring offerings to the Lord. Remember how Abel and Cain brought offerings to the Lord. Adam and Eve had another son, Seth. The Bible tells us that Seth's family called on God too.

But by the time Noah was born, none of the people were seeking after God anymore. Every thought of everyone's heart was evil. That's pretty bad. They had all forgotten God. So God decided to destroy them all, except for Noah and his family.

Talk about It

:: Why would God want to destroy the people he created? *(God wouldn't be a good God if he didn't punish sin. Sometimes God is patient with us and gives us time to turn away, but the people in the world in Noah's day had forgotten about God—that is why God decided to destroy them.)*

:: Why did God save Noah? *(Noah was the only one who followed God. Noah wasn't perfect. He was a sinner too and God could have destroyed everyone. But we will see that, throughout the Old Testament, God always saves at least one family so that one day Jesus could be born into the world through their grandchildren.)*

:: How is our sin today the same as the sin in Noah's day? *(Simply put, sin is disobeying God and doing what we want rather than what God wants. Both our sin and the sin in Noah's day are against God, so they are the same.)*

Pray about It

Ask God to give you the grace to say no to sin and to help you follow him like Noah did.

DAY TWO

Remember It

What do you remember about yesterday's story? What do you think is going to happen today?

Read Genesis 6:9–22.

Think about It Some More

God called to Noah and told him about his plan to destroy all the people. Then he commanded Noah to do something very strange. (Remember the umbrella in the house and how that was strange to you?) God told Noah to build a boat on dry land where there was no water.

This boat, called an ark, was to be bigger than a football field and higher than a three-story building. It would be large enough to hold all of Noah's family and two of every kind of animal, along with enough food for them to eat for a long time. A boat that big would take years and years for one family to build and, once finished, would be impossible to move to water.

Even though this was a very unusual request, Noah believed God and did everything God told him to do.

Talk about It

:: How was Noah different from all the people who lived around him? *(Noah obeyed God's commands, but the people around him did not.)*

:: What did God promise Noah if he obeyed him? *(God promised to save Noah and his family from the flood.)*

:: What do you think the people thought about Noah building a giant boat where there was no water? *(The people probably thought Noah was crazy.)*

:: How would he know how to build the ark and how big to make it? *(God gave Noah all the plans and told him how big the ark should be.)*

 ## Pray about It

Thank God for giving Noah faith to believe in God's plan even though he was building a boat where there was no water.

DAY THREE

Connect It to Jesus

Can anyone guess how our story is about Jesus or points forward to him?

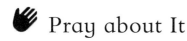 Read 1 Peter 3:18–20.

Think about It Some More

Jesus' disciple Peter, who wrote these verses, tells us something very special about the days of Noah. He said that, while Noah was building the ark, God waited patiently. There was a lot of sin, but God did not bring the flood until the boat was finished and Noah and his family were safe inside.

God had a plan. One day Jesus would be born as one of Noah's great far-off grandchildren. So, when God saved Noah in the ark, he was really saving all of us who come after Noah and trust in Jesus. That is why God waited patiently until the ark was completed.

Talk about It

:: How many people did God save in the ark out of all the people in the world? *(God saved eight people.)*

:: How are Noah and Jesus related? *(Jesus was Noah's far-off grandson.)*

:: Why didn't God bring the flood sooner and destroy all the wickedness of the world? *(He wanted to save Noah so that Jesus could be born one day.)*

:: If you were living in Noah's day do you think you would have believed him that God told him to build an ark? *(Parents, help your children to see that they very well may have made fun of Noah and not believed.)*

Pray about It

Thank God for saving Noah and his family so that one day Jesus could be born as one of his far-off grandsons, making a way for us all to be saved.

DAY FOUR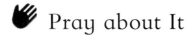

Remember It

What has God been teaching you this week through our Bible story?

 Read Genesis 7:1–10.

Think about It Some More

Noah was six hundred years old by the time he had finished building the ark! That's a lot older than your grandparents. When the ark was complete, it was time for Noah and his family to go inside.

I think it was a good thing God told Noah the rain would not start for seven days. Can you imagine what it would have been like to wait inside with no rain if you didn't know what was going to happen? Just as God said, on the seventh day, the rain started to fall.

Talk about It

:: How did God keep his promise to Noah? *(It started to rain on the seventh day, just as God had said.)*

> KIDS, ask your parents to tell you a time when God was faithful to them.

(Parents, tell your children some of the ways God has provided for you.)

:: On the seventh day, when the rain started, how do you think Noah felt? *(Parents, draw your children out here. Help them think how they might have felt. Point them to God's faithfulness.)*

 Pray about It

Thank God for the way he kept his promise to Noah and for being a God who always keeps his promises.

DAY FIVE

Discover It

Today we look at a passage from a psalm or one of the prophets to see what we can learn from it about Jesus.

 Read Psalm 2:6–8.

Think about It Some More

Last week we read part of this psalm and we learned that it speaks about Jesus. Did you ever hear the story about Jesus' baptism? Do you remember what God the Father said from heaven about his Son Jesus? He said, "This is my beloved Son, with whom I am well pleased" (Matthew 3:17 ESV).

Doesn't that sound a lot like Psalm 2:7 where God says, "I will tell . . .you are my Son" (ESV)? Once again, way before Jesus was even born, God is telling us about Jesus. Even back in Noah's day, God's plan to save the world by sending his Son was set in place all ready to happen in God's perfect time.

Talk about It

:: Who remembers the story and can say what happened when Jesus was baptized? *(You can flip over to Matthew 3:13–17 and give your children a few clues or read those verses to them if they are unfamiliar.)*

:: How is Jesus related to God the Father? *(Jesus is God the Father's only Son.)*

:: Can you think of something else in this psalm that describes who Jesus is? Listen carefully as I read it out loud again. *(Read the passage again and emphasize the word "king" to give your children a clue.)*

 Pray about It

Thank God the Father for giving up his Son to be our Savior.

Week 6

The Rainbow of God's Promise

Collect a pencil, paper, and stopwatch (many cell phones have a stopwatch function) and explain that you are going to draw something and see how fast the children can guess what you are drawing. (You will draw a rainbow.)

Start the timer (assign this task to an older child) when you begin and stop it the moment they guess what you are drawing. They should guess quickly since a rainbow is very recognizable even for young children. Marvel over how quickly they guessed correctly. Then see if they can tell you what the rainbow represents. Say, "This week you will learn how God preserved Noah and his family through the flood, and how God promised to never again destroy the earth with a flood and marked this promise with the rainbow."

DAY ONE

Picture It

What would you do if our next-door neighbor started building a boat the size of a bus in his front yard? At first, you wouldn't know what he was doing. But at some point, after the boat started to take shape, you would realize he was building a large boat on dry ground.

Imagine after he finished building it that he left it sitting there on his front lawn. After a while you would want to ask him, "Why are you leaving your boat in your front yard?" What would you say if he told you it was because there was going to be a flood, the neighborhood was going to become a lake, and he wanted to be certain that he had a ride to work?

Soon, everyone on your block would be laughing at your neighbor. But wouldn't you all be surprised if, the next week, a water main broke, the neighborhood flooded, and there was your neighbor floating off to work in his boat!

Now imagine that you live thousands of years ago and your neighbor's name is Noah and he is building an ark. Wouldn't you think he was a bit crazy?

 Read Genesis 7:11–16.

Think about It Some More

It took Noah a long time to build the ark. Then it took more time to fill it with the animals God brought and more time to bring in the food everyone would eat. But when it was all done, Noah waited.

He probably felt a little silly with an ark full of animals and no water anywhere! Noah was relieved to see that first raindrop fall. God was faithful and kept his promise. Not only did it start to rain, but the earth split open and great fountains of water spouted up from the ground as well. That is how God flooded the earth. Because Noah believed in God's plan, God kept Noah and his family safe inside the ark.

Believing God for things we can't see is called faith. Noah had faith in God's plan. But Noah would have been sad too, sad that the people continued to sin and reject God. The rain also meant they were going to die.

Talk about It

:: What do you think the people around Noah thought when the earth split open and the fountains shot out of the ground? *(The people would have been afraid because they had not see anything like that before.)*

:: Can you remember the word we used to describe someone who believes God for things she can't see? *(Faith. Read Hebrews 11:7 to see how the New Testament remembers Noah's faith.)*

:: What was it Noah believed that he could not see? *(Noah built the ark on dry ground, but he believed that God would flood the earth.)*

 Pray about It

Thank God for giving Noah faith to believe and trust in the Lord. Ask God to give you the same kind of faith.

DAY TWO

Remember It

What do you remember about yesterday's story? What do you think is going to happen today?

 Read Genesis 7:17—8:5.

Think about It Some More

Can you imagine it raining all day and all night for forty days? That is almost six weeks in a row of heavy rain. There was so much rain that even the highest mountains in the world at the time of Noah were covered. Then, even after the rain stopped, the floodwater covered the earth for about a year! But God did not forget Noah, and the water slowly went away. Finally, as the water level got lower, the ark rested on the ground at the top of a mountain.

Talk about It

  :: What would you do in an ark full of animals while you waited for the rain to stop and the flood to go away? *(Parents, let your kids get creative here.)*

  :: How do you think Noah felt when he first felt the ark bump against the ground and stop floating? *(Noah would have rejoiced that God saved him.)*

  :: When we say God is faithful, we mean he keeps his promises. How was God faithful to Noah? *(God did everything he said he would do. God kept all his promises to Noah.)*

 ## Pray about It

Praise God for his faithfulness in keeping his promises to Noah.

DAY THREE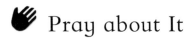

Connect It to Jesus

Can anyone guess how our story is about Jesus or points forward to him?

Read Genesis 8:6—9:1.

Think about It Some More

You might not think that Jesus is anywhere in this story, but he is. The ark is a picture of the way Jesus saves us from God's punishment. Noah was safe from the flood in the ark and we are safe from God's holy anger in Jesus.

Now, we don't live inside of Jesus like Noah lived inside the ark. The way we hide inside Jesus is to believe in him and trust that Jesus died for us when he died on the cross.

When Noah left the ark, God told him and his family to be fruitful and multiply on the earth. That means that God wanted Noah's family to have lots and lots of children. Then their children would grow up and they would have more children.

One day, one of Noah's far-off grandsons named Joseph would have a baby on the very first Christmas and name him Jesus. Did you ever think that God saved Noah so that one day Jesus could come to save us? I guess you could say that by saving Noah God saved us too.

Talk about It

  :: How do you think Noah would have felt to walk on the earth again? *(Parents, draw out your children here.)*

  :: What would Noah have noticed was missing on the earth after the flood? *(There would have been no people or animals except those that had ridden in the ark. God brought judgment on the land just as he said he would.)*

:: What did Noah do that pleased God? *(Noah built an altar and offered on it a sacrifice to the Lord. Remember that every sacrifice offered in worship to God pointed to the day when God would sacrifice his Son Jesus.)*

 Pray about It

After spending all that time on the ark, Noah would have thanked God for some pretty common things, like the dry ground, sunshine, and for helping new plants to grow. Think of some everyday, ordinary things you can thank God for.

DAY FOUR

Remember It

What has God been teaching you this week through our Bible story?

 Read Genesis 9:8–17.

Think about It Some More

Isn't it wonderful that God gave us rainbows to remind us of his promise to never again destroy the world by a flood? God called his promise a *covenant*. That is just another word for promise. They mean the same thing.

The next time you see a rainbow you can tell the people around you that you know why God created rainbows: they are a sign to mark his promise. Rainbows appear in the clouds when a rain shower passes and the sun starts to shine. To see a rainbow after a storm, turn your back to the sun and look up into the sky away from the sun.

Talk about It

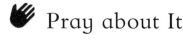 KIDS, ask your mom and dad to tell you a story about a time when they've seen a rainbow.

:: Do you remember why God gave us rainbows? *(Rainbows are signs that mark God's promise to never again destroy the earth with a flood.)*

:: Did the flood take away sin? *(No, the flood did not take away sin. Noah and his family were still sinners who needed a Savior. That is why Jesus still had to come to die on the cross.)*

 Pray about It

Thank God for giving us beautiful rainbows to remind us of his promise.

DAY FIVE

Discover It

Today we look at a passage from a psalm or one of the prophets to see what we can learn from it about Jesus.

 Read Psalm 2:10–12.

Think about It Some More

Today we finish up Psalm 2 which, as we learned over the last two weeks, is about Jesus. In today's portion of the psalm Jesus is described as a person who will rule over all the kings of the earth. The kings of the earth are warned that they should "kiss the Son"—Jesus. This means that they should follow and worship him. If they do, the Bible says that they will find refuge or safety. If they do not worship Jesus, if they go their own way instead, they will perish (die).

In the story of Noah we see how powerful God's judgments can be. The people, including their kings, disobeyed God, so God destroyed them all with the flood. All, that is, except Noah.

Talk about It

:: How can Jesus rule over all the kings of the earth? *(Jesus is God and knows everything. Remember that he holds all things together, even the rulers of the earth. Read Colossians 1:16.)*

:: Can you think of a way Jesus provides a refuge or safety for us? *(Jesus saves us from the punishment we deserve for our sin.)*

:: What will happen to kings who go their own way and do not worship the Lord? *(They will perish or die.)*

:: Who is called the King of kings in the Bible? *(In 1 Timothy 6:15 and Revelation 17:14, Jesus is called the King of kings and Lord of lords. In Revelation 19:16 Jesus is said to have the titles "King of kings" and "Lord of lords" written on his robe.)*

Pray about It

Even though you may not be a king, ask the Lord to help you follow and worship Jesus.

Week 7

The Tower of Babel

If you know a second language (that your children don't know), say to them in that foreign language, "It's time for devotions. Don't forget to bring your Bibles." If you don't know a foreign language, here are those sentences in German: "Es ist zeit für Hingaben. Nicht vergessen, deine Bibeln zu holen." Repeat this several times until your children comment. Then give them the translation. Say, "This week you will learn about how God confused the languages of the people at the tower of Babel."

DAY ONE

Picture It

If we made a list of all our relatives—all of our brothers and sisters, all of our aunts and uncles and all of our cousins and all of their children—how long of a list would it be? We would have many names on our list. Can you remember all the names on the list?

In today's Bible story we are going to read the names of Noah's children and grandchildren.

 Read Genesis 10:1–10.

Think about It Some More

One thing we know for sure is that when God commanded Noah and his sons to be fruitful and fill the earth with children, they obeyed. This is a long list of Noah's grandchildren!

It is clear from reading the Bible that Jesus believed Noah was a real person who survived a real flood and had real children because Jesus taught his disciples about Noah (Luke 17:26).

Talk about It

:: Why do you think God included lists of names in the Bible? *(It shows that the Bible is a book about real people and real events, including Noah and the flood.)*

:: What are the names of Noah's sons? *(Shem, Ham, Japheth.)*

:: Two of Ham's sons were named Egypt and Canaan. Where will we see those names again in the Bible? *(Egypt and Canaan became whole countries. Moses would later lead God's people out of slavery in Egypt into the land of Canaan.)*

 ## Pray about It

Pray for all the people in your family line starting with your grandparents, then your parents, and finally pray for any brothers or sisters that you have and ask God to bless them all.

DAY TWO

Remember It

What do you remember about yesterday's story? What do you think is going to happen today?

 Read Genesis 11:1–9.

Think about It Some More

Notice that the people building the tower in this story didn't mention God. They didn't seem to care about God. They were interested only in making a name for themselves so that they would be great.

People are supposed to worship God and praise his name. When we forget about God, we usually end up praising ourselves instead. Without God, we end up worshiping ourselves or what we do.

In this story, the people wanted to build a tower that reached to the heavens so they would be important. Anytime we make something more important than God, we are sinning against God. That is why God came down and confused their language, so they could not understand each other and the work would stop.

Talk about It

:: Do you remember the name of the tower in today's story? *(The tower was called Babel [verse 9].)*

:: What went wrong in this story? *(The people stopped following God and began to think very highly of themselves.)*

:: Can you think of a time when you were so interested in doing something that you forgot about God? *(Parents, you can help your children reflect on their lives. This could be anything they became obsessed with—a new toy or game, maybe a sports team, etc.)*

 ## Pray about It

Ask God to help you do things to bring glory to him, not to yourself.

DAY THREE

Connect It to Jesus

Can anyone guess how our story is about Jesus or points forward to him?

 Read Revelation 7:9–10.

Think about It Some More

This story comes from the very end of the Bible when God brings people of every language back together again. Jesus is the one who brings the people who were scattered at the tower of Babel back together again. Instead of building a tower for their own glory, the people Jesus brings together will praise God and give him glory.

The book of Revelation tells us that everyone in heaven will worship God with the same words. Today we speak hundreds of different languages, but in heaven we will all sing with one voice.

Talk about It

:: Who is the Lamb this passage is talking about? *(The Lamb is Jesus. He is called the Lamb because he gave up his life on the cross for our sin just like a lamb would be sacrificed as an offering to God.)*

:: At Babel God scattered the people. What does this story tell us God will do with those people? *(God will gather them back together again.)*

:: What will all the people Jesus brings together do in heaven? *(They will all sing praises to God.)*

 Pray about It

Together sing a song of praise to God.

DAY FOUR

Remember It

What has God been teaching you this week through our Bible story?

 Read Deuteronomy 28:63–68 and 30:1–3.

Think about It Some More

After Babel, when God wanted to warn his people, he often said he would scatter them. When God wanted to encourage people to follow him, he promised that he would gather them back together and he would be their God.

Talk about It

> 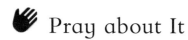 KIDS, ask your parents to tell you how obeying God has been good for them and brought them blessing, or how disobeying God has brought them bad consequences.

(Parents, you can talk about all the blessings that come with obeying God such as not needing to worry that the police will come and arrest you for doing something wrong. Or perhaps you can share a time when you did not follow God's command and received bad consequences like when you get caught speeding and receive a ticket.)

:: What did God say he would do if his people disobeyed him? *(God said he would scatter them.)*

:: What did God say he would do if his people followed him? *(God would gather them back together again.)*

:: Where will all of God's people be gathered together forever? *(We will all be gathered together forever in heaven.)*

Pray about It

Thank God for his promise to gather his people together again.

DAY FIVE

Discover It

Today we look at a passage from a psalm or one of the prophets to see what we can learn from it about Jesus.

Read Isaiah 1:18.

Think about It Some More

If you had a wonderful white shirt and you got a stain on it that you could not wash out, you wouldn't be too happy. The Bible compares our lives to white robes and compares sin to something that stains our white robes and makes them ugly.

In Revelation 7:14, God tells of a group of people whose stains were made clean by the blood of the lamb. That means their sin was washed away by what Jesus did on the cross.

In the Bible verse we just read, Isaiah the prophet is looking far off to the day when the stain of our sin will be washed away by Jesus. He says something scarlet can become the color of snow, and something crimson can become white like wool. Imagine a piece of bright red clothing being washed and coming out perfectly white! Only God can make that happen. There is only one way that the deep, dark stain of our sin can be removed: the blood of Christ washes it away.

Talk about It

:: What is the stain on our white robes? *(The stain on our robes is our sin—the wrong we do against God.)*

:: What can clean away the stain of our sins? *(Jesus' death on the cross—his blood—takes away our sins and makes us white as snow.)*

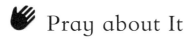 Pray about It

Thank God for taking away the stain of our sin by sending Jesus to die for us.

Week 8

Abram and God's Promise

Say to your children, "What if I told you we were moving? How would you feel?" They might want to know where you are moving, but just answer, "I don't know." They might wonder if you are serious or not. Ask them what the hardest part of moving would be.

Continue, "Imagine if I said to you, 'God is directing us to move, but I don't know where. We are going to start packing, and after we have the truck loaded I think God will tell us where to go.'"

"This week you will learn how Abram moved in a very similar way, and how Abram trusted God."

DAY ONE

Picture It

Imagine that you were writing a book about yourself and your family and how you came to be born. How would you start your book? You could start by telling the story of your parents and how they met. Perhaps you would talk about your grandparents too. You might mention where they all lived and how they got married.

Today we will read the beginning of a story about one of the most famous men in the Bible, Abram. He is the one God later renames Abraham. Listen closely; there is some important information in this beginning part of the story.

 Read Genesis 11:27–32.

Think about It Some More

Terah was Abram's father. But if you follow Terah's family all the way back, the Bible tells us his ancestor was Shem, one of Noah's sons.

If we had a list of all the people who ever came from Noah everyone's name would be on that list. Your name would be on that list too. But God didn't record all the names of Noah's children and far-off grandchildren. He recorded the names of the people who led to Jesus or who played an important part in his plans.

Do you know the special part Abram and Sarai played in God's plan? Well, if you are not sure, keep listening. We are going to learn about it over the next few weeks.

Talk about It

:: Who was Abram's great far-off grandfather? *(Noah and Adam before Noah.)*

:: Where did Terah, Abram's dad, take Abram, Lot, and Sarai to live? *(They were on their way to a place called Canaan when they stopped and settled in Haran.)*

:: The story tells us that Sarai was barren. What does that mean? *(That means she wasn't able to have children even though she wanted some.)*

 Pray about It

Pray for the childless couples you know and ask God to bless them with children.

DAY TWO

Remember It

What do you remember about yesterday's story? What do you think is going to happen today?

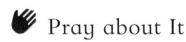 Read Genesis 12:1–9.

Think about It Some More

Imagine what it was like to be Abram when God first spoke to him. He was probably tending his animals or working around his house when suddenly he heard a voice. "Hello Abram, I'm God. I want you to pack up your things, move away from your family, and leave your house and relatives behind."

That's not exactly small talk. But God also gave Abram a promise that would have been very special to him. God said he would make a great nation from Abram. That meant if Abram obeyed God, he was going to give his wife children, and from their children God would make them a nation to bless the whole earth.

Abram and Sarai had wanted children, but so far they had none. So, trusting God's word, Abram left his country and followed God to a new place.

Talk about It

:: What did God promise Abram? *(God promised to make Abram into a great nation. That meant God would give Abram children.)*

:: What did God ask Abram to do? *(God asked Abram to leave his country and his relatives behind and move to a place God would show him.)*

:: Who did God say would be blessed by Abram? *(God said that all the nations of the earth would be blessed by Abram.)*

 Pray about It

Thank God for giving Abram faith to obey and follow God.

DAY THREE

Connect It to Jesus

Can anyone guess how our story is about Jesus or points forward to him?

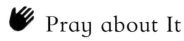 Read Galatians 3:26–29.

Think about It Some More

God made a promise to Abram that through him all nations would be blessed. But Abram himself was not the one to bless all nations. One day, one of Abram's great far-off grandchildren would be the one to bring that blessing.

Can you guess who that great far-off grandchild is? That's right: Jesus. Jesus is the one who fulfilled the promise God gave to Abram to bless the nations.

In our Bible passage today we learn that everyone who has faith and believes in Jesus is one of Abraham's far-off children or offspring. Abraham is the name God gives Abram later in our story. Anyone who is one of Abraham's children gets to share a part of the blessing God promised to him.

Talk about It

:: Who is the great far-off grandson of Abram that brought the blessing God promised to all the nations? *(Jesus.)*

:: How can people today become children of Abraham and share in his blessing? *(If you put your trust in Jesus you can share in Abram's blessing.)*

:: What does this Bible passage say God did with people from different nations like the Greeks and the Jews? *(Parents, if your children do not get the answer that God brought us together and made us all one, read the passage again and emphasize those words to give your children a clue.)*

 Pray about It

Thank God for bringing all different kinds of people together in the family of God.

DAY FOUR_____

Remember It

What has God been teaching you this week through our Bible story?

 Read Genesis 12:10–20.

Think about It Some More

Abram believed God and followed his call to leave his family, but he did not trust the Lord in everything. When he got to Egypt, Abram was afraid the Egyptians might kill him so they could have his wife for themselves. So, instead of trusting God to protect him, Abram hid the fact that Sarai was his wife, saying instead that she was his sister.

But even though Abram did not trust God, he protected Abram anyway. God is always faithful. Even when we sin God always keeps his promises. God's plan was bigger than Abram's sin.

Talk about It

> ● ● KIDS, ask your parents if they can tell you about a time when they
> ● ● had to trust God in a difficult situation.

(Parents, can you think of a time when you didn't know if you would have enough money to pay the bills or a time when you had to trust God in a sickness or trial.)

:: What did Abram do that was wrong? *(Abram didn't tell the full truth that Sarai was his wife.)*

:: What did God do to protect Abram from the Egyptians? *(God made the Egyptians sick until they let Abram go.)*

:: What does this story teach us about God? *(God always keeps his promises. When God said Abram was going to have children, then God protected Abram so that he could have children.)*

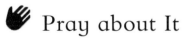 Pray about It

Thank God for always keeping his promises.

DAY FIVE

Discover It

Today we look at a passage from a psalm or one of the prophets to see what we can learn from it about Jesus.

 Read Psalm 4.

Think about It Some More

The psalms are the words to songs that were sung a long time ago. Psalm 4 was written by David. David wrote many of the psalms. They often point us to Jesus or talk about the salvation he offers to us.

In this psalm, David calls God the God of his righteousness. That means that even though David was a sinner he was trusting in God to take away his sin. God took away our sin and became our righteousness by sending his Son Jesus. He lived a sinless life and then died to take the punishment that we deserve for our sin. Jesus takes away our sin and then gives us his perfect righteous life.

Talk about It

:: What is a psalm? *(A psalm is a song that has been saved so we can read it in the Bible.)*

:: Who wrote many of the psalms? *(David wrote many of the psalms.)*

:: What did David mean when he said we should put our trust in the Lord? *(David trusted God to save him from his enemies. He put his trust in God instead of in his own strength. We also must trust God to save us from our sins. There is no way we can take away our sins; we must put our trust in the Lord to save us.)*

Pray about It

Ask God to help you put your trust in the Lord.

Week 9

God Makes a Covenant with Abram

Draw a star on a piece of paper (cut it out, if you like). Show it to your children and ask them what it is. Ask them if they can remember what important ways God used stars in the Bible.

God created the stars to show his glory. God told Abram he would have as many children as there were stars in the sky. One of those stars represented Jesus, a far-off grandson of Abram. A star marked the birth of Jesus. Jesus is called a star (Numbers 24:17 and Revelation 22:16).

Say, "This week you will learn about God's covenant with Abram to make his descendants as numerous as the stars."

DAY ONE

Picture It

Imagine that it is the middle of the night and you are lying on your back in the center of a large grassy field. When you look up, the sky is filled with stars. Some of them are very bright. Some look like they are twinkling. And there are some, the smallest ones, that are so faint you're not even sure they are really there.

What would you say if someone asked you to count them all. There would be way too many stars to count, and it would be very hard to remember which ones you counted and which ones you didn't.

In today's story, that is what God asked Abram to do: count the stars.

 Read Genesis 15:1–6.

Think about It Some More

Once again God reminded Abram of the promise. Abram listened to God but saw one big problem: he still didn't have any children. Without children there was no way for God's promise to come true. Then God told Abram something amazing. Not only was God going to give

Abram a son, he was going to give Abram so many children he would not be able to count them all. He would have as many children as there were stars in the sky!

Even though God's promise seemed impossible, Abram believed God. God counted Abram's faith as righteousness. That means that even though Abram was a sinner, God treated him as though he didn't have any sin because he trusted in God's plan. God's plan was to bring his salvation through one of Abram's far-off grandchildren. That far-off grandchild was Jesus. By having faith in God's plan, Abram was trusting in Jesus.

Talk about It

:: Why was it hard for Abram to understand how God was going to keep his promise? *(Abram did not have any children. Without children he could not become a great nation.)*

:: What does it mean to be righteous? *(Being righteous means that you don't have sin.)*

:: What did Abram do that God counted as righteousness? *(Abram believed or trusted in God's plan.)*

 Pray about It

Ask God to help you have faith in God's plan like Abram did.

DAY TWO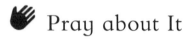

Remember It

What do you remember about yesterday's story? What do you think is going to happen today?

Read Genesis 15:7–21.

Think about It Some More

In Abram's day, if two people made a contract or bargain to do something together they could seal their agreement by making it a special promise called a covenant. To make their covenant they would kill an animal, split it into two pieces, and have each person walk between the pieces. By doing this they were saying, "If I break my part of our bargain I should be killed just as this animal was killed." That made it a very serious promise.

To prove to Abram that God was serious about his promise, God made a covenant with him. Abram killed the animals and set out the pieces, but instead of God and Abram both walking between them, God put Abram to sleep and walked between the animal pieces by himself as a flaming torch. God did this to show that he was going to keep the promise all by himself.

Talk about It

:: What is a covenant? *(A covenant is a special promise that one person makes with another.)*

:: What did God promise in his covenant with Abram? *(God promised to give the land they were standing on to Abram's children. That meant that God was also going to give Abram children.)*

:: Why did God put Abram to sleep and go between the pieces by himself? *(God wanted to show that he was the one who was going to keep the promise. Later, even though Abram's children did not follow God, God still kept his promise.)*

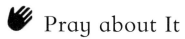

Pray about It

Thank God for keeping his promises even when we sin against him.

DAY THREE

Connect It to Jesus

Can anyone guess how our story this week is about or points forward to Jesus?

 Read Romans 4:13–25.

Think about It Some More

The apostle Paul used the story of Abraham's faith (Abraham is the new name God gave Abram) to teach the people who lived in Rome. He wanted to tell them that as far back as Abraham, God was saving his people because of their faith, not because of their works.

Paul reminded the Romans of the story of Abraham and how he trusted in God's promise even though it seemed hard for him to believe. Today we trust in that same plan. God's plan to take away Abraham's sin and God's plan to take away our sin are the same. God's plan was to use one of Abraham's far-off grandsons to save his people. Now we know who that far-off grandson is: Jesus. He is the wonderful blessing for all of Abraham's children.

If we trust in what Jesus did on the cross, God counts our faith in Jesus as righteousness, just like he did for Abraham.

Talk about It

:: What story did the apostle Paul use to teach the Romans about faith? *(God used the story of Abraham to teach the Romans about faith.)*

:: What is the name of Abraham's far-off grandson who died on the cross to take away our sin and make us righteous? *(Jesus.)*

:: Why is taking our sin away the best blessing God could give us? *(The only way we can be a child of God is to have all our sins taken away. When God takes our sin away he makes it possible for us to go to heaven and be with him.)*

Pray about It

Now that you know God's plan and how he chose to save us from our sins, ask God to help you trust in his plan and believe in what Jesus did on the cross.

DAY FOUR

Remember It

What has God been teaching you this week through our Bible story?

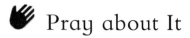 Read Genesis 15:13–15.

Think about It Some More

Hidden in the middle of God's promise to Abraham is another famous Bible story. After God put Abraham to sleep, he told him how his far-off children would live and suffer in a foreign land for 400 years.

Can you guess what God is telling Abraham about? Here are a few clues. One day, Abraham's children would go to Egypt to find food during a famine. While there, they would become slaves. Then God would raise up a man to deliver them from their slavery. What is the man's name? (Moses)

Talk about It

> • • KIDS, ask your parents to remind you what the story of Moses is
> • • about.

(Parents, if you are not sure, you can read the story in the beginning of the book of Exodus.)

:: How could God know about Moses even before Moses was born? *(God knows all things. He knows who is going to be born along with everything that will happen to them.)*

:: How is our faith made stronger when things come true just like God says they will? *(It is easier to believe the promises God gives us when we see that he kept his promises in the past.)*

 Pray about It

Thank God that he knows the future and can take care of us.

DAY FIVE

Discover It

Today we look at a passage from a psalm or one of the prophets to see what we can learn from it about Jesus.

 Read Psalm 6:1–4.

Think about It Some More

In Psalm 6:4, David cried out to God, "Save me for the sake of your steadfast love" (ESV). In the gospel of John, we learn that God sent Jesus, his only Son, because he loved the world (John 3:16). When David cried out for God to save him for the sake of his steadfast love, he was asking for God to send Jesus, for there was no other way David could be saved.

Talk about It

:: How did God show us his love? *(God showed us his love by sending Jesus to die on the cross and take away our sin.)*

:: What danger do we need to be saved from? *(We need to be saved from God's punishment for our sin. Jesus died to take the punishment for the sin of everyone who believes in him.)*

:: We learned this week that Abram believed in God's plan. How do we believe in God's plan? *(We believe that God sent Jesus to take away our sin.)*

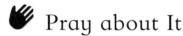 Pray about It

Pray the same prayer David prayed through this psalm: God please save me.

Week 10

God Gives Abram a New Name

Tell your children God gave Abram a new name, Abraham, which means "father of a multitude." God's new name for Abram reflected his plan to bless him with many children.

If you know what your children's names mean, tell them. Then try to come up with new names for your children based on what you know about how God is using them. Here are a few examples: Change Sarah to Servanta because she loves to serve, or change John to Mindfull because his mind is always full of creative ideas.

Say, "This week you will learn about the new names God gave Abram and his wife, Sarai."

DAY ONE

Picture It

Pretend that one Saturday morning we promise to take you out for an ice-cream cone. That would be exciting. You might start to think about which flavor ice cream you would order. But, by the end of the day no one has taken you out for ice cream. "It's okay," you say to yourself, "maybe we will go tomorrow."

A whole week passes, then a month, but still we haven't taken you out for ice cream. Every now and then we remind you that we haven't forgotten our promise. How long would you be willing to wait? One year? Two years? What about 20 years? What if we finally gave you your promised ice cream cone when you graduated from college?

That sounds ridiculous, but that is how long Abram had to wait for the promise God gave him to be fulfilled.

 Read Genesis 16.

Think about It Some More

More than twenty years had passed since God had called Abram and promised to give him children, but no children had come. In those days, people looked down on a wife who could not give her husband a son to carry on the family name. So Sarai, upset that she was still childless, offered her servant, Hagar, as a second wife for Abram.

Instead of refusing a second wife and trusting God's promise, Abram took Hagar and she bore him a son, whom they named Ishmael. God didn't need help from Hagar to fulfill his promise. Even though Sarai was too old to have children, God was about to do a miracle. Ishmael was born normally, without a miracle, and this was not God's plan (Paul explains this in Galatians 4:22–23).

Talk about It

:: Why did Abram take a second wife? *(He didn't see any other way for God's promise to be fulfilled because Sarai was too old to have children.)*

:: How did Sarai feel towards Hagar after baby Ishmael was born, and how did she treat her? *(Sarai felt bad. She was jealous because she couldn't have a child of her own. Sarai treated her so poorly that Hagar took Ishmael and ran away.)*

:: What did God do to encourage Hagar after she ran away? *(God sent an angel to comfort Hagar and encourage her to go back. Even though Ishmael was not the child God promised to give, God still said he would bless Ishmael and make him into a great nation.)*

 Pray about It

Ask God to help you trust the Lord even when things get difficult.

DAY TWO

Remember It

What do you remember about yesterday's story? What do you think is going to happen today?

 Read Genesis 17:1–6.

Think about It Some More

Instead of punishing Abram for taking Hagar, God blesses Abram and reminds him of his covenant promise to bless Abram greatly. Remember, God was the only one to walk between the animals when he made his covenant with Abram. God knew Abram was going to fail but promised to keep the covenant all by himself, even though Abram would sin.

Notice that God's promise to Abram is getting even better. Instead of making Abram the father of one great nation, God tells Abram he would be the father of many nations and that kings would come from Abram's children. To match this bigger promise, God changes Abram's name to Abraham, which means "father of the multitude" or "father of many."

Talk about It

:: Why was Abraham's new name going to be hard to explain to everyone around him? *("Abraham" means "father of a multitude" or "father of many," but Abraham didn't even have one child by his wife Sarai.)*

:: God knew Abraham disobeyed. Why didn't he leave Abraham? *(God's promise didn't depend on Abraham keeping a promise; it depended on God keeping a promise. Even though Abraham was unfaithful, God was still faithful.)*

:: Can you think of any of the kings that will come from Abraham? *(All of the kings of Israel like Saul, David, and Solomon will one day come from the line of Abraham. King Jesus also comes from Abraham's offspring.)*

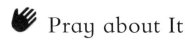 Pray about It

Thank God for being faithful even when we sin against him.

DAY THREE

Connect It to Jesus

Can anyone guess how our story this week is about or points forward to Jesus?

 Read Genesis 17:6–8.

Think about It Some More

There is one word in God's promise to Abraham that points us forward to God's plan to save us through Jesus. Read the passage again and see if you can find it.

Yes, the word that points us to Jesus is *everlasting.* Everlasting is a word used to describe something that will last forever. God was telling Abraham that he was going to be his God forever.

But how was God going to be Abraham's God forever? Abraham was a sinner. God cannot live in heaven with a sinner. That is where Jesus comes in. One day, Jesus would come and die on the cross for Abraham's sin. When Abraham trusted in God's plan he was trusting in Jesus.

Talk about It

:: What does everlasting mean? *(Everlasting is a word we use to describe something that will last forever.)*

:: If you had an everlasting lollipop, how long would you be able to lick it before it was all gone? *(Your lollipop would last forever!)*

:: If we trust in Jesus, how long will we get to be with God in heaven? *(God's promises to everyone who has faith in Jesus are everlasting. That means they will get to live with God in heaven forever.)*

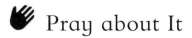 Pray about It

Thank God that his promises are everlasting.

DAY FOUR

Remember It

What has God been teaching you this week through our Bible story?

 Read Genesis 17:9–27.

Think about It Some More

Parents: Note that this passage discusses circumcision. It is usually best to explain circumcision to children before reading the passage. If you think your children are too young, feel free to wait.

Abraham was seventy-five years old when God first promised to give him children. By the time God speaks to him in our story today he is ninety-nine years old. Twenty-four years have gone by. That is why, when God repeats his promise, Abraham laughs. Imagine a man and woman old enough to be great-grandparents having a little baby! God also repeated his promise to Sarai, and he gave her a new name too, Sarah.

Talk about It

> KIDS, ask your parents to tell you about the oldest person they knew who had a baby, then compare her to how old Abraham and Sarai were.

:: What is Sarai's new name? *(Sarah.)*

:: Why did Abraham laugh? *(He thought it was funny that a woman as old as Sarah could have a baby.)*

:: What can we learn from Abraham from this story? *(We can learn that Abraham believed God and trusted God enough to obey him, even before God's promise to give him a son was answered.)*

:: How is Abraham an example for us? *(Abraham had strong, enduring faith. We often have trouble waiting patiently in faith for God's promises to be fulfilled.)*

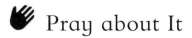 Pray about It

Ask God to give each member of your family a strong faith like Abraham's.

DAY FIVE

Discover It

Today we look at a passage from a psalm or one of the prophets to see what we can learn from it about Jesus.

 Read Psalm 7:6–11.

Think about It Some More

In this psalm David asks God to punish his enemies, be his shield, and save him. David tells God that he is righteous, which means he is good in God's sight. But if David is a sinner, how could he be considered righteous or good?

The only way David could be righteous is if his sins were taken away. That is just what Jesus did for David. Even though David never knew Jesus, he was trusting in God's plan. Today we know that God's plan was to send his Son Jesus to die on the cross to take David's punishment—and then to give David a very special gift. When Jesus took David's sins, he gave David his own righteous life as a gift.

Like David, we are all sinners and are not good at all. That means we are not righteous. But, just like David, we can trust in God's plan to save us. Today we know that God's plan to save all sinners is through Jesus. Jesus will take away our sin and give us his righteous life as a gift.

Talk about It

:: This Bible passage uses a big word: righteousness. What does that word mean? *(Righteousness is our goodness before God. God, for example, is completely righteous so he has no sin at all. We, on the other hand, are sinners and are not righteous; in fact, we are evil or bad. That is why we need Jesus' righteousness.)*

:: Since we are sinners, how can we ever get to the place where God sees us as good or righteous? *(The only way to become righteous, to be good in God's sight, is to have our sins taken away and to receive the gift of God's righteousness by trusting in Jesus who lived a sinless life.)*

:: What kind of things did Jesus do to show us that he was righteous? *(Parents, help your children think of things that Jesus did like heal the sick, worship God and pray to him. Then you can also help them think of things Jesus never did, like lie or fight with his friends or family.)*

 Pray about It

Ask God to help you to live more like Jesus.

Week 11

The Lord Appears to Abraham

Test your children to see how much of Abraham's story they can remember. Ask them the following questions:

    :: *What was Abraham's name before God changed it?*

    :: *What was Abraham's wife's name after God changed it?*

    :: *What did God promise Abraham?*

    :: *What country did Abraham leave to follow God?*

Say, "Sometimes it is hard to remember things we just learned. God often talked to Abraham to help him remember. This week we will learn that God actually came to visit Abraham and ate dinner with him."

DAY ONE

Picture It

Imagine what we would do if the President of the United States walked up to our door right at dinnertime, said he was hungry, and asked if we could prepare him something to eat. What should we serve the president for dinner? How nervous would we be to cook for such an important person?

That is kind of what happened to Abraham in our story today. Only it wasn't the president who came for dinner; it was the Lord! Let's read on to see what Abraham did.

 Read Genesis 18:1–8.

Think about It Some More

When God appeared to men he often came in the form of a man. In this story, God came with two angels. (We learn later in our story that they are angels.) It doesn't tell us what these three visitors looked like, but it is clear that Abraham knew one of them was God because he called him his Lord. Maybe Abraham saw the visitors appear out of nowhere or maybe they looked different from ordinary people.

Talk about It

:: How do you think Abraham knows one of the three visitors is the Lord? *(Your kids can have fun guessing. They may have had a glow about them or, perhaps, God opened Abraham's mind to know.)*

:: Does Abraham ask God to visit or does God decide to come on his own? *(God decides to come to Abraham. In the Bible, God loves to show himself to people he is going to use to do something special, even when they don't ask to see him.)*

:: What does Abraham do when he recognizes that the visitor is the Lord? *(Abraham runs to tell Sarah and starts preparations for a meal.)*

:: Why do you think God would come to visit Abraham? *(Give your children clues by asking them if they remember God's promise to Abraham. We will see in tomorrow's lesson that God comes to remind Abraham of his promise to give him a son.)*

 Pray about It

Thank God for reaching out to us even when we are not calling out to him.

DAY TWO

Remember It

What do you remember about yesterday's story? What do you think is going to happen today?

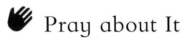 Read Genesis 18:9–15.

Think about It Some More

Once again God reminds Abraham of his promise to give him a son. Only this time God tells him when it will happen. This is good news for someone who has waited a long time for a promise to be kept. Soon Abraham would be a dad. But Sarah, his wife, wasn't so sure. She just laughed.

We shouldn't be too hard on Sarah. After all, Abraham had been telling her about God's promise to give her a child for over twenty years and it still hadn't happened. Even though Sarah laughs and then lies about her laughter, God does not punish her. Not only does God know she will have a son, God also knows that one of Sarah's far-off grandsons, Jesus, will die on the cross to take away her sins. Because of Jesus, Sarah can be forgiven—even for her lying and laughing at God's promise.

Talk about It

:: How long does God tell Abraham that he will still need to wait for a baby? *(One year.)*

:: Why does Sarah laugh? *(She knows her body is worn out and that she is too old to have children. Also, she has heard this same promise for a long time.)*

:: If you were Sarah, what would you have thought about God's promise? *(Help the children identify with Sarah. If we were Sarah we may have sinned worse by mocking God and saying he was wrong.)*

:: What are some promises we need to trust God for? *(Parents, help your children think of some of God's promises. For instance, God promises to children that if they obey their parents it will go well with them, and they will have a long life [Ephesians 6:2–3]. God also promises that he will provide for us [Matthew 6:33], and he will work all things together for our good [Romans 8:28].)*

 ## Pray about It

Ask God to help you believe in the promises he makes to us in his Word.

DAY THREE

Connect It to Jesus

Can anyone guess how our story this week is about or points forward to Jesus?

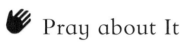 Read Luke 1:26–38.

Think about It Some More

When God visited Abraham, Sarah laughed and said, "Shall I indeed bear a child, now that I am old?" God answered her question by saying, "Nothing is too hard for the Lord" (Genesis 18:13–14).

God wanted her to know he had the power to do everything he said. And a year later, Sarah did have a son, just as God said.

In our Bible story today, we learn that one of Abraham's far-off granddaughters named Mary receives a word from God telling her that she is going to have a baby. Notice how the angel answers Mary when she asks how God could give her a son when she isn't even married yet. The angel's answer is very similar to what God said to Sarah. The angel said, "Nothing will be impossible with God."

Talk about It

:: How is God able to give children to older women like Sarah and women who are not married yet like Mary? *(God is all-powerful and, as the Bible tells us, nothing is too hard or impossible for God.)*

:: How is Jesus related to Sarah's son? *(Jesus is a far-off grandson of Sarah and Abraham.)*

:: How are Sarah and Mary similar? *(Both of these women would not have been able to have children had God not done a miracle for them.)*

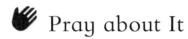 Pray about It

Thank God for the wonderful way he shows us his power through his miracles.

DAY FOUR

Remember It

What has God been teaching you this week through our Bible story?

 Read Genesis 18:16–33.

Think about It Some More

When Abraham heard the Lord's plan to destroy the city of Sodom, he was concerned that good people might be destroyed along with the sinful people who lived there. And since he knew that his nephew Lot was living near the city, he may have been concerned that Lot could be killed when the city was destroyed. God promised not to destroy the city if even ten righteous, or good, people were found there.

Abraham's conversation with God is a good example of how prayer works. God encourages us to pray to him and he promises to hear our prayers. And sometimes God even works them into his wonderful plan.

Talk about It

> ● ● KIDS, ask your parents to tell you a time when they asked God for
> ● ● something and God answered their prayers.

(Parents, think of a time when you prayed for a new job or for a son or daughter or any other prayer request and God answered your prayers.)

:: Why did God say he chose Abraham? *(Reread verse 19 if your children can't remember. God chose Abraham because he knew Abraham would do a good job training his children and teaching them about God.)*

:: How was Abraham's conversation with the Lord a lot like our prayers? *(Prayer is simply talking to God. God encourages us to ask him for the things that we need [John 14:14].)*

:: Can you think of something you could ask God for? *(Help your children to think of something they can ask God to do for them. Be careful to correct them if they ask for things for themselves rather than for others.)*

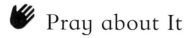 Pray about It

Pray for the things you talked about in answering the last question.

DAY FIVE

Discover It

Today we look at a passage from a psalm or one of the prophets to see what we can learn from it about Jesus.

 Read Psalm 8.

Think about It Some More

The psalm we read today almost sounds like a riddle. For instance, David wrote about someone God made a little lower than the heavenly beings. What does that mean? Then he tells us that God crowned this person with glory and honor and put all things under his feet. Who could that be? God gave us the answer in the New Testament book of Hebrews. Here is what it says:

> But we see him who for a little while was made lower than the angels,
> namely Jesus, crowned with glory and honor because of the suffering
> of death, so that by the grace of God he might taste death for everyone
> (Hebrews 2:9).

David is talking about the Son of God coming down to earth and becoming a man as the baby Jesus. God crowned Jesus with glory because he died on the cross so we could be forgiven. Long before Jesus was born, David sang about him coming to earth and dying on the cross.

Talk about It

:: What other things do we learn about God from this psalm? *(Let your children reread the psalm and tell you things they learn about God. If your children are too young to read, read it again yourself and have them raise their hand when they hear something we learn about God.)*

:: Who made the stars? *(We learned from Colossians that Jesus made everything. So that means Jesus is the one who made the stars.)*

:: David tells us that God's name is majestic. What does majestic mean? *(Probably the best word to help your children understand majestic is "wonderful.")*

 Pray about It

Today's psalm is like a prayer of praise once you understand it.

Week 12

God Rescues Lot

Light a candle and ask your children, "How close can you get to a flame without being burned?" Draw out their opinions and try to decrease the distance by saying, "Don't you think you might be able to get closer?"

Once you settle on a distance, call over one of your children, hold his or her finger, and say you are going to experiment with seeing how close to the flame a finger can get without getting burned. They should object. Of course, you won't follow through. Talk to your children about the foolishness of even asking the question, "How close can I get without getting burned?"

"This week we will learn about Lot, who wanted to find out how close he could live to the evil city of Sodom—and the consequences he and his family experienced."

DAY ONE

Picture It

Did you ever wonder what it would be like to meet an angel? Although some people think angels are only storybook characters, the Bible tells us that angels are real. They are God's messengers and they often look just like other men. They can talk and walk and eat like we do. The Bible even tells us we should welcome strangers into our homes because we never know when a stranger could be an angel (see Hebrews 13:2)! In our story today, God sends two angels to rescue Abraham's relative Lot.

 Read Genesis 19:1–3, 12–14.

Parents: Note that verses 4–11 of this passage speak rather frankly about sexual perversion. They are not absolutely necessary for this lesson. If you wish to include these verses, we suggest a Bible version such as the English Standard Version (ESV), which simply refers to sexual relations as "knowing."

Think about It Some More

God sent two angels to warn Lot that he was going to destroy the city of Sodom. Lot believed the angels, so he went to Sodom to warn the two men who were engaged to marry his daughters. But when Lot told them, they did not believe. They thought he was joking.

We might think they were crazy for not believing, but we need to remember that Sodom was a place where the people forgot about God and were living like life was one big party. Nothing terrible had ever happened to them before. Why should they believe God would destroy their city?

Talk about It

:: Why was Sodom a bad place to live? *(Sodom was a city full of evil.)*

:: Why would God destroy Sodom? *(God is a good judge. Good judges make sure that evil is punished. There was a lot of evil going on in Sodom. That is why God was going to destroy it.)*

:: What would you do if someone came to you and said, "Quick, get out of your town; God is going to destroy it?" *(Parents, help your children sympathize with the two men who didn't believe. If God didn't help us, none of us would believe.)*

 Pray about It

Thank God for sending the angels to save Lot and for helping us to believe.

DAY TWO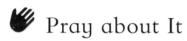

Remember It

What do you remember about yesterday's story? What do you think is going to happen today?

Read Genesis 19:15–16.

Think about It Some More

When God decides he wants to save a person, nothing—not even our sin—can stop him. That is really good news for us because we often turn away from God. But he has a way of grabbing hold of our hearts and saving us anyway. When God reaches out to save us, rather than give us the punishment we deserve, we say he is showing us mercy.

We see a picture of God's mercy toward Lot in our story today. Lot should have listened to the angels and left the night before. Instead of leaving right away, Lot waited until morning. But God had mercy on him. Instead of leaving Lot there to die, the angels grabbed him by the hand and pulled him to safety.

Talk about It

:: *Ask your children to pretend to be the angels and you pretend to be Lot. Have them try to convince you to leave. Keep objecting until they come to the same conclusion as the angels and grab you by the hand to lead you away. Then talk to them about how kind it was of God to not allow Lot to be destroyed.*

:: How did God show Lot mercy? *(God did not allow Lot to stay in Sodom. When he refused to leave, the angels grabbed him and his family by the hand and led them out.)*

:: Is there anyone that is too difficult for God to save? *(No, God can save the most terrible sinners by changing their hearts and drawing them to God. No one can resist God's amazing love once God opens eyes blinded by sin and they see how wonderful he is.)*

 Pray about It

Take time to pray for someone who does not believe in God, and ask God to reach out and pull them out of their sin.

DAY THREE

Connect It to Jesus

Can anyone guess how our story this week is about or points forward to Jesus?

 Read 2 Peter 2:6–9.
(You can skip over verse 8 to make this passage easier to understand.)

Think about It Some More

If God had not warned him, Lot would have stayed in Sodom and been destroyed with the rest of the city. Peter uses the story of Lot to tell us that God can rescue us. If God can rescue Lot from the wicked city of Sodom, then God can rescue us too.

You might not think you need God's rescue, but we all do. Every one of us is a sinner in need of rescue from God's judgment. God has a big rescue plan for his children. God the Father sent his Son to die on the cross so that we could be rescued from the punishment God is going to bring on sinners. God used the angels to rescue Lot, but his big rescue plan for all of us is his Son's death on the cross.

Talk about It

:: Why would God bring his judgment on Sodom and destroy it? *(It was a wicked city full of sin.)*

:: Why would God bring judgment on people today? *(We all have wicked hearts and everyone sins against God.)*

:: What is God's rescue plan for us? *(Jesus died on the cross for our sin. If we place our trust in him we can be saved.)*

 Pray about It

Like Lot, we are all in need of being rescued from our sin. Pray to God that he would rescue you through Jesus.

DAY FOUR

Remember It

What has God been teaching you this week through our Bible story?

 Read Genesis 19:16–29.

Think about It Some More

When we tell you not to do something, you need to be careful to obey. If we warn you not to touch a hot pot and you touch it anyway, you'll get burned. If we don't listen to God's warnings against sin, bad things happen too.

In our story today, Lot's wife doesn't listen to God's warning. He tells her through the angels not to look back. But she doesn't listen. Not thinking there is enough time to reach the mountains, Lot asks the angels if God would protect him in a nearby city. God agrees to spare Lot and hold back the destruction of Sodom until Lot and his family are safe. As soon as they reach the city safely God begins raining down fire on Sodom.

Lot and his daughters trust the Lord and obey God's command not to look back, but Lot's wife disobeys and turns back to look. Instantly she becomes a pillar of salt.

Talk about It

> ● ● KIDS, ask your parents if they ever disobeyed God and something bad
> ● ● happened as a result.

(Parents, you can share about a time when you got a speeding ticket because you didn't obey God when he said obey your leaders, or a time when you got angry and hurt someone with your words.)

:: What happened to Lot's wife? *(She disobeyed by looking back and became a pillar of salt.)*

:: What are some ways that we disobey God? *(Parents, help your children share areas where they sin.)*

:: Does God still punish people for sinning today? *(Yes, God warns us to turn away from our sin and trust in Jesus. But if we don't listen to his warnings, when we die we are sent to a place called hell, which is a place of fire.)*

🖐 Pray about It

Confess the areas of your life where you disobeyed God recently and ask God to forgive you. *(Parents, this is a great place for you to lead in sharing your weaknesses. Then help your children think of things they can confess in prayer to God and ask for his forgiveness.)*

DAY FIVE

Discover It

Today we look at a passage from a psalm or one of the prophets to see what we can learn from it about Jesus.

 Read Isaiah 42:1–3 and Matthew 12:18–21.

Think about It Some More

Long after the prophet Isaiah wrote this Bible passage, Matthew wrote his book about Jesus and said that Isaiah's prophecy was talking about the Lord. Jesus, he explained, is the one Isaiah said would bring God's justice to the nations. That means Jesus would be the one to make sure that God's law was followed, and if anyone sinned the proper punishment would be given.

Jesus did this in at least two ways. First, Jesus died on the cross and took the punishment for everyone who trusts in him. That takes care of justice for those who believe. That is why Matthew says we can place our hope in him. For the rest of the people who do not believe, Jesus will one day return to punish them for their sin. If people refuse to trust in Jesus, they will receive their own punishment so that God's justice will be complete.

Talk about It

:: Even though we are all sinners and deserve punishment, where can we place our hope? *(We can place our hope in Jesus who died on the cross to take our punishment.)*

:: What is the word we use to describe when a judge punishes sin? *(Parents, give your kids a clue and tell them it begins with the letter "J" and we already mentioned it today. "Justice" is a big word but an important one to learn.)*

:: Who is the judge that will bring God's justice to the earth? *(Jesus.)*

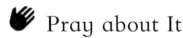 Pray about It

Take time again to pray for anyone you know who is not following or trusting in the Lord.

Week 13

Isaac and Ishmael

Tell your children you want to make them a promise. Friday after dinner you will treat them to homemade ice-cream sundaes. Each day this week during family Bible study, talk about your promise and what a promise feels like. Then, on Friday evening scoop out the ice cream, pour on the chocolate sauce, and ask them what it feels like to finally have their promise fulfilled. Finish the discussion with a review of God's promise to Abraham fulfilled in the birth of Isaac.

Say, "This week you will learn how God fulfilled his promise to Abraham and gave him a son."

DAY ONE

Picture It

There once was a young sailor whose job it was to look after the lowest deck of his ship. One day toward the end of the day, he heard the sound of water splashing at his feet. When he looked down, the hull of the ship was full of water. Rather than report the water to the captain, he went searching for the leak. You see, he was afraid the captain would blame him for the problem.

Hours went by as he searched but could not find the leak. By this time the water had risen to his knees. Now, he thought, I really can't tell the captain. When the ship started to slow and tilt in the water the captain called down to see if everything was okay. The young sailor lied and said that everything was under control. It was a good thing that the captain came for a look himself. As soon as he saw the flooded ship he shouted, "Turn on the pumps," and saved the ship in the nick of time.

Sometimes when we are afraid, we tell lies. That's what happened to Abraham in today's story.

 Read Genesis 20.

Think about It Some More

Abraham is afraid the Egyptians might kill him to get Sarah, his wife. So for a second time he tells her to say that she is his sister. (The first time this happened was in Genesis 12:10–20.)

Even though Sarah is in fact his half sister, it is a lie for Abraham to say that she is his sister instead of his wife.

Even though Abraham waited in faith for God's promise of a son, he was fearful and struggled to trust God to protect him. Now we have his story to help us. How kind of God to show us Abraham's weakness! God knows that all our lives are a mixture of faith and doubt.

Talk about It

:: Why does Abraham lie and say that Sarah is his sister? *(He is afraid that the Egyptians would kill him to get his wife.)*

:: How does God protect Sarah? *(God warns Abimelech in a dream that Sarah is Abraham's wife, and that he should not touch her or he would die.)*

:: When are you tempted to be afraid and not trust God? *(Give your children examples from your life. Then see if they can give you examples from their lives.)*

 ## Pray about It

Ask God to help you to trust the Lord and not lie.

DAY TWO

Remember It

What do you remember about yesterday's story? What do you think is going to happen today?

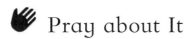 Read Genesis 21:1–7.

Think about It Some More

Finally, Sarah gives birth to the son God promised. Abraham obeys God and names the boy Isaac. Even though they waited a really long time, Isaac was worth the wait.

God likes to do things for us in a way that makes it clear that they come from God. That way we can't steal the credit or glory from God. Today's story is a great example of that.

Abraham and Sarah could not take credit for having a son. They couldn't say they planned to have their son. All they could do is laugh knowing that, without God, having a son at such an old age would have been impossible. They should have been grandparents and there they were holding their own tiny baby boy. Little did they know how God would use that baby to change the world. Jesus would come through Isaac's family.

Talk about It

:: How old is Abraham when his and Sarah's son is finally born? *(He is 100 years old.)*

:: Why does God make Abraham and Sarah wait so long? *(God wants to show that Isaac is a special work of God, so he waits until Sarah is far too old to have children.)*

:: What special blessing does God bring through the far-off grandchildren of Isaac? *(Jesus would be born in the family line of Isaac.)*

:: God kept his promise to Abraham. How can this encourage us as we try to trust God for the things that we need? *(We can believe that God will keep his promises to us, too, no matter what happens.)*

 Pray about It

Thank God for his faithfulness in fulfilling all his promises and ask him to help you to trust him.

DAY THREE

Connect It to Jesus

Can anyone guess how our story this week is about or points forward to Jesus?

 Read 1 Corinthians 1:28–31.

Think about It Some More

God wants all of our boasting (bragging) to be about what God does for us, not what we do for ourselves. God wants us to give him the glory or praise for the blessings in our lives and not act like we brought them on ourselves. That is one of the reasons God waited to give Abraham a son until he was very old. Everyone would say it was God's work, not Abraham's.

God wants us to know that only God can save us—we cannot save ourselves. Abraham and Sarah were too old to have children, so when Isaac came, all of the credit for his birth went to God.

That is the pattern God follows in saving us. There is nothing we can do to take away our own sin. We must depend on Jesus to take it away. When God saves us, we know that all of the credit should go to God.

Talk about It

:: What does this Bible passage mean when it says that God chose the low and despised things? *(God likes to choose the weak things so that he can show his strength.)*

:: How does God choosing the low and despised fit into the story of Abraham and Sarah? *(Since Abraham and Sarah had failed to have children, people would have looked down on them. Because they were too old to have children, their child would have been a clear sign of God's work. God alone would get the credit.)*

:: What is boasting? *(When we boast we are prideful and find our happiness in the things we have done.)*

:: Does God save us because of how good we are? *(No. Our salvation comes completely by grace. It is not based on our works at all.)*

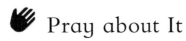 Pray about It

Pray that your boasting will be in the Lord and what he has done.

DAY FOUR

Remember It

What has God been teaching you this week through our Bible story?

 Read Genesis 21:8–21.

Think about It Some More

No one enjoys being made fun of. In our story Ishmael makes fun of Isaac. Sarah gets angry and tells Abraham to send Hagar and her son Ishmael away into the desert. Sarah doesn't want Ishmael to get a share of Abraham's wealth or blessing. So Abraham sends them away, out into the hot sun.

But God takes care of them. When they are tired and out of water, Hagar thinks they're going to die. But God has a different plan, already having promised that Ishmael would be a great nation. So God shows them where to find a well with water and he repeats his promise to Ishmael.

Talk about It

> ● ● KIDS, ask your parents if they ever had a time when they got angry
> ● ● or jealous.

(Parents, take this opportunity to confess your weakness to your children. If we confess our sins so our children see we are sinners too, it will help them on their way to trusting in Jesus for themselves.)

:: How does God keep his promise to Ishmael? *(God doesn't let Hagar and Ishmael die, but provides them with water to drink.)*

:: What do we learn about God from reading this story? *(God always keeps his promises.)*

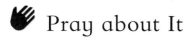 Pray about It

Thank the Lord for caring for Ishmael and caring for us.

DAY FIVE_____

Discover It

Today we look at a passage from a psalm or one of the prophets to see what we can learn from it about Jesus.

 Read Zechariah 6:9–13.

Think about It Some More

In old army movies, soldiers talking on the radio used code names to prevent eavesdropping enemies from knowing what was going on. If you knew the code names, however, you could figure out what they were saying.

The Bible passage we read today is like a coded message. We are introduced to a man called "the Branch" who will build the temple of the Lord. He will be a priest and will sit on the throne at the same time. "Branch" is like a code name given to the Messiah. Some people think that Zechariah probably copied this code name for Jesus from the prophet Jeremiah (Jeremiah 33:15). Jesus would "branch out" from the family tree of David through Jesse, David's father.

Although King Solomon first built a temple for God out of stones, Jesus builds a greater temple by saving people and filling them with his Holy Spirit. Today, all Christians together form the temple of God.

Talk about It

:: Who is the Branch Zechariah is talking about? (*Ultimately, Jesus is the Branch.*)

:: Why did Zechariah call Jesus a Branch? (*Jesus was a branch off of King David's family tree.*)

:: What temple is Jesus building? (*The temple Jesus is building is not made of stones but of God's people. God's presence no longer occupies a building; God lives in the hearts and lives of his people, the church.*)

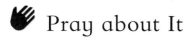 Pray about It

Thank Jesus for dying on the cross so we could become part of God's new temple.

Week 14

Abraham Is Tested

Ask your children to choose two of their favorite toys. Set the toys on the table and ask each child to choose the one toy they want to keep. After they point to one, ask, "What would you say if God asked you to give that toy up and never play with it again? Why might it be difficult? This week you will learn that God called Abraham to give up something very special and valuable."

DAY ONE

Picture It

What would you do if on your very first day of school your teacher gave you a test on a completely new subject? Let's say the first question was, "Name all the parts of the human heart." Then the second question asked you to describe the proper way to rebuild a motorcycle engine. What would you do?

Imagine that you raised your hand and said to the teacher, "I can't answer these questions unless you teach me." Immediately the teacher pulled out a bell, started ringing it, and shouted, "He passed the test." Later she explains that the real test was to see if you could figure out that you needed a teacher to help you learn.

In our story today, we are going to see how God gave Abraham a test he wasn't expecting.

 Read Genesis 22:1–8.

Think about It Some More

Abraham and Sarah waited many years for God to give them a son. Finally, Isaac was born, and it was a miracle because Abraham and Sarah were too old to have children. Now in our story God tells Abraham to kill Isaac!

As we see in verse 1, God was testing Abraham. By now Abraham has learned to trust God even when things look impossible.

If we look ahead to the New Testament, the writer of Hebrews gives us an inside peek into what Abraham was thinking. The book of Hebrews tells us that Abraham believed God could raise Isaac from the dead (Hebrews 11:19). Abraham told the servants that he and his son would both return after the sacrifice. That tells us that Abraham was sure God would do something to save his son.

Talk about It

:: What would you have done if you were Abraham and God asked you to sacrifice and kill your only son? *(Draw the children out here. God asked Abraham a very difficult thing. Remind them of today's opening exercise. Giving up a son is much harder than giving up a toy.)*

:: What do you think helped Abraham to trust God? *(Abraham had learned that God keeps his promises and can be trusted completely. God gives us this story in the Bible so we can see that God has been faithful in the past. That's how we learn to trust God for the future.)*

:: What helps us to trust God? *(Reading these stories out of the Bible helps us to learn that God always keeps his promises.)*

 Pray about It

Ask God to help you love him more than all your other stuff, and to make you willing to give up anything that takes away your love for him.

DAY TWO

Remember It

What do you remember about yesterday's story? What do you think is going to happen today?

 Read Genesis 22:9–14.

Think about It Some More

In this story, Isaac is a strong, healthy boy, but his father Abraham is getting old. It probably would have been easy for Isaac to run away from his father. But it looks like Isaac didn't fight or struggle at all! He allowed his father to tie him up and place him on an altar to be sacrificed.

Imagine a son so filled with faith in God and respect for his dad that he didn't fight even when he thought he was going to die. When his father took out a knife to sacrifice and kill him, he did not open his mouth to say, "Stop, Dad. Are you crazy?" Can you think of another only son in the Bible who did that?

That's right, Jesus did. Isaac's obedience to his father is a foreshadowing—a picture—of what Jesus would do much later as he obeyed God the Father in going to the cross.

Talk about It

:: What did God provide as a substitute or replacement sacrifice for Isaac? *(A ram caught in the thicket took Isaac's place as the offering.)*

:: What do we learn in this story about Isaac's faith? *(Isaac obeyed his father. It seems Isaac's faith in God was as strong as his dad's.)*

:: How should Isaac's example help you to obey your parents? *(If Isaac can obey in such a difficult thing, we should be able to obey in the simple things.)*

Pray about It

Have each of your children ask God to help them obey you. They may even confess specific ways they have disobeyed. Don't require them to do this, but if their hearts seem sensitive, ask if they would like to.

DAY THREE

Connect It to Jesus

Can anyone guess how our story this week is about or points forward to Jesus?

 Read 1 John 4:9–10.

Think about It Some More

In the story yesterday, Isaac was just about to be killed when God told Abraham to stop, and provided a ram as a substitute for Isaac. That means the ram took Isaac's place. Today our Bible passage talks about another substitute, Jesus.

Instead of killing us, God sent his only Son to be our substitute and die in our place. Jesus is like the ram. Like Isaac, he did not fight. Jesus agreed to die on the cross for us.

Today's Bible passage tells us that God sent his Son to be a "propitiation." This means that Jesus died in our place to take our punishment. This time, when Jesus was about to be beaten and killed, no voice from heaven called out to stop it.

Talk about It

:: What does the word "substitute" mean? *(If a person is a substitute they take your place. In baseball, when they want to take out a pitcher because his arm is getting tired, they bring in a substitute pitcher to replace the first one.)*

:: How does the ram in the thicket point to Jesus? *(The ram became a substitute so that Abraham could offer a sacrifice without killing his son. Jesus, our substitute, died in our place so that God the Father didn't have to punish us.)*

:: How does Isaac point to Jesus? *(Isaac, Abraham and Sarah's only son, did not protest when his father was about to sacrifice him. So also Jesus willingly died on the cross so that we could be forgiven.)*

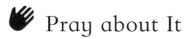 Pray about It

Thank God for sending his Son Jesus to be our substitute and to take our punishment.

DAY FOUR

Remember It

What has God been teaching you this week through our Bible story?

 Read Genesis 22:15–19.

Think about It Some More

The next time you go to the beach or see a sandbox, stop for a minute to look carefully at the sand. Reach down and take a pinch of sand and sprinkle it on your open palm. In that tiny amount you will see hundreds of grains of sand. If you tried to count them it would be pretty hard. If that's hard, imagine trying to count all the grains of sand in a sandbox. What about trying to count all the grains of sand on a beach?

God promised to give Abraham as many far-off grandchildren as there are grains of sand at the beach. So many children would come from Abraham that no one would be able to count them all.

Talk about It

> ● ● KIDS, ask your parents how many grandchildren their parents have.
> ● ● Then figure out how many grandchildren your mom and dad will have if your brothers and sisters each have three children.

:: How many grandchildren and far-off grandchildren did God give Abraham? A thousand? A million? A billion? *(Actually we don't know the number, but we do know that God gave him more far-off grandchildren than we could count.)*

:: Abraham was willing to give up the son God had promised him. How was this similar to what God did in sending Jesus? *(Jesus is God's only Son. God was willing to give up his only Son just as Abraham was willing to give up Isaac.)*

:: Why did God stop Abraham from killing Isaac? *(There was no need to sacrifice Isaac because Jesus would later die in Isaac's place. The ram was a substitute for Isaac, just as Jesus would be the perfect substitute for us—and for Isaac! Jesus died in our place so that we could have eternal life.)*

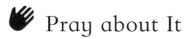 Pray about It

Ask God to give each person in your family a strong faith in God's promises.

DAY FIVE

Discover It

Today we look at a passage from a psalm or one of the prophets to see what we can learn from it about Jesus.

 Read Psalm 5:11.

Think about It Some More

In this verse, David encourages us to take refuge in God. A refuge is a shelter that provides protection from danger. When there is a terrible thunderstorm outside, people run inside to take refuge from the storm so they don't get wet or hit by lightning.

David is saying that when we are in trouble we can take refuge in God and run to him for safety. If we call out to God when we're sick, we are taking refuge in him. When we pray to God for protection before a long car ride, we are taking refuge in him.

Our biggest danger has to do with our sin. Since every person that sins must be punished, we are all in danger of God's punishment. But we have a refuge or shelter from God's punishment. If we place our faith in Jesus he takes the punishment we deserve. Remember how the ram was a substitute for Isaac? Jesus is our substitute.

When David talks about rejoicing because God is our refuge, he is pointing us to Jesus, who himself takes the punishment we deserve. When we think about our sin, we can run to Jesus as our refuge because by trusting in what he did on the cross he takes our punishment.

Talk about It

:: What is a refuge? *(A refuge is a place we can go to protect us from danger.)*

:: When have you ever used our house as a refuge? *(Parents, help your children to see that your home is a refuge from the cold, or from biting bugs, or—as we already mentioned—as a safe place in a storm.)*

:: Why do we need a refuge from God's punishment for sin? *(We are all sinners who deserve to be punished. With no refuge we would be punished in hell forever.)*

:: Who is our refuge from God's punishment for our sin? *(Jesus is our refuge from the Father's punishment.)*

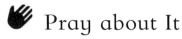 Pray about It

Thank Jesus for being our refuge.

Week 15

God Provides a Wife for Isaac

Ask your children, "Can you remember a way God has been faithful to our family?" Draw your children out or share a testimony of how God answered your prayers or need—perhaps in providing you the home you have, or restoring someone who was sick. Explain to your children that remembering what God has done in our lives in the past can help us trust him for the future. Say, "This week you will see how Abraham remembered God's past faithfulness and drew faith from that for the task of finding a wife for his son."

DAY ONE

Picture It

Imagine that the summer after you graduated from high school a man you never saw before came knocking at your door. He told you that he wanted you to leave your family and go away with him to marry a person you had never met. I'll bet you would think he was strange. If I asked you who was at the door and what they wanted, you would probably reply that it was some crazy guy who I needed to come get rid of.

Believe it or not, the very same thing happened in the story we are about to read. A man came calling for Rebekah, and she ended up going with him to marry a man she had never met before!

 Read Genesis 24:1–9.

Think about It Some More

When Abraham called for his most trusted servant, the servant probably wondered what Abraham was going to ask. "I wonder if he wants me to buy a few more cattle or sell a herd of goats," he may have guessed. But the servant was not prepared for Abraham's request: "Go on a journey to the land I came from and pick out a wife for my son."

Now that was a tough job! How in the world would the servant be able to convince a young woman to return to marry a man she never saw before? Although the servant was not sure Abraham's plan could work, Abraham knew God would help him.

Talk about It

:: What would you have thought if you had been the servant? *(Parents, help your children identify with the servant who was unsure about the assignment Abraham was giving him.)*

:: How did Abraham know God was faithful and would help? *(God had kept his promise to give a son to Abraham and Sarah; therefore, Abraham believed God. Since God said that Abraham would have as many children as there are grains of sand on the seashore, Abraham knew God would provide a wife for his son Isaac so he could have the children God promised.)*

:: How has God been faithful to you? *(Parents, draw out your children here. Remember, every good gift we have is from God, including every breath we take. [See James 1:17].)*

 ## Pray about It

Thank God for all the ways he has been faithful to your family.

DAY TWO

Remember It

What do you remember about yesterday's story? What do you think is going to happen today?

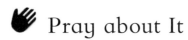 Read Genesis 24:10–14.

Think about It Some More

We know from yesterday that Abraham sent his oldest and most trusted servant to find a wife for his son. In today's story we see the reason Abraham trusted this servant: he was a man who trusted God himself.

We learn this from the servant's prayer to God for help. Perhaps the servant learned how to trust God from watching God work miracles in Abraham's life. Perhaps this is even one of the servants who went with Abraham on his journey to sacrifice his son Isaac. The servant would have known that Isaac's birth was a miracle because he knew how old Abraham and Sarah were.

Talk about It

:: What did the servant do that helps us to know he was trusting God? *(The servant prayed and asked God to help him.)*

:: What can we learn from the servant's faith for our own lives? *(We can call out to God and ask him to help us with our challenges.)*

:: How do you think the servant learned to follow God? *(The servant learned to follow God from watching Abraham follow God.)*

:: Whom has God placed in your life to teach you how to follow God? *(Draw out your children here beyond giving you as an answer. Talk about the other adults in their lives whom God has placed in their lives as an example.)*

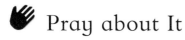 Pray about It

Thank God for the godly examples he has given you to follow.

DAY THREE

Connect It to Jesus

Can anyone guess how our story this week is about or points forward to Jesus?

 Read Genesis 24:15–28.

Think about It Some More

The servant prayed a very specific prayer. He asked God to bring a single woman to the well who would offer water to his camels when he asked her for a drink. Even before the servant had finished praying, Rebekah walked up with her water jar and did just what he'd prayed for.

God planned this even before the servant finished praying. Rebekah was only a part of God's bigger plan. After she married Isaac, their children would carry on God's promise. That way, Jesus would be born through Abraham's family line. In the end, it was Jesus who became the promised blessing from Abraham's family. Through Jesus, Abraham became a blessing to all people.

Talk about It

:: How do we know that Rebekah was God's choice for Isaac? *(Rebekah came to the well before the servant stopped praying, and she did just what the servant prayed God would have her do. She not only gave the servant a drink, but offered a drink to his camels too.)*

:: What can we learn about God from this story? *(God hears our prayers and God is all-powerful, able to work all things according to his plan.)*

:: *Read Matthew 6:8 to your children and ask them how it fits into our story. (God knew what the servant needed even before he asked.)*

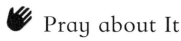 Pray about It

Ask God to provide godly partners for your children.

DAY FOUR

Remember It

What has God been teaching you this week through our Bible story?

 Read Genesis 24:29–67.

Think about It Some More

The story of Rebekah and Isaac is one of the best love stories in the Bible. God sure knows how to match up a man and a woman in marriage! Eve was perfect for Adam, and now we see that Rebekah was perfect for Isaac.

When Abraham's servant told Rebekah's father and brother the whole story of how he found her, they trusted God and gave their blessing for Rebekah to leave to be Isaac's wife. Rebekah trusted God and agreed to go. Then came one last question: would Isaac love Rebekah? Isaac saw her, married her, and loved her. How is that for a love story!

Talk about It

> 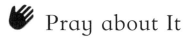 KIDS, ask your parents to tell you a story where they needed to trust God for something.

(Parents, think of a time when you needed to trust God to supply your daily needs, or give your testimony of how you trusted God for your salvation.)

:: What does it mean to trust God? *(When we trust God we believe that what God says is true and we give our lives to God.)*

:: Who in our story trusted God? *(Everyone in this story trusted God. Go through the characters one by one and talk about how each one trusted in God's plan.)*

Pray about It

Thank God for helping your parents trust in him.

DAY FIVE

Discover It

Today we look at a passage from a psalm or one of the prophets to see what we can learn from it about Jesus.

 Read Zechariah 9:9.

Think about It Some More

You might think that a king who was going to save Israel would come into the city riding boldly on a horse or in a chariot, maybe even accompanied by an army. But the king that Zechariah writes about looks very different. He is a humble king who rides into the city on a donkey! Did you ever hear of a king riding a donkey?

Zechariah tells us that this king is righteous (without sin) and that he is going to bring salvation—he is going to save someone. Only one king fits this description, and his name is Jesus.

Talk about It

:: Read Matthew 21:1–9 and ask your children how Jesus riding on a donkey is similar to Zechariah's prophecy. *(Zechariah's prophecy exactly describes Jesus' entry into Jerusalem.)*

:: Zechariah's prophecy tells us to rejoice over the king. What does it mean to rejoice? *(Rejoicing is another word for praising. When Jesus came into the city on a donkey the people shouted, "Hosanna" and "Blessed is he who comes in the name of the Lord." They were rejoicing just as Zechariah said they should.)*

:: Should we rejoice over Jesus coming to earth today? *(Yes, we should rejoice and praise the Lord for coming to earth to save us.)*

Pray about It

Take some time and praise the Lord in words, or sing your favorite praise song to thank the Lord for coming to earth to save us.

Week 16

Jacob and Esau

Place a can of soup on the table and ask your children how much they think the can of soup is worth? Hold a mock auction and get their bids for the soup. Then ask, "If this were your favorite kind of soup, how much would you pay for it?" Finally ask them, "How much would you pay if you were stranded on a desert island and hadn't eaten all week?" Say, "This week you will learn about a young man who sold the most valuable thing he had for a bowl of lentil stew."

DAY ONE

Picture It

Imagine that you are married and about to have your first baby. The big question everyone wants to know is whether it will be a boy or a girl. Finding the answer to that question can help you plan the kind and color of clothes to buy and how to decorate the baby's room.

But imagine the surprise on your face if at your next doctor's visit, the doctor tells you, "Your baby has two different heartbeats." Before you get too upset the doctor adds, "You are not having one baby; you are having twins!" And then the doctor continues to listen to your or your wife's tummy with the stethoscope and says, "You are having one boy and one girl. The girl will be born first and will graduate from medical school. Her brother, born second, will grow up to become a nurse and serve his sister." I think you might wonder how the doctor could hear all that through the stethoscope.

Listen as we read our Bible story today because Rebekah receives that same kind of mind-blowing news from God.

 Read Genesis 25:19–23.

Think about It Some More

Rebekah becomes pregnant and feels her baby moving inside. After a while she starts to feel like a wrestling match is going on inside her. Worried that something might be wrong, she prays to God, and God, who knows everything, tells Rebekah that she is going to have twins. God goes on to tell her that the babies are boys and the one born first, the older son, would serve the younger. He tells her all this before the babies are even born.

Talk about It

:: How does God know that Rebekah is having twins? *(God knows everything and the twins are part of his plan.)*

:: How does God know which boy would be born first, and that the younger son would serve the older son? *(Again, God knows what is going to happen before it happens.)*

:: What does Rebekah do that shows she trusts God? *(When she has a concern about the struggle with her babies, she calls out to God in prayer.)*

 ## Pray about It

Spend some time as a family lifting up your prayer requests to the Lord.

DAY TWO

Remember It

What do you remember about yesterday's story? What do you think is going to happen today?

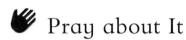 Read Genesis 25:24–28.

Think about It Some More

Our story is getting very interesting. Here is what we know so far. Yesterday we read that Rebekah's older son would serve the younger son, even though that was not the way it normally worked back then. Normally, it was the older son who was in charge. But God said that Esau, who liked to hunt, was going to serve the younger son Jacob, who was content to sit quietly at home.

You would think the boy who stayed around the tents with his mom would serve the stronger son who hunted, but God doesn't always do what we think. Rebekah's favorite son was Jacob, while Isaac's favorite was Esau because he hunted animals to make Isaac's favorite food.

Talk about It

:: Which son was Rebekah's favorite? *(Jacob)*

:: Which son was Isaac's favorite? *(Esau)*

:: Which of the sons do you think should have been the leader? *(Draw your children out to get their opinion.)*

:: Why didn't God follow tradition and have the younger son serve the older? *(God wanted to show that he alone decides who will carry on his promise.)*

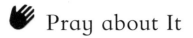 Pray about It

Spend time thanking God for each person in your family.

DAY THREE

Connect It to Jesus

Can anyone guess how our story this week is about or points forward to Jesus?

 Read Romans 9:8–15.

Think about It Some More

Have you been wondering why God told Rebekah that her older son would serve the younger? Here, in the book of Romans, God gives us the answer. God wanted to show that he controls everything. By choosing the meeker son over the stronger son, God was showing us that he didn't need man's strength to accomplish his plans. In the end God wanted everyone to see that his people are saved by our faith in God alone, not because of when we were born or because of anything we do.

God does not save us because we are strong or because we were born first. We are saved by faith (trusting in God's plan), and even our faith is a gift God gives to us. The most important part of God's plan to save us was the death of his Son Jesus, who died to take our sins away.

Talk about It

:: Did Jacob do anything that made God want to choose him over his brother? *(No, God chose Jacob before he had done anything good or bad.)*

:: Why did God choose Jacob to carry on God's promise? *(God chose Jacob because he loved him, but it was not based on anything Jacob had done.)*

:: Why do you think God chooses us to be a part of his family? *(God chooses us the same way he chose Jacob—because he loves us, not because of anything we do.)*

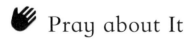 Pray about It

Thank God for loving sinful people and reaching out to save them.

DAY FOUR

Remember It

What has God been teaching you this week through our Bible story?

 Read Genesis 25:29–34.

Think about It Some More

In Isaac and Rebekah's day, the firstborn son was given something called a birthright. That meant that when his father died, the firstborn son would get to keep the family's wealth and take his father's place in leading the family. All the other members of the family would have to serve and obey him.

In Isaac's family, Esau was the firstborn so he held the birthright. But God told Rebekah that her older son would serve the younger. That meant something had to change. God used Esau's foolishness to give away the birthright to Jacob for a bowl of stew. From that day on and for the rest of his life Esau would need to serve Jacob, his younger brother.

Talk about It

> ● ● KIDS, ask your parents if they ever gave something away that they
> ● ● wish they had kept.

:: Why was Esau's decision a foolish one? *(A bowl of stew wasn't worth much, but the son who received the birthright would receive most of what his father owned. That was worth much more than a bowl of stew.)*

:: If someone was going to try to get you to give them something, what favorite thing of yours would they try to get you to trade? *(Parents, this is just a fun way for the kids to identify with Esau.)*

:: How are we sometimes like Esau? *(Every time we disobey God's law we are making a foolish decision, trading obedience for disobedience.)*

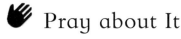 Pray about It

Ask God to help keep you from making foolish mistakes like Esau.

DAY FIVE

Discover It

Today we look at a passage from a psalm or one of the prophets to see what we can learn from it about Jesus.

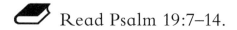 Read Psalm 19:7–14.

Think about It Some More

Let's say that a young man buys a house with money he borrows from a bank. Suppose this man never makes any payments to the bank. After a while, the bank calls the sheriff and the man is evicted from (thrown out of) the house. Even if the man promises to pay back the borrowed money, the bank would not allow him to have the house back.

But suppose the young man's father hears about his son's problem and pays back all the money owed on the house. He could buy his son's house back from the bank. When somebody buys something back like this, they have *redeemed* it.

In this psalm, David describes God as our redeemer. David knows he has broken God's perfect law and therefore deserves punishment. That is why at the end of the psalm he calls out for God to be his redeemer. There is only one way God can redeem any of us, and that is to pay off our debt.

Jesus died on the cross to pay our debt to God, his Father, by taking our penalty upon himself. That is how he redeems us.

Talk about It

:: What is a redeemer? *(Parents, use the illustration you just read to help your children remember this important word. We will come across the word redeemer again. A redeemer is someone who pays your debt so you can be free.)*

:: Who did David call his "redeemer"? *(David called the Lord his redeemer.)*

:: How is God our redeemer? *(Jesus died to pay the penalty we owed for the sins that we committed. We were prisoners to sin but Jesus set us free.)*

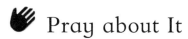 Pray about It

Thank God the Father for sending his Son to be our redeemer.

Week 17

Jacob's Lie

Dress one of your children in your clothes. Pick clothing items the other children (or your spouse) will recognize. Use some cologne or perfume to help fill out the disguise. Ask the others to guess who the child is dressed up as. If they guess correctly, ask them to tell you what clues helped them figure it out. Perhaps they will say they recognized the clothing or the smell of the perfume. Say, "This week you will learn how Jacob steals his brother's blessing by using a disguise and pretending to be his brother, Esau."

DAY ONE

Picture It

Pretend for a moment that you are very old and have only a short time to live. Soon you will die and go to be with Jesus in heaven. If you could make one last request before you die, what would it be? If you could to go to your favorite place one more time, where would you go? If you could choose one final meal, what would you pick to eat?

Today in our story, Isaac has grown old and is making his final request of Esau in his last days.

 Read Genesis 27:1–4.

Think about It Some More

Esau was the firstborn son and the favorite of his father, Isaac. Now Isaac is blind and very old and about to die. He calls his favorite son to his side and gives Esau a last request: to hunt a wild deer or antelope and prepare a meal from it. Isaac plans to bless his son before he dies.

Notice that Jacob is completely left out. Isaac could have called Jacob and asked him to prepare the meal, but he doesn't. Even though God told Rebekah that Esau, the older son, will serve Jacob, Isaac is planning on blessing his older son anyway.

Talk about It

:: What kinds of wild game do we see in our area? *(You might have squirrels, rabbits, or deer.)*

:: Why does Isaac call Esau and not Jacob? *(Esau is Isaac's favorite son.)*

:: How do you think Jacob feels to be left out? *(Draw your children out here and take time to express that you love all of your children and do not have favorites like Isaac did.)*

 ## Pray about It

Ask God to help you love all the members of your family.

DAY TWO

Remember It

What do you remember about yesterday's story? What do you think is going to happen today?

 Read Genesis 27:5–17.

Think about It Some More

Did you ever read a story or see a TV show in which you were not sure who the good guy was? Our story today is like that.

Should we be siding with Isaac? He loves his son Esau more than his other son Jacob, and is going to bless Esau in spite of God's word that Jacob will be the leader. That doesn't seem right. Or should we side with Jacob's mom, who is telling Jacob to lie to his dad and pretend to be his brother, Esau?

It seems they are both wrong. In the end we will see that God works everything out for good, even the sinful things that happen.

Talk about It

:: Did Rebekah, Isaac's wife, trust God to work out his plan? *(No, Rebekah planned to deceive her husband. That was wrong.)*

:: Can you think of a way Rebekah could have trusted God without lying? How could God have worked it out for Jacob to get the blessing? *(Help your children get creative here. For instance, what if God allowed Esau to get lost, or what if he could not find any game? Meanwhile, Rebekah could have reminded Isaac of God's word that their older son would serve the younger.)*

:: When is it okay to sin if it can accomplish something good? *(This is a trick question. It is never okay to sin.)*

:: Why is telling the truth so important? *(The simplest answer is because God tells us we should tell the truth. We are made in the image of God. So as best we can we should be holy, for God is holy [1 Peter 1:15]. In his holiness, God is faithful and true and cannot lie [Hebrews 6:18]. We should always try hard to be like God in these ways.)*

 # Pray about It

Ask God to help you trust him and always tell the truth.

DAY THREE

Connect It to Jesus

Can anyone guess how our story this week is about or points forward to Jesus?

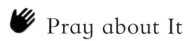 Read Acts 3:12–15.

Think about It Some More

Our Bible story today takes place long after Jacob's day, after Jesus rose from the dead and went back to heaven. The apostle Peter was sharing the gospel story (the story about Jesus) with a group of people. In the middle of his sharing, he gave God an interesting name. He called him "the God of Abraham, Isaac and Jacob."

Did you notice Peter didn't call him the God of Abraham, Isaac, and *Esau?* If you remember from our story this week, God chose Jacob rather than Esau to carry on the covenant promise he made to Abraham. In that covenant, or special promise, God said that Abraham's children would become a blessing to all nations. That promise was passed on to Isaac and then to Jacob.

Then one of Jacob's far-off grandchildren, Jesus, would become the blessing to all nations that God promised. When we trust in Jesus we are adopted into Abraham's family as one of God's children.

Talk about It

:: Why did Peter call God "the God of Abraham, Isaac and Jacob"? *(Abraham, Isaac, and Jacob were the first three to receive God's promise.)*

:: Why isn't Esau's name on Peter's list? *(God chose to bring his promise through Jacob, not Esau.)*

:: Whose family do we get added to when we trust in Jesus? *(When we trust in Jesus we are added to Abraham's family and become God's children too.)*

 # Pray about It

Thank God for giving his promise to Abraham and his son Isaac, and his grandson Jacob and to everyone who trusts in Jesus.

DAY FOUR

Remember It

What has God been teaching you this week through our Bible story?

 Read Genesis 27:18–40.

Think about It Some More

Sometimes we read Bible stories too quickly and don't take time to think about the people in the story. What would we do if we were them? For instance, think of what it was like to be Esau. Even though Esau lost his birthright, his dad wanted to bless him anyway. That must have been encouraging. He probably ran out to the fields, excited to kill some game for his dad.

Did you ever wonder what he was thinking? Perhaps he thought to himself, *I will kill some game quickly, prepare it for my father, and then I will get his blessing. That way I can still rule my younger brother.*

How angry he must have been to find out that, while he was gone, Jacob tricked their father into thinking he was Esau. Esau never forgot how Jacob had tricked him the first time, over the bowl of stew, and now Jacob had cheated him again.

Talk about It

> ● ● KIDS, ask your parents if they can remember a time when anyone
> ● ● cheated them and what it felt like to be cheated.

> *(Parents, think back; did anyone ever overcharge you or rip you off? Tell your children what that felt like. Help them identify with what Esau must have felt when he found out that Jacob cheated him out of his blessing.)*

:: How did God work out his plan for Jacob even though he sinned by lying? *(God always intended Jacob to carry on the promise, and he could even use the sinful decisions of Esau, Jacob, Rebekah, and Isaac to achieve his plan and purpose.)*

:: When Isaac blessed his son Jacob he said, "Cursed be everyone who curses you, and blessed be everyone who blesses you." Do you remember who first said that? *(God first gave this same blessing to Abraham in Genesis 12:3. Parents, look it up with your children.)*

Pray about It

Thank God that even our sin cannot mess up his plans.

DAY FIVE

Discover It

Today we look at a passage from a psalm or one of the prophets to see what we can learn from it about Jesus.

 Read Jeremiah 23:5–6.

Think about It Some More

We have already learned that the code name "Branch" that Zechariah uses in his prophecy stands for Jesus. In today's Bible passage we read that another prophet used that same code name for Jesus.

Jeremiah told the people of Israel that a day was coming when "a righteous Branch" would become king. Righteous means that he would be sinless. He would be called "the LORD is our righteousness." Notice that it doesn't say he would be called "the LORD is *his* righteousness"; it says that this king would be called "the LORD is *our* righteousness." Somehow this king would take away *our* sins and make us righteous (or sinless) like he is.

That matches up with what we know about Jesus. Jesus died on the cross taking the punishment God's people deserved for their sin, and he lived a perfect life so he could give his righteous life as a gift to all those who believe.

Talk about It

:: What does it mean to be righteous? (*If a person is righteous he does not have sin. Either he never sinned—like Jesus who had his own righteousness—or his sins have been taken away and traded for the gift of righteousness that comes from Jesus. If we place our faith in Jesus, he trades our sin for his perfect, righteous life.*)

:: Who is the righteous Branch Jeremiah is talking about? (*Jeremiah is talking about Jesus.*)

:: What did Jesus do to become our righteousness? (*Jesus lived a perfect life and never sinned even once, then died on the cross to take our punishment for sin.*)

Pray about It

Praise Jesus for never sinning, not even once, and for dying on the cross so he could give us the gift of his righteousness.

Week 18

Jacob's Dream

Grab a pinch of dry earth or sand from the garden or from a potted plant. Squeeze the pinch of earth between your thumb and finger and sprinkle it on a sheet of white paper in front of your children.

Ask for a volunteer to count the specks on the paper. (There should be more than they can count.) Soon the children will discover how difficult it is to count all the tiny bits on the page. Now ask them to imagine that their job is to count all the specks of dust not just on the paper, but across the face of the whole earth! Say, "This week you will learn that when God repeated to Jacob the promise he first gave to Abraham, he said that Abraham's descendants would be more than anyone could count."

DAY ONE

Picture It

Imagine for a moment that you are Jacob right after he disguised himself as his brother Esau and received his father's blessing. Quickly, your mom helps you take off the goat skins she placed on your neck and arms. Then, as you take the last one off, you hear a loud scream come from your father's bedroom. You recognize that it is Esau's voice and he is very angry.

Now you are in trouble because you can't give a blessing back like you could something else that you stole. What are you going to do? Your mom tells you Esau wants to kill you. If this happened in our house, where would you hide?

Today we will see what Jacob did to get away from his angry brother.

 Read Genesis 27:41—28:9.

Think about It Some More

Jacob had better look out now! He is in a lot more trouble than he ever imagined with Esau wanting to kill him! It's a good thing that his mom comes up with a plan to help him get away. She plans to send him out of town to find a wife, but she needs Isaac's permission. Isaac agrees and sends Jacob back to Laban (his uncle) to find a wife from among his daughters.

Then Jacob does something surprising: he repeats his blessing to Jacob before sending him on his journey. The first time he was fooled into blessing Jacob, but not this time. This time he blesses Jacob knowingly and repeats the promise God first gave to Abraham. Jacob is not in a disguise, so Isaac must realize that God wants to pass his promise on through his younger son Jacob. Then, before Esau can do Jacob any harm, Jacob is sent off on his journey to find a wife.

Talk about It

:: Why does Rebekah want Jacob to run away from Esau? *(Esau plans to kill Jacob because Jacob stole his blessing.)*

:: Why did Isaac bless Jacob instead of punishing him for lying? *(Isaac realized God was indeed going to continue the promise through his younger son.)*

:: How did Esau's anger grow into other sins? *(Esau's anger led him to want to kill his brother.)*

:: Can you think of a time where you became angry and your sin grew bigger because you didn't turn away from it? *(Parents, help your children to think of a time where in anger they have struck a sibling, broken or ruined something, or spoken disrespectfully.)*

 Pray about It

Ask God to help you turn away from your sins so they don't grow bigger.

DAY TWO

Remember It

What do you remember about yesterday's story? What do you think is going to happen today?

 Read Genesis 28:10–17.

Think about It Some More

Back when Jacob lived, walking alone outside in the dark could be scary. Wild animals made noises and, if you didn't have a weapon for protection, a lion might attack you. A good hunter like Esau could protect himself with his bow and arrows. But Jacob wasn't a hunter like his brother. Imagine him trying to get to sleep using a rock for a pillow.

Well, Jacob did fall asleep and God gave him an amazing dream—a vision of a stairway to heaven. When Jacob woke up, he had something even scarier than lions to be afraid of. God had visited him! But God wasn't going to punish Jacob for his lying. God had visited Jacob to pass on to him the same promise God first gave to Jacob's grandfather Abraham.

Talk about It

:: Why was Jacob afraid? *(Jacob was afraid because God visited him. Remember Jacob had lied to his father and deceived his brother. What if God was coming to punish Jacob for his sins?)*

:: Should we be afraid of God? *(Everyone should be afraid to sin against God because sin deserves punishment. But if we trust in Jesus to take away our sin, we don't have to be afraid of God.)*

:: Why didn't God punish Jacob for lying? *(God doesn't quickly punish us for everything bad we do. God was patient with Jacob. Even though he sinned against God, God planned to bring Jesus into Jacob's future family. God doesn't punish us every time we do something wrong either. God is patient with us so we can learn about Jesus and have our sins forgiven.)*

:: What did God show Jacob in his dream? *(God showed Jacob a stairway to heaven. The stairway showed that God was going to make a way for people on earth to get to heaven.)*

Pray about It

Thank God for being patient with us as he was with Jacob.

DAY THREE

Connect It to Jesus

Can anyone guess how our story this week is about or points forward to Jesus?

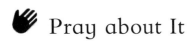 Read John 1:43–51.

Think about It Some More

While Jesus lived on earth, teaching his disciples, he often said things to explain how his life was connected to stories that happened long before he was born.

In today's story, Jesus begins to call his disciples. Even though Nathaniel has known Jesus only a short time, God opens his eyes to understand who Jesus is. Nathaniel calls Jesus "the Son of God" and "the King of Israel." Jesus says something very interesting in reply. Jesus links his life with Jacob's dream from our Bible story this week.

Jacob dreamt about a stairway that started on earth and reached up to heaven, with angels going up and down on it. Here Jesus explains that he himself is that stairway. He says that the angels are going to ascend and descend (go up and down) on him, the Son of Man, which is a name Jesus called himself.

From what Jesus says, we learn that he is the only way we can get from a sinful life on earth to heaven above, where we are forgiven and live with him forever.

Talk about It

:: Who is "the Son of Man"? *("The Son of Man" is the name Jesus uses for himself.)*

:: Who first saw the stairway that connects our world to heaven? *(Jacob first saw it in a dream after he ran away from Esau.)*

:: How can Jesus be the stairway from Jacob's dream? *(When Jesus dies on the cross he makes a way for people to get to heaven. So, in a sense, Jesus provides the way—the stairway—that people can use to get to heaven. Without Jesus we could not get to heaven.)*

Pray about It

Thank Jesus for becoming our stairway or ladder to heaven.

DAY FOUR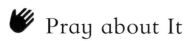

Remember It

What has God been teaching you this week through our Bible story?

 Read Genesis 28:18–22.

Think about It Some More

After his dream about the stairway, Jacob wanted to honor God. But the only way he knew to honor God was to set up a pillar, which was how the people of Canaan worshiped their false gods. To make a pillar, he took the stone he was using as a pillow and stood it on end. That way, if he ever walked by that place again, he could remember what God did. One day in the future God would tell him to return and build an altar, which was the way God wanted to be worshiped (Genesis 35:1).

Talk about It

> ● ● KIDS, ask your parents if they have a special memory of something
> ● ● God did in their lives that they wanted to remember.

(Parents, try to think of a time when God blessed you. It could be the day you became a Christian, your wedding day, or some other important date or event. If there is a particular photo or date in your Bible that helps you remember, share that with your children too.)

:: What name did Jacob give the place where he set up the pillar? *(He called the place Bethel.)*

:: How did Jacob try to bargain with God? *(Jacob said that the Lord would be his God if he provided the things Jacob needed—things like food, clothing, and safety.)*

 Pray about It

Ask God to be your God because he is good.

DAY FIVE

Discover It

Today we look at a passage from a psalm or one of the prophets to see what we can learn from it about Jesus.

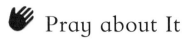 Read Isaiah 11:1.

Think about It Some More

When you cut down a tree, the stump will sometimes try to grow back. Little branches called shoots may grow out of the stump. If you don't cut them off, they will grow into a full-sized tree. If the stump is from an apple tree, the shoots will grow up into apple trees and bear apples.

In this passage, the prophet Isaiah is using the picture of a stump to represent King David's father Jesse, and the shoot growing out of a stump is one of his children or grandchildren. When the shoot grows up, Isaiah tells us, it will become a branch and bear fruit.

Remember our code word "Branch"? It refers to Jesus and we know that Jesus came from Jesse, David's father. Now, Jesus didn't grow up to bear apples or peaches. Bearing fruit simply refers to good deeds. Jesus grew up and did all sorts of wonderful things for people, like healing them, raising the dead, and, yes, dying on the cross so we can go to heaven.

Talk about It

:: What does Isaiah mean by a person bearing fruit? *(Bearing fruit doesn't mean we suddenly start growing grapes out of our ears. It means we do good deeds and obey God.)*

:: What good fruit do you see in your parents' lives? *(Parents, help your children honor your spouse in their comments. If they say something that honors you, thank them.)*

:: How can we tell good fruit from bad fruit? *(The Bible tells us what good fruit is. Parents, turn to Galatians 5:22 and use Paul's description of the fruit of the Spirit for example.)*

 Pray about It

Ask God to help you bear good fruit in your life like Jesus did.

Week 19

Jacob and Rachel

Buy a container of your children's favorite ice cream to enjoy at the end of the week. Before starting Day One, show the ice cream to the children. Stir their appetite by asking them to describe what they like about this particular ice cream. Ask them if they would like to have some—and then say they will first need to work for you for seven years to earn it, but you will keep the ice cream frozen, waiting for them.

After their initial reaction, tell them you will reduce the time to seven days, then seven hours. (If you do your Bible study in the evening, reduce the time to seven minutes and eat the ice cream after you're finished.) Use this as an opener to talk about how Jacob offered to work seven years for Rachel's hand in marriage.

DAY ONE

Picture It

What would it be like to have superhuman strength like Superman for one whole day? What would you do with your power? How about lifting your parents' car up over your head—with one hand?

You would need to be careful, though, with all that strength. If you slammed your bedroom door, it might break right off the hinges and explode into pieces. If you tried to open a tightly closed jar, you might squeeze it too hard and crush it.

Today in our story, we will see how Jacob gets so excited about Rachel that he demonstrates amazing strength by moving a large rock that would normally take many men to move.

 Read Genesis 29:1–14.

Think about It Some More

You might think, from reading the story in the Bible, that Jacob's journey to his uncle Laban's house took only a couple of days. But we know from looking on a map that he walked a distance of over 500 miles! If you walked 25 miles every day, without skipping a day, it would take three weeks to get there. So, by the time Jacob arrived, he must have been very tired. But the moment he saw Laban's beautiful daughter, Rachel, he forgot all about his long journey and moved the large stone covering the well all by himself!

Remember, this is Jacob, the quiet son who stayed by his mother's side and helped her with the cooking. You might have expected Esau, the strong hunter, to be able to move the stone, but not Jacob. Yet move the stone he did. Then he kissed Rachel and told her the story of his journey. She was so amazed that she ran all the way home, leaving her flocks at the well.

Talk about It

:: Where did Jacob get the strength to move the large stone? *(We are not told that God gave him special strength to move the stone, but anything we do is by the grace of God.)*

:: How is this story similar to the one where Abraham sent his servant to find a wife for Isaac? *(Both stories happened at a well, and in both, the very first woman to come to the well was the one the man was looking for.)*

:: How was God at work in this story? *(Parents, help your children to see the different ways God is at work behind the scenes: God helped Jacob find Haran; the shepherds he met knew Rachel was Laban's daughter; God helped Jacob move the large stone; etc.)*

 Pray about It

Thank God for how he works out every detail of our lives for our good.

DAY TWO

Remember It

What do you remember about yesterday's story? What do you think is going to happen today?

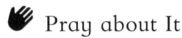 Read Genesis 29:15–20.

Think about It Some More

If you wanted to buy a new bike but you didn't have any money, you could make a deal with the owner of the bicycle store. If you offered to weed his flowerbeds, wash the store windows, and bring all the shopping carts in at the end of the day, and do this for a year, he might agree to exchange your work for the bike you want.

In our story today, Jacob wanted to marry Rachel, but he didn't come with any money. Back in Jacob's day, you had to give the father gifts to get permission to marry one of his daughters. Because Jacob didn't have any money, he offered to work seven years for Laban in exchange for his daughter Rachel.

Talk about It

:: How did Jacob feel about Rachel? *(Jacob loved Rachel, for she was very beautiful.)*

- How long did Jacob agree to work for Rachel? *(Jacob loved Rachel so much he agreed to work for seven years.)*

- Why did Jacob have to work for Rachel? *(Jacob didn't have any money. Because of his sin he left home quickly and his dad was not too happy with his lies. Jacob left without bringing the kind of gifts and money Abraham sent along with his servant to find Isaac a wife.)*

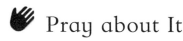 Pray about It

Thank God for loving us so much that he gave his only Son Jesus.

DAY THREE

Connect It to Jesus

Can anyone guess how our story this week is about or points forward to Jesus?

 Read Genesis 29:21–35.

Think about It Some More

Remember how Jacob dressed up like Esau, lied to his dad, and stole his brother's blessing. In our story today, Jacob finds out what it feels like to be tricked.

Instead of keeping his promise to give his younger daughter, Rachel, to Jacob, Laban dresses his older daughter, Leah, as the bride. Jacob doesn't discover the switch until after he is already married to Leah.

When Jacob discovers the truth he complains to Laban, who quickly offers to give Rachel to Jacob if he works for him for another seven years. Jacob agrees and begins to work to take Rachel as a second wife. When God sees that Leah is not loved, he blesses her with four sons.

That is where we find our connection to Jesus in today's story. One of Leah's boys, named Judah, grew up to become the far-off grandfather of Jesus. His people would be called the tribe of Judah.

Talk about It

- How is our story today similar to the story where Jacob steals Esau's blessing? *(Jacob and his mom didn't trust God to work out his plan, and Jacob's mom dressed him up like his brother to steal the blessing. In our story today, Leah dressed up like Rachel in a wedding dress and stole Rachel's place as the bride.)*

- What was wrong with what Laban did in switching his daughters? *(Laban agreed to give Rachel to Jacob, but he deceived him by giving him a different daughter instead. Lying is a sin against God.)*

:: How did God work Laban's sin for good? *(God provided a husband for Leah; he taught Jacob a lesson for deceiving his brother; but most important, Jesus will be born into the future family of one of Leah's sons.)*

 Pray about It

Thank God that our sins cannot stop God's plans.

DAY FOUR

Remember It

What has God been teaching you this week through our Bible story?

 Read Luke 3:23–38.

(Warn your children that you are about to read a lot of names, but ask them to raise their hands each time you read a name they recognize. Slow down when you get to Judah, Jacob, Isaac, and Abraham.)

Think about It Some More

Yesterday we learned that Leah had a son named Judah who would head up the tribe that bears his name, and one day Jesus would be born into that tribe.

Today we are looking ahead to the birth of Jesus. In this passage, Luke records the family tree of Jesus. Notice that it starts with Jesus and goes all the way back to Adam, with Judah's name in the middle.

Talk about It

> KIDS, ask your mom or dad to draw your family tree starting with great-grandparents as the trunk of the tree.

:: Which one of Jacob's sons is listed in Jesus' family tree? *(Parents, you can reread verses 33–34 to see if your children can give you the answer Judah.)*

:: What other names did you recognize? *(Draw your children out to see who they recognized. See if they can tell you something about them.)*

:: Why do you think God gave us this family tree? *(God wanted to show that Jesus was a far-off grandson of Adam, a man like all the others, for only a man could die to take away the sins of men.)*

 Pray about It

Pray for every person in your family tree by name and ask God to help them love Jesus with all their hearts.

DAY FIVE

Discover It

Today we look at a passage from a psalm or one of the prophets to see what we can learn from it about Jesus.

 Read Micah 5:2.

Think about It Some More

About 700 years before Jesus was born, the prophet Micah foretold that a very special ruler would come out of the land and people of Judah. Micah said this ruler would be "from of old, from ancient days." That meant he needed to be a very, very old man. But Israel had never had a ruler like that. There is only one person that fits Micah's description: Jesus, who is the Son of God.

The Son of God has always existed, even before the world was made, so he was surely alive in ancient times. We know this part of the Bible is talking about Jesus because Matthew tells us that it is (Matthew 2:1–6).

Talk about It

:: What do you think will happen 700 years from today? *(Parents, help your children to imagine what might happen far into the future.)*

:: How could Micah know that Jesus would be born into the tribe of Judah 700 years before it happened? *(God spoke through the prophets. God spoke to the prophets and they in turn repeated to the people what God told them.)*

:: Micah tells us that the special ruler he is talking about will come from Bethlehem. How does that fit Jesus? *(Jesus was born in Bethlehem.)*

:: How does Micah's prophecy fit into our story about Jacob's children? *(One of Leah's children was named Judah, who was the far-off grandfather of all the people of Judah. He is the same Judah from Micah's prophecy.)*

 Pray about It

Thank God for sending his Son Jesus to be born into the family of Judah, to save us from our sins.

Week 20

Jacob Flees from Laban

One by one, secretly invite each child to meet you under the dining table. Tell them to be quiet and not to let anyone else see them. (Pull the chairs away from the table in advance.) If you hear any talking, issue an immediate warning by saying, "Somebody may hear you, please be quiet."

Once everyone is gathered, ask the children how they felt sneaking around the house. Then go on to explain that this week they will be learning how Jacob secretly fled from Laban.

DAY ONE

Picture It

Two young boys asked if they could fish in a certain man's pond. Although the man was selfish and never allowed anyone to fish in his pond, he looked down at the boys and thought, *These boys will be lucky to get even one bite, let alone catch a fish.* So he gave them permission.

"Can we keep all the fish we catch?" one boy boldly asked. Convinced that the boys were no threat to his prized collection of large trout, the man answered, "Yes, you can keep the fish you catch." As he walked back to his house, the man chuckled to himself, "Now no one can say that I'm selfish."

The boys, who had been fishing since they were toddlers, quickly cast their lines into the water. One by one they caught all of the man's prize fish and quietly slipped away. What do you think the man will say when he comes back to an empty pond?

Although our story today is not about fishing, it does involve a selfish man. Let's see what happens in our story.

 Read Genesis 30:25—31:9.

Think about It Some More

Jacob watched over Laban's flocks of sheep and goats for fourteen years in return for marrying Leah and then Rachel. Now that he was finished paying off his debt, he wanted to return home. When Laban urged him to stay, Jacob said he would stay if Laban gave him all the animals that had spots or streaks. Laban agreed, but slyly separated out the spotted and speckled animals and sent them far away so Jacob would not get them.

But soon the flocks were having babies again and all of the baby goats and sheep had spots and speckles. So Jacob got to keep them all. When Laban changed the rules and said, "From now on you can have only the sheep and goats with streaks," God made all of them have streaks. When Laban changed the rules yet again and said, "Now you can have only the ones with white spots on their backs," God made all the baby animals have white spots. Every time Laban selfishly tried to cheat Jacob, God blessed Jacob so that his flocks grew larger and larger.

Talk about It

:: How was Laban trying to cheat Jacob? *(Ten times he changed the kind of goats and sheep Jacob could have.)*

:: How did God bless Jacob? *(Even though Laban changed the rules, God changed the kind of animals being born. If Laban said Jacob could have the speckled ones, then all the goats and sheep born were speckled. If he said streaked, then they all had streaks.)*

:: How did God's blessing get Jacob into trouble? *(Laban's sons complained that Jacob had grown rich by taking their father's goats. Laban probably felt like the man with the pond when he saw all his fish were missing.)*

 ## Pray about It

Praise God because he controls all things, even the color of baby sheep and goats.

DAY TWO

Remember It

What do you remember about yesterday's story? What do you think is going to happen today?

 Read Genesis 31:10–21.

Think about It Some More

Back in Bethel, when Jacob had his first dream about the stairway to heaven, he'd made a promise to God. Jacob had said that if God would give him food to eat and clothes to wear and bring him home safely, he would follow God. Since then, God had blessed Jacob with a large family and large herds, making Jacob a rich man. Now it was time for God to bring Jacob home safely.

While Laban was away shearing his sheep, God appeared to Jacob and told him it was time to leave. Jacob realized that since Laban wasn't home, it would be easy to leave without any trouble.

Talk about It

:: Why do you think God told Jacob to leave while Laban was away? *(Laban didn't want Jacob to go, and his sons would try to stop Jacob because they thought he had cheated their father.)*

:: When Jacob first arrived at Laban's he had nothing but his clothes. What does he own now? How has God blessed him? *(Look at verses 17–18 and give your children some clues to help them remember all that Jacob now owned. Help them see how God blessed Jacob while he was away.)*

:: Did God answer Jacob's prayer to give him food and clothes, and to bring him home safely? *(Yes, God gave Jacob all these things.)*

:: What do you think Laban is going to do when he comes home and finds that Jacob left, along with all of his things? *(We will see on Day Four that Laban is not too happy and he runs after Jacob.)*

 Pray about It

Thank God for the way he answered Jacob's prayer.

DAY THREE

Connect It to Jesus

Can anyone guess how our story this week is about or points forward to Jesus?

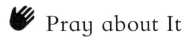 Read Matthew 2:13–16.
(This is a story about baby Jesus.)

Think about It Some More

Yesterday we read how God appeared in a dream to Jacob and told him to flee from Laban. In today's story, God appears to another man, Joseph, and warns him to flee to Egypt to escape evil King Herod. Herod wanted to kill Joseph and Mary's Son, the baby Jesus. God has always planned to save sinners through his Son Jesus, and he will not allow anything to stop his plan—not Laban, not Herod, not anyone.

Talk about It

:: How is the story about Joseph's dream similar to Jacob's dream. *(God told them both to leave the place they were in.)*

:: How is Jesus related to Jacob? *(Jesus is Jacob's far-off grandson.)*

:: How did God know what Herod would do? *(God knows everything, even what people are going to do in the future. Nothing is hidden from God.)*

:: How does this story remind us of Jesus? *(God kept Jacob safe, just like he kept Jesus safe so we could all be saved.)*

 Pray about It

Thank God for protecting Jesus so he could be our Savior.

DAY FOUR

Remember It

What has God been teaching you this week through our Bible story?

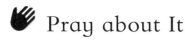 Read Genesis 31:22–55.
(Be aware that verse 35 is an explicit reference to a woman's menstrual cycle.)

Think about It Some More

Laban was upset and angry that Jacob left while he was away, so he chased after him with his men. It took him seven days to catch up with Jacob. It was a good thing that God warned Laban, because Laban felt that everything Jacob owned was really still his. His anger could have led to violence.

When Jacob heard that God appeared to Laban to warn him, he knew God was on his side. God had answered Jacob's prayer to bring him home safely.

Talk about It

> ● ● KIDS, ask your parents if they can remember a time when God pro-
> ● ● tected them from something bad.

(Parents, you might recount a time when God spared you from some danger or calamity.)

:: How did God protect Jacob? *(God appeared to Laban in a dream and warned him not to talk bad about Jacob.)*

:: How does God protect you every day? *(Parents, help your children think of all the ways God protects them.)*

 Pray about It

Thank God for the specific ways he protects you from danger every day.

DAY FIVE

Discover It

Today we look at a passage from a psalm or one of the prophets to see what we can learn from it about Jesus.

 Read Psalm 3.

Think about It Some More

Some of the psalms David wrote are about things that happened to him in his life. Psalm 3 was written when David's son Absalom was trying to kill him. David had to run away. We see from reading what David wrote that he called out to God to be his shield to protect and save him.

It is good to learn how David called out to God because we can use David's prayers to call out to God like he did. You don't have to have someone chasing you to pray these prayers. God gave us these psalms because they teach us something about God.

For example, in this psalm we learn that God is a God who saves. We may not have a person trying to kill us, but we all have another enemy, sin. Sin is always trying to destroy us. God, who saved David from Absalom, can also save us from our sin. So, when David says, "Salvation belongs to the LORD," he is talking about God saving him from Absalom, but he is also telling us about God. God is a God who saves.

Talk about It

:: When we read in this psalm that God is a God who saves, what should that remind us of? *(That should remind us of the cross where Jesus died to save us from our sin.)*

:: Why is David's prayer, "Arise, O LORD! Save me, O my God!" a good prayer for us to pray? *(We need to be saved from our sin as much as David needed to be saved from Absalom.)*

:: Who needs to be saved by God? *(We all need to be saved—every one of us.)*

 Pray about It

Pray David's prayer and ask God to save each person in your family.

Week 21

Jacob's Wrestling Match

Challenge your children one by one to an arm-wrestling competition. (You may want to skip challenging your teenage son who plays offensive tackle.) With each child apply only as much strength as is needed to keep them from winning. Let each match go long and encourage them to keep trying to win. As they tire, overpower them and win each match. Explain that this week you will learn how Jacob wrestled with God.

DAY ONE

Picture It

Pretend that you are a knight in armor on your way home to your castle. But you have a problem: there is a dragon that lives between you and the castle walls. There is no way to escape the dragon; you will have to confront him. And to make matters worse, the last time you traveled along the dragon's road you stole some of his treasure, making the dragon very angry.

Now wouldn't you feel better if two of the strongest knights from the neighboring castles met you along the way and offered to walk along with you? With three knights traveling together, the dragon might not be so quick to fight and might allow you to pass.

Today in our story, Jacob has solved the problem of Laban chasing him, but he has a dragon awaiting him: his brother Esau. Let's see who he meets along the way to help him.

 Read Genesis 32:1–2.

Think about It Some More

With Esau not too far away, Jacob was glad to see the angels! The last he had heard, fifteen years before, his brother Esau wanted to kill him. As Jacob traveled closer to home, he knew he would have to deal with his brother. When God told Jacob to leave Laban God promised to go with him (Genesis 31:3). Now that he saw the angels, Jacob knew God was with him in that place.

Talk about It

:: What did Jacob say when he saw the angels? *(Jacob called the place "God's camp.")*

:: How can God's faithfulness in keeping his promise to Jacob encourage us? *(God does not change. He was faithful to Jacob and he will be faithful to us as well. We can trust his promises.)*

:: Can you think of something that can cause us to fear and forget God's faithfulness? *(Parents, first confess your weaknesses and then draw out your children.)*

 ## Pray about It

Ask God to help you to trust him anytime you are afraid.

DAY TWO

Remember It

What do you remember about yesterday's story? What do you think is going to happen today?

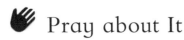 Read Genesis 32:3–21.

Think about It Some More

When Jacob heard that Esau was coming to meet him with four hundred men, he thought that Esau was coming with an army to kill him. There is no way Jacob, with wives and children, could fight four hundred men, but he knew God could.

Knowing there was no way he could win a battle against his brother, Jacob did three things. First, he called out to God and asked for help. Next, he prepared to send on ahead a whole parade of animals as gifts for his brother. Finally, he split his group in half so that if Esau attacked one group, the other group might still escape.

Talk about It

:: What did Jacob do that was good? *(Jacob called out to God for help.)*

:: What should we do when we are in trouble today? *(We can still call out to God for help today.)*

:: What do you think will happen in our story? *(Draw out your children to see if they remember what happened in this story. If they're unsure, have them guess.)*

 ## Pray about It

Ask God to help you remember to call out to the Lord in times of trouble.

DAY THREE

Connect It to Jesus

Can anyone guess how our story this week is about or points forward to Jesus?

 Read Genesis 32:22–32.

Think about It Some More

Can you imagine what Jacob must have thought when, in the middle of the night, a stranger appeared and began to wrestle with him? Jacob may have thought it was a robber or one of Esau's men. They wrestled all night, but Jacob did not give in. Then, toward morning, the man put Jacob's hip out of joint with one small touch. Suddenly Jacob realized he had been wrestling with God.

Despite the pain, Jacob held on and refused to let go until God blessed him. So God blessed Jacob and gave him a very special name: Israel. From that time on, God's people would be known as the people of Israel.

When Jesus came riding into Jerusalem just before going to the cross, the crowds waved palm branches and shouted, "Blessed is…the King of Israel" (John 12:13).

Talk about It

:: What did the man whom Jacob wrestled with do that made Jacob realize he was no ordinary man? *(The man touched Jacob's hip and put it out of joint.)*

:: Who was Jacob wrestling with? *(Jacob was wrestling with God who had come down in the form of a man. That is why Jacob said he saw God face-to-face.)*

:: Can you think of a time when God became a man and walked on the earth? *(Jesus is God the Son who came down to earth to die on the cross.)*

 Pray about It

Thank God for reaching out to Jacob, and thank him for sending Jesus to reach out to us so we could know God too.

DAY FOUR

Remember It

What has God been teaching you this week through our Bible story?

 Read Genesis 33:1–11.

Think about It Some More

When Jacob saw Esau coming with all of his men, he moved ahead of his family and bowed down seven times, hoping to appease Esau. How surprised he was when Esau ran up to him, welcoming him and kissing him!

Fifteen years earlier, Esau had wanted to kill Jacob. But now Esau welcomed him back warmly. It was such an amazing change that Jacob praised God and said, "God has dealt graciously with me."

Talk about It

> 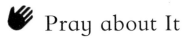 KIDS, ask your parents if they can remember a time when someone forgave them for something they did.

(Parents, this is a great time to share a time when your spouse forgave you for something you did. Communicate to your children how wonderful forgiveness feels. Then connect that to the gospel where Jesus forgives us of our sins.)

:: What did you think was going to happen the first time you heard this story? Did you think there was going to be a war? *(Parents, draw out your children as to what they thought would happen.)*

:: How do you think Jacob felt when he realized his brother was not mad? *(Jacob would have felt happy and relieved.)*

:: Was God faithful (did he keep his promises) to Jacob? *(Yes, God kept his promise to protect Jacob.)*

Pray about It

Thank God for his faithfulness to protect Jacob.

DAY FIVE

Discover It

Today we look at a passage from a psalm or one of the prophets to see what we can learn from it about Jesus.

Read Zechariah 10:3–6.

Think about It Some More

To erect a stone building, the very first stone to be laid is the cornerstone. All the other stones in the building line up with that first one. In this prophecy (word from God) Zechariah tells of a day when God will care for the house of Judah. From the house of Judah he will raise up a cornerstone.

The apostle Paul tells us that this cornerstone is another code name for Jesus. He says that the house of God is built on the foundation of the apostles and prophets, and that Jesus Christ is the cornerstone *(see Ephesians 2:20–21)*. That means that Jesus is the most important part of the church.

Talk about It

:: Who was Judah? *(Judah was one of Jacob's sons, born to Leah.)*

:: Who is Zechariah talking about when he says that a cornerstone will come out of the house of Judah? *(He is talking about Jesus who is the most important part of the church.)*

:: If Jesus is the cornerstone, can you guess who are the other stones that make up the walls of God's church? *(Read 1 Peter 2:4–5 to your children. We are the stones that make up the walls of God's church.)*

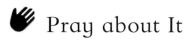 Pray about It

Thank God for sending Jesus to be the cornerstone of God's church.

Week 22

Joseph's Dream

Collect a variety of brightly colored crayons, markers, or pencils, along with a sheet of paper. Tell your children that you want them to raise a hand when they think they know what you are drawing. Start drawing Joseph's multicolored robe. As each child raises a hand, have her whisper her guess in your ear. See if they can guess that the lesson for this week is about the life of Joseph, Jacob's son.

DAY ONE

Picture It

Small children often have a favorite blanket or toy that they take everywhere they go. They may even have a special name for it; for example, "blankie" for a blanket. Maybe you can remember when you had such a blanket or toy. If a child loses his special blanket or toy, he can get pretty upset because he doesn't feel safe without it.

You don't see adults still carrying around those kinds of things. As we grow older we realize that those blankets and toys can't really help us. We need to depend on God for our help and learn to do without them. Sometimes parents need to help their children give them up by saying, "Don't you think it's time to leave blankie behind?"

In our story today, Jacob trusts the Lord and helps the people give up their "blankies." See if you can pick up from our story what things they are depending on for comfort.

 Read Genesis 35:1–7.

Think about It Some More

When Jacob first met God at Bethel, he made a pillar out of the stone he was sleeping on. Here in our story God instructs Jacob to build an altar for him in Bethel. An altar is a pile of stones used for presenting an offering to God. Every time an animal is killed on God's altar, God is reminded how one day his only Son Jesus will be sacrificed and will die for the sins of his people.

Before Jacob built the altar, he told all the people to put away their false gods. Back when God first spoke to Jacob, Jacob promised that he would make the Lord his God if the Lord would protect him and safely bring him home. Now Jacob keeps his end of the bargain. By ordering all the idols to be left behind he is saying to his family, "We are not going to trust in these false gods anymore. We are going to trust the Lord."

Talk about It

:: What was the people's "blankie"? (*The people carried false gods with them much like a child carries a blankie. But false gods are powerless to help anyone.*)

:: What about us—who should we trust to keep us safe? (*We should trust the Lord like Jacob did. There is nothing wrong with a little child holding onto a blankie, but as we get older we need to place our trust in the Lord.*)

:: What reason did Jacob give his family for putting away their false gods and trusting the true God? (*If you have young children you can repeat verse 3 and then ask them the question. Jacob said that God answered him when he was in trouble and God had been with him wherever he went.*)

 ## Pray about It

Ask God to help each person in your family trust in him.

DAY TWO

Remember It

What do you remember about yesterday's story? What do you think is going to happen today?

 Read Genesis 37:1–4.

Think about It Some More

Sometimes we make the same mistakes our parents make. In our story today, that's what Jacob did. When Jacob was a young boy his father Isaac loved Esau more than him. You would think Jacob would have learned a lesson from that, but he didn't.

Jacob loved Joseph more than his other sons, and he gave Joseph a special coat. The other brothers were envious—angry that their father didn't give them special coats too. It didn't help that Joseph reported on his brothers' behavior. They probably thought of him as a tattletale.

Talk about It

:: How would you feel if you were one of Joseph's brothers? (*Parents, draw out your children here to help them identify with the way Joseph's brothers felt.*)

:: Can envy work the same way in our hearts too? (*Yes. The Bible warns us against envy in Galatians 5:19–21, showing that envy is a common but serious sin.*)

:: Can you think of a time when you were envious of someone? (*Have the children share their own struggles with envy. Perhaps there was a time when one of their siblings received a birthday gift and they wanted to have one as well.*)

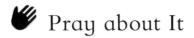 Pray about It

Ask God to help you not be envious of those around you.

DAY THREE

Connect It to Jesus

Can anyone guess how our story this week is about or points forward to Jesus?

 Read Genesis 35:9–12.

Think about It Some More

After Jacob built his altar to God at Bethel, God spoke to him. He reminded Jacob of the new name God gave to him after his wrestling match. From then on, God didn't want him to use the name *Jacob*. Instead, he wanted him to use the name *Israel*.

In time, all of God's people would use the name *Israel* as their family name. They would be called the people of Israel. Their rulers would be called the kings of Israel, and the greatest king of Israel was Jesus. The name *Israel* always points to Jesus, the king of Israel.

Talk about It

:: What did God promise Jacob when he spoke to him? *(God promised to give Jacob the land just as he had promised Abraham and Isaac before him. Also, God promised to make Jacob a great nation and said that kings would come from him.)*

:: When God gave Jacob the new name *Israel,* he told him to be fruitful and multiply. Do you remember what that means and who else God gave that command to? *(It means to have a lot of children. God first gave that command to Adam and to Noah again after the flood.)*

:: What do we learn about God from today's story? *(Once again we learn that God is faithful to keep his promises.)*

 Pray about It

Take some time to lift up your prayer requests to God, and while you do, praise him for being faithful.

DAY FOUR

Remember It

What has God been teaching you this week through our Bible story?

 Read Genesis 37:5–10.

Think about It Some More

What would you do if you dreamt that you got a whole bag of little chocolate bars, but your brother or sister didn't get any and you ate all of your chocolate bars by yourself? How would your brother feel if you shared your dream with him? He might not be too happy. It might be better to keep that dream to yourself.

In our story today, God gave Joseph two dreams. The first one was about sheaves (bundles) of wheat stalks and the second was about stars. In both dreams, Joseph was at the center with his family bowing down to him.

Rather than keep his dreams to himself, Joseph announced them boldly. But that only made his brothers so full of envy that they hated him. Even his father corrected Joseph.

Talk about It

> :: KIDS, ask your parents if they were ever envious of someone.

(Parents, try to remember what it was like growing up and if there were any rivalries in your family.)

:: What did Joseph's brothers think of his dreams? *(They didn't like his dreams and were all the more angry and envious.)*

:: Who gave Joseph his dreams? *(God gave Joseph his dreams.)*

:: Why did Joseph's father keep his dreams in mind (think about them more)? *(God spoke to Israel [Jacob] through dreams when he was a young man. Perhaps he wondered if God might be speaking to his son.)*

:: Later in our story we will learn that some bad things happen to Joseph. How might these dreams help Joseph during tough times? *(Joseph could remember the dreams and be encouraged that God would help him.)*

Pray about It

Ask God to help you to love your brothers and sisters (or your friends if you are an only child) and treat them with love and respect.

DAY FIVE

Discover It

Today we look at a passage from a psalm or one of the prophets to see what we can learn from it about Jesus.

 Read Genesis 49:1–2, 8–10.

Think about It Some More

When Jacob as an old man was close to death, he called all his sons together to tell them what was going to happen to them when they got older. We have already learned that Jesus was one day going to come from Judah's family. Now listen to what Jacob tells Judah.

Jacob tells Judah that the scepter (the thing a king holds in his hand) will not depart or leave Judah. That means that Judah will always have a king. The Scripture also says that all the different peoples of the world will be obedient to him—he will be the ruler of all nations. Jesus is the king Jacob spoke about who sits on heaven's throne ruling the nations. Jesus will rule on his throne forever.

Talk about It

:: Who is the king that Jacob says will be the ruler over all the nations? *(Jesus is the King that will come from Judah.)*

:: How could Jacob know the future to tell his sons what was going to happen? *(God gave Jacob the words to say.)*

:: What animal did Jacob say Judah was going to be like? *(A lion's cub.)*

:: *(Read Revelation 5:5.)* What word matches up with Jacob's words to Judah? *(Revelation 5:5 calls Jesus "the Lion of the tribe of Judah.")*

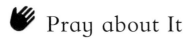 Pray about It

Thank God for working out his plan to bring Jesus to save us and be our King forever.

Week 23

Joseph Is Attacked by His Brothers

Prior to Bible study, secretly prepare an old colorful shirt in the following way: cut the shirt in several places, smear it with ketchup or red food coloring, and set it aside to dry. Gather and ask if you ever told the story about the day you were attacked by a shark. Tell how you were swimming when the shark nearly ripped your shirt off your back. Tell your children to wait a minute while you bring in the shirt. Show it to them and ask if they believe your story.

Finally, confess that you made up the whole story. Ask if your prop helped the story seem more believable. This should serve as a helpful illustration for the lesson you are learning this week, particularly the part where Joseph's brothers deceived their father.

DAY ONE

Picture It

Imagine that you are a detective for a police department and get a call that a man was found dead. You go to his apartment to try to figure out how he died. When you arrive, you find the man's body lying at the bottom of the stairs. "Poor guy tripped over his robe and fell all the way down and hit his head on the table," one of the policeman concludes, pointing to a small smudge of blood on the table.

But you are not so sure. Why put a table at the bottom of the stairs? When you see four table leg marks in the carpet over by the window, you realize that the table had recently been moved. After a closer look, you discover the red stuff on the table isn't blood—it's ketchup! Writing out his report, the policeman asks, "Should I say it was an accident?" You respond, "It was not an accident; it was murder. You will find the killer's fingerprints on a ketchup bottle in the refrigerator." Sure enough, the prints on the bottle lead to the killer who wanted the crime to look like an accident.

In today's story, Joseph's brothers plan to kill him and then think of a way to cover it up so no one will know that they did it.

 Read Genesis 37:12–20.

Think about It Some More

Israel (remember that is the name God gave to Jacob) called for his son Joseph and sent him to check up on his brothers to see if they were doing what they were supposed to be doing. But his brothers spotted him coming while he was a still long way off. They were tired of their little brother always checking up on them and envied their father's love for Joseph. So they planned to kill him to put an end to his dreams.

We need to be careful. Our boasting can provoke others to sin.

Talk about It

:: At first Joseph's brothers only envied him. How has their sin grown? *(What started out as envy has grown to murderous hatred.)*

:: Can our sins grow and get worse if we don't turn away from them? *(Yes, for example, we can start out angry and then move to hitting someone.)*

:: Can you remember a time when your sin started out as anger and grew to something more serious? *(Parents, help your children identify with the brothers and how their sin grew because they did not turn away from it. If ever your children hit one another, you can be almost certain that it started with smaller sins.)*

 Pray about It

Ask God to help you turn away from your sins so they don't grow into bigger sins.

DAY TWO_____

Remember It

What do you remember about yesterday's story? What do you think is going to happen today?

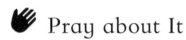 Read Genesis 37:21–30.

Think about It Some More

While Joseph was still a way off, Reuben, one of his brothers, tried to talk some sense into the others. He wanted them to throw Joseph into a pit instead of kill him. Secretly Reuben was hoping he could come back later to rescue Joseph. They listened to Reuben and threw their young brother into a pit. Then Reuben left for a while. The story doesn't say why he left, but he may have gone for a pole or some rope to drop down to Joseph for his rescue.

The rest of the brothers sat down to eat their lunch and discuss what they would do with Joseph. Judah convinced them not to kill Joseph, but to sell him as a slave to a group of traders that were traveling by. Later, when Reuben returned and saw that Joseph was gone, he tore his clothes because he was very sad. His planned rescue had failed.

Talk about It

:: What would you have done if you were Joseph? *(Draw your children out to help them identify with the story. There are no wrong answers here.)*

:: How did God protect Joseph? *(Not all of Joseph's brothers wanted to kill him, and they were able to convince their brothers not to harm Joseph.)*

:: Why did God allow Joseph to be sold as a slave in Egypt? *(We have not read how God will use Joseph in Egypt yet. It your children don't already know, hold off telling them what is going to happen. Tell them that sometimes God uses bad things to bring about good things.)*

 Pray about It

Thank God for protecting Joseph from his angry brothers.

DAY THREE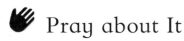

Connect It to Jesus

Can anyone guess how our story this week is about or points forward to Jesus?

Read Matthew 27:1–10.

Think about It Some More

Today we've taken a break from the story of Joseph to read about Jesus, who was also betrayed.

Do you see how the life of Joseph and the life of Jesus are similar? Joseph was captured by his brothers and thrown into a pit. Jesus was arrested by his own people and sent to die. Joseph was betrayed by the sons of Israel (his brothers) for twenty pieces of silver. Matthew tells us that Jesus was also betrayed by one of the sons of Israel (Judas, his disciple) for thirty pieces of silver.

Although these stories look very sad at first, God used both Joseph and Jesus to save his people. Jesus saved us by dying on the cross for our sin. In the next few weeks, we will see how God uses Joseph to save Israel.

Talk about It

:: How are Jesus and Joseph similar? *(Both men were betrayed by those closest to them.)*

:: Did Judas' thirty pieces of silver make him happy? *(No. Money can never bring us true happiness. Judas ended up killing himself.)*

:: How did God use the bad things Judas did for our good? *(In the end Jesus was lifted up on a cross to die, which seemed very bad. But while he was on the cross he took the punishment we deserved for our sins so we could go to heaven. That is how God used his death for our good.)*

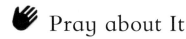 Pray about It

Ask God to help you to love Jesus more than anything or anyone else.

DAY FOUR

Remember It

What has God been teaching you this week through our Bible story?

 Read Genesis 37:31–36.

Think about It Some More

Did you ever notice that covering up one sin often leads you to commit others?

Let's say you take a cookie after mom tells you not to, and then you run into the next room. Your first sin is disobeying mom; your second sin is hiding what you did. If she calls to you and asks, "What are you doing in there?" you will be tempted to sin again by lying. Imagine that you quickly gobble the cookie down. But when you come back into the kitchen mom notices a bit of cookie on the corner of your mouth. How many times might you lie as she questions you again and again?

Joseph's brothers have to lie over and over to cover up what they did to their brother.

Talk about It

 KIDS, ask your parents if they have ever lied to cover up a sin.

(Parents, it is important that our children see that we are sinners too. If you can't remember a story from when you were a child, at least acknowledge that you have lied to cover up bad things that you have done.)

:: Why does one sin often lead to another? *(Once we commit one sin, we need to keep sinning to cover up our first sin.)*

:: What are the lies that Joseph's brothers had to tell to cover up their sin? *(They had to tear Joseph's robe, kill one of their father's goats, and fabricate a story suggesting that Joseph had been killed by wild animals.)*

:: What about you, have you ever lied to cover up something you did? *(Parents, this is where you can help your children identify with Joseph's brothers.)*

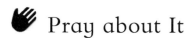 Pray about It

Ask God to help you not to sin in the first place. If you do, ask him to help you not to cover it up with more sins.

DAY FIVE

Discover It

Today we look at a passage from a psalm or one of the prophets to see what we can learn from it about Jesus.

 Read Numbers 24:15–17.

Think about It Some More

A prophet named Balaam heard the words of God and the knowledge of the Most High, and then gave this prophecy about a king who would come from Israel. David is the king that Balaam is talking about who defeated the enemies of God. But this prophecy and the picture of a conquering king foreshadows (or points ahead to) Jesus, who will put all his enemies under his feet until his final triumph over death itself. *(See 1 Corinthians 15:22–26.)*

Talk about It

:: Who is the king that Balaam's prophecy speaks of? *(King David, the one who would kill the giant Goliath.)*

:: How does this prophecy also remind us of Jesus? *(Jesus was also a king that came from Israel. Jesus defeated the enemies of sin and death.)*

:: Balaam also talks about a star. *(Read Revelation 22:16.)* Who does the writer of Revelation say the star is? *(Jesus is the bright morning star that comes from the line of David.)*

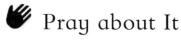 Pray about It

Praise God for sending Jesus, the bright morning star.

Joseph Interprets the Dreams

Give each person a chance to tell the group about a dream they had. Share with them some of the dreams you remember. Perhaps you dreamt of finding a treasure and the dream was so real you woke up feeling rich! Explain to them that, in the Bible, God sometimes used dreams to speak to people.

Say, "This week, you will learn how God gave Joseph the amazing ability to interpret people's dreams."

DAY ONE

Picture It

Picture yourself walking with two of your friends into a grocery store. They each pick up a candy bar and slip it into their pockets. What would you do if they picked up a third candy bar, held it up in front of you, and said, "Quick, drop this into your pocket, and let's get out of here"? Let's say that rather than steal something you didn't pay for, you decide to turn and run. But just before you do, they drop the candy into your pocket.

As soon as you leave the store, you feel the manager's hand grab you by the shoulder while his other hand pulls the candy bar from your pocket. Do you think he is going to believe you when you tell him you didn't steal it?

Sometimes people are accused of crimes they did not commit. That is what happened to Joseph in our story, and it landed him in jail.

 Read Genesis 39.

(You may want to review this chapter before reading it to your children, because of Potiphar's wife telling Joseph to "come to bed with me" [NIV] or "lie with me" [ESV]. Younger children are generally satisfied with the explanation that Potiphar's wife was dishonoring her husband.)

Think about It Some More

When you read about Joseph's life one of the things you notice is that he has a "good news, bad news" story. That is, every time he gets good news, bad news is not far behind.

Joseph was his father's favorite son. That's the good news. The bad news is that his brothers were jealous that he was the favorite, and they tried to kill him. The good news is that one of his brothers stopped them and was going to rescue Joseph. The bad news is that he came too late and Joseph had already been sold as a slave. The good news is that Joseph was sold to a wealthy man, had a great job, and God prospered him. But now more bad news: the wealthy man's wife falsely accused Joseph of a crime and he was thrown into prison.

Just when you think things are starting to go well for this guy, something bad happens again. But through all the trials, God had a plan for his life.

Talk about It

:: Why did Potiphar like Joseph and put him in charge of his whole house? *(Potiphar could see that God was with Joseph and everything Joseph did was a success.)*

:: What did Joseph do when Potiphar's wife wanted him to sin? *(Joseph refused to spend time with her because she was married to another man. Finally, he ran away.)*

:: Why was Joseph thrown into prison? *(Potiphar's wife lied to her husband saying Joseph was trying to steal her from him.)*

:: How did God bless Joseph in prison? *(Just like while he was working in Potiphar's house, God blessed Joseph and enabled him to succeed at whatever he did.)*

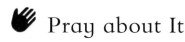 Pray about It

Thank God for protecting Joseph while he was in prison.

DAY TWO

Remember It

What do you remember about yesterday's story? What do you think is going to happen today?

 Read Genesis 40.

Think about It Some More

Most people would be discouraged if they were thrown into prison for something they didn't do, but not Joseph. He continues to trust God while looking for opportunities to find a way out.

When the cupbearer needs someone to tell him the meaning of his dream, Joseph says that his God knows the meaning of every dream and asks the cupbearer to tell him his dream. Joseph interprets his dream and asks the cupbearer to speak well of him when he returns to Pharaoh. After the cupbearer is released from prison, he forgets about Joseph, leaving him in prison. Even so, Joseph does not lose his faith in God, whom he continues to serve.

Talk about It

:: Why did Pharaoh send the cupbearer and the baker to prison? *(Pharaoh sent them to prison because he was angry with them.)*

:: Who gave the dreams to the cupbearer and the baker? *(God gave them the dreams.)*

:: How can you tell from what Joseph said that he was following God? *(Joseph points the men to God when he tells them about their dreams.)*

 Pray about It

Ask God to help you follow him like Joseph did, even when times are tough.

DAY THREE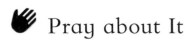

Connect It to Jesus

Can anyone guess how our story this week is about or points forward to Jesus?

Read Genesis 41:1–14.

Think about It Some More

Can you imagine staying in prison for two whole years for something you didn't do? That's what happens to Joseph. But God has a plan. God plans to use Joseph to save Israel from a terrible famine that is soon to come. Saving Israel is very important because Jesus would one day be born into the family of Israel.

To get Joseph out of prison, God gives Pharaoh a dream that only Joseph can interpret. The cupbearer remembers Joseph and, in a flash, Joseph is released from prison. He is cleaned up and given new clothes to wear. By saving Joseph out of prison, God saves Israel from the famine; and by saving Israel, Jesus is born so we can be saved.

Talk about It

:: Why did God save Joseph? *(God saved Joseph so Joseph could save Israel from the famine and Jesus could be born into the family of Israel.)*

:: How is God faithful to Joseph? *(The simple answer is that God helps Joseph get out of prison, but the bigger answer is that God is going to use Joseph to save Israel, which means that Jesus could be born. Jesus would one day die for Joseph's sins so he can go to heaven.)*

:: Joseph trusts God to get him out of prison. What do we need to trust God for? *(We need to trust God for everything—our food, clothing, and everything else that we need.)*

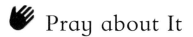 Pray about It

Ask God to help you trust him when things are difficult like Joseph did.

DAY FOUR

Remember It

What has God been teaching you this week through our Bible story?

 Read Genesis 41:15–36.

Think about It Some More

A famine is a time when there is not enough food for everyone to eat. Famines are usually caused by long periods with no rain. If it doesn't rain, plants can't grow. If the plants do not grow, then all the animals die of hunger because there are no plants to eat. If the animals and plants die, the people die too because they have nothing to eat.

The famine Joseph warned Pharaoh about was going to last seven years. If God had not warned Pharaoh through Joseph, all of Egypt could have died.

Talk about It

> ● ● KIDS, ask your parents how long they think you could survive on the
> ● ● food you have stored up in your house.

(Parents, take a guess as to how long the food you have would last. Then try to estimate how much space a seven-year supply of food would require.)

:: What is a famine? *(A famine is when there is not enough food to eat.)*

:: Why did God give the dream to Pharaoh? *(God gave the dream to Pharaoh to warn him about the famine in order to save Egypt and all of Israel, as we will see next week.)*

:: After Joseph told Pharaoh what his dream meant, what else did he tell him? *(Joseph told Pharaoh how to save the food in the years of plenty to provide for the years of famine.)*

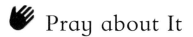 Pray about It

Thank God for all the food you have to eat every day.

DAY FIVE

Discover It

Today we look at a passage from a psalm or one of the prophets to see what we can learn from it about Jesus.

 Read Isaiah 42:5–9.

Think about It Some More

Isaiah was one of God's prophets, which meant he received messages from God to give to his people. This part of Isaiah's book has some wonderful promises in it that point us to Jesus.

The easiest one to pick out is the one in which Isaiah tells us that the servant God is going to send will open the eyes of the blind. Jesus did that. Isaiah also said that God's servant would be a light for the nations. Jesus said, "I am the light of the world" (John 8:12). A flashlight showing the way in the darkness is a little bit like what Jesus does. Our sin is the darkness and Jesus shines the light of his truth to lead us out of darkness into heaven to be with him.

Jesus also came to free us from the prison of our sin and give us his righteousness, which means his sinlessness.

Talk about It

:: How could Isaiah know all about Jesus way before Jesus was even born? *(Even though Isaiah was writing this part of the Bible, God was helping Isaiah, giving him the words to say.)*

:: How is Jesus a light to the nations? *(Jesus didn't just come to save Israel. Remember God's promise to Abraham, Isaac, and Jacob? God promised to bless all nations through them. So, Jesus came to die for people from every nation so their sins could be forgiven.)*

:: How was our story about Joseph getting out of prison like Isaiah's prophecy? *(In Isaiah's prophecy God promises to bring the prisoners out of the dungeon as part of his plan of salvation. In our story this week, God brought Joseph out of prison.)*

Pray about It

Thank God for sending Jesus to be our light and show us the way to God.

Week 25

God Provides for the Israelites in Famine

Have on hand a bag of candy or some other treat (try to use a candy or snack with a lot of small pieces like raisins). Each day for seven days give each child a generous amount to eat and a cup with his or her name on it. (Next week you will be finishing the story of Joseph.) Have your children decide how many pieces to eat and how many to save, but let them know they will receive the treats for only seven days. Encourage your children to save a bit for when the seven days are up.

Next week, when you don't offer any more treats, count out what each of your children have stored in their cups and divide by seven. Each day allow them to eat one-seventh of their store. Those who have saved more will, each day, enjoy a larger portion than the others.

Say, "In this week's lesson you will learn how God helped his people through years of famine the very same way."

DAY ONE

Picture It

Did you ever refuse to eat something because you didn't like it? Most people in the world do not have a lot of different foods to pick from, so they have to eat what they have. Often they eat the same thing day after day. If they refuse to eat, they go hungry. Soon, they are glad to eat whatever there is.

When the famine hit, all of Egypt had to eat bread made of grain for seven years! Can you imagine what it would be like to eat the same thing every day for seven years!

 Read Genesis 41:38–57.

Think about It Some More

Pharaoh was so glad that Joseph knew what his dream was about and liked his plan so much that he put Joseph in charge of all Egypt. Joseph was so wise that Pharaoh knew God was helping Joseph *(Genesis 41:38–39)*. When the years of plenty came, Joseph stored the extra grain away so none of it was wasted or spoiled. Then, when the famine came, Egypt had plenty of food. They had enough for themselves and more to sell to people in the surrounding country.

All the world came to buy food from Joseph in Egypt. All the people in Egypt who had laughed at Joseph for building large places to store grain were now in line to buy food like everyone else and were grateful for his insight.

Talk about It

:: What did the people during the famine do who didn't like to eat bread every day? *(They had to eat it anyway; otherwise they would starve to death.)*

:: How would you like eating the same thing for seven years? *(Parents, draw out your children here. If you want to have a little fun, think of a food they don't like and ask them what they would do in a famine where all there was to eat was that particular food.)*

:: When do you think Pharaoh realized Joseph was right about his dream? *(If he didn't believe Joseph was right in the years of plenty, surely he was appreciative of Joseph and believed when the famine started.)*

 Pray about It

Thank God for the food he provides for your family every day.

DAY TWO

Remember It

What do you remember about yesterday's story? What do you think is going to happen today?

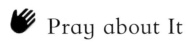 Read Genesis 42.

Think about It Some More

Because of the famine in the land, Jacob has to send his sons to Egypt to buy grain for food. As soon as Joseph sees his brothers, he recognizes them. When they bow down to him he remembers the dream God gave him in which his brothers' bundles of grain bowed down to his.

Joseph recognizes his brothers, but they do not recognize him. Instead of welcoming them, Joseph tells the guards that his brothers are spies, and has them thrown into prison. Three days later Joseph has them released from prison. He overhears them talking about how they believe God is judging them for what they did to Joseph. When they are finally sent home and find their money in the top of their grain sacks, they are even more afraid.

Talk about It

:: Why didn't Joseph's brothers recognize him? *(Joseph would have been all grown up and dressed like a king.)*

:: Why did Joseph put their money back in their sacks? *(Joseph wanted to teach his brothers a lesson for the poor way they treated him.)*

:: What do you think the brothers thought when they opened their sacks and found the money? *(They were afraid and did not know what to do. They needed to return with Benjamin to prove they were honest men and get their brother Simeon back. But if they went back, they could all be accused of stealing and be thrown in prison.)*

 Pray about It

Ask God to help you share your sins and not hide them like Joseph's brothers did.

DAY THREE

Connect It to Jesus

Can anyone guess how our story this week is about or points forward to Jesus?

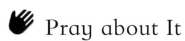 Read Genesis 43.

Think about It Some More

The food that Joseph's brothers got from Egypt runs out and they need more. After all, the famine has only just started and it was going to last seven years! They are afraid to return, but they have to go back or starve, so Jacob instructs his sons to return the money left in their sacks and bring along special gifts for the Egyptian ruler. Then he prays for them: "May God Almighty grant you mercy."

When a person asks for mercy, they are asking for forgiveness. The brothers need the ruler of Egypt to forgive them for stealing the money that was left in their sacks. But even more than that, they need God's mercy for selling off their brother and lying to their father. You will see in our story that Joseph does grant them mercy—because God is granting them mercy.

It was God's plan to provide food for their family so Jesus could be born into the family of Judah, one of the brothers. God could have killed the brothers for what they did to Joseph, but God forgave them, knowing that one day his Son Jesus would die for their sins.

Talk about It

:: Why did Joseph's brothers run out of food? *(The famine was going to last seven years. They didn't bring back enough food to last that long.)*

:: What does it mean to show mercy to someone? *(If you show mercy, you don't punish them for the wrong things that they do. Instead you forgive them. God showed us mercy by sending Jesus to die on the cross for our sins so we could be forgiven.)*

:: How did Joseph show mercy to his brothers? *(Joseph was in charge of all Egypt. He could have had his brothers punished in prison for the rest of their lives for what they did to him. He could also have refused to give them food. Knowing that the famine would last seven years, they would have starved to death.)*

 ## Pray about It

Thank God for his mercy in that he does not punish us for our sins like he should.

DAY FOUR

Remember It

What has God been teaching you this week through our Bible story?

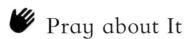 Read Genesis 44.

Think about It Some More

In our Bible story today, Joseph's brothers return to Egypt to buy more grain. As they prepare to return home with their grain, Joseph orders that his own silver cup be placed in Benjamin's grain sack. (Benjamin is Joseph's youngest brother and loved very much by his father, so Joseph knew his brothers would not leave him behind.) While the brothers are on their journey home, Joseph sends his men to arrest them for stealing the cup.

Even though the brothers believe their troubles are God's punishment to them for what they did to Joseph, they still don't tell Joseph what really happened. Instead, when they talk about the brother who was lost, they say he was torn to pieces *(verse 28)*. Isn't it interesting that even when they feel God correcting them they still try to keep up with their lie?

Talk about It

> ● ● KIDS, ask your parents to explain why Joseph's brothers should have
> ● ● told the truth.

(Parents, use your own words to talk about telling the truth and how when we tell the truth we are trusting God, but when we keep the truth hidden we are trusting ourselves, not God.)

:: Whose sack contained the cup? *(It was in Benjamin's sack.)*

:: Why did Joseph have the cup put in Benjamin's sack? *(Benjamin was Joseph's youngest brother and Joseph knew his brothers would not go home without him.)*

:: Which was more important to Joseph's brothers, telling the truth or hiding their sin? *(They were more concerned with hiding their sin.)*

Pray about It

Have everyone confess an area of sin that they might be tempted to hide. Then ask God to help everyone trust in Jesus and the gospel, which can free us from our sins. *(Parents should begin this time of confession and help draw out the children.)*

DAY FIVE

Discover It

Today we look at a passage from a psalm or one of the prophets to see what we can learn from it about Jesus.

Read Psalm 110.

Think about It Some More

Can you imagine having a long name like Melchizedek? Imagine when you first go to school and have to learn how to spell your name. Melchizedek has eleven letters, and nine of them are different! Even though Melchizedek is a hard name to say and spell, he is an important guy to know about because there is something special about him.

The New Testament writer of the book of Hebrews tells us that Melchizedek's life points us to Jesus. Just like Jesus, Melchizedek is both a priest and a king of the city called Salem (that city later became Jerusalem, the same city where Jesus would one day be called king). So, when you see the long name Melchizedek, think about Jesus.

Talk about It

:: What does a king do? *(A king rules over people. Both Melchizedek and Jesus were kings over Jerusalem.)*

:: What does a priest do? *(A priest prays to God on behalf of the people, often to ask God to forgive them for their sins. Both Melchizedek and Jesus are priests.)*

:: Read Hebrews 5:5–10 and try to find out where it connects Psalm 110 to Jesus. *(Parents, have your children raise their hands when they hear words from Hebrews that are also in Psalm 110.)*

Pray about It

Thank God that Jesus will remain a priest forever for us. That means he is always there to ask God to forgive us.

Week 26

Joseph Reveals Himself to His Brothers

Collect a few 5 x 7 or 8 x 10 photos of family members and place them on a table, picture side up. Cover the photos with one-inch squares of construction paper. Finally, take one or two squares off each photo to reveal a clue to who is in the picture (choose more obscure parts of the photo to make guessing more difficult). Call your children in and see if they can guess the identities of the people in the photos. Take away a square at a time until they guess correctly. Say, "This week you will learn how Joseph revealed himself to his brothers."

DAY ONE

Picture It

Imagine that you are sitting down together around your dining room table when Dad comes home from work right in time for dinner. He is all dressed up in a button-down shirt and tie. Just before dessert, Dad announces he has something to show you that he has been keeping a secret.

Suddenly he rips open his shirt, popping the buttons, revealing a Superman costume. Imagine your surprise when, after he tells you he is the real Superman, he opens a nearby window and flies out. You would be about as shocked as Joseph's brothers are in the next part of our story.

 Read Genesis 45:1–5.

Think about It Some More

Last week we learned that Joseph's brothers were brought back to Egypt because the Egyptian ruler's silver cup was found in the youngest brother's sack. When they see Joseph, they beg for mercy. Then they await his decision, not knowing what will happen. Perhaps they think they will be thrown into prison or even killed for their crime. But none of them would have guessed what happens next.

When Joseph reveals himself as their brother, they are terrified. Not only has the cup been found in Benjamin's sack, now the brother they sold into slavery was going to decide their fate. He might even have them killed.

Talk about It

:: Why are the brothers concerned when they see that the Egyptian ruler is their brother Joseph? *(Joseph could have them all cast in prison for the rest of their lives. They may have thought he was going to get even with them.)*

:: How does Joseph treat his brothers? *(Joseph has mercy on them, not punishing them for what they did to him.)*

:: Who does Joseph say is in control of everything that happened? *(Joseph understands that God sent him to Egypt to save lives during the famine.)*

 Pray about It

Pray that God would help you to be forgiving toward others.

DAY TWO

Remember It

What do you remember about yesterday's story? What do you think is going to happen today?

 Read Genesis 45:16–28.

Think about It Some More

There is one interesting thing missing from this story: Joseph's brothers never tell their father what they did to him. That is why it is so difficult for Jacob to believe that his son Joseph is still alive.

Joseph was so forgiving of his brothers and so sure God had planned it for good that he never accuses them or holds what they did against them.

Talk about It

:: How does Pharaoh treat Joseph's family? *(Pharaoh is so glad things are going well in the famine that he welcomes Joseph's family to Egypt and is very kind to them.)*

:: Why does Joseph tell his brothers not to quarrel or argue? *(The Bible doesn't tell us why Joseph says that, but we can guess. See what your children think. It could be that Joseph doesn't want them blaming one another for what they did to him, but wants them to rejoice about all that God has done.)*

:: Why doesn't Jacob, Joseph's father, believe at first that Joseph is alive? *(His sons have not told him the whole truth. Remember that he thought Joseph had been killed because of the blood they put on his robe.)*

 Pray about It

Ask God to help you confess and not hide your sins.

DAY THREE

Connect It to Jesus

Can anyone guess how our story this week is about or points forward to Jesus?

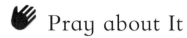 Read Genesis 45:6–15.

Think about It Some More

We saved this part of Joseph's speech to his brothers for today because it tells us how our story is connected to Jesus. Joseph says that God sent him to Egypt to preserve a remnant on earth. A *remnant* is another word for a leftover piece or a part of something.

God knew the famine was coming and all of Joseph's family would die if they didn't get food. So God sent Joseph ahead to Egypt so Jacob and his sons could be saved from the famine. They were important because God made his covenant with Jacob and his father Isaac, and grandfather Abraham before them.

When Joseph says that God wanted to preserve a remnant, he is simply saying that God wanted to keep a part of Abraham's family safe because one day Jesus would be born into that family.

Talk about It

:: What is a remnant? *(A remnant is a leftover part or piece of something.)*

:: If God had not sent Joseph to Egypt, what terrible thing would have happened? *(Most of the people would have died, including Jacob and all his children. That would mean that God's promise to Abraham would have failed.)*

:: Even though Joseph's brothers sold him as a slave to traders going to Egypt, who did Joseph say really sent him to Egypt? *(Joseph said that it was God, not his brothers, who sent him to Egypt.)*

 Pray about It

Thank God for always keeping his people safe so one day Jesus could be born as a far-off grandson of Israel.

DAY FOUR

Remember It

What has God been teaching you this week through our Bible story?

 Read Genesis 46:1–7, 26–30.

Think about It Some More

Once again God repeats his promise to Jacob and calms his fears. When God said that Joseph, his son, would close his eyes, that meant that Joseph would be there when he died. Now for sure Jacob knew his son was alive.

What an amazing sight it must have been to watch Joseph ride up in a royal chariot, bow before his father, and give him a great big hug. Remember, Joseph was Jacob's favorite son, the one to whom he gave the colorful coat. Jacob was so glad to see his son that he said he was ready to die. That tells us that he must have been praying to God to bring his son back before he died. If that's true, God answered his prayers and he was ready to go home to be with God.

Talk about It

> ● ● KIDS, ask your parents if they can remember the things God said to
> ● ● Jacob.

(God told him that he did not need to be afraid, that he would see Joseph before he died. God repeated his promise to make Jacob into a great nation, and said that he would lead his family back out of Egypt.)

:: How do you think Jacob felt when he saw Joseph climb down from the chariot and come over to greet him? *(Draw your children out here. Talk about some of the memories they might have had together.)*

:: Do you know whom God would use to lead his people out of Egypt? *(Moses, who we will be learning about next week.)*

Pray about It

Thank God for keeping Joseph safe and using him to save his people during the famine.

DAY FIVE

Discover It

Today we look at a passage from a psalm or one of the prophets to see what we can learn from it about Jesus.

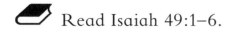 Read Isaiah 49:1–6.

Think about It Some More

Sometimes when we read a Bible passage it sounds more complicated than it really is. This part of the Bible is like that. Isaiah is describing Jesus as God's servant in this passage.

Look for the clues that help us to know Isaiah is talking about Jesus. The most important one is in the last verse, where Isaiah describes what God's servant will do. He says he will be a "light for the nations" and will bring salvation "to the end of the earth." That is just what Jesus did. Remember that Jesus called himself "the light of the world" *(John 8:12)*, and Jesus said that his disciples were to take the message of his life into all the world for all nations *(Mark 16:15)*. Jesus is the only one who can bring salvation.

Talk about It

:: What did Jesus do that brought salvation to the ends of the earth? *(Jesus died on the cross and took our punishment so we could be saved—have our sins forgiven so we can go to heaven.)*

:: Why do you think the Bible describes Jesus as "the light"? *(Parents, you can talk about what the light does in the darkness. It sends the darkness away. Light also helps us to see. Jesus is the light because he sends the darkness of sin away and helps us to see the truth.)*

:: Why is Jesus described as a servant? *(Jesus came to serve us by dying on the cross for us. When someone does something for you, they are serving you.)*

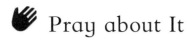 Pray about It

Thank Jesus for coming to bring salvation to the whole earth.

Week 27

God Protects Baby Moses

Hide ten nickels and one quarter around the room. Place the nickels out in the open where everyone can see them. Place the quarter in a very difficult place to find, like in a plant. Tell your children that you have placed the coins around the room and, when you give them the signal, you want them to try to find them.

Once they find the nickels, assuming they don't find the quarter, give them clues. You can do this by telling them they are hotter when they get close or colder when they move farther away from the hidden coin. Explain to them how the quarter was more difficult to find because you took extra care to keep it hidden.

Say, "This week, you will learn how Moses was hidden from Pharaoh's soldiers as part of God's plan."

DAY ONE

Picture It

Imagine that you and your brother or sister are throwing a ball back and forth at breakfast in your kitchen, and each time you pass the ball you throw it a little bit harder. Then, it happens. You throw the ball so hard the other person can't catch it, and it knocks a bottle of cooking oil off the counter. The bottle breaks on the floor next to the refrigerator with a loud crash. Pieces go everywhere.

Mom comes in and immediately begins to clean up the mess. You and your sister think, *We are in big trouble now,* but what you don't know is that God is going to work your foolishness for your good. As Mom wipes up the mess, she realizes she needs to move the fridge because the oil has run underneath it. When she does, she finds a diamond earring she lost two months ago. Although you were disobeying, God was able to work your sin for good! That doesn't mean we should sin to test God, but God can work our sins for good.

In our story today, Joseph reminds his brothers that God used their sin for good to save a lot of people from dying.

 Read Genesis 50:15–26.

Think about It Some More

After Jacob dies, Joseph's brothers start to worry. They think Joseph may now try to get even with them for what they did to him. Instead of asking for forgiveness straight out, they say that, before he died, their father asked that Joseph forgive them.

However, they need not worry—Joseph has already forgiven them. He can see how God used their evil deed to save a lot of people, including their whole family.

Joseph's faith in God is an example for us all. Even when someone does something bad to us, God can use it to make our lives better.

Talk about It

:: Why were Joseph's brothers afraid? *(They thought he might try to punish them for what they did now that their father was dead.)*

:: Do you think Joseph's father really asked Joseph to forgive the brothers, or do you think they were making up the story? *(We don't know for sure, but the way the story is written it seems like the brothers made it up. Jacob is already dead and they become afraid before they mention it.)*

:: What did Joseph say God was going to do in the future? *(God was going to bring them out of Egypt, back to the land he promised to give his father Jacob, grandfather Isaac, and great-grandfather Abraham.)*

 Pray about It

Ask God to help you forgive people who sin against you.

DAY TWO

Remember It

What do you remember about yesterday's story? What do you think is going to happen today?

 Read Exodus 1.

Think about It Some More

The people of Israel have now been in Egypt for more than 300 years. The new king (in Egypt, called the pharaoh) knows nothing about Joseph and how he had served Egypt. Pharaoh is afraid of the Israelites because there are so many of them, so he decides to kill their baby boys. In this way, the Hebrew nation will not become too strong, and Pharaoh can keep them as his slaves to do whatever he wants. ("Hebrews" is the name Pharaoh calls the Israelites.)

But Pharaoh is fighting against God, who had promised Abraham that everyone who blessed him would be blessed and everyone who harmed him would be harmed *(Genesis 12:3)*. The midwives who deliver the babies refuse to obey Pharaoh's order and the Israelites grow stronger. Then Pharaoh makes a new law that every Hebrew son born should be thrown into the Nile River.

Talk about It

:: Why isn't Pharaoh grateful for all that Joseph did to save Egypt during the famine? *(By now, 300 years later, Joseph has been forgotten.)*

:: Why does Pharaoh want to kill all the baby boys? *(He is afraid the Hebrews [that is what he calls God's people] will rise up like an army and fight against the Egyptians.)*

:: What do you think God is going to do? *(God is going to raise up a deliverer who will lead his people out of Egypt. Remember that when Joseph was dying he told his brothers that God would lead them out of Egypt and take them back to the land God promised to give Abraham.)*

:: Why don't the Hebrew midwives follow Pharaoh's command to kill the baby boys? *(They fear God and refuse to do what they think is against God's word.)*

 ## Pray about It

Thank God for giving us grace to obey even when it is difficult.

DAY THREE

Connect It to Jesus

Can anyone guess how our story this week is about or points forward to Jesus?

 Read Exodus 2:1–10.

Think about It Some More

Where in the world do you hide a baby for three months, and what do you do if a baby you are trying to hide starts to cry? What if your neighbor asks, "Hey, is that a baby I hear crying in your house?" Do you reply, "No, that is only the cat"?

Moses' mom had to hide him, because Pharaoh ordered that all of the Hebrew baby boys should be thrown into the Nile River. But you can't hide a growing boy forever, so she finally gives in to Pharaoh's command and places him in the Nile—gently, in a basket boat—trusting the boy to God. Then she sends his sister along to watch over him.

God saves baby Moses so that when he grows up he can save God's people. That's how Moses is like Jesus. God is going to use Moses to rescue his people from the evil of Egypt, and that points forward to how God would use another baby, Jesus, to grow up to rescue his people from the evil of their sin.

Talk about It

:: Why does Moses' mom try to hide him? *(Pharaoh ordered that all the Hebrew baby boys be thrown into the Nile River. She hid Moses so he would not be killed that way.)*

:: What happens to Moses in the river? *(Parents, allow your children to retell the story of how Pharaoh's daughter finds him.)*

:: Who takes care of baby Moses in the end? *(In the end, Moses' mom takes care of him and actually gets paid by Pharaoh's daughter for doing so. Parents, this is an amazing provision by God that many children don't realize. Moses' mom released her son into the river, trusting him to God, and that very day God returns him to her to raise with the blessing of Pharaoh's own daughter.)*

 ## Pray about It

Thank God for saving baby Moses' life.

DAY FOUR

Remember It

What has God been teaching you this week through our Bible story?

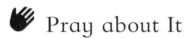 Read Acts 7:2–22.

Think about It Some More

This story is a part of a speech given by a Christian named Stephen. He is trying to explain God's plan to save his people to a group of Jewish leaders who are angry with the Christians. They are upset because they believe that Jesus was destroying their Jewish faith. But Stephen knows that God's promise to Abraham and God's raising up Moses was part of a bigger plan that pointed to Jesus. So, in order to help them understand, Stephen shares the whole story with them.

One of the things we learn from Stephen's speech is that Moses was born at a special moment in time when God was ready to bring his people, who had grown into a great nation, out of Egypt, back into the land he had promised to Abraham.

Talk about It

> ● ● KIDS, ask your parents if they can tell you about a time when they
> ● ● had an opportunity to talk to someone about Jesus.

:: What did Stephen say God thought about Moses? *(Parents, if necessary, reread verse 20.)*

:: What happened to God's people while they were in Egypt? *(They had a lot of children and increased in number [verse 17].)*

 Pray about It

Ask God to give you opportunities to share about God with others.

DAY FIVE

Discover It

Today we look at a passage from a psalm or one of the prophets to see what we can learn from it about Jesus.

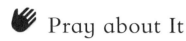 Read Isaiah 7:10–14.

Think about It Some More

There are two special things Isaiah foretold about Jesus. First, he would be born of a virgin, which means that Mary, his mother, would have her baby before she had a husband. (Joseph married Mary after the baby Jesus was already growing inside her.) The second thing we learn about Jesus from this passage is that he would be called *Immanuel.* The name *Immanuel* means "God with us."

So we see that long before Mary was even born God gave Isaiah a picture of Jesus, a man who was born by a miracle of God. He was no ordinary man—he was the Son of God who came down from heaven to us to save us from our sin.

Talk about It

:: What does the name *Immanuel* mean? *("God with us.")*

:: Why is *Immanuel* a good name for Jesus? *(Jesus was not an ordinary man—he was the Son of God with us. So Jesus was "God with us.")*

:: Do you remember how Mary got the baby Jesus inside of her? *(The Holy Spirit caused the baby Jesus to start to grow inside of her.)*

 Pray about It

Thank Jesus for leaving heaven to come as Immanuel—"God with us."

Week 28

God Calls Moses

Call your children to gather for Bible study time, but instead of calling their real names, call different names. For example, if your child's name is Bob, call for Frank. If your child's name is Mary, call for Susan. Try several different names, then go gather your children. Ask them why they didn't come when you called.

They may say that you called the wrong names, or they might just be confused. Tell them the names you called and ask why they did not respond. They of course will explain that you need to call their real names if you want them to come.

Say, "That is just what God did to Moses in the story we're looking at this week. God had a job for him and he called him by name."

DAY ONE

Picture It

Imagine that we are all going to a professional baseball game. When we get to the stadium entrance Dad passes out the tickets so that we each can hand them to the ticket taker at the gate.

As soon as you give the man your ticket he shouts, "We have a winner!" People with cameras take your picture, and you find out that you are the one-millionth visitor to the stadium and have won a ticket to a special box seat in the front row. The ticket is good for all the free food you want and, after the game, you'll get to meet the baseball players.

At first it sounds exciting, but then you realize your family is going to be sitting far away up high in the outfield. What would you do? Take the special seat or turn it down to sit with your family?

In our story today, Moses has the special seat, living in the palace of Pharaoh, but his family lives as slaves along with the other Israelites. Let's see what he does.

 Read Exodus 2:11–25 and Acts 7:23–29.

Think about It Some More

The story of Moses is recorded in at least three places in the Bible. We read from two of them today. By putting them together we get a more complete picture of what happened to Moses.

Although Moses lived in the palace of Pharaoh, his people (the Hebrews) were the Egyptians' slaves. They were treated cruelly and beaten. Moses turned down the treasures of Egypt when he sided with his people and killed the Egyptian. He hoped the Hebrew people would accept him as rescuer, but they mocked and rejected his leadership. They spread word of his crime all the way to Pharaoh, so Moses ran away from Egypt.

Talk about It

:: Why wasn't Moses happy living in the palace with Pharaoh? *(Moses was kind of like the child in the baseball game story. Although he was very blessed, he wasn't with his family. Although Moses was living in a palace, his people were living in slavery. He could not enjoy the pleasures of Egypt while his people were suffering.)*

:: Why did Moses run away from Egypt? *(Pharaoh found out he had killed an Egyptian and wanted to kill Moses.)*

:: If you were Moses, what would you do when you saw that your family were slaves? *(Parents, draw out your children and help them to see how hard it must have been for Moses to live in comfort while his people suffered.)*

:: Who did Moses worship, the gods of Egypt or the true God of Israel? *(Moses worshiped the true God of Israel.)*

 Pray about It

Ask God to help you love and worship him instead of the treasures of this world.

DAY TWO

Remember It

What do you remember about yesterday's story? What do you think is going to happen today?

 Read Exodus 3.

Think about It Some More

There is something about a fire that draws our attention. People love to sit around campfires and cook marshmallows, or watch a fire crackle in their fireplace in the fall. But can you imagine walking along and seeing a bush on fire, but with it not burning up?

That is what happened to Moses. When he stepped closer to the fire to get a better look, he discovered that God was in that burning bush. God called Moses by name and told him that he was going to send him to deliver his people from slavery in Egypt. But Moses wasn't so sure. First, he had already tried to deliver the Hebrews when he killed the Egyptian, and they had only mocked him. Second, Moses was eighty years old. He was forty when he ran away from Egypt and had been living in Midian for another forty years.

God encouraged Moses and told him that he would strike the Egyptians with his power. Moses would not have to go alone.

Talk about It

:: What is your favorite part of today's story? *(Parents, draw out your children and remind them of the different parts of the story.)*

:: Why did God tell Moses to take off his sandals? *(God said the ground was holy. If you went into a house with white carpet, the owner would likely tell you to take off your shoes because you would get the carpet dirty. That is the same idea here. God wanted Moses to know that God was very different from him. Moses was a sinner standing next to God who had no sin.)*

:: God told Moses that his name was "I AM WHO I AM." What kind of a name is that? *(It is a name that is different from every other name. It shows that God is above everyone and all other gods and doesn't need anyone's help because he is powerful all by himself.)*

 Pray about It

Praise God that he is awesome and powerful.

DAY THREE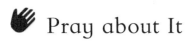

Connect It to Jesus

Can anyone guess how our story this week is about or points forward to Jesus?

 Read Hebrews 11:23–26.

Think about It Some More

Here in the book of Hebrews the story of Moses is told again. Once more we learn something about Moses that we didn't know from reading his story in the book of Exodus or the book of Acts—Moses was a man of faith.

Unsure how it would all work out, Moses still had a sense that God wanted to deliver his people from slavery. He did not follow the false gods of Egypt. Instead of living a sinful life serving the gods of Egypt, Moses joined God's plan to save his people and trusted God to be his reward.

Each one of us must make the same decision that Moses made, to love God and trust in his plan or to love the pleasures of sin more.

Talk about It

:: What did Moses give up when he killed the Egyptian and sided with God's people? *(Moses gave up all the treasures of Egypt. He had everything he could possibly want when he was living with Pharaoh. He gave all that up when he killed the Egyptian.)*

:: What does the word *faith* mean? *(Faith is believing something that you cannot see. Faith is required to believe that God is real because we cannot see him.)*

:: How did Moses demonstrate faith? *(Moses was willing to give up the wonderful things of Egypt and side with his people, the slaves, because he believed their God was the one true God.)*

 ## Pray about It

Ask God to help each member of your family place their faith in Jesus and not be drawn to the pleasures of the world.

DAY FOUR

Remember It

What has God been teaching you this week through our Bible story?

 Read Exodus 4:1–17.

Think about It Some More

Did you ever argue with Mom when she wanted you to do something you didn't want to do? That is what happens to Moses in our story.

Although Moses believes in God, he doesn't want to go to Egypt to save God's people. Moses is a sinner like we all are. Though God is patient with him, Moses keeps arguing until at one point God's anger against Moses begins to show. Still, God is patient and helps Moses to see that God will go with him and help him.

It is a good thing for Moses that God's plan to save Israel out of Egypt was meant to lead to Jesus dying on the cross for our sins. Although Moses is a great Bible hero, he is just a sinner like we are who needs to trust in God's plan to save so his sins can be forgiven.

Talk about It

> ● ● KIDS, ask your mom and dad if they can remember a time when you
> ● ● argued with them because you didn't want to do what they were asking you to do.

(Parents, this should not be difficult. Think back to something your children were reluctant to do, like clean their room or eat their vegetables.)

:: Why doesn't Moses think he is the right guy to go to Egypt? *(He doesn't think the people will believe him. He doesn't think he is a very good speaker.)*

:: Why does God get angry with Moses? *(Moses doesn't want to obey God and tells God to send someone else. When Moses doesn't trust God he is sinning. God is good and must punish sin, and gets angry when Moses disobeys.)*

:: Why doesn't God destroy Moses when he sins? *(God has a plan to send Jesus to take the punishment that Moses and the rest of his people deserve for their sins.)*

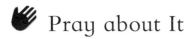 Pray about It

Thank God for being patient with Moses and us in our sin.

DAY FIVE

Discover It

Today we look at a passage from a psalm or one of the prophets to see what we can learn from it about Jesus.

 Read Isaiah 8:11–15.

Think about It Some More

Did you ever walk along a path and trip over a stone that was sticking out? Well, that is what a stumbling stone is. There you are, walking along fine, following the way home when bam! You hit the stumbling stone and fall down.

In today's Bible passage, Isaiah compares Jesus to a stumbling stone. Remember how we compared the prophets to people who were sending messages by code? "Stumbling stone" is another code word for Jesus in the Bible. Isaiah prophesies that one day the Lord will become a stumbling stone for Israel.

In Jesus' day, the religious leaders of Israel wanted everyone to follow their laws. They had added their own laws to God's laws. They made their laws more important than God. When Jesus came, he disagreed with the religious leaders and told them to follow him instead of all their manmade laws. The religious leaders didn't like that very much. Jesus was like a stone in their path that made them stumble. Instead of following him they fell away from God.

Talk about It

:: Was there ever a time when you were walking along the woods on a path and you tripped over a stone? *(Parents, draw out your children to help them remember if they ever tripped over a stone. If not, keep this story in mind the next time you go for a hike.)*

:: This passage also says that Jesus will become our sanctuary. Do you know what a sanctuary is? *(A sanctuary is a safe place where no one can hurt you. A bird sanctuary, for instance, is a place where birds can be safe and not fear hunters shooting them.)*

:: How is Jesus our sanctuary or safe place? *(Jesus died on the cross to take the punishment for everyone who believes in him. By believing in Jesus, he becomes our safe place from God's punishment.)*

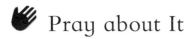 Pray about It

Ask Jesus to help you trust in him and make him your safe place.

Moses Confronts Pharaoh

Place a dozen rocks in one small paper bag and a dozen cotton balls in another. Pass around the bag containing the rocks and ask your children to put their hands in and describe the way they feel without guessing what they are. Do the same with the bag containing the cotton balls.

Explain to the children that God describes our hearts as either soft and obedient to God or hard and rebellious toward God. Explain that in our sin we all have hearts of stone, and God is the only one who can soften them to cause us to trust him.

Say, "This week you will learn about Pharaoh's hardened heart and his refusal to obey the command of the Lord from Moses."

DAY ONE

Picture It

Imagine Mom announcing that she is taking you all to your very first movie at a theater. Everyone is excited about the news and quickly gets ready to leave. You all jump in your car and head out. You wonder what it will be like to see a movie on the big screen.

Then all of a sudden traffic stops—there has been an accident on the highway. After about ten minutes your hopes for the movie start to fade. When Mom turns on the radio you hear that a mile in front of you a truck full of sand has turned over, blocking all traffic. With at least 100 cars behind you, there is no way to get out. When the clock reaches 7:40, the time your movie starts, you realize there won't be any movie tonight.

Sometimes our plans run into roadblocks. That is what happens to Moses in our story today.

 Read Exodus 4:18–23, 27–30 and Exodus 5.

Think about It Some More

When Aaron first tells the people about Moses and what God said, they are excited. They have been in harsh slavery all their lives, waiting for God to deliver them.

At first, the people praise God for sending Moses and Aaron. But then they run into a roadblock: Pharaoh refuses to let the people leave Egypt. Not only that, but he also makes them start looking for their own straw. That means that after a hard day making bricks they would have to search out the land and gather straw for the next day's work. Instead of trusting God, they begin to be discouraged and complain.

This pattern of Israel first believing God then turning away in unbelief will happen over and over again throughout her history.

Talk about It

:: Can you think of a time when God brought a roadblock into your life and you didn't get something you wanted? *(Parents, help your children remember a time when they were going to go somewhere and it got rained out or cancelled, or maybe they got sick and couldn't go. Draw them out to see how they felt. Did they get angry or complain? Help them identify with the Israelites.)*

:: How are we similar to the Israelites? *(It is easier to say we believe God than to live like we believe God. Every time we grumble and complain, we show that we do not fully trust God.)*

:: How do you think Moses felt when the people complained? *(Moses had a tough job. If you remember, he didn't think the people would listen to him.)*

 Pray about It

Ask God to help each person in your family to trust him through the roadblocks of life when we don't get what we want.

DAY TWO

Remember It

What do you remember about yesterday's story? What do you think is going to happen today?

 Read Exodus 5:22—6:1.

Think about It Some More

Nobody likes a difficult job. We don't want to clean up the dishes when the food has been baked on and they need to be scrubbed. When we want to go for a bike ride, we don't like finding out we have a flat tire. We like things to go smoothly.

Life was no different for Moses. He obeyed God and told Pharaoh to let God's people go. But Pharaoh refused, punishing Israel instead. Moses wasn't too happy that his job was getting hard. But sometimes God allows difficulty in our lives to help us learn to trust him.

God was kind to Moses: even though Moses complained, God did not punish him. Instead, God encouraged Moses to trust him to bring his people out of Egypt with a strong hand.

Talk about It

:: Why did Moses complain to God? *(Pharaoh did not listen to Moses and did not let the people go. Instead, he punished them by making them work even harder.)*

:: If you can remember a time when something you were trying to do did not go well, share it with each other. *(Parents, see if you can help your children remember the trouble they had learning something difficult, like how to ride a two-wheeler or how to read.)*

:: What does God teach us as he helps us get through difficult times? *(God teaches us that we can trust him to help us get through difficult times.)*

:: What is God trying to teach Moses? *(God is trying to teach Moses to trust in him even when it looks like nothing is working out. God always has a plan.)*

 ## Pray about It

Ask God to help you not complain when things don't go the way you want them to.

DAY THREE

Connect It to Jesus

Can anyone guess how our story this week is about or points forward to Jesus?

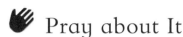 Read Exodus 6:2–9.

Think about It Some More

Yesterday we learned how Moses was upset that God had not saved his people right away. In our Bible story today, God answered Moses' complaint and told him that he would bring them out of slavery. Then God said something extra special: in addition to ending their slavery, he was going to redeem his people and make them his own.

By saying he was going to redeem them and make them his own, he was welcoming them back into a friendship. Now remember, God is sinless. He can't just overlook sin. Sin is evil and must be punished.

That is where Jesus comes into our story. God the Father knew that one day he would take care of sin by sending his Son Jesus to die on the cross. That is what the promise God keeps repeating is all about.

Talk about It

:: What special person was God pointing to when he said he would redeem his people? *(God was pointing to Jesus. He was talking about how he would rescue his people from slavery in Egypt, but the greater slavery God would save them from was their slavery to sin. One day he would send Jesus to die on the cross for their sins.)*

:: *Read verse 9 again.* How did Israel respond to Moses? *(They didn't listen to him. They were discouraged from all the years of harsh slavery.)*

:: How are we sinners like the people of Israel? *(We have a hard time obeying and trusting God like they did.)*

Pray about It

Thank God for sending Jesus to die in our place.

DAY FOUR

Remember It

What has God been teaching you this week through our Bible story?

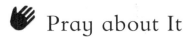 Read Exodus 7:8–13.

Think about It Some More

Anyone can do a magic trick if he knows the secret of how to do it. Magicians can make it look like rabbits come out of hats or large objects disappear right before your eyes.

When Aaron threw down his staff and it turned into a snake, it was not a trick. And to prove it, the snake that came from Aaron's staff ate up the magicians' snakes. God showed that he was greater. God won over the magicians of Egypt!

Talk about It

> ● ● KIDS, ask your parents if they remember reading or hearing about
> ● ● this story when they were little.

(Parents, you may have seen the movie, The Ten Commandments, or read this story from the Bible.)

:: How was God's power greater than the magicians of Pharaoh's court? *(Aaron's staff swallowed up the staffs of the magicians. Pharaoh's magicians tried to overcome the power of God, but could not.)*

:: What does it mean to have a hardened heart? *(Parents, if you did the activity from this week remind your kids about it. A hard heart is one that doesn't want to let God's Word in.)*

Pray about It

Ask God to soften your heart so you won't say no to God.

DAY FIVE

Discover It

Today we look at a passage from a psalm or one of the prophets to see what we can learn from it about Jesus.

 Read Isaiah 9:2, 6–7.

Think about It Some More

Three times in the gospel of John (1:9; 8:12; and 12:46) Jesus is described as a light that has come into the world. Jesus is the light Isaiah is talking about.

In verse 6, Isaiah describes a person who was born a man but was also "Mighty God." There is only one man ever born who was both man and God—Jesus. It was important for Jesus to be both God and man. By being a man, he could die in our place and take our punishment. Because he was also God, he could live a sinless life and rise again from the grave.

When Jesus died he took away our punishment so we could have peace with God. That is why Jesus is called the "Prince of Peace." He made a way for God to redeem his people and make them his own, just like he promised Moses he would do in our story this week.

Talk about It

:: What is the name of the child whom Isaiah is talking about? *(Jesus)*

:: How many of the names that Isaiah gave Jesus can you remember? *(Parents, feel free to give your children some clues or point them back to verse 6 to read them back to you.)*

:: In John 8:12 Jesus says, "I am the light of the world. Whoever follows me will not walk in darkness, but will have the light of life." How do Jesus' words fit in with what Isaiah said? *(If they can't find the answer, give them the clue to look in the first verse you read today.)*

:: What "enemy" does Jesus give us peace from? *(This is a trick question but an important truth to help your children understand that while we are sinners, we are God's enemy. If it were not for Jesus, God would punish us for our sin. When Jesus gave us peace, he gave us peace from God because he took our punishment upon himself.)*

Pray about It

Thank God for sending Jesus to give us peace with God so that everyone who trusts in Jesus can change from being God's enemy to becoming God's friend.

Week 30

God Sends Plagues against Egypt

This week you will be learning about the first nine plagues God sent on Egypt. Read the following list of plagues and ask your children to guess which ones are correct. They should answer true or false with a show of hands for each one. See who gets the most correct.

- :: *God sent a plague of blood. (True)*
- :: *God sent a plague of wasps. (False, he sent a plague of flies.)*
- :: *God sent a plague of death to livestock. (True)*
- :: *God sent a plague of darkness. (True)*
- :: *God sent a plague of snow. (False, he sent a plague of hail.)*
- :: *God sent a plague of salamanders. (False, he sent a plague of frogs.)*
- :: *God sent a plague of boils. (True)*
- :: *God sent a plague of bats. (False, he sent a plague of gnats.)*
- :: *God sent a plague of grasshoppers. (True)*

DAY ONE

Picture It

Imagine what it would be like in Egypt when the first plague hit. There you are, out with your family for a nice day at the river, swimming and splashing. The sun is high but you are shaded by trees along the riverbank, and everyone is having a great day.

Then out of nowhere people start to shout, "There's something red in the water!" Looking down, you notice the water has turned deep red. People all along the river start yelling, "Blood, blood, there is blood in the river!"

You join the mad rush to get out of the river. The water feels different and when a bit splashes into your mouth you realize that the water *has* turned into blood. The white shirt you are wearing to protect you from the sun is now deep red, dripping with blood. All along the bank, fish are floating belly-up.

That's what it would have been like during the first plague. Let's see what Pharaoh thinks of this plague and if he will let God's people go.

 Read Exodus 7:14–24.

Think about It Some More

If you have ever gotten a whiff of a foul-smelling garbage can full of rotting food scraps on a hot day, then you know what Egypt smelled like after the Nile turned to blood and all the fish died. Some people who don't believe the Bible is true might try to explain away this plague by saying that it really wasn't blood, or the fish got a disease and lost their blood in the river so it only looked like it had turned to blood. But notice, God even turned the water in the stone jars to blood. You can't explain that away.

Someone else didn't believe in the plagues: Pharaoh. Pharaoh was right there to see it all happen, but when his magicians also changed water into blood, Pharaoh turned away from Moses and didn't care.

Talk about It

:: List the different places where God turned the water into blood. *(The list is found in verse 19. See how many your children can remember. Give them a clue or two and see if they can guess them all.)*

:: Why do you think God changed even the water in jars to blood? *(By changing the water in jars to blood God was making sure that everyone knew it was a miracle. God didn't have Moses dump a load of red coloring into the Nile.)*

:: How do you think the magicians did their trick? *(It would be easy to use red dye in a jar to make it look like the water turned into blood. Parents, you can demonstrate this by placing some cherry powdered drink mix or food coloring into a clear glass and pouring water on top of it.)*

 Pray about It

Ask God to help you believe the message of the Bible, which is God's Word to us.

DAY TWO

Remember It

What do you remember about yesterday's story? What do you think is going to happen today?

 Read Exodus 9.

Think about It Some More

How would you like to have Pharaoh as your leader if you were a farmer trying to make a living in Egypt? You have already had plagues of frogs, gnats, and flies, which made it hard for you to get your work done. But now the plagues are really starting to destroy your farm.

First, your animals all die, then you get sores (called boils) on your face, and then terrible thunderstorms unleash a fury of lightning and hailstones that destroy your crops. All this because your leader has hardened his heart against God and refused to set the Hebrew slaves free.

If plagues like this happened today, we wouldn't have any meat or vegetables in the grocery stores for months. We would be forced to eat canned food or boxed cereal for a year. Even then, the price of meat and fresh vegetables would be so expensive we still wouldn't have them to eat very often.

Talk about It

:: Which of these plagues do you think was the most terrible and why? *(Help your children to understand the consequences of the plagues and what would happen if we had similar plagues today.)*

:: Why did Pharaoh agree to let the people go during the hail? *(Pharaoh just wanted the hail to stop. But as soon as the hail stopped he turned back to his sin. He only agreed to Moses' demands to get what he wanted.)*

:: What happened to God's people during the plagues? *(God protected them from the plagues. None of their animals died, they didn't get sick, and the hail did not fall on their crops.)*

:: Reread verses 12 and 34. Who hardened Pharaoh's heart? *(Verse 12 tells us God did, but verse 34 says Pharaoh did. Pharaoh was clearly responsible for his own willing disobedience to God. None of us deserve anything better from God than the awful judgments Pharaoh received. Without grace from God to soften our hearts, we all would have hard hearts. None of us would obey God's commands.)*

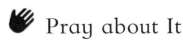 Pray about It

Thank God for the way he protected his people during the plagues.

DAY THREE

Connect It to Jesus

Can anyone guess how our story this week is about or points forward to Jesus?

 Read Exodus 10:1–2.

Think about It Some More

Here in the middle of the story, God tells us the reason he hardened Pharaoh's heart and brought so many devastating plagues against Egypt: he was writing a story for our children. God wanted to create a story about himself and how he saved his people that was so amazing and wonderful that everyone would want to tell their children about it. Then when their children heard all that God did and how powerful he was, they would believe he was the Lord and God was a saving God.

While God brought plagues on Egypt, he saved his people. There is an important reason God saved Israel from the plagues: Jesus would one day come from the family line of Israel.

Next week we will read about the last plague and how it points directly to Jesus, and shows us how God would save his people from their sins.

Talk about It

:: When God was saving Israel, who was he thinking about? *(God was thinking about all the children who would come in the future. He wanted to create a story that would help them believe he was the Lord and he was a saving God.)*

:: Since we know God is powerful enough, why didn't he use one big plague to force the Egyptians to let his people go? *(God used all the plagues to create a wonderful story that no one would forget so they could pass it on for all generations.)*

:: Why did God include this story in the Bible? *(So we could read it for ourselves and then tell our children.)*

 ## Pray about It

Thank God for giving us a story that helps us believe that he is real.

DAY FOUR

Remember It

What has God been teaching you this week through our Bible story?

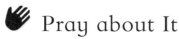 Read Exodus 10:3–20.

Think about It Some More

The terrible plague of hail destroyed all the plants that were already growing, but the wheat survived. It had only started to sprout from the ground.

Instead of allowing all of God's people to go, Pharaoh agreed to release the men, but he refused to let the children go. We learned yesterday that the children were special to God. There was no way God would agree to let his people go but leave the children behind. Pharaoh made a big mistake.

In the eighth plague, locusts (flying grasshoppers) swarmed and ate everything left by the hail, even the young shoots of the wheat plants. That meant Egypt would not have any food to eat. The animals were destroyed and then all the crops were destroyed. Once again Pharaoh cried out for forgiveness, but then as soon as the locusts were gone he hardened his heart again.

Talk about It

> ● ● KIDS, ask your parents to tell you what they would do if someone
> ● ● tried to keep you and not let you go.

(Parents, use this as an opportunity to tell your children how special they are, how much you love them, and how you would never let anyone take them or keep them.)

:: What is a locust? *(A locust is a flying grasshopper that loves to eat plants and can eat them all the way to the ground.)*

:: Why were the locusts so bad for Egypt? *(The locusts ate all the plants not destroyed by the hail. That meant that all the Egyptians and their animals didn't have any plants to eat. Soon the animals and then the people could starve to death.)*

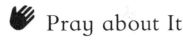

Pray about It

Thank God for protecting and saving the children of Israel from Pharaoh.

DAY FIVE

Discover It

Today we look at a passage from a psalm or one of the prophets to see what we can learn from it about Jesus.

 Read Deuteronomy 18:15–19 and Acts 3:18–23.

Think about It Some More

Moses didn't only lead God's people out of Egypt, he also became a great prophet. A prophet is someone who speaks to the people for God. God speaks to prophets, then they in turn deliver the message to God's people. You could call them God's messengers.

In this story, Moses tells the people that one day God would raise up another prophet. Later, in the New Testament, when Peter addresses the crowd he tells them the name of the prophet Moses spoke about—Jesus. So way back in Moses' day, God was already letting people know Jesus was coming.

Talk about It

:: What does a prophet do? *(He speaks to the people the words God gives him.)*

:: Who did Peter say the prophets were talking about? *(Peter said the prophets were looking forward to a day when Jesus would come and were talking about him in what they wrote.)*

:: How was Jesus a prophet? *(Jesus spoke the words of God. He also said what God would do in the future, and those things came true. For example, in Matthew 16:21, Jesus prophesied his own death and resurrection.)*

Pray about It

Thank God for sending Jesus to tell us God's Word.

Week 31

The Last Plague
and the First Passover

Make a list of all the firstborn sons in the families you know from among your relatives, families in church, and neighbors. Explain that this week you will be talking about the last plague on Egypt.

Ask them to imagine for a moment that the plague was coming tonight. All the families that do not put the blood of a lamb on their front door as God instructed will lose their firstborn son. If that were the case, how important would it be to reach all the families on our list with God's instructions?

Say, "This week, you will learn that only the blood of Jesus can cover sin to allow the judgment of God to pass over."

DAY ONE

Picture It

How would you like to help a beekeeper take the honey from his beehive? Imagine going up to the hive with ten thousand bees flying around, all trying to protect their honey. When beekeepers tend to their beehives they often wear a screen mask over their heads. As long as they wear it they are protected and the bees cannot sting them.

Let's say you got to wear one the day you went after the honey. Don't you think you might be a bit scared seeing the bees land right in front of your face and hear them buzzing all around you?

Today in our story, we will learn what the children of Israel had to do to protect themselves from the last plague, which was so close some of them could hear the loud crying in Egypt.

 Read Exodus 11.

Think about It Some More

You would think that Pharaoh would have given up when Moses said God was going to kill all the firstborn sons of Egypt. After all, Pharaoh had a son too. But Pharaoh didn't even say one word to Moses. He was angry and had a hard heart. His country of Egypt, the land he ruled, was ruined. The people had few animals left, no crops for food, and they suffered sickness and pests worse than anything they ever imagined.

Even though God knew Pharaoh wouldn't listen, he sent Moses to warn him anyway.

Talk about It

:: What did God say would happen after the last plague? *(Pharaoh would finally let God's people go.)*

:: How do we know sin had a strong hold on Pharaoh? *(Pharaoh completely refused to obey God even after all the plagues.)*

:: Who can break the strongest hold sin has upon our lives? *(Jesus can break the hold of sin on our lives. Jesus died on the cross to break the power of sin.)*

 ## Pray about It

Ask God to help you obey his Word and to never harden your heart like Pharaoh did.

DAY TWO

Remember It

What do you remember about yesterday's story? What do you think is going to happen today?

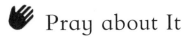 Read Exodus 12:1–30.

Think about It Some More

At first you might think that the people of Israel escaped death in their homes. But when you think about it, death came to every home, both in Egypt and Israel. In Egypt, the firstborn sons of every family died—loud cries and wailing could be heard everywhere. But with God's people, a lamb died in the firstborn son's place.

To show God that a substitute had been killed, the blood of the lamb was painted on the doorpost as a sign. When the angel of death came through and saw the blood, he knew that a lamb had been killed. The blood pointed forward to the day when Jesus, the Lamb of God, would die for our sins. So when the angel saw the blood, he passed over those homes.

Talk about It

:: What did the Israelite families put on their doorframes? *(They put the blood of the sacrificed lamb on the doorposts.)*

:: Where does the name "Passover" come from? *(The name comes from God passing over the houses that had the blood on them.)*

:: Why did God tell the Israelites to celebrate the Passover every year? *(God did not want them or their children to ever forget what he had done for them. See verses 26–27.)*

 Pray about It

Thank God for passing over the houses with the blood on their doorposts.

DAY THREE

Connect It to Jesus

Can anyone guess how our story this week is about or points forward to Jesus?

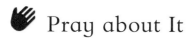 Read 1 Corinthians 5:7–8.

Think about It Some More

In sports, when a player is hurt or tired, the manager will put in a substitute player to take his place. This week we read a Bible story where God told Israel to use a lamb as a substitute. Instead of killing the firstborn son, the lambs were killed as a substitute in place of the sons.

In today's reading, we learn that we have a substitute. There was a lamb killed in our place too. Jesus is the Lamb of God that was killed in our place. He took the punishment for our sins so God's judgment would pass over us. When God told Israel to kill the Passover lambs and put the blood on the doorframes of their homes, he was creating a picture of what he would one day do with his Son Jesus for us. Jesus Christ is our Passover lamb.

Talk about It

:: What part of the Passover story points to Jesus? *(The lamb that is killed points to Jesus.)*

:: Who does the apostle Paul say is our Passover lamb? *(The apostle Paul tells us that Jesus is our Passover lamb.)*

:: How do we remember the Passover story in church on Sunday? *(We celebrate communion and in it remember our Passover Lamb, Jesus, who was sacrificed in our place on the cross.)*

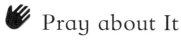 Pray about It

Thank God for giving Jesus as our Passover Lamb.

DAY FOUR

Remember It

What has God been teaching you this week through our Bible story?

 Read Exodus 12:30–42.

Think about It Some More

Since we have not experienced the hard life of slavery, it can be hard to imagine how excited the people of Israel were to be leaving Egypt. Every day they had to work making bricks, never getting paid for their work. They had to do what they were told or risk being whipped or even killed. They didn't get days off when they were sick, and they didn't get to rest when they were tired. The children of Israel had lived this way all their lives.

When Pharaoh gave the order for them to leave, they did not waste any time. They were finally free! God had rescued them from slavery just the way he said he would, and they were ready to run.

Talk about It

> ● ● KIDS, ask your parents what it felt like when they were finally free
> ● ● from a large debt or bank loan, and how getting out of debt is a little bit like Israel getting out of slavery.

(Parents, the Bible says that the borrower is a slave to the lender [Proverbs 22:7]. Tell the story of how you or someone you know paid off a loan and what it felt like to be free from the payment. Explain that you had to work and work to pay it off, and if you didn't the bank could come after you or make you pay a lot more.)

:: Did the Israelites leave Egypt the way God planned? *(Yes, it happened exactly as God had foretold, including the Egyptians giving the Israelites treasures.)*

:: How many people left Egypt? *(The Bible says there were six hundred thousand men. Add to that all the women and children and there could have been two million people or more! God told Abraham that he would make him a great nation. That promise was being fulfilled.)*

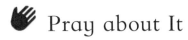 Pray about It

Thank God for rescuing the Israelites from slavery.

DAY FIVE

Discover It

Today we look at a passage from a psalm or one of the prophets to see what we can learn from it about Jesus.

 Read Psalm 45:1–6.

Think about It Some More

Picture a king riding on a horse, a sword at his side. The king is victorious. That means he won a battle. The battle was between good and evil and the king fought for good—for truth and righteousness.

In this psalm we have a picture of Jesus. Jesus fought for good against Satan and won the battle over sin and death when he died on the cross for our sins and rose again from the grave in victory. One day Jesus will return to judge everyone who refuses to believe and who disobeys God's commands.

The last book of the Bible, Revelation, talks about Jesus returning victoriously. It says, "Then I saw heaven opened, and behold, a white horse! The one sitting on it is called Faithful and True, and in righteousness he judges and makes war. His eyes are like a flame of fire, and on his head are many diadems, and he has a name written that no one knows but himself. He is clothed in a robe dipped in blood, and the name by which he is called is The Word of God" (Revelation 19:11–13).

Talk about It

:: How long does this Psalm 45 say the king's throne will last? *(Parents, have your children reread verse 6 if they aren't sure. It says the king's throne will last forever and ever.)*

:: How long is forever and ever? *(This is kind of a trick question to see if the kids realize that it will never end.)*

:: There is only one king who has a throne that will last forever and ever. What is his name? *(Jesus is the name of the king whose throne lasts forever and ever.)*

 Pray about It

Thank God that his throne will last forever and ever.

Week 32

God Parts the Red Sea

Pour two tablespoons of water on a large dinner plate and bring it to Bible study time. Challenge the children to see if they can use their hands to separate the water by placing their hands, palms together in a praying position, and then slowly separating their hands to push the water toward the sides of the plate, leaving the middle between their hands dry. Their hands can squeegee the water apart but it soon comes rushing back around their hands.

Say, "We can't part even two tablespoons of water, yet God parted the whole Red Sea! This week you will learn about the awesome power of God, which is able to deliver his people to safety."

DAY ONE

Picture It

Pretend that it is the 4th of July, the birthday of the United States of America. What does your family do to celebrate Independence Day? How do you make the 4th of July different from the other days in July? (If you live in a different country you can substitute one of your nation's holidays.) Most people get a vacation day from work on the 4th of July. A lot of folks grill hamburgers and hot dogs outside, go to parades, and then shoot off fireworks high into the air when it gets dark. Is there anything else you might do to celebrate?

In today's lesson, we will learn how God told Israel to celebrate the Passover so they would never forget their own independence day from Egypt.

 Read Exodus 13:1–16.

Think about It Some More

The problem with celebrating things that happened in the past, like the 4th of July, is that we can get so excited about the celebration that we forget why we are celebrating. Many people don't know what actually happened on the 4th of July in 1776. The truth is, nothing much happened on that day. We declared our independence on July 2nd, then signed the declaration on August 2nd. When we celebrate on July 4th, we are actually celebrating the day people found out about our independence being declared.

In our story today, God wanted to make sure the children of Israel would never forget the Passover and the last plague. That is why God said that every firstborn boy and firstborn male animal belonged to the Lord and had to be redeemed (bought back) by killing a lamb. This tradition would make sure that Israel never forgot how the firstborn of Egypt died the night of the Passover, but God spared the people of Israel who killed a lamb in the place of their firstborn and painted the blood of the lamb on the doorpost.

Talk about It

:: Why was it so important that Israel remember the last plague and the Passover? *(The killing of the lamb instead of the firstborn son and the blood on the doorpost point forward to Jesus.)*

:: How does the last plague and the Passover point forward to Jesus? *(The lamb that was killed during the first Passover in place of the firstborn son enabled Israel to escape God's judgment. Jesus died on the cross in our place so we could escape God's judgment. When we trust in Jesus and his death on the cross, God passes over our sin because Jesus took our punishment.)*

:: Why don't we celebrate the Passover by killing animals today? *(The Passover was a picture pointing forward to Jesus. After Jesus came and died and rose from the dead, the church started celebrating his resurrection.)*

:: What holiday helps us remember Jesus' death and resurrection? *(Easter Sunday)*

 ## Pray about It

Thank Jesus for dying on the cross so God's judgment might pass over us.

DAY TWO

Remember It

What do you remember about yesterday's story? What do you think is going to happen today?

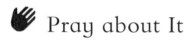 Read Exodus 14:1–7.

Think about It Some More

Moses instructed the Israelites to celebrate the Passover dressed and ready to leave, as if they were about to go on a journey (Exodus 12:11). The people obeyed Moses so, after the death of the firstborn sons and Pharaoh's permission to leave, all of Israel was ready to go. All Israel poured out of their houses and left Egypt, and God led them into the wilderness.

At first, the Egyptians were glad to let the people go and even gave them gifts as they left (Exodus 12:35–36). But it wasn't long before the Egyptians started to realize their workers were all gone. Now they would have to do all the work. No one was gathering straw, no bricks were being made, and no one was hauling or cleaning or cooking or washing their clothes.

When Pharaoh realized the whole work force of Egypt was gone, he got angry again, forgot about the plagues, and gathered his army to chase down the Hebrews and bring them back to Egypt.

Talk about It

:: How did Israel's obedience to God allow them to leave Egypt safely? *(Since everyone was ready to go, they were able to leave Egypt very quickly before Pharaoh could change his mind.)*

:: What can we learn from Israel's obedience to God's Word? *(If we obey what God says to us through his Word, God will guide us through our trials. But if we disobey the Lord, it will only bring us trouble.)*

:: Who did Pharaoh take with him to catch Israel? *(He took six hundred of his best chariots along with all the other chariots of Egypt. There could have been thousands of chariots.)*

 ## Pray about It

Ask God to help you to obey his Word like all of Israel did.

DAY THREE

Connect It to Jesus

Can anyone guess how our story this week is about or points forward to Jesus?

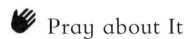 Read Exodus 14:8–9 and Romans 9:17.

Think about It Some More

In today's two Bible passages, we learn once again that God is in control of everything, even Pharaoh's heart. Paul tells us in the book of Romans that God put Pharaoh on the throne of Egypt to show his power through Pharaoh's life and that God's name would be proclaimed in all the earth.

Now here we are today, thousands of years later, reading all about it and we too are rejoicing over God's amazing plan to save his people. The story of Pharaoh and God's power to deliver his people has been told many, many millions of times. But the greatest celebration comes when we remember that Jesus was born to the sons of Israel in the Promised Land, in a town called Bethlehem. So when we celebrate Israel's salvation from slavery in Egypt, we can also celebrate our salvation from slavery to sin.

Talk about It

:: Pharaoh thought he was in control, but who was really in control of everything? *(God)*

:: What does God's control over Pharaoh's heart tell us about God? *(God is all-powerful. He even controls the lives of sinful men. God is not responsible for their sins, but he can use their sins for his good.)*

:: What is the message God wanted to be proclaimed in all the earth? *(The story of Jesus is the message God wanted to be proclaimed in all the earth. God didn't save only Israel from slavery; God's plan of salvation was bigger than that. God's salvation includes Jesus saving us from our sins. After all, if God had not delivered Israel from Egypt, Jesus would not have been born in Bethlehem.)*

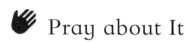 Pray about It

Thank God for saving Israel, and thank God for saving us through Jesus.

DAY FOUR

Remember It

What has God been teaching you this week through our Bible story?

 Read Exodus 14:10–31.

Think about It Some More

Have you ever played a game of tag and had someone chasing you when you found yourself cornered by a fence or a wall with nowhere to go? Well, that is what happened to God's people. They got a big head start running away from Egypt, but they were stopped when they came to the Red Sea. It seemed to them like they were trapped with nowhere to go. When they saw the army of Egypt approaching, they cried out in fear because they thought they were going to die.

But God had a plan. He put a pillar of cloud between the Egyptians and his people to protect them while Moses stretched out his hand and God parted the Red Sea. When the cloud lifted, the Egyptians must have been shocked. Israel had escaped! Their tracks led down the sandy bank into the sea. Giant walls of seawater stood to the left and right of the path.

Pharaoh dared to go in after the slaves. But once Israel was safe on the other side, Moses stretched out his hand and God closed the sea, destroying Pharaoh and his army. Not only did God save his people; he also destroyed their enemy.

Talk about It

> ● ● KIDS, ask your parents if they can remember a time when God provided a way through a difficult time for them.

(Parents, think of a time when God delivered you from a difficult situation. This could be a financial provision or another answer to prayer.)

:: How can our faith in God's plan be made stronger by reading how he saved Israel? *(God is all-powerful and he can save us when we need his help, just like he helped Israel.)*

:: Can you think of an area of your life where you could use God's help to get you through? *(We need God's help every day. Parents, help your children see where they need God's help with chores, school, and even their play)*

Pray about It

Ask God to watch over you like he watched over Israel.

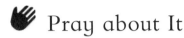
DAY FIVE

Discover It

Today we look at a passage from a psalm or one of the prophets to see what we can learn from it about Jesus.

 Read Psalm 45:6–9.

Think about It Some More

Who was the oldest person that ever lived in your family? Although they may have been blessed to live a long time, they didn't or won't live forever. We all die—unless we are around when Jesus returns. So when God tells us about a throne that lasts forever, we know the king can't be an ordinary guy because we all die. The king who sits on that throne must be a very special person.

There is only one king who lives forever—Jesus. Jesus also fits the description of a king who rules in righteousness and gladness. Hebrews 1:8–9 quotes this psalm and tells us that it is about Jesus.

Talk about It

:: How is this psalm talking about Jesus? *(Jesus has an everlasting throne. He alone could love righteousness and hate wickedness perfectly.)*

:: What does it mean that the king on the throne loves righteousness? *(It means the king loves what is right and what is good.)*

:: *Read Hebrews 1:8–9.* How is Psalm 45 like the passage in Hebrews 1:8–9? *(Hebrews 1:8–9 is a direct quote and tells us Psalm 45 is about God's Son Jesus.)*

Pray about It

Ask God to help you to follow Jesus' example by loving righteousness.

Week 33

God Provides Food and Water for Israel

Bring a golf-ball-sized rock, a washcloth, and a small basin half filled with water to Bible study. Soak the washcloth in the water, and give it to your youngest child to wring out. Pass the cloth up the ranks of your children from youngest to oldest, and see how each successively older child can wring a bit more water out of the cloth into the basin. (If you have only one child, you can include yourself and your spouse.) By the time you get to your oldest child, he will celebrate how much stronger he is by the amount of water he can produce from the already wrung-out cloth.

Finally, pass the rock around, and ask each person to squeeze water from the rock. Hold the basin below their hands in anticipation of what might come out. The lesson, of course, is to show that the greatest strength in man is no match for the power of God, who provided water out of the rock for his thirsty people.

Say, "This week you will learn how God miraculously provided food and water for Israel in the desert."

DAY ONE

Picture It

Imagine that while on vacation in the mountains we get stuck in heavy traffic. By the time we break free of the jam it is late. Dad says he is going to push on through and not stop to eat until we arrive at our vacation home.

When we finally reach our destination, we are all talking about food. Someone suggests that we send out for pizza, while someone else wants to eat hamburgers; but everyone agrees that we want to eat, and fast. But there's a problem: it is so late that everything is closed, including the grocery stores.

Suddenly everyone's mood changes. People start getting irritated; they complain saying that we should never have gone on vacation in the first place.

Have you ever had an experience like that? We are quick to complain when we don't get what we want. Today we'll see how Israel is tested when they don't get what they want.

 Read Exodus 16:1–8.

Think about It Some More

In this Bible passage, we learn that complaining is a sin against God. The story starts out with the people grumbling against Moses and Aaron, but later Moses and Aaron tell the people that their complaining is not against man but against God.

So, the next time your favorite flavor of ice cream runs out, or Mom won't let you play outside, remember that any complaint to Mom is really a sin against God. After all, it is God who provides all the milk for ice cream in the world, and God is the one who brings the rain that grows the grass to feed the cattle. When we complain, we are really saying, "God, I don't like the way you are running the world."

Talk about It

:: Why did Israel complain? *(They complained because they were hungry and didn't have any food to eat.)*

:: What could they have done instead of complaining? *(Instead of complaining they could have asked Moses to ask God for some food to eat. If God could provide a way through the Red Sea, he could provide food.)*

:: How was God merciful to Israel? *(Remember that mercy is when you don't give someone the punishment they deserve. In this story not only did God not punish Israel for their sins, he even gave them what they wanted.)*

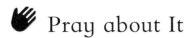 Pray about It

Ask God to help you to trust him and not complain.

DAY TWO

Remember It

What do you remember about yesterday's story? What do you think is going to happen today?

 Read Exodus 16:9–35.

Think about It Some More

God can provide for our needs in amazing ways. The Israelites complained in the wilderness because they didn't have any food and they didn't see any way to get food. They didn't have flour so they couldn't make bread. There were no plants or wild animals to eat, and they didn't have enough of their own animals to feed them all.

They forgot that God was all-powerful and can do anything. He doesn't need flour to make bread, and he commands all the animals of the earth. To show the Israelites his mighty power, God made bread out of nothing at all and commanded quail to fly to them to provide meat—enough to feed the million-plus people who left Egypt.

Talk about It

:: What did Israel call the bread that God provided? *(They called the bread manna.)*

:: How does this story speak of God's kindness and patience? *(In spite of their grumbling, God gave the Israelites food. God gave them manna for forty years, even though they continued to sin.)*

:: How did God honor the Sabbath? *(God allowed the Israelites to gather twice as much manna on the day before the Sabbath. On every other day of the week, if they tried to keep more manna than they needed for the day, it would spoil. But not on the Sabbath! To the Israelites, this was a sign that God was taking care of them.)*

 Pray about It

Take time to pray for something you would like God to provide.

DAY THREE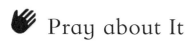

Connect It to Jesus

Can anyone guess how our story this week is about or points forward to Jesus?

Read John 6:31–40.

Think about It Some More

Jesus was full of surprises when he taught. He loved to show how stories in the Old Testament were actually about him. For forty years the people of Israel wandered in the desert and ate manna. That heavenly bread saved them from starving. But they didn't know that every time they took a bite, they were pointing forward to a day when God would save his people from a greater danger, their sin.

Just as the people needed the manna to survive, so we need Jesus. He is our bread from heaven! If we place our trust in Jesus, his death on the cross, and his resurrection from the dead, God forgives our sin and opens a way for us to live with Jesus in heaven.

Talk about It

:: Who is the Bread of Life? *(Jesus)*

:: Why did Jesus call himself the bread of life? *(Bread is a basic food that can keep us alive. Without food and water we would die. Jesus is spiritual food and water because without Jesus and his sacrifice on the cross, we would die a spiritual death and be separated from God forever.)*

:: Who did Jesus say would never get thirsty again? *(Parents, if your children don't know the answer, read verse 35 again and see if they can answer "those who believe in Jesus.")*

:: What do we need to believe about Jesus? *(We need to believe that Jesus was God and lived a sinless life, and that Jesus died for our sins and rose again from the dead. All that together is the basic gospel message.)*

 Pray about It

Ask God to help every person in your family believe and put their trust in Jesus.

DAY FOUR

Remember It

What has God been teaching you this week through our Bible story?

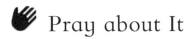 Read Exodus 17:1–7.

Think about It Some More

At some point the people of Israel ran out of water and got very angry. They seemed to forget that God was creating bread for them out of nothing every day. If God provided bread out of nothing, he could provide water as well. But the people argued, complained, and finally wanted to stone Moses to death.

Instead of punishing the people, God showed them mercy and gave them water to drink. Instead of striking the people for their sin, God told Moses to strike the rock and gave them water to drink.

In the New Testament, Paul tells us that the rock is a picture of Jesus (1 Corinthians 10:4). God overlooked Israel's sin and gave them water because he knew that one day Jesus would stand in their place and take their punishment.

Talk about It

> ● ● KIDS, ask your parents if they were ever in a situation where they
> ● ● complained because they didn't get what they wanted.

(Parents, think of a time when a store ran out of something you wanted to buy.)

:: Why did the people want to stone Moses? *(They believed they were about to die. They blamed Moses and wanted to stone him for it.)*

:: Who were the people really angry with? *(The people were really angry with God for not giving them what they wanted.)*

:: Instead of punishing Israel, what did God do? *(God stood on a rock and told Moses to strike the rock where he stood. God knew that one day his own Son would die for their sins.)*

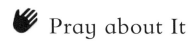 Pray about It

Ask God to help us remember that he gave us Jesus, so the next time we don't get something we want we are not so quick to complain.

DAY FIVE

Discover It

Today we look at a passage from a psalm or one of the prophets to see what we can learn from it about Jesus.

 Read Psalm 72:1–2 and 2 Timothy 4:8.

Think about It Some More

The Old Testament is filled with Scriptures that point to Christ. Jesus is the royal Son. He is the one who will judge people in righteousness and justice. Solomon, who wrote this psalm, was a very wise judge who made godly decisions, but Jesus is the only truly righteous judge. Paul, in writing to Timothy, described Jesus as the righteous judge who will one day give a crown of righteousness to everyone who believes in him.

Talk about It

:: Who is the judge Psalm 72 is telling us about? *(Jesus is the judge.)*

:: What kind of a judge is a righteous judge? *(A righteous judge is one who doesn't commit crimes and stands for what is right and true, for good and not for evil. A righteous judge punishes sin but rewards good.)*

:: How is Jesus a righteous judge? *(Jesus never sinned and always judges correctly.)*

:: If Jesus is a judge that punishes sin, why doesn't he punish our sins? *(When Jesus was on the cross dying, God punished him in our place. Now if we trust in Jesus we can be forgiven.)*

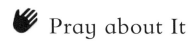 Pray about It

Thank Jesus for being a righteous judge and for taking our punishment.

Week 34

God Gives Moses
the Ten Commandments

Before moving into the Bible study for this week, ask your children the following questions:

"Why do we have to stop at stop signs?"

"What would happen if the police gave special permission to go through red lights to every driver whose name begins with the letter M, so they could get where they were going faster? Would that be a blessing to them? Would that work for the other drivers?"

Say, "Laws are passed for the good of the people. This week we will learn the ten laws (or commandments) that God gave us. Each of these commandments is designed for our good and God's glory."

DAY ONE

Picture It

Imagine that you were playing catch with a friend and the ball you were throwing accidentally flew over a fence into the electric company's power station. Along the fence are signs in big red letters that say, "Danger, high voltage! Do not enter." I don't think you would want to climb the fence to get your ball because you could get electrocuted.

In today's Bible story, God tells Moses to warn the people about Mt. Sinai. He was to put up a boundary to protect the people from stepping onto God's mountain because, like the power station, if they wandered too close, it could kill them.

 Read Exodus 19.

Think about It Some More

Most people don't realize that if they saw God's face or touched God they would die. They think of God as a good guy, like a good friend, but they don't realize that God is also holy.

God's holiness means that he doesn't have any sin at all and he must remain set apart from sin. If sin comes near, God destroys it because sin is evil and he is good.

That is why God warned Moses to set up a boundary around the mountain where he was. That way, the people would not accidentally get too close and have God punish them for their sin. God had a plan to save them from their sin, but if they didn't follow his plan they would die.

Talk about It

:: Why didn't God want the people to touch the mountain? *(God's holy presence came down upon the mountain. If the people went there, they would die.)*

:: Why did God speak to Moses so the people could hear? *(Then the people would believe and put their trust in Moses as their leader [verse 9].)*

:: Why didn't Moses die when he walked on the mountain? *(Moses didn't die because God chose Moses and gave him faith in God's plan. God's plan was to save his people through his Son Jesus. So when Moses had faith in God's plan he was trusting in Jesus. God knew that one day Jesus would die for Moses' sins and he overlooked them.)*

 Pray about It

Thank God for saving Moses and allowing him to go up on the mountain to talk to God.

DAY TWO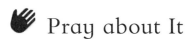

Remember It

What do you remember about yesterday's story? What do you think is going to happen today?

Read Exodus 20:1–21.

Think about It Some More

When the people heard the commandments God gave, they were afraid because they didn't think they could obey them all (Hebrews 12:19–20). They were also terrified of the thunder and lightning that came along with God's voice.

If you have ever been in a terrible thunderstorm, you know how frightening the lightning and thunder can be. You can imagine what it would be like if, in addition to that thunder and lightning, you heard a booming voice say, "Honor your father and mother," and you knew if you didn't you could die.

Talk about It

:: Which of God's commandments have you disobeyed? *(Parents, help your children here. It should be easy for them to see that they have disobeyed parents, or coveted—wanted something that someone else has.)*

:: What is the punishment for breaking one of God's commands? *(The punishment for breaking one of God's commands is having to spend forever in hell. Parents, this answer is shocking but nonetheless true.)*

:: Is there any way for sinners to go to heaven? (Yes, if we trust in Jesus who died on the cross to take the punishment that we deserve for our sin, we can be forgiven and go to heaven.)

 ## Pray about It

Ask God to help you remember what Jesus did for you each time you sin and break God's commands.

DAY THREE

Connect It to Jesus

Can anyone guess how our story this week is about or points forward to Jesus?

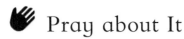 Read Galatians 3:23–24.

Think about It Some More

Paul describes God's laws (the Ten Commandments are a part of God's law) as a prison. That might sound like an odd thing to say, but here is why. The law tells us what we must do, for example, worship God and obey parents; or what we must not do, for example, steal or lie. If we break God's law even once, we are not free to go to heaven to be with God but are held as prisoners for judgment. This is bad news.

But this bad news was a part of God's plan so that when he brought us the good news about Jesus, we would be excited to follow him. Jesus never broke God's law, and now he offers to trade his perfect life for the sinful lives of all who will believe in him as their Savior. Once we come to Jesus and believe, we are no longer held prisoners by the law and we are free to go to heaven.

Talk about It

:: How many of us are sinners? *(We all are sinners.)*

:: Why did God give us the law? *(God gave us the law to show us how sinful we are so we would want to run to Jesus to be saved.)*

:: What is the bad news? *(The bad news is that we have all broken God's law and cannot save ourselves.)*

:: What is the good news? *(The good news is that Jesus Christ died on the cross for our sins, so everyone who places their trust in him is forgiven and can avoid the bad news.)*

Pray about It

Take time to confess some of the ways you have broken God's laws and ask God to forgive you.

DAY FOUR

Remember It

What has God been teaching you this week through our Bible story?

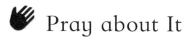 Read Exodus 20:22–23.

Think about It Some More

When you want to make sure someone remembers something important, you can repeat it so he doesn't forget. For instance, the day before a test your teacher might remind you to study, or the day before your first game your coach might tell you not to forget your uniform. Mom or Dad might tell you three times to clean your room before they leave, to make sure you don't forget while they are gone.

God knew which commands Israel needed to hear more than once to make sure they did not forget. So God told them again not to make false gods of silver or gold. But even though God repeated this command, we will see that Israel soon forgot what he said.

Talk about It

::

> ● ● KIDS, ask your parents what kinds of things you have to hear more
> ● ● than once to make sure you do them.

(Parents, remind your children of the times when you asked them to do something and they didn't follow through. This will help them identify with Israel.)

:: Why do you think God repeated to Israel the command not to make gods of silver and gold? *(God knew they would be tempted to make false gods.)*

:: What did God do for Israel to help them stay away from false gods? *(God spoke to them from heaven. Idols made of silver and gold cannot speak. God wanted to show that he was all-powerful and not the same as false idols.)*

 Pray about It

Ask God to help you remember his commands and not forget what your parents ask you to do.

DAY FIVE

Discover It

Today we look at a passage from a psalm or one of the prophets to see what we can learn from it about Jesus.

 Read Jeremiah 31:31–34 and Luke 22:19–20.

Think about It Some More

Jeremiah wrote about a wonderful day when the covenant (or promise) God made with Abraham would be replaced by a new covenant. Instead of writing his law on tablets of stone like he did with Moses, God was going to write his law on the hearts of people.

The new covenant, or promise, Jeremiah wrote about came true in Jesus' day. Luke told the story for us to read. At the last supper before he died, Jesus talked about the new covenant. The new covenant he talked about was God's new promise to us.

Talk about It

:: How did Jeremiah know about the new covenant hundreds of years before Jesus was even born? *(God told Jeremiah what would happen and Jeremiah wrote down God's words for us to read. Whenever we read the Bible we should remember that although men wrote the words, God inspired them to write what they wrote down.)*

:: What makes the new covenant wonderful? *(Parents, have your children reread the passage. If you have young children, read the verses again to see if they can pick up the benefits of the new covenant, like the forgiveness of sins, an all-knowing God, and being God's people.)*

:: What did Jesus do to make a way to forgive our sins? *(Jesus died on the cross to take our penalty and then he rose again in victory over sin and death.)*

Pray about It

Thank Jesus for giving us a new covenant where God's law is written on our hearts and we become God's people.

Week 35

The Tabernacle

Bring an umbrella to Bible study, open it up, and point it toward your family so no one can see you. Continue talking with your children as normal, but move the umbrella so it always blocks them from seeing you. They of course will ask you why you have an umbrella opened between you. Explain to the children that the tabernacle had a curtain in the middle separating the holy place from the Most Holy Place, and you wanted to give them an idea of what it would be like if they were separated from you by a curtain.

Draw them out for a bit, asking them a few questions, including what it feels like to be talking to an umbrella. Explain that the curtain of the tabernacle hid the presence of God from the people until after Jesus died and the curtain of the temple was torn in two. Say, "This week you will learn about the construction of the temple and the curtain that prevented the people from approaching God."

DAY ONE

Picture It

If you were going to build a house today, what materials would you need? A list might include cement and block for the bottom part, wood and nails for the top, bricks for the outside, drywall for the inside.

Can you think of anything that is missing from that list? We would still need shingles for the roof, wire for the electric, pipes for the plumbing, carpet for the floors, paint for the walls, cabinets and appliances for the kitchen, wood for the trim inside, windows, doors, toilets and sinks, heating and air conditioning. Overall it is a very long list—and that doesn't include the furniture.

Today we will read about the materials God wanted his people to use to build his house.

 Read Exodus 25:1–8.

Think about It Some More

In today's passage, God called Moses to collect the items needed to build a very special tent called a tabernacle. The tabernacle was where God would live among his people.

God wanted to show Israel and the surrounding nations that he was different from their false gods. None of the other gods lived with their people. Sure, they might have an idol carved of stone in a temple, but idols are fake. God actually came down and lived in the tabernacle with his people, and all of Israel would see his presence in the form of the pillar of cloud or fire over the tabernacle.

Talk about It

:: In Egypt, the Israelites had been poor slaves. Where did they get the gold and silver Moses was asking them for? *(Just before the Israelites left Egypt, they asked for gold and silver and other valuable things from the Egyptians. They did this because God had told them to. God knew all along that he wanted to use these things to build the tabernacle.)*

:: What is a tabernacle? *(A tabernacle is a tent. The word is also used to describe the way God lives among his people. God is said to "tabernacle" among his people. That is what John was talking about in the New Testament when he said God "dwelt" among us [John 1:14].)*

:: Why did God have his people build the tabernacle? *(God wanted to live with his people.)*

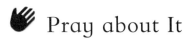 Pray about It

Praise God for the way he loves to live among his people.

DAY TWO

Remember It

What do you remember about yesterday's story? What do you think is going to happen today? Read Exodus 26. *(Parents, take a look at this passage before you read it. If it seems too long and detailed to hold your children's attention, you may want to read just verses 1, 7, 15, 26–27, and 31–37.)*

Think about It Some More

If Mom asked you to bake a cake, what ingredients would you use? You would want to follow a recipe to make sure the cake came out the way it was supposed to. If you didn't follow directions but put in whatever you wanted, you would find out the hard way that you made a big mistake when your cake came out as flat as a pancake or tasted terrible.

In today's story, God gave Moses very detailed instructions on how to build his special tent. God planned every part of the tabernacle so it would turn out just the way he wanted. If you follow the directions we have in the Bible, you could make a tabernacle very much like the one Moses made.

Talk about It

:: What kind of materials did God want Moses to make his tabernacle out of? *(Parents, see how many of the items mentioned in the story your children can remember.)*

:: God wanted two rooms in his tent. What are they called? *(Parents, if your children can't remember, have them look at [or reread] verse 33. The two rooms are the Holy Place and the Most Holy Place.)*

:: Which room do you think God was going to live in, the Holy Place or the Most Holy Place? *(God was going to live in the Most Holy Place.)*

 ## Pray about It

Thank God that he is a holy God, not a sinner like us. That way we can always trust that he will do the right thing.

DAY THREE

Connect It to Jesus

Can anyone guess how our story this week is about or points forward to Jesus?

 Read Exodus 27:1–8.

Think about It Some More

In addition to the tabernacle, God also gave Moses instructions for his furniture. One of the pieces of furniture was called the altar. The altar was so holy that it had to be carried using poles so no one would touch it. Thousands and thousands of lambs would be sacrificed on the altar for the sins of the people, year after year. But all those lambs were still not enough to take away the sin of God's people. All they did was point forward to a day when the Lamb of God, Jesus, would be sacrificed by dying on the cross for our sins.

Talk about It

:: Can you remember another Bible story where something was sacrificed on an altar? *(Abraham was going to sacrifice Isaac on an altar, but God provided a ram instead.)*

:: Why did God build an altar for Israel? *(Israel would sacrifice lambs on it as offerings to God so that God would not kill them for their sin. The lambs were sacrificed in their place.)*

:: Why don't we need an altar today? *(We don't need an altar today because Jesus was the perfect sacrifice for sin. Once we trust in Jesus, no other sacrifice is needed.)*

Pray about It

Thank God for sending Jesus to be our perfect sacrifice.

DAY FOUR

Remember It

What has God been teaching you this week through our Bible story?

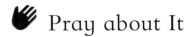 Read Exodus 28:1–30.

Think about It Some More

Not only did God have special instructions for the tabernacle and the furniture, he also gave special instructions for the clothes of the priest who would offer the sacrifices to God.

One of the most interesting parts of the outfit was the breastplate. The priest's breastplate had the names of the twelve tribes of Israel on it. God even gave it a special name: the breastplate of judgment. Every time the priest would go into the tabernacle, he carried the names of Israel close to his heart. That way, he wouldn't forget them since he was responsible to offer sacrifices for them all.

Talk about It

> ● ● KIDS, ask your parents if they have a story of a time when they for-
> ● ● got someone's name.

:: Whose names were placed on the breastplate? *(If your children can't come up with the answer have them look at [or reread] verse 21 to find that the names of the sons of Israel were placed there.)*

:: Why do you think God wanted the priest to remember all the sons of Israel when he went into the tabernacle? *(The job of the priest was to pray for the sins of all of Israel and ask God to forgive them and accept the animals that were killed in their place.)*

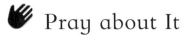 Pray about It

Thank God for providing a way for Israel's sins to be forgiven

DAY FIVE

Discover It

Today we look at a passage from a psalm or one of the prophets to see what we can learn from it about Jesus.

 Read Psalm 72:4–8.

Think about It Some More

We already learned that this psalm described Jesus as the righteous judge (verses 1–2). Today we learn that Jesus would bring peace to and rule the whole earth.

Talk about It

:: There is only one king who could rule for all generations. What is his name? *(Jesus is the only king who could rule for all generations, so we know Psalm 72 must be talking about him.)*

:: What else do we see that points to Jesus in this psalm? *(If you have young children, you can reread the psalm and have them raise their hands when they hear something that points to Jesus. Only Jesus will be able to reign and have peace abound, and rule from sea to sea.)*

:: How long does it say Jesus will bring peace to the earth? *(Verse 7 says peace will abound until the moon is no more.)*

Pray about It

Thank God for sending Jesus to be our king who will defeat evil and bring peace to everyone for all time.

Week 36

The Golden Calf

Print out a picture of a cow from the Internet or copy one out of a picture book. Gather your children, show them the picture, and ask, "Whose dog looks most like this cow?" You can play this up a bit by asking if any of their friends' dogs have a cowlike nose or ears. They will likely laugh. If they object, point out the similarities. The cow has two eyes, two ears, a mouth, and some hair just like dogs do.

After a moment share that you are only joking and there is really little resemblance between a cow and a dog. Explain that it would be even worse to ask which person looks like this cow.

Say, "When Israel made a golden calf as an idol and said it was their god, it was an even greater insult to God. They were calling the creator of the universe a cow. This week, you will learn about their idolatry."

DAY ONE

Picture It

Imagine that Dad returns home from a moving sale and announces that he has bought a new dresser for the master bedroom, which has white furniture. The dresser he bought is black and scratched up; it will need a coat of paint. Excited to surprise Mom, you and Dad pick up a can of paint along with brushes and some sandpaper and get started on the project.

First, you take out all the drawers and remove the knobs. Then Dad directs you to sand the fronts of the drawers to make sure the new paint sticks well, while he does the same to the body of the dresser. After laying down a drop cloth, he opens the paint can and you both paint the old black dresser bright white. Carefully you brush the paint on, transforming the scratched-up black dresser into a beautiful white one.

Even though the dresser was ugly black, now the bright white is all you see.

In today's story, we learn what God uses to cover up sin. You can't cover up sin with a coat of paint; but there is something that does the job. Let's read and find out what can cover up our sin.

 Read Exodus 29:1–21, 35–37.

Think about It Some More

God gave Aaron and his sons a long list of things to do to prepare them to serve God as priests. First, they had to wash themselves and put on special clothes. Then they were anointed with oil, which was a way to show that God chose them for the job out of all the others. Finally, animals were killed and their blood was painted on their ears, fingers, and toes and sprinkled all over their clothes. Like the dresser painted white, the blood was meant to cover their sins so they could serve in God's holy presence.

The animal blood didn't take away their sins; it only pointed ahead to the day when Jesus would shed his blood for their forgiveness.

Talk about It

:: Why did Aaron and his sons place their hands on the animals before they killed them? *(This was to show that the animals died in their place taking their sins.)*

:: Why did God have blood sprinkled on brand-new clothes? *(Aaron and his sons were sinners. By sprinkling the blood on their clothes, God was showing us all that we need blood to cover over our sins. This idea points to Jesus and how he shed his blood to cover our sins.)*

:: Why don't we need to kill animals today and use their blood to cover our sins? *(We have Jesus. When we trust in Jesus and his death on the cross, his blood covers our sins.)*

 Pray about It

Thank God that we no longer have to kill animals to cover our sin because Jesus died for us.

DAY TWO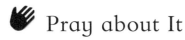

Remember It

What do you remember about yesterday's story? What do you think is going to happen today?

Read Exodus 32:1–8.

Think about It Some More

Do you remember the one command God repeated after he gave the Ten Commandments to Israel? We learned about it in Exodus 20:22–23. God told Israel not to make gods of silver or gold, but it didn't take Israel long to disobey. This is why God repeated that command.

When Moses delayed in returning, the people were impatient and asked Aaron to make for them gods to worship. Instead of reminding them of God's command and saying no, Aaron foolishly agreed and helped them make an idol, sinning along with the people.

Rather than look down on Israel for disobeying, we need to remember that sin works the same way in our hearts and lives today.

Talk about It

:: Can you think of a time when you disobeyed Mom or Dad? *(Parents, remind your children of the last time they disobeyed. See if you can remember a time when they disobeyed shortly after you warned them.)*

:: Who saw what Israel did when Moses was not around to see their sin? *(God was watching and knew everything they did.)*

:: Why were the sins of Aaron and the people so evil? *(God had just warned them not to worship other gods. Aaron, of all people, should have known better.)*

:: We can try to hide our sin from parents, but why can't we hide our sin from God? *(God sees all our sins because he is all-knowing—we can't hide anything from God.)*

 Pray about It

Ask God to help you obey and not hide your sin.

DAY THREE

Connect It to Jesus

Can anyone guess how our story this week is about or points forward to Jesus?

 Read Exodus 32:9–14.

Think about It Some More

While God was on one side ready to punish Israel for their sin and Israel was on the other side worshiping their golden calf, Moses was in the middle standing between God and his sinful people.

When Moses heard God say he was going to destroy Israel, he spoke up to help them and reminded God of his promises. God listened to Moses and did not destroy Israel.

Moses acted as the mediator—the person in the middle—between God and his people. One day God would send Jesus to become our mediator—to stand between God the Father and us, taking our punishment. Unlike Moses, who sinned, Jesus could stand in our place to take our punishment because he never did anything wrong.

Today, Jesus still stands in the middle in heaven praying for us. Each time we sin, he reminds his Father that he died for all our sins so we can be forgiven.

Talk about It

:: What does a mediator do? *(A mediator stands between two parties or people and helps them find a way to settle their conflict.)*

:: What did Moses do as a mediator? *(Moses stood in the middle and reminded God of his promises.)*

:: Who stands in the middle as the mediator between us and God? *(Jesus stands in the middle for us. Jesus stands ready to defend us when we sin by showing his Father the nail marks in his hands. His nail marks declare to God that Jesus died for our sins and took our punishment so we can be forgiven.)*

 Pray about It

Thank God for sending Jesus to be our mediator and to stand in the middle for us.

DAY FOUR

Remember It

What has God been teaching you this week through our Bible story?

 Read Exodus 32:15–35.

Think about It Some More

When Mount Saint Helens, a volcano in the state of Washington, erupted in 1980, it blew out sideways and knocked down trees for fifteen miles. Millions of trees were left lying down, all facing away from the blast. After it was safe to return to the area, people went to see the results of the explosion. But even though they had heard reports of the damage, they were shocked when they saw the terrible destruction for themselves.

That's what happened to Moses when he came down from the mountain. Although God had told him, Moses was shocked to see the terrible way Israel was sinning and breaking God's commandments. He realized more than ever that his people needed a mediator, so he went back up the mountain to stand in the middle and continue pleading for God to save them.

Moses is a wonderful picture of Jesus. Jesus is our perfect mediator, who died for our sins, rose again, and forever stands between us and God to plead for our forgiveness (Romans 8:34).

Talk about It

> ● ● KIDS, ask your mom or dad if they ever heard about something they
> ● ● were later shocked to see for themselves.

:: Why did Moses go back up the mountain to talk to God? *(Moses saw how evil the sin of the people was and knew they needed a mediator—someone to stand in the middle for them.)*

:: What did Moses offer to do for the people? *(Moses offered to give his own life to save the people. When he asked that his own life be blotted out instead of the people, he was asking to take their punishment on himself.)*

:: How was Moses acting like Jesus? *(Moses offered to take Israel's punishment to save them, which was like Jesus who died on the cross to take our punishment.)*

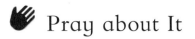 Pray about It

Thank God for the forgiveness he shows his people.

DAY FIVE

Discover It

Today we look at a passage from a psalm or one of the prophets to see what we can learn from it about Jesus.

 Read Isaiah 53:12.

Think about It Some More

There are a lot of big words in this prophecy, but when you know what they mean it is not too difficult to understand. Isaiah 53:12 is one of the clearest prophetic passages pointing to Jesus. This verse tells us four things about the Savior: 1) Jesus "poured out his soul to death" when he died on the cross for our sins; 2) Jesus was considered to be a transgressor—a sinner; 3) Jesus bore, that is, he took on himself, the sins of many; 4) Jesus makes intercession for the transgressors, which simply means that he stands in the middle praying for us because we are sinners.

Talk about It

:: Can you think of one thing Isaiah tells us about Jesus in this part of the Bible? *(Parents, help walk your children through the above list. Give them as many clues as they need or reread the passage, and have your younger children raise their hands when they think it is talking about Jesus.)*

:: What is a transgressor? *(A sinner or somebody who disobeys God's law.)*

:: Who does Jesus remind you of from our story this week? *(Jesus reminds us of Moses who prayed to God not to destroy Israel for their sin. Jesus is always praying for us, thus he is a mediator for us like Moses was a mediator for Israel.)*

:: When Jesus died, he was hung on the cross between two criminals. Which part of today's verses point to Jesus being crucified with sinners? *(To be "numbered with the transgressors" means to be treated like a sinner. If you had asked someone who watched Jesus being crucified, how many criminals had been killed that day, they would have answered three, counting Jesus with the two robbers.)*

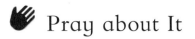 Pray about It

Thank Jesus that he was willing to die like a criminal on a cross between two robbers.

Week 37

God Has Mercy on Israel

Prior to your Bible study, pull your oldest child (or spouse if you have only one child) aside and explain that you are going to use her as a mediator for Bible study. You will use her to communicate with the others. Tell her she can speak on behalf of the others.

Instruct the mediator to call the family together. If one of your children arrives without a Bible, or comes late, or fails to pay attention, suggest a penalty for him to the mediator. Remind the mediator of her appeal rights on behalf of the other children.

Use this exercise to demonstrate what a mediator does. Say, "Moses stood as a mediator for the people of Israel before God. This week, you will learn how Moses interceded on Israel's behalf before God."

DAY ONE

Picture It

One day a family decided to go on an outdoor hiking vacation to a clear mountain lake. Since they didn't know the way, they hired a guide to take them through the forest and up the mountain. Because there were wolves and bears, the guide brought along a gun for protection and carried a special radio to call for help in an emergency.

After hiking for about one hour the family stopped to take a rest and one of the boys wandered off to explore on his own, disobeying the guide's instructions to stay together. When the boy returned, the guide warned the family that if they didn't follow his directions he would leave. During their next stop another of the boys wandered off. This time the guide turned to the father, gave him the map and compass, and left to go back to town.

Now imagine that you are that dad. Would you continue on your own and hike to the lake or would you stop and go back? Even though the map can show you the way, you probably wouldn't want to go without the protection of your guide.

In our Bible story today, we will see that Israel was facing the same problem as the family on the trail.

 Read Exodus 33:1–11.

Think about It Some More

God didn't destroy Israel for making the golden calf, but he did say he would no longer go with them as their guide. God told Moses he would send an angel ahead of them instead. God called Israel "stiff-necked," which meant they were stubborn and would not listen to God.

When the people heard God's decision, they were sad. They had come to enjoy seeing God's presence in the pillar of cloud that rested on the tent where Moses met with God. If God left, who would protect them? What would they do for water or food? God had provided all their needs.

Talk about It

:: Why were the people sad? *(They were going to lose the living presence of the one true God, who had lived among them ever since they were delivered from Egypt. God's presence made them different from all the other peoples of the earth.)*

:: Why did God say he would not go with them? *(God told Moses that if he went and the people kept on disobeying, he would end up destroying them because they disobeyed so much.)*

:: How did the people know that Moses was meeting with God? *(A pillar of cloud would come down over the tent where they were meeting.)*

:: How does God live among us today? *(We don't have a pillar of cloud anymore, but the same God who met with Moses comes to live in us when God places his Holy Spirit in our hearts.)*

 Pray about It

Thank God for his Holy Spirit, who lives inside all who place their hope and trust in Jesus.

DAY TWO

Remember It

What do you remember about yesterday's story? What do you think is going to happen today?

 Read Exodus 33:12–23.

Think about It Some More

From the moment Israel left Egypt, God traveled with them in the pillar of cloud by day and the pillar of fire by night. So when Moses heard that God was not going with them anymore, he was sad. Once again he stood in the middle as Israel's mediator. He told God that his presence was what made Israel different from all the other peoples, and Moses reminded God of his promise to go with his people. God heard Moses' prayer and agreed to stay with Israel.

Emboldened by God's answer, Moses asked to look upon God's face, but he didn't know that he would die if God were to show Moses his full glory. Sinful people think that they can look at God like they look at anyone else, but the only way we can stand before God in heaven is if our sins have been washed away.

Talk about It

:: How did Moses act as Israel's mediator in this passage? *(Remember that a mediator is someone who stands in the middle between two parties. Here Moses is speaking for Israel, pleading with God not to leave them.)*

:: What did Moses say made God's people different from all the other people on the earth? *(Moses said that God made them different. All the other peoples had false idols that could not speak or hear, but God was different. He was real and alive and could speak and help his people.)*

:: Why couldn't Moses see the face of God? *(Moses was a sinner with a sinful body. The holy presence of God would kill any sinful person who looked upon him.)*

 ## Pray about It

Pray the same prayer that Moses prayed and ask God to go with your family.

DAY THREE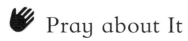

Connect It to Jesus

Can anyone guess how our story this week is about or points forward to Jesus?

Read Hebrews 12:18–24.

Think about It Some More

Did you notice the writer of the book of Hebrews is comparing Moses with Jesus? The mountain mentioned is the mountain of God where God gathered all his people and gave them his commandments. When God spoke, the people became afraid and asked Moses to talk to God in their place. So Moses became their mediator and spoke to God for them.

This passage tells us that all Christians have a new mediator and his name is Jesus.

Talk about It

:: Do you remember what a mediator is? *(A mediator is someone who stands in the middle to help two parties resolve a problem. In this case, Jesus died on the cross so we would not be enemies with God anymore.)*

:: Abel is mentioned in this passage. Do you remember his story? *(Abel was Adam and Eve's son. His brother Cain killed him because Cain was envious.)*

:: How is Abel like Jesus? *(Both men were wrongfully killed.)*

:: Why is Jesus' death better than Abel's death? *(Parents, this is a complicated idea. When Abel was killed, the Bible tells us that his blood [his death] called out for God to bring judgment because murder is a terrible sin. But when Jesus died on the cross, taking the punishment we deserved, his death spoke a different message. It called out to God to forgive men because Jesus took our punishment for our terrible sins on the cross.)*

 ## Pray about It

Thank Jesus for taking our punishment when he was on the cross so we could be forgiven.

DAY FOUR

Remember It

What has God been teaching you this week through our Bible story?

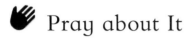 Read Exodus 34.

Think about It Some More

Can you remember a time you asked your parents for a second chance after you disobeyed? In our story today, God gives Israel a second chance. He even gives them new stone tablets with the Ten Commandments written on them and repeats his law and his promises.

When Moses returns from meeting with God, his face is lit up like a light bulb and the people are afraid. Although Moses did not see God's face, just being in God's presence is enough to cause his face to glow.

Talk about It

> ● ● KIDS, ask your parents if they can remember a time when someone
> ● ● gave them a second chance.

(Parents, think of a time when a policeman let you go with a warning, or someone forgave a debt, or an employer let you try again to do something you failed at.)

:: What important commandments did God repeat to Israel? *(God reminded Israel not to have false gods and to keep the Sabbath holy.)*

:: What did God remind Israel they needed to do for their firstborn sons and animals? *(Israel needed to kill a substitute in their place to redeem them.)*

:: How did killing a lamb in place of the firstborn son point forward to Jesus? *(Jesus was God's Son who died for us, just as the lamb died for the firstborn son.)*

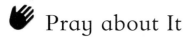 Pray about It

Thank God for being slow to anger and abounding in steadfast love and faithfulness.

DAY FIVE

Discover It

Today we look at a passage from a psalm or one of the prophets to see what we can learn from it about Jesus.

 Read Psalm 16:8–10 and Acts 2:25–31.

Think about It Some More

After Jesus rose from the dead he taught his disciples how the Old Testament pointed forward to him. His disciples in turn taught others what Jesus had told them, and some of what they said was written down and preserved for us to read in our Bibles. That way, we can all learn which passages in the Old Testament point to Jesus.

Today's story contains one of those passages that point us to Jesus. It says that one day there would be a man who would die, but his body would not decay in the grave and he would come to life again.

In the book of Acts, Peter tells us that David was talking about Jesus rising from the dead way before Jesus was ever born.

Talk about It

:: Who did Peter say David was talking about? *(Peter said David was talking about Jesus in this psalm.)*

:: What did David say would happen to Jesus after he died? *(Jesus would not stay in the grave but be raised to life again.)*

:: *Read Acts 13:34–39.* How is this passage similar? *(Paul quoted the same psalm and connected it to Jesus.)*

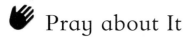 Pray about It

Thank God that Jesus did not stay in the grave, but rose again so that we too would one day rise from the dead.

Week 38

The People of Israel Complain

Purchase a can of vegetables that your children do not like very much and serve it for dinner one night. (Keep your normal dinner hot on the stove on standby.) Give them a larger than normal portion, then see if anyone complains. Once they do, draw them out about what it means to complain, then ask your children to think of a food they would be most likely to complain about if they had to eat a large spoonful of it every day. How might their opinion change if it was the only food they had to eat to avoid starving?

Say, "We, like Israel, often complain about our food. When we read the story of Israel we can be self-righteous and judge them for their complaining, but we often do the very same things. This week you will learn how Moses once again served as a mediator between God and Israel in the midst of their complaining."

DAY ONE

Picture It

Imagine that you are walking along a rocky path when all of a sudden you hear a loud rattling noise ahead. Immediately you slow down and cautiously move a step closer to see where the noise is coming from. Then you see it—a large rattlesnake, coiled up on a rock to the right of the path ahead.

The closer you get, the louder the snake rattles. To avoid the danger, you step carefully far around the snake. Today we will read about the warning God gave Israel when they started down a sinful path.

 Read Numbers 10:11–13 and 10:33—11:3.

Think about It Some More

When God wanted to move his people to a new location, the pillar of cloud would lift from the tabernacle and start to move. When the cloud lifted, everyone had to stop what they were doing, take down their tents, and pack up everything. God's people didn't have cars or buses to ride in; most people had to walk. Each time the cloud lifted there was a lot of work to do.

So, much like we complain, Israel began to grumble about all their troubles. When God heard their complaining he set fire to the ground around their camp as a warning not to complain.

Talk about It

:: Can you think of something you complain about? *(Parents, help your children identify with Israel here. Perhaps they complain when you ask them to clean their room or do their homework.)*

:: When Israel complained, whom were they sinning against? *(Israel was sinning against God because they didn't like the way he was leading them.)*

:: When we complain, whom are we sinning against? *(Although we may be sinning against parents or another person, we are mostly sinning against God who daily gives us good things and provides us with everything we need. When we complain we are telling God that what he has given us is not good enough.)*

 Pray about It

Ask God to help you not to complain today.

DAY TWO

Remember It

What do you remember about yesterday's story? What do you think is going to happen today?

 Read Numbers 11:4–17.

Think about It Some More

If you ate oatmeal every day for breakfast, lunch, and dinner for a whole year, you would get pretty tired of oatmeal. That's what happened to God's people. They were eating manna for breakfast, lunch, and dinner every day. The people were mostly doing okay, until a few troublemakers started complaining, loudly reminding the people of all the foods they had left back in Egypt.

But the troublemakers never said anything about the cruel slavery that was back in Egypt. Their complaining spread as it was repeated throughout the camp.

Talk about It

:: Instead of complaining, what should the people have been doing? *(The people should have been thanking God for what he gave them instead of complaining.)*

:: Can you remember a time when you complained about the food you had to eat instead of being grateful? *(Parents, help your children to remember a time when they complained. If you did the activity at the beginning of this week's lesson, remind them of how they reacted. Another idea is to serve them the same food for all three meals, but don't tell them what you are doing. If they complain, help them identify with the Israelites.)*

:: How did God help Moses? *(God gave Moses a plan to spread the workload out among seventy men in Israel and placed his Spirit upon them to serve Moses.)*

 ## Pray about It

Thank God for the kind way he cared for Israel even though they were complaining.

DAY THREE

Connect It to Jesus

Can anyone guess how our story this week is about or points forward to Jesus?

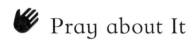 Read Numbers 11:24–29 and Acts 2:14–18.

Think about It Some More

When God's Spirit fell on the seventy men they began to prophesy. That means God gave them a message to share with the people. Even the two men who missed the meeting at the tent started speaking prophecies back in the camp. When Joshua heard what was happening he wanted to stop them, but Moses said it was okay and told Joshua that he dreamed of a day when God would pour his Spirit on all people so everyone could prophesy.

That is how our story is connected to Jesus. After Jesus rose from the dead and went back to heaven he did exactly what Moses hoped for. He poured out his Spirit on all people, men and women, young and old. Now, every person who believes in Jesus is filled with God's Spirit.

Talk about It

:: Why did God pour out his Spirit on the seventy men? *(God poured out his Spirit on the seventy men so they could help Moses care for the people.)*

:: What did Moses hope would happen one day? *(Moses hoped for a day when God would pour his Spirit out upon all people.)*

:: When does God pour out his Spirit upon us today? *(God pours out his Spirit on us when we first believe in Jesus.)*

Pray about It

Ask God to pour out his Spirit on everyone in your family so they will place their hope and trust in Jesus.

DAY FOUR

Remember It

What has God been teaching you this week through our Bible story?

 Read Numbers 11:31–34.

Think about It Some More

When God tells you that he is going to give you a lot of something, look out because he can really give you a huge amount. In our story, God used the wind to bring in so many quail they were knee deep as far as you could see.

But once again Israel sinned. Instead of trusting God for the quail they needed for each day, especially because there were millions all around them, the people got greedy. They gathered quail all day long. Those who got the least still collected about sixty laundry baskets full. If it takes about 100 quail to fill a laundry basket then each person captured at least 6,000 quail!

When God saw their greed he brought a terrible sickness on those who craved the quail and many died. They named the place Kibroth-hattaavah, which is a Hebrew name that means "graves of craving."

Talk about It

> ● ● KIDS, ask your parents if they ever greedily took more of something
> ● ● than they needed.

(Parents, think of a time when something was on sale and you bought more than you needed, or when something was free and you took more than you needed.)

:: Why would God's people gather so many quail? *(They didn't trust God to give them more the next day, so they gathered as many as they could in order to provide for themselves.)*

:: Who did the Israelites love more, the quail or God? *(The Israelites seemed to love the quail more than God.)*

:: Is there anything that you enjoy that you are tempted to want and love more than God? *(Parents, help your children to see that anything we crave or desire more than God, even a good thing, is an idol.)*

👋 Pray about It

Ask God to help you love him more than anything else.

DAY FIVE

Discover It

Today we look at a passage from a psalm or one of the prophets to see what we can learn from it about Jesus.

 Read Malachi 4:1–3.

Think about It Some More

Malachi is the last book of the Old Testament. Malachi was one of God's prophets. In this passage, Malachi describes the sun, but there is something different about the sun in his prophesy. Instead of shining with light, the sun Malachi is talking about will shine with righteousness or goodness and bring healing and judgment to the earth.

Malachi isn't really talking about the sun. He is talking about a man, a very special man. Jesus is the sun that Malachi told Israel about. Jesus brought righteousness and healing and takes away our sin.

Malachi compares us in our sin to a calf who starts out life locked in a stall. When the door is opened and the calf is allowed to go out, it jumps for joy in the freedom it has to run around. That is what it is like for us when God sets us free from sin—we jump for joy and celebrate God's salvation.

Talk about It

:: Who is the sun in Malachi's prophecy? *(Jesus is the sun in Malachi's prophecy.)*

:: Why did Malachi say we were like calves leaping out of a stall? *(The stall represents our sin. When God forgives our sin, we get so excited that we jump and dance and praise him.)*

:: How does this passage point to Jesus? *(Malachi tells us that the sun will bring righteousness, healing, and judgment. Jesus brought all those things. Jesus never did anything wrong and then died on the cross for our sins. Now he offers us his goodness or righteousness, and he heals us from our sins by forgiving them. Once we are forgiven our sins, we are free like the calves from the stall.)*

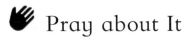 Pray about It

Thank God for sending his Son Jesus to die on the cross so we can be free from our sins.

Week 39

Miriam

Ask your children, "Who of you is the fastest?" (If you have one child, ask about the children in his class or neighborhood. Then ask if the other children ever boast about their abilities or brag about their accomplishments.) Ask, "Who is the best singer?" "The smartest?" "The greatest?"

Help them through these discussions. Hopefully, they will be kind toward one another and the questions will pose some level of discomfort. Be on the lookout for children either exalting themselves, saying "I'm the best," or humbling themselves, pointing out the strengths of another.

Discuss your observations with your children and share that God lifts up the humble, but he brings down the proud. Say, "In this week's lessons you will learn how God humbled Miriam because of her prideful complaining."

DAY ONE

Picture It

A family went to the ocean to enjoy a day playing on the beach. After swimming a while, the younger son began creating a beautiful sand castle. The older two children, seeing their younger brother having so much fun, decided to build their own castle.

As time went on, the younger son's castle was so fantastic it became the talk of the beach. The two older children rushed to catch up to their brother, but their castle looked sloppy compared to his. They became so jealous of their younger brother's castle that they pretended to trip and spilled a bucket of water that tore down the left side of his work. But God taught them a lesson, for as soon as they stood up from the staged accident a huge wave crashed onto shore and destroyed their own castle.

Today in our Bible story, we will read how the sin of envy affected Moses' brother and sister.

 Read Numbers 12:1–2.

Think about It Some More

Aaron and Miriam were Moses' brother and sister. They were upset that he was getting all the attention. They probably were called Moses' brother and sister all the time. They were envious.

They didn't want Moses to get all the attention. They wanted people to know that God spoke through them too and that Moses wasn't the only important person around.

So they pridefully lifted themselves up, while they tore Moses down and criticized his choice of a wife. But God heard every prideful word and complaint they brought.

Talk about It

:: What does the word "envy" mean? *("Envy" is when you wish you had something that someone else has. It could be a thing or an ability or talent like singing or running.)*

:: Can you think of a time when you felt envious of your brother or sister or friend? *(Parents, draw out your children here.)*

:: Why do we become envious of people? *(We want people's attention for ourselves. When others do things better than us, then the attention we want goes to them instead. That is when envy rises up in our hearts and tempts us to tear them down with our words or actions.)*

:: Even when parents are not around to catch you in your sin, who is always watching? *(God is always watching and hears everything we say and knows everything we do.)*

 Pray about It

Ask God to help you not sin by being envious of others.

DAY TWO

Remember It

What do you remember about yesterday's story? What do you think is going to happen today?

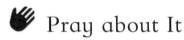 Read Numbers 12:3–10.

Think about It Some More

Can you remember a time when you won an award or did something that turned out well and you wanted to boast about yourself? Or a time when after a sports game you made fun of the losing team? That is what pride is: boasting about how good we are or making fun of those who are not as good.

Moses had a reason to brag, but he didn't. After all, Moses met with God face to face, yet we learn that Moses was the most humble man in the world. That is why God's anger burned against Aaron and Miriam. Even though Moses walked in humility, they were trying to tear him down.

That's the reason God gave Miriam leprosy, which was a terrible disease. In another place in the Bible, God said that he "opposes the proud, but gives grace to the humble" (James 4:6). God punished Miriam because in her pride she was envious of a humble man. God defended Moses so he did not need to defend himself.

Talk about It

:: If God were to give leprosy to everyone who complained, how many of us would be sick with the disease? *(We would all be sick, because we all complain.)*

:: Why did God give Miriam leprosy? *(God gave Miriam leprosy because she was complaining about a humble man and she was proud, trying to exalt her own reputation.)*

:: What can we learn from Miriam and Aaron's lives? *(We can learn that we should not tear other people down with our words and that God will judge the sin of envy.)*

 ## Pray about It

Ask God to help us encourage one another, not tear one another down.

DAY THREE

Connect It to Jesus

Can anyone guess how our story this week is about or points forward to Jesus?

Read Philippians 2:1–11.

Think about It Some More

In our story this week, God called Moses the most humble man on the face of the earth. His humility as a leader pointed forward to a day when God would give Israel a leader with even greater humility.

Jesus put aside (gave up) his glory as the Son of God and came down to earth as a man. Then he died on the cross and took our punishment so we could be forgiven. That is the most humble thing anyone has ever done.

Talk about It

:: Pride is when we consider ourselves more important than others. What is humility? *(Humility is when we consider others as more important than ourselves.)*

:: How did Jesus show humility? *(Even though he was God, he became a man and died on the cross for our sins.)*

:: Name some ways we can show humility. *(Parents, help your children think of ways they can think of others as more important than themselves. This could be as simple as serving one another or respecting parents.)*

 ## Pray about It

Ask God to help you show humility like Moses and Jesus did.

DAY FOUR

Remember It

What has God been teaching you this week through our Bible story?

 Read Numbers 12:11–16.

Think about It Some More

Once again Moses acted as a mediator for Israel. Remember that a mediator is a person in the middle. Aaron and leprous Miriam were on one side; God who judged her was on the other; Moses was in the middle. Aaron pleaded with Moses to ask God for mercy, so Moses prayed.

God heard Moses' prayer and healed Miriam, who then had to remain outside the camp for a week to show she was healed and not contagious. When Miriam was healed, Israel could move to a new place.

Talk about It

> 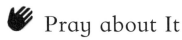 KIDS, ask your parents if they can remember a time when God humbled them for their pride.

(The Bible tells us that pride "goes before destruction" [Proverbs 16:18]. See if you can remember a time when you fell after giving in to pride.)

:: What lesson do you think God taught Miriam through giving her the terrible disease? *(God taught Miriam to be humble and not to complain about others.)*

:: How do we know God healed Miriam? *(She is allowed to come back into the camp after seven days.)*

Pray about It

Thank God for his mercy toward Miriam and toward us to forgive us for our sins.

DAY FIVE

Discover It

Today we look at a passage from a psalm or one of the prophets to see what we can learn from it about Jesus.

 Read Haggai 2:20–23.

Think about It Some More

In ancient days, a king's signet ring was very important. It was engraved with the special mark of the king and was a symbol of his authority and power. When the king made a law, he would drip hot wax on the paper and press his ring into the hot wax, leaving the mark of his ring. If you had the paper sealed by the king's ring, it was as good as having the king there saying it himself. Everyone had to honor what it said.

Haggai, the prophet who wrote our Bible passage today, said that Zerubbabel, a king in David's family line, would become the signet ring of God. Now Jesus is not a ring you can put on your finger, but he is the answer to this prophecy. Jesus' words carried the same power and authority as God's words because Jesus was God. Just as a signet ring carried the authority of the king, so Jesus carried the authority of God the Father. That is why Jesus said, "If you knew me, you would know my Father also" (John 8:19), and "I and the Father are one" (John 10:30).

Talk about It

:: What would a king do with his signet ring? *(He would melt wax onto an important paper and press the ring into the wax to make the king's mark. When the king marked a paper with his ring, everyone knew the words on the paper were the king's words.)*

:: Jesus was a real man, but what else was he at the same time? *(Jesus was also God.)*

:: How can Jesus and the Father be one? *(This is a mystery that is impossible for us to fully explain, but the Bible teaches there are three persons in our one God.)*

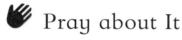 Pray about It

Thank Jesus for coming to earth to show us the way to God.

Week 40

Israel Spies Out the Land

Send your children into your backyard or another location if you don't have a backyard. Or if the weather is poor have them look through the back windows of your home. Tell them you want them to observe and report as much as they can. If they see any animals or people, you want to know all about it. Give them a two-minute time limit, and say you are going to give a prize to the spy who can give you the most information.

Reassemble in two minutes and interview them for their details. Award a prize to the person who brought back the most information. (If you have only one child, write down three or four things you can see. If he gets them all, award him a prize.)

Say, "This week you will learn about the spies whom Moses sent into Canaan and the reports they came back with."

DAY ONE

Picture It

While on vacation, a father took his three-year-old son swimming for the first time. The little boy didn't mind splashing his toes in the shallow children's pool and even worked up the courage to walk in the knee-deep water. But every time he looked over at the adult pool, he became afraid. The water was so deep that he saw the people disappear under the surface when they swam.

The next day, after about an hour in the children's pool, the dad picked up his son and began walking over to the adult pool. "Daddy is going to take you swimming with him," the father told his son. But as soon as they got close and the boy saw people jumping in and swimming underwater, he became afraid and started to cry. The father tried to reassure him by telling him that as long as he was with Daddy he was safe, but the little boy cried all the louder.

Sometimes fear keeps us from trusting. That is what happened to Israel in our story today.

 Read Numbers 13:1–3, 17–33.

Think about It Some More

There was one important thing the fearful spies forgot. They forgot about God's power. God said he was going to give them the land. Even though the cities had high, thick walls for protection and even though the people seemed as big as giants, no one could stop their all-powerful God.

Caleb didn't think Israel was strong enough to win battles all by themselves either. But he didn't forget about God, and he knew Israel could win with God on their side. The ten fearful spies made a terrible mistake when they forgot about God. Anytime we are afraid, a good question to ask is, "Have I forgotten about God?"

Talk about It

:: What did most of the spies do wrong? *(The spies forgot about God.)*

:: How did the spies' bad report affect the people? *(Their bad report caused the people to fear too.)*

:: How was Caleb's report different from the others? *(Caleb had faith. Even though the cities were strong and fortified, Caleb knew the cities could be defeated with God's help. Caleb had faith that with God all things are possible.)*

:: Why didn't the spies need to be afraid? *(The spies didn't need to be afraid because God was going to go with them and give them the land.)*

 Pray about It

Ask God to help you remember him when you are afraid.

DAY TWO

Remember It

What do you remember about yesterday's story? What do you think is going to happen today?

 Read Numbers 14:1–10.

Think about It Some More

When you see how quickly the bad report of the spies spread through all of Israel you can understand why God earlier punished his people for complaining. What started out as a bad report among a few, ended with many people saying God was trying kill them and would leave their wives and children to die alone. Some even suggested they pick a new leader who could take them back to Egypt.

It got so bad that, when Joshua and Caleb defended God, the people picked up stones to throw at them. They would have killed them if the glory of the Lord had not appeared to save the two courageous spies.

Talk about It

:: Make a list of the ways the people sinned against the Lord instead of trusting him. *(Parents, help your children by giving them clues to find the answers. They accused God of trying to kill them, their wives, and their children. They said life in Egypt was better than life with God. They tried to stone and kill the men who trusted God.)*

:: Out of the thousands of Israelites how many men trusted God? *(Four men are listed as trusting God: Moses, Aaron, Joshua, and Caleb.)*

:: What did Joshua and Caleb warn the people not to do? *(They warned them not to rebel against the Lord.)*

:: When Israel rejected Moses as their leader who else were they rejecting? *(They were also rejecting God.)*

 Pray about It

Ask God to help you have the courage and faith to trust him like Joshua and Caleb did.

DAY THREE

Connect It to Jesus

Can anyone guess how our story this week is about or points forward to Jesus?

 Read Numbers 14:11–24.

Think about It Some More

Once again Moses stood in the middle for his people and prayed to God saying, "Please forgive the sins of your people, according to your great steadfast love." God granted Moses' prayer because Moses prayed for the one thing that could save Israel: God's steadfast love and forgiveness.

Although God didn't allow Israel into the Promised Land, he forgave Israel because he knew that one day his Son Jesus would stand in the middle as their true mediator and die on the cross for their sins. Centuries later, in a letter to Timothy, the apostle Paul called Jesus the one true mediator (1 Timothy 2:5) who stood in the middle between sinful man and a holy God. Even as Moses prayed, God saw ahead to the day when he would send his Son.

Talk about It

:: Why did God want to punish Israel? *(The people rejected God and were even going to stone Joshua and Caleb.)*

:: Why didn't God destroy Israel for their sins? *(Jesus' death on the cross is the only reason God forgives anyone. For Israel, God looked forward to the day when he would send his Son to die for their sins. For us, we look back to the sacrifice of Jesus on the cross.)*

:: How can Moses' example help us when we sin? *(Moses gave us a great prayer to pray when he asked God to forgive Israel because of his great love. And we can add, "For you have sent your Son Jesus to take away my sin.")*

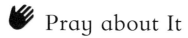 Pray about It

Think of some of the ways that you have sinned. Confess them to God and ask him to forgive you and take your sin away.

DAY FOUR

Remember It

What has God been teaching you this week through our Bible story?

 Read Numbers 14:26–45.

Think about It Some More

If you are baking a cake and accidentally mix into the batter a cup of salt instead of a cup of sugar, there is nothing you can do to save your cake. You have to throw it away and start all over again. Once the salt is in it, no amount of pretty icing on top can hide the bad taste.

In our story today, Israel's disobedience was like putting salt in the cake. They tried to make up for their sin by going into the Promised Land by themselves and attacking the Canaanites. But there was no way they could change the fact that they had disobeyed. By going in without God, they only added to their sin. The Canaanites defeated them because God did not go with them.

We can't cover over our sin by doing things. The only way to cover our sin is by believing in Jesus who shed his blood to cover our sins. But Jesus doesn't cover over our sin like icing covers a salty cake—Jesus actually takes our sin away.

Talk about It

> ●● KIDS, ask your parents if there is an area in your life where you dis-
> ●● obey again and again.

(Parents, help your children think of an area of their lives where they struggle and repeat the same sins again. Help them identify with Israel.)

:: Ask your parents what you can do about your repeated sins? *(Parents, this is where you can help your children to see that no amount of good behavior can ever fix their bad behavior. What they really need is to trust Jesus to take their sin away.)*

:: What punishment did God bring to the people more than twenty years old? *(God said they would not be allowed to go into the Promised Land.)*

:: Whom did God allow to go into the land? *(Only Joshua, Caleb, and the children of Israel under twenty years old were going to go into the land.)*

:: How did God keep his promise to Abraham in this story? *(He was keeping his promise to Abraham by giving them the land he'd promised Abraham long ago.)*

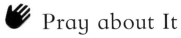 Pray about It

Tell God that you know your good behavior won't get you into heaven. Then ask him to help you trust in Jesus who died to take the punishment for your sin. His death takes your sin away so you can go to heaven.

DAY FIVE

Discover It

Today we look at a passage from a psalm or one of the prophets to see what we can learn from it about Jesus.

 Read Zechariah 2:10–12.

Think about It Some More

In this passage, God promised through a prophecy of Zechariah that he would dwell (live) among his people. But then it goes on to say that God would also draw other nations to join Israel and they would be God's people too. This would have been very strange for Israel to hear because they believed God loved only Israel. They would have wondered how God was going to draw foreign nations who worship idols into God's family.

Jesus provides the answer of Zechariah's prophecy. As the apostle John wrote in his gospel regarding Jesus, "And the Word became flesh and dwelt [lived] among us" (John 1:14). With "many nations," Zechariah is pointing forward to a day when Jesus would make a way for people of every nation, language, and tribe to be saved. The salvation of Jesus Christ is available to everyone. Through Christ, people of every nation are today being gathered to become the people of God. In the end, God will live among people of every tribe and nation in heaven (Revelation 5:9).

Talk about It

:: What did Zechariah say we should do in response to God bringing all different kinds of people to join his family? *(Parents, if your children don't get the answer, reread verse 10 to discover that we should sing and rejoice that God is coming to live with his people.)*

:: How did God make Zechariah's words come true? *(Jesus came to live on earth and, after he rose again from the dead, he promised to send the Holy Spirit to live with everyone who believes. Even though Jesus is now back in heaven, God still lives with his people in the person of the Holy Spirit.)*

:: Compare Zechariah 2:10 with John 1:14. How are they related? *(In Zechariah, God made a promise to live with his people. In John, we see how he kept the promise by sending Jesus to live on earth.)*

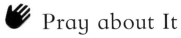 Pray about It

Thank God for keeping his promise by sending his Son Jesus to die for our sins and filling everyone who believes with his Holy Spirit.

Week 41

Moses Disobeys God

Gather your children and bring along two pieces of paper. Tell your children you are going to act out two scenes with the paper and you want them to describe each one.

Take the first piece of paper and fold it back and forth, slowly and carefully, every half inch or so, to form a fan. Ask the children to describe your actions and attitude. Begin to do the same with the second piece of paper, but pretend to get frustrated as you try to fold it. After a few sloppy folds, crumple the paper into a ball and angrily throw it down. When the children describe this last demonstration they should connect it with anger.

Talk about how our attitudes often affect the result of what we try to accomplish. If we are careful, we get a good result. If we are careless or angry, we do not. Ask the children if they have seen this at work in their own lives. Say, "This week you will see how Moses' anger resulted in him disobeying God by taking things into his own hands."

DAY ONE

Picture It

Imagine that we send out for two pepperoni pizzas from a local pizza delivery place; let's call it Pizza Express. When the pizzas arrive, we notice they have mushrooms on them instead of pepperoni. Reluctantly we eat the pizzas.

The next time we send out for pepperoni pizza, instead of changing restaurants and ordering from, say, Tony's Pizza, we order again from Pizza Express. This time, instead of pepperoni, we get sausage and green pepper. Two weeks later, instead of pepperoni, they deliver anchovies and ham pizzas.

When you call them back and complain, they offer to send you free pizzas. When they arrive they are not pepperoni either. This time they send you broccoli and ham pizzas. How many times would you order from Pizza Express before you gave up on them and changed to Tony's Pizza?

In today's story, Israel is complaining again, but no matter how many times they complain, God never gives up on his people.

 Read Numbers 20:1–5.

Think about It Some More

Reading this story in the Bible is like watching a remake of an old movie. When you heard today's Bible story you may have thought, *Hey, we already did this one.* But no, this is yet another time when Israel complains about not having water to drink.

Israel is on the edge of the Promised Land, a fertile land with plenty of water, but because they disobey, God leads them back into the wilderness. Instead of asking God for water, they again complain and long for Egypt. Their attitude is an insult to God, who had rescued them from slavery.

Talk about It

:: How are we like Israel? *(We often repeat the same sins. Parents, help your children identify patterns of repetitive sinful behavior in their own lives. You may consider confessing your own struggles, as appropriate.)*

:: With all you know about God, what would you say Israel should do instead of complain? *(Parents, draw your children out on this one. Help them remember that God is merciful and forgiving. Even in the wilderness, if Israel had asked God to provide for them, he would have provided everything they needed.)*

:: What can we learn from Israel's mistakes? *(Again draw out your children. We should not forget that when we sin against God we often get bad consequences. And if we ask, God will supply what we need.)*

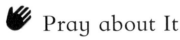 Pray about It

List some things that you or others you know need; then present your requests to God.

DAY TWO

Remember It

What do you remember about yesterday's story? What do you think is going to happen today?

 Read Numbers 20:6–9.

Think about It Some More

When the people complain, Moses and Aaron go to the tent of God and fall on their faces. Many other times when Israel had sinned, Moses had prayed to God for them, but this time all Moses can do is fall down before the Lord. Even though he doesn't say a single word, God knows what Israel needs. God tells Moses to speak to the rock, promising that it will produce water for his people and their animals.

Talk about It

:: How does God show Israel mercy instead of judgment? *(Even without Moses asking, God offers to provide water for the Israelites in spite of their grumbling and complaining.)*

:: Does Moses tell God what the people need or does God already know? *(God already knows. Matthew 6:8 tells us that our Father knows what we need even before we ask!)*

:: How should this story encourage us when we pray? *(Parents, draw out your children. God always wants us to bring before him our concerns and troubles. But he does not require us to pray perfect prayers before he will provide what we need.)*

Pray about It

Thank God for knowing what we need even before we ask.

DAY THREE

Connect It to Jesus

Can anyone guess how our story this week is about or points forward to Jesus?

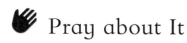 Read Hebrews 4:14–16.

Think about It Some More

Even though Moses was Israel's leader, he wasn't perfect; he was a sinner like the rest of the people. Tomorrow we will see how Moses disobeyed God. When Israel sinned, Moses called out to God for them, but when Moses sinned there was no one to call out to God for him. Moses needed a Savior.

The writer of Hebrews tells us that with Jesus we have a priest who is perfect and never sinned even once. A priest is someone who stands in the middle for sinners and offers up prayers and sacrifices so God will not punish them. Jesus offered up his life as a sacrifice for our sin so we can be forgiven. Because Jesus never sinned he is able to lead all his children into a better promised land, called heaven.

Talk about It

:: How is Jesus different from Moses? *(Both men led God's people but, unlike Moses, Jesus never sinned. Moses was a mere man; Jesus was God.)*

:: Who was Moses supposed to lead into the Promised Land? *(If Moses had not sinned he would have led Joshua and Caleb, along with all the children of Israel, into the Promised Land. Remember the Israelites had sinned earlier, so only their children were allowed to go into the land.)*

:: What promised land is Jesus going to lead his people to? *(Jesus will one day lead us to a new heaven and new earth. Read 1 Thessalonians 4:16–17.)*

 Pray about It

Praise the Lord for preparing a place for us in heaven, and ask him to return soon.

DAY FOUR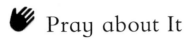

Remember It

What has God been teaching you this week through our Bible story?

Read Numbers 20:10–13.

Think about It Some More

Instead of speaking to the rock as God had commanded, Moses strikes the rock with his staff in anger. This is a serious sin against God. First, Moses disobeys God because he is angry with the people, calling them "rebels." Second, Moses and Aaron take credit for producing the water when they say, "Shall we bring water for you?"

Because of his sin, God doesn't allow Moses into the Promised Land either. Even though Moses was a godly man, he was still a sinner. That means that even Moses needed a Savior.

Talk about It

> ● ● KIDS, ask your parents to tell you about a time when they got angry
> ● ● because things didn't go the way they wanted.

(Parents, this is a great time to confess how sometimes you get angry when your children disobey.)

:: Why didn't Moses obey God? *(Moses, like us, was a sinner who didn't trust in God's plan. He struck the rock instead of speaking to it, and spoke about it as if he were the one who would bring water from it.)*

:: How can we fall into the same pattern of sin in our lives? *(Children often get angry at one another. In particular, when dealing with a younger child an older child is often tempted to act as a judge.)*

:: How did God demonstrate his mercy to Israel in spite of Moses' sin? *(God caused water to flow from the rock anyway. In today's world, God shows us mercy through the cross of Jesus, and does not judge us according to what we deserve.)*

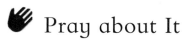 Pray about It

Ask God to show mercy to the people you know who do not believe in Jesus and help them to believe and trust in him.

DAY FIVE

Discover It

Today we look at a passage from a psalm or one of the prophets to see what we can learn from it about Jesus.

 Read Malachi 3:1.

Think about It Some More

Hundreds of years before John the Baptist and Jesus were born, Malachi gave this prophetic promise to his people. Mark, who wrote one of the Gospels, said that John the Baptist was the messenger, whom Malachi and the other prophets had spoken about, who would come to prepare the way for Jesus.

John the Baptist told the people to turn away from their sins and be baptized. This would prepare them for the more powerful prophet whom God would send, who would baptize them with the Holy Spirit. Soon after, Jesus himself came to John to be baptized at the start of his ministry.

Because of prophecies like this one, Israel began to look for the day when God would send someone to help them. By the time Jesus came, some people in Israel were waiting for his arrival.

Talk about It

:: Who does Malachi say is going to come? *(God is the one who is going to come. Basically, God says, "I will send a messenger to announce my coming.")*

:: How does this Bible passage point to Jesus? *(Jesus is the person Malachi said would be announced by the messenger.)*

:: Why did God give Israel hints about what he was going to do? *(Parents, there are a number of answers to this question. God wanted them to know about his plan to encourage them during difficult times. God also wanted some people like Simeon and the three wise men to know and greet Jesus as a little baby. Scriptures like this gave them clues about what God was going to do.)*

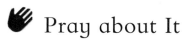 Pray about It

Thank God for giving us hints in the Bible that tell us that God always had a plan to save his people by sending his Son Jesus.

Week 42

God Heals Israel with a Bronze Snake

Prior to your Bible study, list several complaints you could make about your life. Try to list small, petty things like the weather being too cold or too hot or that you don't have enough time or money to do everything you could ever possibly want to do. When you gather your children together, pretend to have a little pity party for yourself and rattle off your complaints.

Ask the children to describe what you were doing, and tell you whether it was good or bad. Help them to see that when we complain and grumble, we have forgotten about God and his blessings. Say, "This week you are going to read about another instance of Israel's complaining."

DAY ONE

Picture It

The air force is one of the army's best friends in a battle. Imagine that ten soldiers are walking along a road when they notice three hundred enemy soldiers marching toward them in the distance. The ten quickly run and hide in a nearby stone house. They can't fight three hundred enemies by themselves, so they call for help. They are near the ocean and not too far offshore is an aircraft carrier full of warplanes ready to go. Within seconds of their call the ship sends six fighter-bomber planes to help them.

The enemy commander sees the men run into the old house and thinks he has them trapped, so he gives the order for his men to attack. But before the enemy soldiers can get close to the house, the fighter planes come to the rescue and scare the enemy soldiers away.

In today's story, Israel's enemies make a mistake. They think they can defeat Israel, but they don't realize that Israel has a friend to help them in battle, someone even better than the air force—they have God!

 Read Numbers 21:1–3.

Think about It Some More

For once, instead of complaining when they need help, Israel calls out to the Lord instead. The last time they had fought a battle, they'd lost because they had tried to fight without God. Remember the story? After God told them they were not allowed to go into the Promised Land, they decided to go in and attack anyway and lost the battle. But this time they do it right.

Talk about It

:: What did Israel do before they went into battle? *(They prayed and asked God to give them victory.)*

:: What do you think happened to the Israelites who were captured by the Canaanite king? *(The story doesn't tell us, but because God is with Israel in this battle maybe they were rescued.)*

:: What can we learn from this story for our lives? *(We should always depend on Jesus and not try to live our lives apart from God.)*

 # Pray about It

As a family try to think of at least one thing you need God's help with, then pray and ask God for help.

DAY TWO

Remember It

What do you remember about yesterday's story? What do you think is going to happen today?

 Read Numbers 21:4–6.

Think about It Some More

There is no guarantee that if we obey God today we will also obey him tomorrow. We need God's grace to follow him every day.

Not long after their deliverance from King Arad, the Israelites began to complain again. Instead of asking God for help like they did before the fight, they complained about the lack of water and about food they didn't like. Because of this, God punished them by sending poisonous snakes to bite them.

Talk about It

:: What should Israel have done differently? *(Israel should have called out to God for help like they did against King Arad. If God had given them victory in battle, surely he would have provided water to drink.)*

:: How are we weak like Israel? *(We can fall into the same pattern of sin as they did—one day obeying and the very next day disobeying.)*

:: Is there a sin that you repeat over and over again? *(Parents, help your children answer this question. You probably have an idea of the areas of sin they regularly fall into.)*

 Pray about It

Ask God to forgive you for the sins you repeat over and over again.

DAY THREE

Connect It to Jesus

Can anyone guess how our story this week is about or points forward to Jesus?

Read Numbers 21:7–9 and John 3:9–15.

Think about It Some More

Even though Israel sinned, God provided a way for them to escape his judgment. God told Moses to put a bronze snake up on a pole. All those who complained and were bitten by the real snakes could look up at the bronze snake to be healed and saved from death.

Later, in another part of the Bible, the apostle John explains that God used the snake on the pole to point to Jesus. Just as the people were healed who looked upon the snake, so we are saved from death when we look to Jesus who was lifted up on the cross.

Talk about It

:: Who does the bronze snake on the pole point forward to? *(The bronze snake on the pole points forward to Jesus who was lifted up on a cross and died for our sins so we could be forgiven.)*

:: What happened when the people who were bitten by the snakes looked up at the bronze snake on the pole? *(They were healed.)*

:: What happens when we look to Jesus who was lifted up on the cross and died for us? *(When we place our trust in Jesus and believe that God lifted him up to take our punishment, we are forgiven of our sins. This is like being healed of our worst disease.)*

 Pray about It

Thank Jesus for being willing to be lifted up on the cross to die so we could be forgiven.

DAY FOUR

Remember It

What has God been teaching you this week through our Bible story?

 Read Numbers 21:10–20.

Think about It Some More

After the people of Israel looked up at the snake on the pole and were healed, they continued their wandering in the wilderness. When they needed water to drink, God provided a well for them. And in this part of the story, there is no record of Israel complaining.

Though Israel had been quick to say that God was leading them into the wilderness to die, that wasn't true. God provided everything they needed to follow him. The problem with Israel was that they often loved food and water more than God, and they quickly complained.

Talk about It

> ● ● KIDS, ask your parents which they like better: when you ask them for
> ● ● what you need, or when you complain that you don't have what you
> want.

:: What is different about this story from some of the others we read about Israel? *(The people of God did not complain.)*

:: What did the people do when God provided water for them? *(They sang.)*

:: What lesson can we learn from this story? *(We should not complain, but trust God to give us everything we need to do his will.)*

:: Will God always give us what we want? *(No, God doesn't always give us what we want, but God will give us everything we need—to obey him. Sometimes God calls us to suffer, but when he does, he always gives us the strength to endure.)*

 Pray about It

Make a list of the things you want to ask God to provide, then lift those requests up to God.

DAY FIVE

Discover It

Today we look at a passage from a psalm or one of the prophets to see what we can learn from it about Jesus.

 Read Malachi 3:2–3.

Think about It Some More

Remember that the first verse of this chapter in Malachi is speaking about John the Baptist announcing the ministry of Jesus. In today's verses, Malachi tells Israel that Jesus will come to purify his people so they can bring offerings or gifts of righteousness or goodness to God.

But there is one big problem. How is God going to take away the sin of his people so that they will be pure and able to bring God gifts of righteousness? Well, if you know the gospel, you know the answer. Malachi is talking about what Jesus will do by living a perfect life and then dying for our sins on the cross. When Jesus died on the cross, he took the punishment for the sins of everyone who trusts in him. Then Jesus gives them his perfect life in exchange for taking their sins.

That's how sinners get the righteousness Malachi is talking about. It is not about our goodness; Jesus gives us his own goodness as a free gift.

Talk about It

:: Who is Malachi talking about in today's Bible passage? *(Malachi is talking about Jesus.)*

:: What does it mean to purify something? *(To purify is to take away anything bad that has spoiled something. For instance, when you purify water you take out all the dirt and germs [the bad things] and make it clean.)*

:: How can Jesus purify sinners to make them righteous or good? *(Jesus died on the cross to take away their sin and lived a perfect life, which he offers to trade for the sins of anyone who trusts in him.)*

✋ Pray about It

Ask God to purify your heart and take away your sin.

Week 43

Rahab's Help

Collect two steel washers, a penny, a saltshaker, a skillet or cooking pan, a plate, and a fork. You will also need three ice cubes. Once you have everything together, call your children into the kitchen.

Take the ice cubes out of the freezer and place them on the plate. Tell your children that the ice cubes are the enemy, and you want to see what will melt them the quickest. Place the steel washers in the skillet on the stove and turn it on high. Then have one of the children place the penny on the first ice cube. Have another child liberally shake salt on the second. Finally, bring the skillet to the table and, using the fork, slide the two washers onto the last ice cube. Which ice cube melts the fastest?

Say, "This week, you will learn how God's fame among his people caused Israel's enemies to melt—with fear."

DAY ONE

Picture It

Imagine that we are about to go on a trip to the ocean to swim. When a friend hears about our trip, he warns us to be careful of the jellyfish because they can sting. Then, on the way to the ocean, we turn on the radio and hear the announcer say, "If you're headed to the beach today, make sure you keep an eye out for jellyfish because they have a painful sting." Finally, when we arrive at the beach, we see a sign that reads, "Danger! Jellyfish Present at High Tide."

Guess what we would be looking out for when we got to the water. That's right, jellyfish. When something is repeated to us again and again it gets our attention.

Listen as we read today's story to see what God is repeating to Joshua.

 Read Joshua 1.

Think about It Some More

Israel spent forty years wandering in the desert until every last person who had rebelled against God was dead, even Moses. By that time, the children had grown up and, when God gave his command to Joshua, they were ready and filled with faith to take the land. The good news is that God promised to go with them and give them every inch of ground they walked on.

Can you imagine playing in a baseball game and the Lord told you that every time you stepped up to bat you would hit a home run? Wouldn't that be exciting! But what if you then had to face the world's fastest pitcher who was throwing 100-mile-an-hour fastballs? It could be a little scary. You would need to be strong and courageous and stand at the plate and swing. Even though God said he would give you a home run, you would still have to swing the bat.

Talk about It

:: What was the command that the Lord repeated to Joshua? *(Be strong and courageous.)*

:: Why do you think the Lord told Joshua to be strong and courageous? *(Like the batter in the illustration needed courage to face the fast pitcher, Joshua needed courage to attack the enemies in the land.)*

:: What is different about the attitude of this generation of Israel? *(They are filled with faith to go into the land, while their parents were filled with fear and rebelled.)*

:: Why can trusting in God give us courage? *(God is the same today as he was back in Joshua's day. We can always place our trust in God because he is still in control of all things.)*

 ## Pray about It

Ask God to give you a strong faith to trust him like Joshua did.

DAY TWO_____

Remember It

What do you remember about yesterday's story? What do you think is going to happen today?

 Read Joshua 2:1–7.

Think about It Some More

The account of the spies in Jericho has all the excitement of a good spy movie. There is a manhunt, a beautiful woman, sneaky tricks, and quick escapes.

In a spy movie, the good guy always wins in the end because the story is written that way. But unlike an author's fictional characters, God writes his stories about real people. So, even though Rahab hid the spies under the flax and sent the king's men on a false chase, it was really God who hid the spies and sent the king's men away. He wanted it to happen that way. God is in control of all things, everywhere, all the time. So if we trust God and put our faith in him, we can be sure he is in control and will take care of us.

That is why the two spies from Israel could enter Jericho, an enemy city, with such confidence. With God in control they didn't have to worry. Their confidence was not in themselves, a pocketful of gadgets, or a fast car to get them out of town. Their confidence was in the Lord.

Talk about It

:: How many spies did Joshua send into Jericho? *(Joshua sent two spies.)*

:: Why weren't the spies afraid to go into an enemy city? *(The spies knew that God would protect them.)*

:: Who wrote the story of your life, where you would be born and what you would do? *(God wrote the story of every person's life, and everything they would do.)*

 Pray about It

Thank God for the way he is in control of all things.

DAY THREE

Connect It to Jesus

Can anyone guess how our story this week is about or points forward to Jesus?

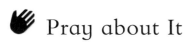 Read Matthew 1:1–6.

Think about It Some More

You may not have heard it on the first go-round, but there is an interesting name listed in the family tree of Jesus—someone from our Jericho spy story. Listen as I read the passage again, and raise your hand when you hear a name you recognize from the story.

When the two spies were hidden under the flax by Rahab, they had no idea she was going to play a key role in God's saving plan. As we will see in the rest of our spy story, Rahab and her family are the only survivors after Jericho is destroyed. Rahab joined God's people and became the far-off grandmother of King David, who was the far-off grandfather of Jesus. So that means that Rahab was the far-off grandmother of Jesus.

Talk about It

:: *Reread today's Bible passage and have your children raise their hands the moment they recognize a Bible character they know. Then have them tell you something about what that person did in the Bible.*

:: Why do you think this family tree for Jesus begins with Abraham? *(Abraham was the man who received the promise that God would bless all nations through him. Jesus is the fulfillment of that promise. It would be Jesus' death on the cross that would bless the nations.)*

:: Matthew's family tree of Jesus only goes back to Abraham. But if you went all the way back in Jesus' family tree, who would be his very first far-off grandfather? *(Adam is the first person in Jesus' family tree; he is Jesus' far-off grandfather.)*

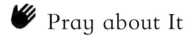 Pray about It

Thank God for saving Rahab so that Jesus would one day be born.

DAY FOUR

Remember It

What has God been teaching you this week through our Bible story?

 Read Joshua 2:8–24.

Think about It Some More

In the first weeks of studying the Bible, we learned how God promised to bless all nations through Abraham. Rahab's life gives us a hint of that promise because she is not an Israelite, yet she trusts in the Lord, and God uses her in the family line leading to Jesus.

Even though Rahab was not an Israelite, she had a strong faith in God's plan. She told the spies, "I know that the LORD has given you the land," and asked that she and her family be saved when the Israelites invaded Jericho. The spies promised that if she didn't turn them in, her whole family would be saved.

Talk about It

> KIDS, ask your parents what their favorite part of this story is.

(Parents, think about the story and come up with your favorite part and why. Thinking about Bible stories and what you like best about them forces you to think more carefully about the story.)

:: How does Rahab get the spies out of Jericho? *(She tells the spies to escape out of a window by climbing down a long rope.)*

:: What do the spies tell her to do so that she is saved when Israel attacks Jericho? *(She must tie a scarlet [red] cord outside her window, so the Israelite soldiers see it and know she and her family are the ones they are to save.)*

:: What in our story tells us that Rahab was trusting in God? *(Parents, if you have small children, reread the story and have them raise their hands the moment something you read tells about Rahab's faith in God.)*

:: How is the scarlet cord like the blood on the doorposts during the last plague? *(When God saw the red blood on the doorframes, he did not bring destruction on the firstborn son of that house. In our story of Rahab in Jericho, when the Israelite soldiers see the scarlet cord, they do not bring judgment upon her.)*

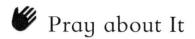 Pray about It

Ask God to help you to trust in him when it is difficult like Rahab did.

DAY FIVE

Discover It

Today we look at a passage from a psalm or one of the prophets to see what we can learn from it about Jesus.

 Read Isaiah 41:8–14.

Think about It Some More

There are many promises in this prophecy from Isaiah. In it, God calls the children of Abraham his friends and tells them that he will not cast them away. He will be their God to strengthen, uphold, and help them; and in battle the Lord will give them victory.

Now, if you were an Israelite listening to Isaiah's words, you would really be encouraged. But there is a hidden promise in this prophecy too. The last verse we read tells them that God is their helper, but then it says that a "Holy One" is going to come from Israel as their "Redeemer." Isaiah's words came true when the angel came to Mary.

The angel said Jesus was the Holy One whom God promised to send (Luke 1:35). Later, when the demons met Jesus, they called him the "Holy One of God" (Luke 4:34). So you see, Isaiah was talking about Jesus and pointing to a day when he would come.

Talk about It

:: Who is the Holy One of Israel Isaiah mentioned in his prophecy? *(Jesus is the Holy One of Israel.)*

:: Isaiah calls this Holy One a Redeemer. What does the name "Redeemer" mean? *(A redeemer is someone who pays the price to buy something back. If a person is thrown into jail for stealing, a redeemer could repay the price of what they stole, pay their penalty or fines and, by doing that, redeem them from prison.)*

:: Why do we need a redeemer? *(We need a redeemer because we are sinners who must pay the penalty for our sin. The problem is, we can't afford to pay that penalty. Jesus died on the cross to pay the penalty for us.)*

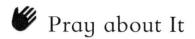 Pray about It

Thank Jesus for paying our penalty on the cross and bringing us victory over sin and death.

Week 44

Jericho Falls

Find something to use as a pretend trumpet: a length of pipe, hose, or even the cardboard roll from paper towels can work. Bring your trumpet, along with a few blocks to stack up. Place the blocks one on top of the other in the middle of a table; then gather your children.

Walk around the table seven times blowing your trumpet. After the seventh time, give the loudest blast of all, and ask your children to give a shout. They are going to think you are crazy, especially if you have older children. After you and the children give a shout, look to them and say, "That proves it." When they ask you, "Proves what?" tell them it proves that it really was God's power—not the trumpets or the shouting—that knocked down the walls of Jericho, because your blocks remained standing.

Say, "This week, you will learn of God's awesome power in the defeat of Jericho."

DAY ONE

Picture It

What would it be like if you could control the flow of a river with a traffic light? Instead of building a large bridge over a river or a tunnel under it, you could install the special light, push a button, and the river would stop flowing so you could walk or drive across. Once you were safely on the other side, the river would start flowing again.

We know that it is impossible to control the flow of a river with a traffic light, but opening up a river is not impossible for God. That's what he did to the Red Sea when Israel fled from the Egyptians, and that is what he does in today's Bible story.

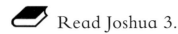 Read Joshua 3.

Think about It Some More

Rahab told the spies that the people of Jericho melted with fear when they heard how God opened up the Red Sea. Imagine what the king of Jericho thought when his spies returned with new reports of Israel's God parting the waters of the Jordan River and all Israel advancing to their city!

The Jordan was a raging river at flood stage; no army would dare try to cross it until the dry season. When the people of Jericho heard reports of the God of Israel opening up the flooded river, they would have really melted with fear.

The city of Jericho had huge, thick walls, but if the God of Israel could split open the Jordan River at flood stage, all of Jericho would have feared he could do the same to their city's walls.

Talk about It

:: How did opening up the Jordan River help Israel to trust God? *(When they saw the power of God open up the river, they knew God would be with them and would help them conquer their enemies.)*

:: If you lived near Jericho and heard that Israel was coming through the Jordan River towards you, what would you have done? *(You would want to get behind the thick walls of the city for protection.)*

:: How can the miracles God did for Israel help make our faith strong? *(We worship the same God, so when we pray we know God can do great things.)*

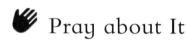 Pray about It

Thank God for his mighty power that pushed back the waters of the Jordan River.

DAY TWO

Remember It

What do you remember about yesterday's story? What do you think is going to happen today?

 Read Joshua 4:1—5:1.

Think about It Some More

God cares about the children and grandchildren of his people. The Passover celebration was set into place so the children of Israel would never forget how God had rescued his people from the last plague. In the same way, God gave the children of Israel a reminder of the day their fathers crossed over the Jordan River into the Promised Land.

Even though those stones are gone now, we have something even better than those twelve stones: we have God's Word that tells the whole story of the crossing for us to read.

Talk about It

:: Who took over for Moses as the leader of Israel? *(Joshua took over and God spoke to him as he had spoken to Moses.)*

:: Why did God have the twelve tribes of Israel set up a pile of stones where they crossed the river? *(It was to be a reminder for their children of the day God dried up the waters of the Jordan River.)*

:: What happened when kings of the Ammonites and Canaanites heard about the crossing? *(Their hearts melted with fear.)*

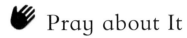 ## Pray about It

Thank God for bringing Israel safely through the Jordan River.

DAY THREE

Connect It to Jesus

Can anyone guess how our story this week is about or points forward to Jesus?

 Read Joshua 5:10–15.

Think about It Some More

How would you like to be the commander of an army getting ready for battle, when all of a sudden a strange soldier you have never seen before slips through your security force and stands beside you with his sword drawn, looking ready to cut you down? You would want to know if he was a friend or an enemy!

That is exactly what Joshua wanted to know. As soon as he heard the Lord identify himself as the commander of God's army, Joshua fell on his face.

By jumping ahead to the last book of the Bible, we can find out just who this mystery commander was. The last book of the Bible describes Jesus as the commander of God's army (Revelation 19:11–19). It tells us that Jesus has a sharp sword, which he will use to strike down the nations. His robe is dipped in blood and the words "King of kings and Lord of lords" are written on it.

Talk about It

:: Once Israel crossed the Jordan, they celebrated the Passover. What is the Passover? *(The Passover is a celebration that remembers the meal the Israelites ate in Egypt on the night of the last plague. God told his people to celebrate that day once a year so they would never forget how he spared their firstborn sons.)*

:: Why did God stop sending the manna? *(Once they were in the Promised Land there was plenty of food for them to eat. Remember, the spies brought back a huge bunch of grapes to Israel and said that Canaan was a land flowing with milk and honey.)*

:: What did Joshua do when he met the commander of the Lord's army? *(Joshua immediately fell on his face and worshiped. We are similarly called to worship the Son. Let us not become so familiar with Jesus that we lose sight of his mighty power. Let us worship the Lord!)*

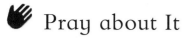 Pray about It

Follow Joshua's example and take time to worship and praise Jesus as the mighty commander of God's army.

DAY FOUR

Remember It

What has God been teaching you this week through our Bible story?

 Read Joshua 6.

Think about It Some More

As Israel approached the great walls of Jericho, the watchmen would have called out, "Here come the Israelites. They have crossed the Jordan and they are marching upon our great city." With that, all the people of Jericho would prepare for battle. But instead of attacking Jericho, Israel only marched around their city.

Imagine the confusion inside the city as the watchmen reported that Israel wasn't attacking. The people inside the city heard the trumpets of Israel sound, then stop. The Bible doesn't tell us what the people inside the city were thinking, but by the seventh day of this some in Jericho may have laughed, "Do they think they are going to destroy our great walls with their trumpets?"

But when the walls came tumbling down, the people of Jericho were not laughing anymore. By defeating Jericho this way, everyone in Israel would know that their victory came by God's power, not the strength of their army.

Talk about It

> ● ● KIDS, ask your parents to tell you about a time when God provided
> ● ● something for them in a way that they knew it was by God's grace,
> not their own effort.

(Parents, can you think of a time when God gave you a job or provided something you needed that you didn't work for?)

:: What caused the walls of Jericho to fall down? *(The power of God caused the walls to fall.)*

:: Why was it important that Rahab be saved? *(She was going to become the far-off grandmother of King David and Jesus. It is interesting to note that even though the walls came tumbling down, and Rahab's house made up a part of the walls, no one in her family was hurt.)*

:: How are we like Rahab? *(Rahab was a sinner whom God saved. We too are sinners whom God saves. Like Rahab, we deserve God's judgment for our sin, but receive his mercy and forgiveness instead.)*

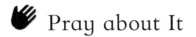 Pray about It

Thank God for the way he saved Rahab and thank God for saving us.

DAY FIVE

Discover It

Today we look at a passage from a psalm or one of the prophets to see what we can learn from it about Jesus.

 Read Zephaniah 3:14–20.

Think about It Some More

Anytime our punishment is taken away it is a time for rejoicing. Let's say that Dad gets stopped by a policeman for speeding. At first everyone in the car would be sad. But if the policeman decided to give Dad a warning instead of a ticket, everyone in the car would rejoice.

In today's Bible passage, Zephaniah is calling Israel to rejoice and celebrate because the Lord has taken away the judgments against them. Zephaniah tells them that they never have to fear again because the King of Israel is with them. When Zephaniah tells Israel that God has cleared away their enemies, he is referring to battles like the one at Jericho; but he is also pointing forward to a day when Jesus would clear away our greatest enemies: sin, death, and the judgment of God.

Jesus was the mighty one who Zephaniah said would save Israel, and Jesus is the one who saves us from punishment too. That is why we should rejoice with all of our hearts.

Talk about It

:: Who did Zephaniah say was going to save Israel from their enemies? *(The Lord their God who was the mighty one.)*

:: How does this passage point to Jesus? *(Jesus is the mighty one who came to earth, lived among his people, and defeated their enemies for good.)*

:: What did Jesus do to defeat the enemies of Israel? *(Jesus died on the cross for all those who would trust in him. Israel had earthly enemies, but their biggest enemy was a holy God who was going to punish them for their sin. When Jesus died he brought peace between Israel and God.)*

:: How is the description of God in Zephaniah similar to the description of the commander of the army of the Lord we read a few days ago in our story about Jericho? *(Both are powerful and both have come to be with and help God's people.)*

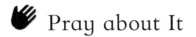 Pray about It

Thank Jesus for defeating our enemies, and pray that Jesus returns soon to destroy all evil.

Week 45

Israel and Ai

Plan your Bible study for the end of dinner. Prepare a special dessert. Collect a straw or stick for each person in the family, and cut one of them an inch shorter than the others. When you bring out dessert, also bring out the straws. Show your children that one of the straws is shorter than the rest, and explain that the person who draws the short straw will be the first to get dessert.

Mix up the straws, hiding their length in your closed fist so the shorter one is hidden among the others. Have each person choose a straw, then compare their lengths to reveal the person who was chosen by lot to get dessert first. Repeat this exercise with one fewer straw each time (but always include the short one) until everyone is served.

Then explain to your children that this week God will have Israel use lots (similar to drawing straws) to find a thief.

DAY ONE

Picture It

There once was a family who planned a birthday party for their grandfather. The day before the celebration, the mom made a chocolate birthday cake. Early the next day, the family discovered that the cake was missing a slice.

The mother called her children into the room and lined them up. One by one she stood in front of them and asked them if they took the cake. When she came to the last child, a five-year-old boy, she said, "You are the one who took the cake." Then she sent her oldest daughter to check his room for a knife and a dish. Soon the girl returned with a crumb-covered knife and plate, which she had found hidden under his bed.

The children were amazed and wondered, *How did Mom know?* Later she told them she saw a bit of chocolate in the corner of her little son's mouth. She could tell the cake had been cut with a knife, but since no crumbs were left on the table she guessed that he used a plate to carry the cake away.

In our story today, a man name Achan stole a bar of gold and 200 silver coins and hid them in his tent. He thought he'd gotten away with the theft, but God knew exactly what he'd done.

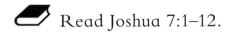 Read Joshua 7:1–12.

Think about It Some More

A good detective can solve a crime using clues. That is what the mom in our story did when she discovered the clue of the chocolate in the corner of her son's mouth. But God is more amazing than a good detective. He doesn't need any help from clues because he knows everything.

God told Israel to destroy Jericho, but to save the silver and gold for him. Even though Achan hid the gold and thought he had gotten away with his theft, God knew what he did. Because God knows everything, he didn't need a single clue to know what happened. We might be able to hide our sin from people, but we can't ever hide our sin from God.

Talk about It

:: Why did Israel lose the battle with Ai? *(Achan stole some things that were supposed to be devoted to [set aside for] God.)*

:: How did God know someone had stolen some of the devoted things? *(God knows everything.)*

:: Have you ever stolen something that did not belong to you and hid it so no one would know? *(Parents, draw your children out here. They may have taken a piece of candy without asking or a toy from a friend. Help them identify with Achan.)*

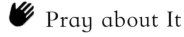 Pray about It

Ask God to help you remember he knows everything, and that it is useless for you to try to hide your sin.

DAY TWO

Remember It

What do you remember about yesterday's story? What do you think is going to happen today?

 Read Joshua 7:13–26.

Think about It Some More

God used lots to find Achan—and to show his great power to Israel. Not only did he know who stole the devoted things, God was also able to control the lot—each time the lot was taken, it fell to Achan's group. First Achan's tribe was chosen, then Achan's clan, and finally his family.

Did you notice that each time they picked lots they were getting closer to Achan, but he didn't confess until the very end when he was found out? The whole time, he was trying to hide his sin, hoping the lot would fall on someone else. It could have gone differently for Achan if he had confessed his sin and asked God for mercy. Because he hid his sin, God punished him.

Talk about It

:: Can you explain how choosing by lots works? *(Parents, remind your children of the casting lots activity from earlier this week. If you skipped that activity, you might consider doing it here.)*

:: How could God control the lots to make sure the correct tribe or clan was chosen? *(God is in control of all things. He is also all-powerful and makes everything work according to his plan.)*

:: What do you think God may have done if Achan had confessed right away and asked God to forgive him? *(God may have forgiven Achan. Joshua could have stood in the middle for him and prayed to God, asking him to spare Achan.)*

:: Did Achan deserve to be killed? *(Yes, in fact, the punishment for sin is always death. We all deserve to be killed for our sin, but God in his mercy sent Jesus to die for our sins so we could be forgiven.)*

 Pray about It

Ask God to help each person in your family confess their sins and ask God for his mercy.

DAY THREE

Connect It to Jesus

Can anyone guess how our story this week is about or points forward to Jesus?

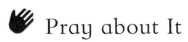 Read Joshua 8:30–35.

Think about It Some More

Tomorrow we will read how Israel attacked Ai again and won. But we skipped over the battle today because our connection to Jesus comes after the battle. When the fight was over and Israel had won, Joshua built an altar to the Lord with uncut stones. That meant he used only stones he found and didn't shape them with chisels into blocks.

Once he had carefully stacked the stones to make an altar, he sacrificed a peace offering to God. The animal sacrificed as a peace offering pointed forward to a day when Jesus would die for our sins and take away our punishment so we would have peace with God. God commanded that an altar be made of uncut stones to remind us that all our work is sinful; even the cutting of stones for his altar was affected by our sin.

Talk about It

:: What did Joshua write on the stones? *(Joshua wrote the law, the Ten Commandments, on the stones.)*

:: What did Joshua read to the people? *(Joshua read the book of the law to the people to remind them of what God commanded.)*

:: What commandments did Achan break? *(Achan loved money more than God; Achan coveted the gold and silver that did not belong to him; and Achan stole a robe, a gold bar, and silver coins.)*

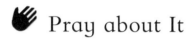 Pray about It

Ask God to help you obey his commands, not hide your sin like Achan did.

DAY FOUR

Remember It

What has God been teaching you this week through our Bible story?

 Read Joshua 8:1–29.

Think about It Some More

If you have ever been caught in a sudden storm without an umbrella, you know that there is no way to stay dry unless you run for cover. But if you are in the middle of a field with nowhere to go, there is no protection for you and you get soaked.

That's kind of what happened to the people of Ai. All of Ai was lured out into the open wilderness beyond the protection of the city walls. After setting the city on fire, the men of Israel attacked from all sides, and the army of Ai had nowhere to run. Israel defeated Ai with the Lord's help.

God allowed the first attack on Ai to fail because Achan had stolen the devoted things. But this time God was with Israel in battle, and no army can defeat Israel with God on their side.

Talk about It

> KIDS, ask your parents to explain what an ambush is.

(Parents, an ambush is a surprise like when you hide some of your army then bring them out for a surprise attack. If you get the opportunity, wait for one of your children around a corner and snatch them up in your arms when they walk by, explaining that you ambushed them to give them hugs.)

:: Why did the men of Ai leave the protection of the city to chase the Israelites? *(They remembered the earlier battle and thought they could win again. They didn't know that a large part of Israel's army was hidden, waiting for them to leave.)*

:: What is different about this attack on Ai from the first one that failed? *(The first time, because of Achan's sin, God did not go into battle with Israel. This time, God promised to go with them and give them victory. In the first battle the fighting men of Israel did not get to keep anything. This time they got to keep all the livestock for food.)*

 Pray about It

Ask God to help you remember that it is always best to trust in him.

DAY FIVE

Discover It

Today we look at a passage from a psalm or one of the prophets to see what we can learn from it about Jesus.

 Read Jeremiah 33:14–15.

Think about It Some More

Do you remember the code word "branch" and what it means? That's right; anytime we read in the Bible about a righteous branch springing up from David, we know that it is referring to Jesus.

In this Bible passage, Jeremiah tells us that Jesus will execute (bring) justice and righteousness. The way Jesus brought righteousness was to live a perfect life and die on the cross for our sins. Now everyone who believes in Jesus can have their sins removed. But for all those who refuse to believe in him, a day will come when Jesus will return to execute justice and punish them. In that day, everyone who refused to believe will be cast into the fires of hell.

Talk about It

:: Who is the righteous branch that Jeremiah is talking about? *(The righteous branch is Jesus.)*

:: What did Jesus do to bring goodness or righteousness to us? *(Jesus died on the cross to take our sins away.)*

:: What is the promise that God made to the house of Israel? *(The promise goes back to Abraham's time when God said that he would bless all nations of the earth through Abraham [Genesis 17:5; 18:18].)*

 Pray about It

Thank God for keeping his promise to send a king from the family of David who would become our righteousness.

Week 46

God Calls Gideon

Into a paper bag, place just enough rope to fill the bottom. Then gather your children. Ask them, "If I told you there was a snake in this bag and I wanted you to put your hand in without looking, would you do it? What fears would you have? What would give you confidence to do it anyway?" They will likely say that any confidence to put their hand in the bag would come from trusting you as their parent. In effect, they are drawing their faith from your past faithfulness to them.

Now, tell them to go ahead and put their hand in the bag. Tell them that it is safe but dramatize things a little, pretending you are trying to keep a snake from coming out. In the end, have a child pull out the rope, your pretend snake.

Say, "This week you will learn how God worked out his plan using a fearful man."

DAY ONE

Picture It

There once was a boy whose grandfather kept honey bees in a field next to his house. He called the field the ball diamond because it was nice and flat and the children loved to play baseball on it. But he always warned the children not to play ball near the bees.

One day a group of children didn't obey the rule. The batter hit a foul ball high in the air in the direction of the beehives. The young boy playing third base ran to catch it and crashed right into one of hives. Immediately a swarm of bees flew out of the hive and started stinging him and the others who were playing in the field, so the children ran away. That day they learned how important it is to obey the rules set in place to protect us.

In today's story, we will see the consequences that came upon Israel because they didn't obey God's rules.

 Read Judges 6:1–10.

Think about It Some More

When God gave the Promised Land to Israel, he gave them one important rule to follow: destroy the idol worshipers who live in the land. God gave them this command so they would not be led astray to worship false gods (Deuteronomy 20:16–18). But unfortunately, Israel did not obey the Lord and, as God predicted, they turned away from him and worshiped the idols of the Canaanites.

Because Israel walked away from God, he allowed their enemies to grow strong and attack Israel so they would return to God. The idol-worshiping Midianites attacked Israel and took their crops and animals. When the Israelites cried out to God for help, he sent a prophet to explain to them that they were suffering because they did not obey God's laws.

Talk about It

:: How did God use the trouble and suffering caused by the Midianites to help Israel? *(The suffering helped Israel remember the Lord and their need for him.)*

:: How does God use trials and suffering in our lives to draw us near to him? *(When we don't obey his rules, God can use trials to bring us back to himself. Not all trials are the result of our sin, but some can be. Parents, you can give the example of a child who runs away from his mom and dad, only to trip and fall and return crying. Even a small trial like that can help us realize we are wrong.)*

:: Can you think of a trial God brought to your family to help you call out to God for help? *(Parents, help your children here. Every time we are sick and call out to God for help, the sickness is actually helping us to remember and trust in God.)*

 Pray about It

Ask God to help each person in your family to trust and obey God.

DAY TWO

Remember It

What do you remember about yesterday's story? What do you think is going to happen today?

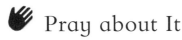 Read Judges 6:11–16.

Think about It Some More

Isn't it interesting that God chose one of the weakest men of Israel to save them from the Midianites? When the Lord appeared to Gideon, he was hiding from the Midianites inside a winepress grinding wheat.

By choosing the weakest man of Israel, God made sure that everyone would know it was really God's power that had saved them.

Talk about It

:: Who appeared to Gideon while he was hiding in the winepress? *(God appeared to Gideon.)*

:: Why was Gideon hiding? *(He knew that the Midianites attacked at harvest time and he didn't want them to take his wheat, so he was hiding from them.)*

:: What was God going to help Gideon do? *(God was going to use Gideon to attack the Midianites and save Israel.)*

 ## Pray about It

Ask God to reach out to you and call you as a part of his wonderful plan.

DAY THREE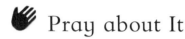

Connect It to Jesus

Can anyone guess how our story this week is about or points forward to Jesus?

Read Judges 6:17–24.

Think about It Some More

When the Angel of the Lord burned up the basket of food and disappeared, Gideon realized it was God and was afraid and thought he would die. But God called out to Gideon to comfort him.

Even though Gideon was a sinner and deserved to die, God didn't kill him because Gideon was a part of God's plan to save Israel. Each time God saved Israel he was preparing the way for Jesus to be born.

Talk about It

:: What happened after the Angel of the Lord touched the food with his staff? *(Fire burned up the food and the Lord vanished.)*

:: Why was Gideon concerned when he realized it was really God who came to speak with him and he saw God face to face? *(Read Exodus 33:20 to your children if they don't have the answer, then ask them again.)*

:: If Gideon was a sinner, why didn't God judge Gideon's sin and kill him? *(Gideon was a part of God's plan to save Israel, so one day Jesus could be born. God was looking ahead to the day Jesus would come to save his people. Jesus came to save Gideon.)*

Pray about It

Thank God for the wonderful mercy he showed us in saving Israel through Gideon.

DAY FOUR

Remember It

What has God been teaching you this week through our Bible story?

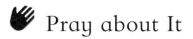 Read Judges 6:25–40.

Think about It Some More

When the people discovered that Gideon tore down the altar to Baal, they were angry and wanted to kill him. Joash, Gideon's father, stopped them and said that if Baal was a real god then he could punish Gideon himself. But since Baal was a false god, nothing happened to Gideon.

Baal was a god that people made up, not a real God like the Lord. Anyone can make up a false god and carve a statue, but only the true God can fight his enemies.

Talk about It

> ● ● KIDS, ask your parents if they think they would have had more or less
> ● ● courage than Gideon.

(Parents, think through Gideon's actions. He broke down the altars at night and set out the fleece multiple times. What do you think you would have done?)

:: Why didn't Baal go after Gideon for tearing down his altar? *(Baal was a false God. There is only one real God; all the others are fakes.)*

:: How did the Spirit of God help Gideon when he was afraid? *(The Spirit of God helped Gideon to trust God and gave him boldness to fight.)*

:: Why did Gideon lay out a fleece? *(Gideon's faith in God was weak. He laid out the fleece to be sure God would be with him.)*

 Pray about It

Praise God for answering Gideon's prayers; praise him for being a real, live God that we can trust.

DAY FIVE

Discover It

Today we look at a passage from a psalm or one of the prophets to see what we can learn from it about Jesus.

 Read Jeremiah 33:16.

Think about It Some More

Last week we learned that this part of Jeremiah's prophecy talked about Jesus as the righteous Branch. Today Jeremiah says that Jesus the Lord is our Righteousness. Remember, righteousness is goodness. That is important because as sinners we have lost our goodness or righteousness, and righteousness is the very thing we need to be able to go to heaven and live with God.

That is why Jeremiah's prophecy is good news. God is promising that he will give his people who are sinners God's righteousness so they can go to heaven.

Now we know, from reading the story of Jesus, that the way God gave us his righteousness was by sending Jesus to live a perfect life on earth in our place. Then Jesus traded with us. He took our sins and gave us his perfect life.

Talk about It

:: What is righteousness? (*Righteousness is goodness. Even one sin ruins any chance a person might have to be righteous.*)

:: Who is the only person who never sinned at all and is the only one who is righteous? (*Jesus is the only person who is righteous because he never sinned.*)

:: If Jesus was already perfect, he didn't need to live a righteous life on earth for himself, so why did he come as a man to live a perfect life? (*He did it as a gift for us. He came to live a perfect life on earth in our place so that he could give us his perfect life, his righteousness, as a gift.*)

Pray about It

Thank Jesus for giving up the awesome glory of heaven to become a man like us to save us.

Week 47

Gideon's Victory

For this exercise, find something very heavy. The ideal object would weigh too much for your youngest child to lift, but be light enough for your oldest child to lift. (If you are working with only one child, pick something too heavy for him or her to lift without your help. If you have a stronger child, pick a larger piece of furniture like a sofa.)

Ask for a volunteer to carry the object from one end of the room to the other. Say, "Let's see, who would be perfect to carry such a heavy object?" Then choose your youngest child. When the child cannot pick the object up, add your strength so the two of you move it together.

Explain to your children that you wanted to pick someone who could not boast in her own work, but would need your help to complete the task. Say, "This week you will see how God used Gideon as a deliverer in a way that would show God's power and give God the glory."

DAY ONE

Picture It

Imagine that our family takes a trip with another family and stops at a hotel for the night. After checking in, Dad asks for help with the luggage. You and two others volunteer to carry the suitcases up to your rooms, but Dad tells the others that you and he can handle the job without them. Now, you were already wondering if the five of you could handle the nine suitcases, but with just you and Dad there is no way you can carry the bags up in one trip.

After the others turn to go up in the elevator, you follow Dad off to the left; he comes out of a small room with a huge luggage cart on which the suitcases fit easily. As you roll the luggage over to the elevator, you realize that the cart was Dad's plan all along.

In our story today, God sends most of Gideon's army home. We will have to see what God has in mind for these 300 men. Certainly he can't think they will be able to defeat a whole army.

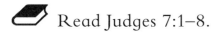 Read Judges 7:1–8.

Think about It Some More

When the Bible mentions tens of thousands of people, it can be hard to imagine how many people that is. To make it easier to understand, think about it this way. When Gideon called the men of Israel to fight, so many men answered his call that you could have filled a whole baseball stadium with them.

With such a large army, the Israelites would think they had won the battle by their own strength, without God's help. But God wanted them to know he was the one who brought them victory in the battle. So he told Gideon to send most of them home. That way, all Israel would know that their victory came because of God's strength, not because of the size of their army.

Talk about It

:: Why did God send most of Gideon's men home? *(He wanted Israel to know he was the one who would bring them victory.)*

:: How many men were left after God sent the others home? *(Only 300 men were left.)*

:: How were only 300 men going to defeat the Midianite and Amalekite armies? *(God told Gideon that he was going to be with him [Judges 6:16]. With God on their side, Gideon could have won the battle all by himself.)*

 Pray about It

Praise God for the wonderful way he teaches us to trust in him.

DAY TWO

Remember It

What do you remember about yesterday's story? What do you think is going to happen today?

 Read Judges 7:9–15.

Think about It Some More

Now, it is easy to say you are going to defeat a whole army with only 300 men, but imagine what Gideon thought when he saw how large the Midianite army was. There were so many soldiers that it looked like a swarm of locusts—way too many soldiers to even count. Gideon was probably thinking that he needed all the men God sent home.

Even though God called him and had answered Gideon's prayer about the fleece, Gideon still did not trust God. But instead of leaving Gideon, God helped his weak faith again. God sent him to spy on the enemy and hear what they were saying. God was already planning to defeat the enemy, and he knew how to encourage Gideon for the fight. After hearing the fearful soldiers talk, Gideon finally realized God would help him.

Talk about It

:: How many enemy soldiers were there? *(There were so many that you could not count them all.)*

:: Who gave the dream to the enemy soldier? *(God gave the dream to him.)*

:: Why did God send Gideon to the enemy camp? *(Gideon was fearful and did not trust God to help him. God knew that when Gideon heard the enemy soldiers talking about how God was going to help Gideon win, it would strengthen his faith, and his courage would rise.)*

:: What did Gideon do when he heard the soldiers talking about the dream? *(He worshiped God.)*

 Pray about It

Take time to ask God to help you with your most difficult challenges. Consider praying for family and friends who seem very far from God or something else that seems like a really big need. If God could do all he did through Gideon to save Israel, he can answer prayers for the things we need too.

DAY THREE

Connect It to Jesus

Can anyone guess how our story this week is about or points forward to Jesus?

 Read Judges 8:22–35.

Think about It Some More

Not long after the battle, Gideon fell into sin. Although Gideon told the people that God should be their king, Gideon asked the people to bring him an offering of gold. Gideon also took many wives, like the pagan kings of his day would do.

Gideon made a golden ephod (a vestlike jacket or breastplate) from the gold that the people gave him and he put it up in his own city for everyone to see. Now the priests of Israel were the ones God said should wear a golden ephod to show their special position. So Gideon's ephod confused and distracted the people from their worship of God. Instead of paying attention to God, they all came to look at Gideon's ephod.

As soon as Gideon died, the people returned to worship false gods again. God used Gideon to save Israel in battle, but Gideon, being a sinner, could not save them from their sin and he led them astray. One day, however, God would raise up another Savior—Jesus—who would not fall into sin, but would lead God's people to righteousness.

Talk about It

:: What did Gideon love more than God after he won the battle? *(It seems from our story that Gideon loved the things of the world—like gold and many wives—more than he loved God.)*

:: How was Jesus like Gideon? How was he different? *(God used both Gideon and Jesus to save Israel. God used Gideon to save Israel in battle, while God sent his Son Jesus to save us from our sins. But unlike Gideon, Jesus never sinned.)*

:: Gideon was distracted from serving God with gold and many wives. What kind of things could distract you from following God? *(Parents, help your children to see that we can long after the things of the world more than we long after God. For children, toys, candy, playtime, and other things can distract them from serving God.)*

 Pray about It

Ask God to help you love him more than anything else in the world.

DAY FOUR

Remember It

What has God been teaching you this week through our Bible story?

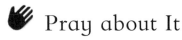 Read Judges 7:15–25.

Think about It Some More

If you have ever been alone at night and heard a strange noise, you know how quickly a person can become afraid. It is different when it's light outside. If a coat slips off a hanger in your open bedroom closet in the daytime, you can see that it is only a coat. But if that same coat slips off the hanger at night, it could look like there is someone crouching down in your closet.

So you can imagine, when Gideon's men broke their jars and sounded their trumpets in the black of night, the enemy soldiers didn't know what was going on and began to panic. They drew their swords, and God confused them so much that they started fighting each other. In the black of night they didn't realize they were killing each other. Then Israel chased after them and won the battle.

Talk about It

> ● ● KIDS, ask your parents if they can think of a time when they became
> ● ● afraid late at night.

(Parents, think back to growing up. When were you the most afraid? Did you panic?)

:: Even though Gideon's men fought the battle, who helped Israel win? *(God helped Israel win.)*

:: How did God use the trumpets, jars, and torches to scare the Midianites? *(The Midianites thought each trumpet, jar, and torch represented a large group of men surrounding them. In their fear and confusion, they began to fight each other and then fled.)*

:: How do you think the dream God gave the enemy soldiers helped Gideon? *(Because of the dream, the enemy soldiers were already afraid of Gideon. When Gideon's men broke their jars, the enemy soldiers probably remembered the dream and what it meant and were all the more afraid.)*

:: What can we learn about God from this story? *(Parents, give your children clues and see if they can give you an answer. God kept his promise to Gideon to give him victory, and we also learn that God is powerfully in control of dreams and the outcome of battle.)*

 ## Pray about It

Thank God for saving Israel and showing them his power by using so few men to defeat the enemy.

DAY FIVE

Discover It

Today we look at a passage from a psalm or one of the prophets to see what we can learn from it about Jesus.

 Read Jeremiah 33:17.

Think about It Some More

We know from the past two lessons that Jeremiah is talking about Jesus in this part of the Bible. (If you would like to, reread verses 14–16.) In today's verse, God promised Israel through Jeremiah that they would always have a king on the throne of David.

Hundreds of years later, the people of Jesus' day remembered what Jeremiah said. They knew that Jesus was born in the family line of David, and they saw that he was a great teacher and had power to perform miracles. That is why some of them wanted to make Jesus their king.

But they didn't realize that Jesus had a different plan. They were right to think of Jesus as the king Jeremiah talked about, but Jesus didn't come to sit on a throne here on earth. Jesus came to defeat sin and death, and then to sit on a throne in heaven where he would rule over God's people forever, just as Jeremiah said would happen.

Talk about It

:: How does Jeremiah's prophecy point forward to Jesus? *(Jesus is the eternal King who sits upon the throne forever, thus fulfilling this promise.)*

:: *Read Luke 1:26–33.* How does this passage fit with what Jeremiah said? *(The angel Gabriel told Mary that Jesus would be given the throne of David and would reign over Israel forever, fulfilling the promise of Jeremiah for David to always have a king on his throne.)*

:: What do we need to do to make Jesus our king? *(Jesus is king over all men, whether they want him to be or not. But, if we believe that God sent Jesus to die on the cross for our sins and that Jesus rose again from the dead and we trust in him to save us, then we are welcoming Jesus as our king.)*

 ## Pray about It

Ask God to help each person in your family to believe and welcome Jesus as his or her king.

Week 48

God Gives Samson Strength

Snip a small lock of hair from you or your spouse and place it in a plastic bag. Pass it around to your children and ask, "How could growing long hair make a person strong?" Your children will probably look at you as if you're a bit crazy. Perhaps some of them will remember the story of Samson in the Bible. The correct answer is that hair, all by itself, cannot make a person strong.

This week we will read the story of Samson and how God told his mother not to cut his hair. Samson's hair wasn't the key to his strength—God was. Samson's hair was a sign that he was following God's plan. The power wasn't in the hair; the power was in God.

DAY ONE

Picture It

Did you know that God invented superheroes? Superman and Spider-Man are not in the Bible, but God did create a man named Samson and gave him superhuman strength to win battles against the Lord's enemies.

If you could have one superhuman ability, which one would you choose? Super strength would probably be close to the top of the list for most people, right alongside flying. Today we will learn about one of God's superheros and how he got his superpowers. He couldn't fly, but he did have superhuman strength.

 Read Judges 13:1–5.

Think about It Some More

Even though God's people were disobeying God and not calling out to him for help, God had a plan to save them from their enemy, the Philistines. God appeared as an angel of the Lord to the wife of a man named Manoah and promised to give her a son who would begin to save Israel from the Philistines. God told her that this boy would be a Nazirite.

A Nazirite was a person who gave his life in service to God. God gave Manoah's wife three instructions for raising her son: don't let him drink wine, don't let him eat anything unclean, and don't ever cut his hair.

Talk about It

:: Why did God allow the Philistines to win battles against Israel? *(Israel disobeyed God's commands. We know from our story about Gideon that after he died they started worshiping idols.)*

:: Can you think of a reason why God wanted to save Israel even though they were disobeying him? *(God loved his people. That is the reason why he saved them, and that is the same reason why God saves us today.)*

:: What Nazirite rule about hair did God give Manoah's wife that he wanted her son to follow all his days? *(God told Manoah's wife that her son's hair should never be cut.)*

 ## Pray about It

Thank God for showing his love to Israel even when they were not calling out to him.

DAY TWO

Remember It

What do you remember about yesterday's story? What do you think is going to happen today?

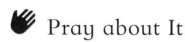 Read Judges 13:6–18.

Think about It Some More

It is easy to believe in something you can see, but it takes a lot more faith to believe in something you can't see. Even though Manoah didn't see the angel of God who visited his wife, he believed her and then prayed for God to send the man again.

When the angel of God returned, Manoah believed what he said and wanted to know his name so that after it all came true he could honor the man.

Talk about It

:: What does it mean to have faith in something? *(When you have faith, you believe something is true, even if you can't see it for yourself. For instance, even though we have never seen Jesus, we believe that he is real and he died for our sins.)*

:: How did Manoah show that he had faith? *(Manoah believed what the angel of the Lord told his wife.)*

:: What did the Lord tell Manoah his name was? *(The angel never gave Manoah his name, but said it was too wonderful to share. God can't be described with just one name like we can. It takes a lot of names to describe God.)*

:: Can you think of some of the names God is called? *(God, Jesus, Spirit, Father, Son, Comforter, Creator, Savior, etc.)*

 Pray about It

Use some of the names of God in prayers to thank God for all he does. For instance, you could thank God for being our Father in heaven, the Creator who made the earth, and our Savior who rescued us from sin.

DAY THREE

Connect It to Jesus

Can anyone guess how our story this week is about or points forward to Jesus?

 Read Judges 13:19–25.

Think about It Some More

Did you ever notice how sacrifices (the killing of animals as an offering to God) seem to be a part of nearly every Bible story? In the story we are reading this week, Manoah wanted to prepare a meal for the angel of the Lord, but the Lord asked him to kill an animal as a burnt offering instead. Then when Manoah presented the offering, God burned it up in a blaze of fire.

The reason there are so many animal sacrifices is because they all point forward to Jesus. Each time an animal was sacrificed to God, it pointed forward to the day when God would sacrifice his only Son for our sins.

As soon as God burned up the offering, Manoah realized that it was God and not an ordinary man who had visited them, and he thought their lives were in danger. But his wife knew that if God had intended to kill them, he would have already done it. God burned up the offering, but he let them live.

Talk about It

:: What happened to the offering Manoah presented to the Lord? *(God burned it up.)*

:: What do all the animal sacrifices in the Old Testament point to? *(The animal sacrifices point to Jesus who was sacrificed in our place.)*

:: Why did Jesus have to die on the cross in our place? *(Parents, this is a wonderful opportunity to see how well your children understand the gospel. We have all broken God's law and deserve to be punished. But God sent his Son Jesus to die in our place so we could be forgiven.)*

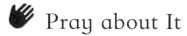 Pray about It

Thank Jesus for dying on the cross for some of the specific sins you have done in your life. For example, you might thank him for dying on the cross to take away your angry attitudes toward your mom.

DAY FOUR

Remember It

What has God been teaching you this week through our Bible story?

 Read Judges 14:1–9.

Think about It Some More

Years have passed in our story. Manoah's wife had a baby boy and she named him Samson. We don't know anything about Samson's childhood because the story jumps to when he is a young man. The Lord is with Samson and has given him super strength. But instead of being a humble and godly man, Samson is proud and disrespectful.

Talk about It

> ⬤ ⬤ KIDS, ask your parents if they remember a person whom God blessed
> ⬤ ⬤ with wonderful abilities but who became proud.

(Parents, think back to growing up. Did you know someone who was really good in sports or a particular academic subject, but who was proud and boastful about what they could do? Explain how we should always remember that it is God who gives us our gifts and not use them to puff ourselves up.)

:: Who helped Samson kill the lion? *(The Spirit of God rushed upon Samson and gave him his strength.)*

:: Did Samson honor the Lord for helping him kill the lion? *(No, Samson seemed to do whatever he wanted and did not honor the Lord. He was disrespectful to his parents and wanted a wife from among the Philistines.)*

:: Why did God bless Samson even though he was full of pride? *(God wanted to use him to judge the Philistines and deliver his people.)*

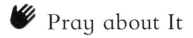 Pray about It

Thank God for the way he helps you every day even when you sin.

DAY FIVE

Discover It

Today we look at a passage from a psalm or one of the prophets to see what we can learn from it about Jesus.

 Read Jeremiah 33:18 and Hebrews 7:23–25.

Think about It Some More

Last week we read how Jesus fulfilled the promise made in Jeremiah 33:17. That verse says that a descendant of David will be king of Israel forever. In a similar way, verse 18 tells us that there will always be a priest to offer sacrifices for the people.

Back when God gave his law to Moses, God said that whenever the people sinned and deserved to be punished, they should bring a lamb to the priest for him to kill. The priest would offer a sacrifice up to God to make a payment for their sin. The lamb would be killed in their place.

When Jesus came, he became a priest for us all. Only, instead of a lamb, he gave up his own life as the perfect sacrifice for us. So Jesus is both the priest who offers up the sacrifice and the lamb who died in our place.

Talk about It

:: Why couldn't Jeremiah's prophecy be talking about the priests of old? *(The priests of old were ordinary men who died. Jesus is the only priest that lives forever.)*

:: What sacrifice did Jesus offer for our sins? *(Jesus died on the cross for our sins.)*

:: Why is the death of Jesus on the cross better than the lambs that died as sacrifices? *(The lambs didn't really take away sin; they only pointed to Jesus. Jesus' sacrifice really takes away our sins because he took the punishment we deserved.)*

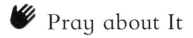 Pray about It

Thank Jesus for serving as our priest forever in heaven. The wounds on his hands and feet tell God the Father that the punishment for our sin was paid by Jesus.

Samson Loses His Strength

Bring a large stack of books and call your children together. Ask an older child to stand up and hold out a hand, palm up, waist high. Place the books on his hand until he can't support the load and the books fall.

Then ask one of your younger children to try. Place one hand under the smaller child's hand while you load the books with the other. Load the full number the first child held and then add more. Then celebrate the smaller child's victory.

Someone will say the test was not fair because you helped. Agree that the only reason the smaller child won was because of your help. Then repeat the exercise with your older child so he is able to do it with your help too.

Say, "This week you will see that Samson did not learn the lesson that God was the source of his strength until after he lost his powers. Samson's pride was his greatest enemy."

DAY ONE

Picture It

Imagine that your best friend has a beautiful white cat named Princess who looks so fluffy that you want to pet her. After asking your friend for permission, you walk over slowly to pet the cat. At first the cat purrs loudly and her fur feels so soft, but then out of nowhere she hisses and whacks your hand with her paw to scratch you. Quickly you move your hand away.

The next time you go to your friend's house the cat is lying in the same place and you decide to try to pet her again. After a couple of purrs, the cat changes moods and tries to scratch you. Once again you escape without harm, but this time you feel the sharpness of her claws across the back of your hand. If, on your third visit, the same thing happens, you would stop trying to pet the cat no matter how soft her fur looked and felt.

In our story today, Samson did not learn his lesson. Even though Delilah was tricking him and turning him over to the Philistines again and again, he did not leave her.

 Read Judges 16:4–14.

Think about It Some More

By this time in our Bible story, Samson has overpowered the Philistines with great feats of strength and has become the ruler over Israel. But he has also become very proud of his strength and very confident of himself.

The Philistines, on the other hand, are tired of being ruled by Samson, and they don't like him very much. So they offer his girlfriend Delilah a huge amount of money to betray Samson and see if she can discover the secret of his great strength.

Three times Delilah asks Samson to tell her what makes him so strong, but each time Samson tells her a lie. When the Philistines rush upon Samson he defeats them easily. But Samson's pride blinds him so that he is unable to see Delilah as a traitor.

Samson isn't trusting in God to help him. Instead, Samson trusts in his own strength to save him. God has blessed him with superhuman strength to save Israel, not to play games with Delilah.

Talk about It

:: What is pride? *(Pride is when we think more highly of ourselves than we should; when we lift ourselves up over others or God.)*

:: How does Samson's pride blind him? *(Samson thinks that his strength is enough to get him out of any danger. He relies on himself, not on God.)*

:: How can pride still blind us today? *(Pride blinds us by fooling us into thinking we can do things by ourselves without God. Think about it: when was the last time that you prayed to ask God to help you with school? Or when was the last time you thanked God for helping you do a good job in something? It is easy to think that we should get the credit for the things we do well, when it is God who helps us to do everything we do.)*

:: Can you think of an area of your life where you have been proud? *(Parents, help your children here. Remember, we often cannot see our own pride.)*

Pray about It

Confess where you have pride in your life and ask God to help you grow in humility.

DAY TWO

Remember It

What do you remember about yesterday's story? What do you think is going to happen today?

Read Judges 16:15–22.

Think about It Some More

Samson tries to "pet the cat" one too many times and this time he gets "scratched." Samson's pride blinds him to Delilah's traps so, after she pressures him, Samson tells her about his

Nazirite vow not to cut his hair. Delilah knows that Samson is finally telling her the truth, and after he falls asleep she has his head shaved.

But notice, before she calls the Philistines, Delilah mocks Samson. She doesn't really care for Samson; she only wants the money. Samson's strength disappears with his hair, and he cannot stop her from turning him over to the enemy.

Talk about It

:: Who does Samson love more than God? *(Samson loves Delilah more than God, and Samson loves himself more than God.)*

:: What does Delilah love more than God? *(Delilah loves money more than Samson or God. In the end she betrays Samson for 1,100 silver coins. While that is a lot of money, it is not enough to buy your way to heaven. When you die you leave all your money behind.)*

:: What are we tempted to love more than God? *(Parents, help your children think of the things that most cause them to sin. If they like a toy so much that they would fight over it, they love it more than God. If they angrily refuse to do chores, they love ease more than God. Often our anger helps us to see where our false loves live. Anything that leads us to sin rather than obey God is usually connected to something we love more than God.)*

 Pray about It

Ask God to forgive you for the things you love more than God.

DAY THREE

Connect It to Jesus

Can anyone guess how our story this week is about or points forward to Jesus?

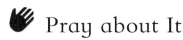 Read Judges 16:23–31.

Think about It Some More

As now-blind Samson is led into the banquet hall, the Philistine rulers mock God. Although Samson was blinded by the Philistines, God has used his defeat to open the eyes of his heart to see his pride. Samson's defeat by the Philistines has helped him realize that God is the real source of his strength.

Now, with his hair growing long again, Samson has reason to think his strength has returned. But this time, instead of trying to fight the Philistines by himself, he calls out to God for help. This is the first time Samson calls on the Lord before a fight.

God answers his prayer and Samson's awesome strength returns to him one last time. In the end, Samson gives up his own life to save Israel by destroying their enemies. That is what Jesus did for us—he gave up his life to destroy our enemies.

Talk about It

:: How is Samson different in this part of our story from the way he was before? *(Samson is no longer proud, thinking he can do things without God, in his own strength.)*

:: Who does Samson kill when he knocks down the pillars? *(The lords [rulers] and important officials of the Philistines were killed.)*

:: How is Samson like Jesus? *(God uses Samson to deliver Israel from their Philistine enemies. Jesus came to deliver us from our enemies, sin and death.)*

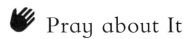 ## Pray about It

Thank God for forgiving Samson and restoring his strength one last time.

DAY FOUR

Remember It

What has God been teaching you this week through our Bible story?

 Read Hebrews 11:32—12:3.

Think about It Some More

Some stories end with, "And they lived happily ever after." Here in the book of Hebrews, there is a wonderful ending to Samson's sad life.

For the first part of his life Samson was a bad example, but at the very end Samson turned away from his pride and gave up his life for God's people. Because of that, Samson finished well and his life points us to Jesus. Even though Samson had many failures, he is named in the book of Hebrews as a hero of our faith. The men and women listed in this part of the Bible trusted God through some difficult trials. The writer of the book of Hebrews tells us about them so we can follow their example.

Talk about It

> ● ● KIDS, ask your parents who their favorite Old Testament hero is and
> ● ● why.

:: Why is Samson's name listed among the faithful? *(Samson repented or turned from his sins in the last part of his life, and in the end saved Israel from their enemies.)*

:: What can we learn from Samson's life? *(Parents, draw out your children here to see if they have picked up on the evil of pride and our need to trust God, not ourselves.)*

:: What did Jesus do to show his faith? *(Jesus endured the cross and suffered in our place so we could be forgiven.)*

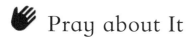 Pray about It

Praise God for giving us so many wonderful examples of faith, especially Jesus.

DAY FIVE

Discover It

Today we look at a passage from a psalm or one of the prophets to see what we can learn from it about Jesus.

 Read Ezekiel 34:20–24 and John 10:14–15.

Think about It Some More

A long time before Jesus was even born, Ezekiel, a prophet of God, spoke of a shepherd who would be born into the family line of David. Instead of caring for sheep, this shepherd would watch over God's flock, his people. Ezekiel said that he would feed and protect them from all harm.

But Ezekiel never mentioned who the shepherd was. It is not until Jesus explained that he was the Good Shepherd that Israel learned who Ezekiel was talking about. Jesus was the one who laid down his life for God's sheep, the people of God. Jesus was the shepherd born into the family of David whom Ezekiel had prophesied about. If we trust in Jesus, we become a part of his flock too.

Talk about It

:: Who is the shepherd Ezekiel said would come to God's people and become their prince? *(Jesus is the shepherd Ezekiel talked about.)*

:: Why is Jesus called David in Ezekiel's prophecy? *(Jesus is called David because he comes from the family line of David.)*

:: How is Jesus a shepherd? *(The simple answer is that Jesus takes care of us. But you can explain to your children that a shepherd leads his sheep to good food and he protects them from danger. If a wolf attacked, the shepherd would sacrifice his own life to protect the sheep. Jesus leads us to our heavenly food, God's Word; and he sacrificed his own life to protect us from the dangers of sin and death. By taking our punishment upon the cross, he also protects us from God's judgment.)*

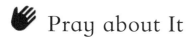 Pray about It

Thank Jesus for being our shepherd and for laying down his life for the sheep.

Week 50

Ruth

Bring your children together and ask them if they know who their grandmothers are. Then ask if they know who their great-grandmothers are (or were). You may need to explain what a great-grandmother is. Share a story from when you were a child about one of your grandmothers (their great-grandmothers). One fun exercise is to share that their great-grandmother lived in a time before many familiar modern conveniences and inventions. If you have a photo of your grandmother, show it to them.

This week, you will learn about King David's great-grandmother. Her name was Ruth.

DAY ONE

Picture It

Think of the three most special things you own. Can you name them? Now imagine that while you are away visiting relatives a tornado whips through town and slams right into your house, destroying it. All three of your most special things are carried away and lost forever. How would you feel if that happened?

In our story today, we will read about a woman who lost the three most special things she had: her husband and her two sons. All three were killed, leaving only her son's wives.

 Read Ruth 1.

Think about It Some More

After Naomi's husband died, her two sons had to care and provide food for her. But after they both died there was no one to care for Naomi. Apart from God, Naomi lost the three most important things she had. Without her husband and two sons, she would be forced to beg in the streets. That is why she decided to go back home to Israel where at least she had a hope that someone from her own people would reach out with care.

Her daughters-in-law (her son's wives), Ruth and Orpah, had family they could go live with now that their husbands were dead. That is why Naomi told them to return to their families. But one of them, Ruth, loved Naomi so much she refused to leave. As part of Naomi's family, she had given up the false gods of the Moabites and wanted to make Naomi's God, the God of Israel, her God too.

Talk about It

:: Which of her daughters-in-law wanted to stay with Naomi, Orpah or Ruth? *(Ruth was the one who wanted to stay with her.)*

:: Reread what Naomi said in verses 8 and 9. What do we learn about Naomi's faith from these verses? *(Naomi trusted the Lord to care for Ruth and Orpah, showing that she had a strong faith.)*

:: What did Ruth do to show she trusted the Lord? *(She said Naomi's God would be her God.)*

:: Ruth learned about the true God from Naomi and her husband. Who are you learning about God from? *(Parents, take time to help your children see all the people who are helping them learn about the Lord, the one true God.)*

 Pray about It

Pray for each of the people in your life who are teaching you about God.

DAY TWO

Remember It

What do you remember about yesterday's story? What do you think is going to happen today?

 Read Ruth 2.

Think about It Some More

Often people say they got lucky when good things happen to them that they did not plan. If you and a friend are walking along on a hot day and you find a dollar on the ground, and then you pass a man who is selling drinks for a dollar, you might say to your friend, "This is my lucky day." Or if Mom dropped her fork in the trash can, only to find that her car keys had been accidentally thrown away, she might say, "It's a lucky thing I dropped my fork in the trash can so I could find my car keys."

But when you understand that God is in control of all things, you realize that there is no such thing as luck. All things happen exactly the way God planned them. It is much better for us to thank the Lord for his provision when we are blessed, rather than say we got lucky.

It wasn't luck that Ruth happened upon Naomi's relative Boaz's field—it was God who led Ruth there. And it was God who brought Boaz along at the very same time that Ruth was there. These things didn't happen by accident, chance, or luck; they were planned by God.

Talk about It

:: How did God use Boaz to care for Ruth? *(Boaz told his men not to chase Ruth away and to leave some of the barley in the field for Ruth to find. Then he also gave her lunch to eat.)*

:: Why do you think Boaz cared for Ruth? *(He heard all about her story and he also knew that Naomi was related to him, so he treated Ruth like family.)*

:: When Naomi heard that Ruth picked the barley from Boaz's field, she didn't say, "Wow, were we lucky!" Who did Naomi say took care of them? *(Naomi said it was by the Lord's kindness that these things happened this way [verse 20].)*

 ## Pray about It

Make a list of the things that people you know need; then ask God to provide for them.

DAY THREE

Connect It to Jesus

Can anyone guess how our story this week is about or points forward to Jesus?

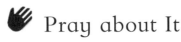 Read Ruth 3.

Think about It Some More

In yesterday's story, when Ruth returned from gleaning in Boaz's fields, Naomi told her that Boaz was one of their redeemers. Naomi knew that if a person's land was sold because he needed the money, God said that someone in the family should redeem it or buy it back for him. God also told Moses that if a woman in Israel lost her husband, one of her husband's brothers should marry her (Deuteronomy 25:5–6). Naomi wanted Boaz to redeem them and marry Ruth so they could be cared for again.

This picture of a redeemer is meant to point us to Jesus. The Bible tells us that Jesus is our Redeemer (Luke 1:68). By his death, he purchased our salvation so we could live with God in heaven. The Bible also tells us that Jesus is a bridegroom and all the people he saves are his bride.

Talk about It

:: What is a redeemer? *(A redeemer is a person who buys back something that is lost. In our story, a redeemer is a person who would buy back land that was sold because a family needed money.)*

:: Who did Naomi want to redeem them? *(Naomi wanted Boaz to be their redeemer.)*

:: Who is our redeemer? *(Jesus is our Redeemer.)*

:: How did Jesus redeem us? *(Jesus died on the cross to pay the penalty for our sin. Once the penalty was paid, all those who trust in Jesus get a home in heaven with God. Jesus bought us back with the blood he shed on the cross.)*

Pray about It

Praise God for redeeming us so we can live with the family of God in heaven and never have to be alone.

DAY FOUR

Remember It

What has God been teaching you this week through our Bible story?

 Read Ruth 4.

Think about It Some More

Boaz was not the first person in line to redeem Naomi and marry Ruth. There was another man who was a closer relative who first had to refuse to redeem them before Boaz could marry Ruth.

Boaz wanted to marry Ruth, so he reminded the other man that there would be a high cost to buy back their land and redeem them. He told him that if he didn't want to spend so much money, Boaz would gladly redeem them instead. The other man quickly agreed to allow Boaz to redeem Naomi and Ruth. On the spot, Boaz announced that he would buy Naomi's field and marry Ruth!

Talk about It

> ● ● KIDS, ask your parents if your mom was surprised when your dad
> ● ● asked her to marry him.

:: Why was Boaz glad to redeem Naomi and Ruth? *(In addition to it being the honorable thing to do, it seems that Boaz loved Ruth and wanted to make her his wife.)*

:: What did it cost Boaz to redeem Naomi and Ruth? *(He had to buy Naomi's land and pay for the wedding, and agree to take care of them for the rest of their lives.)*

:: What did it cost Jesus to redeem us? *(Jesus had to die on the cross to pay the penalty for our sins.)*

:: Why was Jesus glad to redeem us from our sins? *(The Bible tells us that God gave up his only Son Jesus to be our Redeemer because he loved us. Jesus shares in the Father's love for all of us. In fact, the Bible calls Jesus the bridegroom and us, his bride.)*

 ## Pray about It

Praise God for sending his Son Jesus, and ask God to help you to love the Lord with all of your heart.

DAY FIVE

Discover It

Today we look at a passage from a psalm or one of the prophets to see what we can learn from it about Jesus.

 Read Isaiah 54:5–7.

Think about It Some More

In this passage, Isaiah compared God's people in their sin to a woman who needed a redeemer. He encouraged Israel by saying that the Holy One of Israel would be their redeemer.

These words were written for us as well. God would send a redeemer for us, too. We know from reading the Bible that Jesus is the one Isaiah was talking about. Jesus was even called "the Holy One of God" during his ministry. So, long before Jesus was even born, Isaiah foretold a day when Jesus would come as the redeemer of God's people.

Talk about It

:: Who did Isaiah say would become the redeemer for God's people? *(Isaiah called him the Holy One of Israel.)*

:: *Read John 6:69.* Who does Peter say is the Holy One of Israel? *(Jesus is the Holy One of Israel.)*

:: How could Isaiah know that Jesus would become Israel's redeemer long before Jesus was even born? *(God spoke through the prophets. Since God knows everything, he could tell his prophets what was going to happen long before it took place.)*

 ## Pray about It

Praise God for the way he used the prophets to tell Israel about Jesus, long before he was even born.

Week 51

God Hears Hannah's Prayers

As parents, we often pray for our children, but sometimes we don't think of telling them about those prayers. Did you pray for your son or daughter before he or she was born? Perhaps you asked God for a safe delivery. Or perhaps you've prayed recently for your children that God would draw them to himself and save them.

Take time today to share with your children some of the prayers you've prayed for them. Perhaps you would also like to pray for your children at the beginning of your Bible study. Share your prayers with your children to encourage them. If you have multiple children, share about a different child each day. Say, "This week you will learn how God answered Hannah's prayers."

DAY ONE

Picture It

Imagine that you know a family that buys expensive birthday gifts for their children every year. The kids are always bragging that their birthday presents are better than yours. When you got a bike for your birthday, they said their bikes were faster. When you got a baseball glove, they showed you theirs, signed by professional baseball players, and said yours was a cheap one. How do you think you would feel when they made fun of the gifts you received?

In our Bible story, today a man named Elkanah has two wives. One of them makes fun of the other, which causes her to be very sad.

 Read 1 Samuel 1:1–11.

Think about It Some More

When someone is making fun of us there are two different paths we can take. One is to get angry and maybe say bad things back. The other path is to pray and ask God for help.

In today's story, Hannah prays. Instead of saying bad things about Peninnah, Hannah calls out to God, asking him to give her a son. Not only is God going to answer her prayers, but he will also use her son as a great prophet in Israel.

Talk about It

:: What do we learn about Elkanah and Hannah's relationship with God from this story? *(Both were faithful to God, as is shown from their trips to the temple, their sacrifices, and Hannah's prayers.)*

:: How did Hannah feel about not having children? *(This was very difficult for Hannah and she was sad. But God had a plan to bless her.)*

:: Can you think of a time when you didn't get something you wanted? How well did you do in that trial? *(Parents, most of our children don't go through huge trials, but sometimes a rained-out baseball game or a cancelled party can help us to see how much they want something.)*

 ## Pray about It

Ask God to help you respond like Hannah when you don't get what you want.

DAY TWO

Remember It

What do you remember about yesterday's story? What do you think is going to happen today?

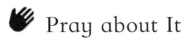 Read 1 Samuel 1:11–23.

Think about It Some More

God doesn't always give us what we want, even if we pray real hard for it. But in our story today, God answered Hannah's prayers and gave her a son. Hannah loved God and remembered her promise to give her son to God. So as soon as her son was finished nursing, she planned to take him back to Eli the priest to serve the Lord at the tabernacle.

Talk about It

:: Why did Eli think Hannah was drunk? *(He could see her mouth moving, but she wasn't actually saying anything; she was just mouthing the words.)*

:: Once Eli understood Hannah's problem he prayed for her. How did Eli's prayer affect Hannah? *(She was very encouraged that Eli the high priest prayed for her.)*

:: Name something that you could pray for and trust God to answer? *(Parents, help your children think of something to pray about. Perhaps you have an unsaved relative, or someone you know is having trouble conceiving a child. If so, lead your children to pray for them.)*

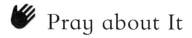 Pray about It

Pray for the requests mentioned in the last question.

DAY THREE

Connect It to Jesus

Can anyone guess how our story this week is about or points forward to Jesus?

 Read 1 Samuel 1:24—2:2.

Think about It Some More

Hannah keeps her promise to God and brings her young son to Eli the priest to serve the Lord at the tabernacle. After giving her son to Eli, she sings praise to God. Her song sounds a lot like the prayer Mary sings after learning that she is going to have the baby Jesus. Mary says, "My soul magnifies the Lord, and my spirit rejoices in God my Savior" (Luke 1:46–47).

Both Hannah and Mary see God as their Savior, and God gives special sons to each of them. Samuel grows up to be a great prophet and priest. God uses him to anoint David as king over Israel. Mary's son, Jesus, grows up to bring the salvation both women pray for. By dying on the cross, Jesus takes Hannah and Mary's sins away.

If we believe in and place our trust in Jesus, he will take away our sins too. Then we can sing a song that says God is our salvation, just like Hannah and Mary did.

Talk about It

:: How did Hannah keep her promise to God? *(Hannah gave her son Samuel to Eli to serve with him as a priest.)*

:: Who did Hannah honor in her wonderful prayer? *(Hannah honored the Lord in her prayer.)*

:: Why was Hannah willing to give her son to Eli? *(Hannah knew it was God who gave her a son and she knew Samuel belonged to the Lord, so she was excited to have him serve Eli. She could go and visit Samuel each year when they went to worship the Lord at the tabernacle.)*

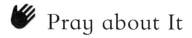 Pray about It

Ask God to help you trust him like Hannah did. Then ask him for the things someone you know needs.

DAY FOUR

Remember It

What has God been teaching you this week through our Bible story?

 Read 1 Samuel 2:12–21.

Think about It Some More

Even though Hannah gave up her son Samuel, the Lord blessed her with three more sons and two daughters. God also blessed Samuel, who served the Lord faithfully with Eli.

While Samuel grew stronger in his love for God, Eli's sons were wicked men. They didn't love the Lord and were stealing parts of the offering that did not belong to them. They were not afraid of the bad consequences that come to those who disobey God.

Talk about It

> KIDS, ask your parents to tell you their favorite part of this week's story.

(Parents, you could talk about God answering Hannah's prayer, or Hannah's faithfulness, or the way that she trusted God.)

:: How did God bless Hannah for giving up her son Samuel? *(God blessed Hannah with three more boys and two girls.)*

:: How was Samuel different from Eli's sons? *(Eli's sons did not love the Lord but Samuel did.)*

:: What do you think will happen to Eli's two sons? *(Parents, you can accept any answer. They will eventually be killed for their disobedience.)*

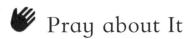 Pray about It

Ask God to help you trust in him like Samuel did.

DAY FIVE

Discover It

Today we look at a passage from a psalm or one of the prophets to see what we can learn from it about Jesus.

Read 1 Samuel 2:10 and Revelation 6:10.

Think about It Some More

The last part of Hannah's powerful prayer points forward to Jesus. Hannah spoke of an anointed king who will be used by God to judge the whole earth. That is exactly what God tells us Jesus will do on the Day of Judgment. On that day, Jesus will judge the secrets of all men's hearts (Romans 2:16). Hannah also called God's judge his king and his anointed. Both of these also point to Jesus.

Talk about It

:: Who was the last part of Hannah's prayer about? *(The last part of Hannah's prayer was about Jesus.)*

:: Whom did Hannah say the Lord would judge? *(Parents, you can reread verse 10 to give your children a clue. For younger children, use voice inflection to give away the answer.)*

:: Hannah said that the one who would judge the ends of the earth would also be a king. How does that point to Jesus? *(Jesus was a king. When he was crucified, a sign was attached to the cross naming him "the King of the Jews.")*

 Pray about It

Pray a prayer modeled after Hannah's. Think of the things that God says he will do in the Bible and put them together in a prayer. For instance, you could pray that God would save all his children, destroy sin, and live as King in heaven forever.

Week 52

God Calls Little Samuel

Call your children together and ask them if anyone has seen a pizza delivery guy come to the house. When they say no, repeat the question, saying you want to make sure they didn't see a pizza guy around. When they say no again, explain that you started feeling hungry for pizza an hour ago, so there must be a pizza guy coming with pizza. Tell them you think the pizza guy will come just because you want some pizza. Ask if they agree. Play along for a while, but then agree that the pizza guy would never deliver a pizza unless you ordered one.

Say, "That is the same with us. Unless God calls us, we would never come to him. This week we will learn how God took the initiative and called little Samuel."

DAY ONE

Picture It

There once was a family that lived next to an apple orchard. Every summer they watched beautiful apples grow from little green balls into big red apples. The owner of the orchard told them that they were free to collect any apples that fell to the ground, but he asked them not to pick any apples off the tree.

The boys of the house, Bob and Tom, didn't care about the rule. They didn't like the apples that fell to the ground, so they picked the best apples off the trees instead. Although their father often corrected them, he loved the taste of the sweet apples they brought home. The boys knew that if they brought some of the apples home to their dad, they wouldn't get into trouble. The dad scolded them, but because he ate the apples too, his poor example spoke louder than his words. In the end, he was just as guilty as his sons were for stealing the farmer's apples.

In today's story, we will read how Eli ate the meat his sons stole from God. Although he corrected them, his poor example spoke louder than his words.

 Read 1 Samuel 2:12–17, 27–36.

Think about It Some More

During the time when Samuel was a young boy serving the Lord, most of Israel was disobedient to God. Eli's sons, Hophni and Phinehas, didn't care about God and stole meat from the

Lord's sacrifices. The priests were permitted to have some of the meat for their families, but Eli's sons were taking the best parts of the meat before the sacrifice was even offered up to God. That meant they were stealing what belonged to God. And Eli ate it too.

Instead of punishing them on the spot, God was kind to Eli and his sons and first sent a prophet to warn them. The prophet told Eli that he was honoring his sons above God by eating the meat they were stealing.

Talk about It

:: How would you describe Hophni and Phinehas? *(Parents, draw out your children and have them describe in their own words that Eli's sons were wicked men who did not care about God.)*

:: What should Eli have done to correct his sons? *(Eli should have removed his sons from serving as the Lord's priests until they turned away from their sin.)*

:: Have you ever disobeyed one of God's commands? *(Help your children to see that they are sinners too. It is easy to look down on those who are sinning in the Bible stories that we read and not realize that we are sinners like they are.)*

 Pray about It

Confess your sins to God and ask him to forgive you.

DAY TWO

Remember It

What do you remember about yesterday's story? What do you think is going to happen today?

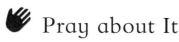 Read 1 Samuel 3:1–14.

Think about It Some More

Even though it was rare in those days for God to speak through a prophet, God sent one to Eli. But after hearing the Lord's warning, neither Eli nor his sons turned away from their sins. Eli didn't remove his sons from serving as the Lord's priests, which he should have done, and he said nothing about the meat they were stealing from God. So in our story today, the Lord called to young Samuel and gave him a second warning for Eli.

Talk about It

:: What do you think it would have been like to be Samuel when the Lord called him at night? *(Draw out your children here. Ask them if they would have been afraid, or confused. Remind them that we can still talk to God through our prayers.)*

:: Why do you think God warned Eli a second time? *(Eli didn't listen to God's first warning and discipline his sons.)*

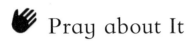

:: Did Eli still have time to repent of (turn away from) his sins? *(Yes, there is always time for us to stop sinning and ask God to forgive us, but we will see in this story that Eli never does.)*

:: Did you ever have a time when Mom or Dad had to give you more than one warning to turn away from your sins? *(Parents, remind your children of a time when you had to repeat a warning to them twice because they did not follow your correction.)*

 Pray about It

Ask God to help you turn away from your sin after the first warning from your parents.

DAY THREE

Connect It to Jesus

Can anyone guess how our story this week is about or points forward to Jesus?

Read 1 Samuel 2:35–36 and Hebrews 7:20–25.

Think about It Some More

The high priest in Israel was the man who offered sacrifices in the presence of God for the sins of the people. But we know from our story that Eli and his sons were not faithful priests. That means they were not careful to obey God.

When God sent the prophet to warn Eli, he said he was going to raise up a faithful high priest. That message was about Jesus. Jesus is the faithful high priest God raised up to replace the sinful high priests of Israel. Did you notice the prophet said the faithful high priest would serve as a priest forever? Jesus is the only one who fits that description. All the other high priests were normal men who died.

Jesus was a special high priest. He didn't offer animals to cover sins—he gave his own life as an offering to God. Now Jesus lives in heaven and the nail marks in his hands speak of his sacrifice to God the Father in heaven forever.

Talk about It

:: What does it mean to be faithful? *(To be faithful means that you do what you are supposed to do or what you promise to do, and you don't give up or quit.)*

:: Why is Jesus the only one who could be a faithful priest forever? *(All the other priests died. Even if they were faithful while they lived, and we know they all sinned in some way, they all died. Jesus is the only priest who never sinned and who lives forever.)*

:: What does a priest do? *(A priest offers sacrifices for the people to God so God will not punish them for their sins. Jesus offered up himself as a sacrifice. Now he stands before God always asking God to forgive us for our sins.)*

Pray about It

Thank Jesus for being our faithful high priest forever. Thank him for dying on the cross as our sacrifice.

DAY FOUR

Remember It

What has God been teaching you this week through our Bible story?

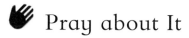 Read 1 Samuel 3:15–21.

Think about It Some More

The morning after God spoke to Samuel, Eli persuaded him to tell him everything. Even after hearing of God's coming judgment, Eli did not turn away from his sins. He could have confessed his sin and removed his sons from serving at the tabernacle. Instead, Eli gave up, did nothing, and waited for God's judgment to fall upon him.

God's word to Samuel came true: the iniquity (the sin) of Eli's house would never be atoned for (taken away and forgiven). Because Eli did not turn away from his sin, nor did he call out to God to save him, his sin would never be forgiven.

Talk about It

> ● ● KIDS, ask your parents what they would have done about their dis-
> ● ● obedient sons if they had been Eli.

(Parents, think of how you may have handled the situation better than Eli and then give your children some ideas of what Eli could have done, the least of which was remove his sons from serving God in the temple.)

:: How are we all like Eli? *(We are all sinners who need to call out to God to forgive us for our sins.)*

:: What happens to us if we refuse to turn away from our sin? *(Like Eli, if we don't turn away from our sin and call out to God to save us, we will be lost forever.)*

:: How can we be saved from our sin? *(We need to call out to God to save us. Jesus died on the cross to take the punishment of everyone who would trust in him. If we believe that Jesus died on the cross for our sins, we can call out to God and ask him to forgive us and help us to turn away from our sin.)*

 Pray about It

Pray for any friends and relatives who you know are not following God, and ask God to change their hearts.

DAY FIVE

Discover It

Today we look at a passage from a psalm or one of the prophets to see what we can learn from it about Jesus.

 Read Psalm 94:1–4 and Acts 17:30–31.

Think about It Some More

Many Old Testament passages, such as Psalm 94, speak of God as a judge over the wickedness of man. In the New Testament, we learn that Jesus is the judge that these Old Testament Scriptures are pointing forward to. That means that Eli and his two wicked sons Hophni and Phinehas will stand before Jesus on the final day of judgment.

In fact, we will all stand before Jesus on that day. The Bible tells us that he will separate all those who believed in God's plan and called out for forgiveness, from all those who rejected God and did not call out to him. Each time we read a psalm that talks about God as a judge, we should remember that we are all sinners who deserve to be judged.

But there is good news for everyone who believes in Jesus! The good news is that Jesus stood in our place and took the punishment for everyone who calls on him to be saved.

Talk about It

:: What does a judge do? *(A judge decides if a person is guilty or innocent of doing something wrong.)*

:: Who is the judge described in this psalm? *(Jesus is the judge. Whenever we read in the Bible about someone who will judge the earth, it is referring—at least indirectly—to Jesus.)*

:: Are we guilty of doing something wrong? *(Yes, we are all guilty of sinning against God. Parents remind your children that God said they should obey their parents in everything [Colossians 3:20]. If we have disobeyed our parents, even one time, we are guilty of sinning against God.)*

:: How can we escape God's judgment? *(We can escape God's judgment if we trust in Jesus and what he did on the cross. Jesus died to take our sin upon himself and trade it for his sinless life. If we trust in Jesus he will make that trade with us, and when judgment day comes we will have Jesus' righteousness instead of our sins.)*

 Pray about It

Praise God that he has made a way for us to escape his punishment so we can live in heaven with him.

Week 53

The God of Israel Cannot Be Captured

Look for a smooth rock or a small piece of scrap lumber. Using a permanent marker, draw a face on it. Tell your children that you are doing an experiment to see if you can make it talk. Explain that to do this you have drawn a face on the rock, giving it a mouth. Take a vote to see how many believe it can talk. They will, of course, all say it cannot talk.

Remind them that people made idols out of wood and stone and then worshiped them as gods even though they could not talk, could not hear, and had no power. But we serve a God who speaks to us through his Word, listens to our prayers, and is powerful enough to save us from our sin!

Say, "This week you will learn how our living God is more powerful than idols."

DAY ONE

Picture It

A young boy was going away to camp for the very first time. He brought a tent, a sleeping bag, extra clothes, food, a flashlight, and a number of other items. By the time he finished setting up his tent, it was already getting dark. It was a long walk to the bath house and he was a little afraid of the dark, so he double-checked to make sure his flashlight was in his backpack.

By the time he had stowed his belongings in the tent, it was time for the flashlight. He pulled it out of his backpack. But as he took a step away from his tent in the darkness and turned on the flashlight, nothing happened. He'd forgotten the batteries. Without batteries, the flashlight had no power.

Today in our story, Israel is going to find out that God's ark (not Noah's boat, but the box the Israelites carried through the wilderness) had no power apart from God's presence, just as the flashlight wouldn't work without batteries.

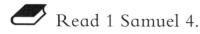 Read 1 Samuel 4.

Think about It Some More

The Israelites made a big mistake. They thought the ark could help them win a war without God. The ark was only a fancy wooden box that had no power by itself. God, not the ark, was the power of Israel. It is true that God's presence and his power did rest on the ark; that is why God told the people not to touch the ark and why they had to carry the ark with long poles. But this time, the Israelites used the ark like it was a god or a good luck charm.

They found out soon enough that the ark could not save them in battle without the power of God. In the end, Israel lost thousands and thousands of men—along with Hophni, Phinehas, and Eli. It all happened just as God had told Samuel it would.

Talk about It

:: What big mistake did Israel make going to war? *(They did not ask God to help them win the battle. Instead, they took the ark, thinking that all by itself it would help them win.)*

:: Why were the Philistines afraid? *(They had heard what God did to the Egyptians and were worried that they would lose the battle.)*

:: Who did not go to battle with Israel? *(God did not go to battle with Israel. That is why they lost.)*

:: What can we learn from Israel's mistake? *(We need God to help us in everything that we do. We can't assume God will help us—we need to ask him.)*

 ## Pray about It

Thank the Lord for the ways that he helps your family, and ask God to be with you in the challenges you will face today.

DAY TWO

Remember It

What do you remember about yesterday's story? What do you think is going to happen today?

 Read 1 Samuel 5.

Think about It Some More

The Philistines made a big mistake capturing the ark of God. They treated it like a false idol and placed it alongside the statue of Dagon in their temple. When they returned the next day and found their idol of Dagon on the floor, they probably thought it was an accident. But when they came in the following day, they must have been shocked to see their god Dagon on the floor again, with his hands and face broken off. Then when large lumps (called tumors) began to grow on the Philistines' bodies, they really began to fear that the ark was the cause of their problems.

Talk about It

:: Why didn't Dagon fight back when the Lord knocked him down? *(Dagon was not a real god. Our God is the only real God. There are no other gods. Dagon was only a statue made by man.)*

:: Why did God knock Dagon down and break off his arms and legs? *(God was showing the Philistines that Dagon was a fake and he alone was God. Read Psalm 115:4–8 for God's description of pagan idols.)*

:: Why did God punish the Philistines with tumors? *(God was keeping his promise to Abraham. God told Abraham that he would make him into a great nation, and he would bless anyone who blessed Israel and curse anyone who cursed Israel.)*

 Pray about It

Praise the Lord, for he is the one true God; all other gods are idols.

DAY THREE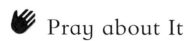

Connect It to Jesus

Normally we connect our story to Jesus today, but we are going to save that for tomorrow's reading.

Read 1 Samuel 6:1–16.

Think about It Some More

Even though the Philistines thought God was punishing them, they wanted to be sure, so they set up a test with a couple of milk cows and a cart.

The Philistines knew that if you take a cow away from its newborn calf and hitch it up to a wagon, it will turn around and go back to its baby and carry the wagon along with it. So the Philistines thought that if the ark, which they set on a cart hitched up with milk cows, went back to the barn, they would be okay. But in our story, after the Philistines hitched up two milk cows to the wagon, they left their calves and took the wagon straight back to Israel.

When the wagon reached Israel, the men of Israel who saw it celebrated by offering a sacrifice to God for bringing the ark back home.

Talk about It

:: Why did the Philistines use cows with baby calves instead of oxen to pull the cart? *(The Philistines were setting up a test. If the cows turned around, left their calves, and went to Israel, the Philistines would know the God of Israel was against them.)*

:: Who controlled where the cows would take the ark? *(God controlled the cows. They never once turned to the left or the right, but walked straight home to Israel.)*

:: Why were the people so excited to see the ark back in Israel? *(The ark was where God's presence rested. When the people saw the ark they would have understood that God was returning to Israel.)*

 Pray about It

Thank God for returning to Israel and keeping his promises even though the Israelites sinned against him.

DAY FOUR

Remember It

What has God been teaching you this week through our Bible story?

 Read 1 Samuel 7:1–11.

Think about It Some More

We waited until today to connect our story to Jesus because of the lamb Samuel offered up to the Lord as a sacrifice. Samuel's offering of the lamb was a picture of Jesus, the Lamb of God, who died on the cross to save us from our sins.

While Samuel was doing this, the Philistines were marching against Israel to attack. But because Israel confessed their sins and offered up a lamb, God remembered his promises to Israel and turned against the Philistines and defeated them.

Every time we see a lamb sacrificed for sinners in the Bible, it should remind us of God's plan to send Jesus to die on the cross in our place.

Talk about It

> ● ● KIDS, ask your parents to tell you something they have given up to
> ● ● serve and follow the Lord.

(Parents, we give up a lot to follow the Lord. We don't do what we want without considering whether it is pleasing to God. For example, you might like to keep all the money you make for yourself, but instead you give some of your money to the church.)

:: What did Samuel say the people of Israel needed to do? *(Samuel told them to get rid of their idols and serve God alone.)*

:: Did Israel try to fight the Philistines alone, or did they ask for God's help? *(They asked for God's help.)*

:: Who was the lamb that Samuel offered up meant to remind us of? *(The lamb is supposed to remind us of Jesus who died so we could be saved from our sins.)*

 Pray about It

Ask God to help you love him more than anything else in your life.

DAY FIVE

Discover It

Today we look at a passage from a psalm or one of the prophets to see what we can learn from it about Jesus.

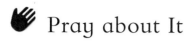 Read Isaiah 52:10 and Luke 2:25–32.

Think about It Some More

In our story this week, the Philistines were afraid of the God of Israel because they heard how he saved Israel from the Egyptians (1 Samuel 6:6). In the passage we read today, Isaiah told Israel that a day was coming when the whole earth would see God's salvation.

It was Jesus who brought the salvation Isaiah spoke about. When Mary and Joseph brought Jesus into the temple as a small baby for his dedication, they met an older man named Simeon. Simeon recognized Jesus as the Savior of the world, and he announced that the salvation Isaiah foretold was going to come through their little baby.

Talk about It

:: Who was Isaiah talking about in this passage? *(Isaiah was talking about Jesus.)*

:: How was God going to save his people through Jesus? *(Jesus died on the cross to take our sins away so we could be saved from the punishment we deserve.)*

:: What did Simeon say about Jesus? *(If your children can't remember, have them reread Luke 2:25–32; or if you have younger children, you can read it again. Simeon took the baby in his arms and said he saw God's salvation. God showed Simeon his salvation, which one day will be seen by all.)*

 Pray about It

Tell God how different things in the world can't save us. For instance you could pray, "God I know money cannot save me. I know I can't work my way to heaven." Then thank God that he gave you Jesus, our salvation.

Week 54

Israel Demands a King

Prior to your Bible study this week, purchase for your children a selection of small treats—things you would not normally have. Hide the treats around your home in places where a set of lost keys might be found. Put your keys in your pocket.

Then call your children together and ask them to help you look for your keys. As they look around they will find the treats. Have them place the treats in a pile and keep on looking. At some point, pull your keys out of your pocket and say that you found them, that they were in your pocket the whole time.

Explain that you wanted them to find the treats, not the keys. Say, "This week you will learn how Saul went on a search for donkeys, but God intended him to find the prophet Samuel instead."

DAY ONE

Picture It

A young boy received a plastic model car kit for his birthday. There were thousands of little pieces that had to be glued together, so the boy's mom suggested he wait for his dad to help.

At first the little boy was happy to wait, but when he thought about his friends and all the cars they displayed on their bedroom dressers, he longed to have one for his dresser. Knowing how much fun it would be to glue the parts together, he begged his mom to allow him to do it himself. His mom warned that he could make a mistake that would be difficult to fix, but the little boy insisted, so his mom gave him the car.

Sure enough, as his mom predicted, the boy soon ran into trouble. He got glue on the wheels, which kept them from turning and then put a big glue fingerprint on the front windshield that would not come off. The boy was sad that he didn't listen to his mother's warning.

In our story today, God warned Israel against choosing a king, but they didn't listen either.

 Read 1 Samuel 8.

Think about It Some More

Young Samuel, who grew up with Eli at the tabernacle, is now an old man. Under Samuel's rule as a judge over Israel, God has defeated the Philistines and restored peace to Israel. When

Samuel grew old, his sons took over as leaders, but they did not do a good job and the people of Israel were angry. They longed to have a king like the other nations around them. So they asked Samuel to give them a king.

Samuel was upset with their request and warned them that a king would force them to work and would take their money away. He knew that God was their king and warned them against choosing another, but they demanded a king who would fight their battles. This was very sad because God had always fought their battles and cared for them. By asking for a king, they were rejecting God.

Talk about It

:: Why did the people of Israel want a king? *(They wanted a king so they could be like the other nations around them. Instead of God, they wanted a king they could see lead them out into battle.)*

:: By asking for a king to lead them, who was Israel rejecting? *(They were rejecting God who had led them into battle.)*

:: What are some of the things Samuel warned them a king would do? *(Parents, if your children don't remember, read through the list in verses 11–18.)*

:: Can you think of a time when you didn't listen to your parents' warning? *(Parents, try to help your children remember a time when you warned them but they did not listen. Perhaps you warned them not to wear their good shoes outside and they got them muddy. Or you warned them to put their toys away, but they didn't and someone stepped on one and broke it.)*

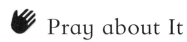 Pray about It

Praise God for all he has done for you and your family.

DAY TWO

Remember It

What do you remember about yesterday's story? What do you think is going to happen today?

 Read 1 Samuel 9.

Think about It Some More

The story about Saul and his donkeys shows us the wonderful providence of God. *Providence* is a big word that means that God controls all things and makes them work according to his plan. Nothing happens by accident. Every bird that lands on the ground, every star twinkling in the sky, and every hair on your head is placed exactly where God wants it to be.

God is like a great orchestra conductor directing the musicians in a concert hall. Even though the musicians are each able to play on their own, they all follow the waving baton of the conductor to create beautiful music. That is how God directs everything in our lives. So when Saul's father lost his donkeys, it didn't happen by accident—it was directed by the providence of God, as a part of his plan, to lead Saul to Samuel.

Talk about It

:: Describe what God's providence means. *(Parents, you may need to help your children through repeating a definition. God's providence is his control over every part of creation, moving them according to his plan.)*

:: Where do you see God's providence in our story today? *(God wanted the donkeys to be lost and not found right away. God wanted Samuel to be at just the right spot. God worked it out so that they had silver for a gift to give to Samuel, even though they didn't originally have plans to visit him, etc.)*

:: Where do you see God's providence at work in your family? *(This is a fun exercise. The makeup of your family, the address where you live, the color of your eyes, and the church you are a part of are all governed by the providence of God.)*

 ## Pray about It

Thank and praise God for his providence (for how he controls all things and makes them work according to his plan).

DAY THREE

Connect It to Jesus

Can anyone guess how our story this week is about or points forward to Jesus?

 Read 1 Samuel 10:1–8.

Think about It Some More

When the prophets of God anointed a man to be king, they poured oil on him. The oil was a symbol that God's blessing, his favor, and his Spirit were upon him. Anytime a man is anointed to be God's king in the Scriptures, it points forward to Jesus who is called "God's Anointed" (Acts 4:26).

Even though Israel was rejecting God and wanted a king for the wrong reasons, God could still work that for good. Later we will see that God used their new king, Saul, to defeat the Philistines and save his people.

Talk about It

:: What does it mean to anoint someone? *(When you anoint someone you pour or rub oil on them. God did this to show whom he chose to be king, and to show that God's presence would be on that person like the oil was on them.)*

:: Who is called "God's Anointed"? *(Jesus is God's Anointed.)*

:: How is God's providence at work in our story today? *(Even though Israel sinned by asking for a king, God used their new king to defeat the enemies of Israel.)*

 Pray about It

Praise God for his powerful control over everything, even our sin. He is able to make all things work just as he planned.

DAY FOUR

Remember It

What has God been teaching you this week through our Bible story?

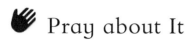 Read 1 Samuel 10:17–27.

Think about It Some More

Once again our story shows us the providence of God at work. Did you notice how God controlled the casting of lots so that Saul was the man chosen? Although it looked like it happened by chance, God is so powerful that he controls everything, even the casting of lots.

Talk about It

> ● ● KIDS, ask your parents if they have a story of how God's providence
> ● ● worked in their lives.

(Parents, often the circumstances surrounding how you met your spouse can be a great example of God's providence because God used it to bring your son or daughter into your family.)

:: Where do you see God's providence at work in our story today? *(Have your children explain how God controlled the casting of lots so Saul was the one man chosen out of all the men in Israel.)*

:: We don't cast lots to guide our choices today. What do we use? *(We use the Bible to help guide our choices today. God's Word contains everything we need to make wise decisions that honor God.)*

 Pray about It

Thank God for giving us his Word to guide us every day.

DAY FIVE

Discover It

Today we look at a passage from a psalm or one of the prophets to see what we can learn from it about Jesus.

 Read Daniel 9:24–26.

Think about It Some More

This passage in the Bible sounds like a big riddle when you first read it. But if you look for a few key words, you can figure out that it is talking about Jesus.

First, it tells us about a time when sin will come to an end. Second, it speaks of a day when righteousness (goodness) will last forever. Finally, Daniel tells us about a prince who will come in that day and rebuild Jerusalem (God's city where his people live). The prince will be anointed, which means he is picked by God to do God's work.

Jesus is the only one who fits this description. He is "the Anointed One" who can rebuild God's city, do away with sin, and bring righteousness that will last forever.

Talk about It

:: How is this passage about Jesus, "the Anointed One," like Saul from our story this week? *(Saul was anointed by God to be king over Israel, and Jesus was anointed by God to be king over Israel. That is why Jesus is called "the Anointed One" in this passage.)*

:: What did Jesus do to put an end to sin? *(Jesus died for our sins on the cross so we could be forgiven. One day Jesus will come again and put an end to all sin. He will judge the wicked and take all those who trust in him to heaven.)*

:: Daniel 9:26 says that the anointed one is "cut off." How was Jesus cut off? *(When Jesus was on the cross, God the Father turned away from his Son and gave him our punishment.)*

 Pray about It

Thank Jesus for allowing himself to be cut off from his Father in heaven when he took our punishment on the cross.

Week 55

Saul Disobeys the Lord

Ask your children if they will give you their opinion about a change you would like to make in a recipe for French toast. Explain that the directions say to mix four eggs with a cup of milk, but you were thinking of mixing the eggs with orange juice or, perhaps, vinegar instead of milk, and doing it your own way.

Draw them out as to why that would be a bad idea. Then tell them that the directions say to mix in a teaspoon of cinnamon, but you were thinking that chili powder or mustard might work just as well. When they object, ask them why it is important to follow directions.

Say, "There are often bad consequences when we disobey directions. There are also bad consequences when we disobey God. This week you will hear how King Saul disobeyed the clear instructions of the Lord and what the consequences were."

DAY ONE

Picture It

Termites love to eat wood. If they get into the walls of your house, they can turn your house into sawdust. It is important, if termites come into your home, that you kill them all, especially the queen. If you don't get them all, they will multiply again and continue eating away at your house.

In today's story, the enemies of Israel are a lot like the termites. That is why God tells Israel to completely wipe them out.

 Read 1 Samuel 15:1–3.

Think about It Some More

The king of Amalek and his people, the Amalekites, were idol-worshipers who rejected the one true God of Israel. They also attacked Israel when they were escaping from Egypt. That is why God gave Saul very specific instructions to attack them and completely wipe them out. God knew that if Saul didn't destroy them all, they would rise up again to come against his people and lead Israel astray with their idolatry.

When we read that God said all the Amalekites should die, we might think his judgment was too terrible. But God is holy (that means God doesn't have any sin at all) and because of his holiness he must punish sin. We all deserve the same punishment he gave the Amalekites, but God sent his Son Jesus to take that punishment for everyone who trusts in him. The Amalekites rejected God's plan and followed idols instead—that is why they were judged.

Talk about It

:: Why does God bring his punishment upon people? *(Since God is holy he must punish sin and evil. God brings his punishment on all those who sin against him.)*

:: Since we are all sinners, why don't we all get God's punishment? *(God sent his Son Jesus to die on the cross and take the punishment of everyone who places their hope and trust in him.)*

:: What did God tell Saul to do with the animals of the Amalekites? *(He was supposed to destroy all the animals, but he disobeyed.)*

 Pray about It

Thank God for sending Jesus so we could escape the punishment we deserve for our sins.

DAY TWO

Remember It

What do you remember about yesterday's story? What do you think is going to happen today?

 Read 1 Samuel 15:4–12.

Think about It Some More

When I tell you to clean your room and pick up everything off the floor, should you obey me or shove half of your stuff under your bed where I can't see it?

Of course we know that it is not a good thing to shove your stuff under your bed, but sometimes we do what we want instead of obeying. When I say "pick up everything," I don't mean for you to push half of it aside.

When God told Saul to destroy everything, he meant everything. By sparing the king of Amalek and not killing all the animals, Saul and his men were disobeying God's command. Even worse, Saul set up a monument to himself; he was supposed to give glory to God, but he kept the glory for himself.

Talk about It

:: How did Saul disobey? *(He didn't kill the king of the Amalekites, nor did he kill all the animals. Also, he set up a monument to himself.)*

:: Why did Saul and the soldiers of Israel keep some of the animals alive? *(They kept the best of the animals for themselves. They killed only the weak ones. The animals would be useful for food, clothing, or sacrifice.)*

:: Can you think of a time when you disobeyed God? *(Parents, help your children remember a time when they disobeyed God by disobeying you.)*

 ## Pray about It

Ask God to help you to obey his commands every day.

DAY THREE

Connect It to Jesus

Can anyone guess how our story this week is about or points forward to Jesus?

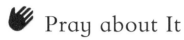 Read 1 Samuel 15:13–23.

Think about It Some More

King Saul failed to follow God's command. God told him to destroy all the animals, but Saul said that he and the men thought they would keep the animals and offer them as a sacrifice to the Lord. It could be that they just wanted to keep them for themselves. On top of that, Saul lied and said he had obeyed God's command when he really hadn't.

When Samuel heard the bleating of the captured animals, he knew Saul had disobeyed God. He corrected Saul, telling him that God had rejected him as king. God had anointed Saul as king; however, Saul disobeyed God, failing to deliver his people from their enemies.

When Jesus came as the King of Israel, he did what Saul could not do. Jesus obeyed God the Father perfectly. Then Jesus died on the cross so that our sins could be forgiven.

Talk about It

:: How did Samuel know Saul had sinned? *(Even before he heard the bleating of the sheep, God told Samuel that Saul had disobeyed.)*

:: What did God say was better than offering sacrifices? *(God said that obedience was better than offering sacrifices.)*

:: What was Saul's punishment? *(God rejected Saul as king.)*

:: Who did God raise up as a king who followed all the Lord's commands? *(God the Father raised up Jesus as King. Jesus followed all of God's commands and never sinned.)*

Pray about It

Think of ways that you have not followed God's commands, and ask God to forgive you and help you to obey.

DAY FOUR

Remember It

What has God been teaching you this week through our Bible story?

 Read 1 Samuel 15:24–35.

Think about It Some More

Saul did not tell the truth and confess his sin until after Samuel said God had rejected him as king. Only then did Saul admit that he kept the animals because he was afraid to tell the people no. The Bible tells us that the fear of man (fearing what people think of us) can capture us (Proverbs 29:25).

Instead of thinking about what God wanted and what God thought of him, Saul thought more about what the people wanted and what they thought about him. Saul wanted the people to like him, to think he was a great king. That is why he built a monument to himself. Because he didn't obey God, God was going to give the kingdom to someone else.

Talk about It

> KIDS, ask your parents if they ever struggled with the fear of man.

(Parents, think of an example of the fear of man. Sometimes we are afraid to share the gospel because we are afraid of what people will think. Sometimes we might join in a sinful discussion because we don't want to be seen as the "religious one.")

:: Are there any areas in your life where you struggle with the fear of man? *(Parents, now turn the discussion to your children. See if you can help them think of ways they fear the opinions of others. Perhaps they are afraid to be expressive in worship because they are afraid of being made fun of. Or perhaps they are afraid to walk away when their friends engage in sinful behavior.)*

:: Who are we supposed to fear instead of fearing man? *(We are supposed to fear God. That doesn't mean we run away from God like we would run away if a bear was chasing us. It means that we fear God's judgment and holiness, which helps us obey and not sin against God.)*

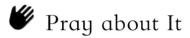 Pray about It

Ask God to help you to fear God and obey his commands.

DAY FIVE

Discover It

Today we look at a passage from a psalm or one of the prophets to see what we can learn from it about Jesus.

 Read Isaiah 28:14–16 and 1 Peter 2:5–9.

Think about It Some More

In this prophecy, Isaiah corrects Israel's leaders. Instead of trusting God, they have made a bargain with Egypt to help them. Fearing that the Assyrian army was going to attack them, they called out to Egypt for help. They forgot that God is the best help in a time of trouble. Isaiah corrects Israel and warns them by saying they had made lies their refuge instead of God.

Hidden in Isaiah's correction is a message of hope that points forward to Jesus. Remember that we said the word *cornerstone* is one of our code words for Jesus. Later in the Bible, Peter confirms that Isaiah is talking about Jesus.

Talk about It

:: What is a cornerstone? *(A cornerstone is the first stone laid in a wall, which all the other stones line up with. If it is placed correctly and all the other stones line up with it, the whole foundation will be built correctly.)*

:: Who is the cornerstone that Isaiah is talking about? *(Jesus is the cornerstone that Isaiah is talking about.)*

:: What can we do to become a part of the house that Jesus is building? *(According to both Isaiah and Peter, we must believe. We get connected as a stone in God's house when we place our faith in the cornerstone.)*

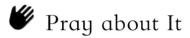 Pray about It

Ask God to help the people you know to place their trust in Jesus.

Week 56

God Chooses a New King

Fold up a twenty-dollar bill as small as possible and wrap it up with a scrap of gift wrap. Keep the small package hidden.

Ask your children to imagine that they invite two friends over for a birthday party and both friends bring gifts. The first friend brings a present so large it can barely fit through the door. The second friend brings a very tiny present. (At this point, pull out your tiny present and show them.) What present do your children think they would be most excited about?

Tell them that the big present was filled with happy birthday balloons. The little present, even though it was small, was very special. (Open the gift to reveal the money.) Explain that we can't tell what is inside a present by the way it looks on the outside.

Say, "This week you will learn that man looks on the outside, but God looks at the heart."

DAY ONE

Picture It

A father took his young daughter to the zoo for her birthday. First, they went into the reptile house. Though she didn't like snakes, she could see they were held securely behind thick glass so she wasn't afraid. Next, they saw a peacock that ran across the path. Although it wasn't in a cage, the little girl knew that peacocks were gentle so she wasn't afraid.

But before she got to the next display, she heard the deafening roar of a lion. When she got closer and saw that there were no bars on the lion's cage, she became afraid. She told her father that the lions were so strong they could swim across the water, climb the high wall, get out, and eat them both. But her father assured her that no harm would come to her. He held her hand and brought her closer to the lions. She was afraid, but she trusted her dad and walked up safely to see the lions.

In our story today, you will see how, although Samuel is afraid of Saul, he trusts God.

 Read 1 Samuel 16:1–3.

Think about It Some More

Samuel was not excited when God told him to anoint one of Jesse's sons as the new king—because Saul, the previous king, was still alive. If Saul found out what Samuel was doing he would be very angry.

Samuel had to give bad news to Saul once before—God was going to rip the kingdom away from Saul. In most countries, if you are part of a plan to overthrow the president or king and you get caught, the punishment is death. No wonder Samuel was afraid.

Talk about It

:: Why was Samuel afraid to anoint a new king? *(He was afraid that if Saul found out, he would be killed.)*

:: Why didn't Samuel need to be afraid? *(Samuel did not need to be afraid of Saul because God was the one telling him to go. Samuel could trust God.)*

:: Who were Jesse's grandparents? *(Parents, you can give your children clues to lead them to remember that Boaz married Ruth and had a son named Obed, who was Jesse's father. So Boaz and Ruth were Jesse's grandparents. It is interesting to note how God works his plan all together for good.)*

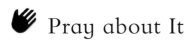 Pray about It

Thank God for the wonderful way he works all things together in his plan to save us.

DAY TWO

Remember It

What do you remember about yesterday's story? What do you think is going to happen today?

 Read 1 Samuel 16:4–10.

Think about It Some More

In our activity this week, we learned that a small present could be more valuable than a large one. It just depends on what is inside. A diamond ring, for example, is very small and could be wrapped in a tiny package, but would still be very valuable. Although a stuffed animal toy would take a much bigger box, it doesn't cost as much.

When Samuel went to anoint a new king for God, he was thinking that the Lord was going to choose a person who was tall and strong on the outside—like Saul. That was why Samuel thought Eliab, Jesse's oldest son, would be king. But God wasn't looking at the outside; God was looking at the heart of a man. He wanted a king who would obey him.

Talk about It

:: Why did Samuel think Eliab was the one God chose to be king? *(Eliab was the oldest son, and apparently he was tall and impressive looking.)*

:: What is more important than outward appearance? *(The heart is more important than outward appearance. When we talk about "the heart," we mean our loves and passions, the things that motivate us. God wanted a king who loved God and would follow him and obey his commands.)*

:: Which should we be more concerned about, our outward appearance or our heart for God? *(We should be more concerned about our heart for God.)*

 ## Pray about It

Ask God to help you to be more concerned about what is in your heart than what you look like on the outside.

DAY THREE

Connect It to Jesus

Can anyone guess how our story this week is about or points forward to Jesus?

 Read 1 Samuel 16:11–13.

Think about It Some More

Once God told Samuel not to look at the outward appearance of a person, Samuel looked more carefully at Jesse's sons. One by one they were brought before Samuel, but Samuel refused them all, for none of them had a heart for God. When all had passed, Samuel was confused and asked if Jesse had any more sons. Jesse answered that only one son remained, the youngest son, who had been left behind to tend the sheep.

David was young, but he loved God. So Samuel anointed David as the next king of Israel and the Spirit of God came upon him. David became the first king in a line of kings that led all the way to King Jesus. Jesus became the last King in David's line because he sits upon the throne of David forever in heaven.

Talk about It

:: Why wasn't David invited to the sacrifice? *(It's as God told Samuel: man looks at the outward appearance. David's father had left him behind because he was the youngest and smallest. He didn't think David was important enough to bring. By choosing the youngest, God shows us again that it is not man's power, but God's power that brings the victory.)*

:: What are some ways David was like Jesus? *(David was chosen by God as a king to lead his people Israel. David and Jesus are in the same family. David was a shepherd; Jesus is called the Good Shepherd of God's people.)*

:: What did God give David to help him from the day he was chosen? *(God gave David his Holy Spirit to be with him.)*

Pray about It

Ask God to save you from your sin and fill you with his Holy Spirit.

DAY FOUR

Remember It

What has God been teaching you this week through our Bible story?

 Read 1 Samuel 16:14–23.

Think about It Some More

Yesterday we read how God's Spirit rushed upon David. Today we discover that God's Spirit left Saul and an evil spirit began to bother him. One of Saul's servants suggested he find a skillful musician to play for him. David, Jesse's son, was recommended. When David played his songs on the harp, the evil spirit left Saul.

You may not know that many of the words to David's songs have been saved for us to read. We don't have the music, but we still have the words. They are written down in the book of Psalms. Some of the psalms even tell us they were to be sung with stringed instruments playing. One of them, Psalm 61, starts out like this. *Read Psalm 61:1–4.*

Talk about It

> KIDS, ask your parents if they have a favorite psalm.

(Parents, share your favorite psalm with your children. If you can't think of one, consider sharing Psalm 23. It is one of the most familiar psalms and we will be reading it in a later lesson.)

:: What happened when David played music for king Saul? *(When David sang for Saul and played his instruments, the evil spirit left the king and he felt better.)*

:: What special role did Saul give David? *(Saul made David his armorbearer—David helped Saul put his armor on.)*

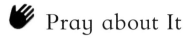 Pray about It

Thank God for saving the words to David's songs for us to enjoy today.

DAY FIVE

Discover It

Today we look at a passage from a psalm or one of the prophets to see what we can learn from it about Jesus.

 Read Psalm 95:1–3.

Think about It Some More

Our Bible passage today is a part of one of the songs we talked about from the book of Psalms. We don't know if David wrote this one, because it doesn't say, but it sure sounds like one of his songs.

One of the lines says, "Make a joyful noise to the rock of our salvation." That leads to a question: Who is the rock of our salvation? If we are supposed to sing and shout loudly to the rock of our salvation, we need to know who this person is.

Peter tells us in 1 Peter 2:6–9 that the rock of our salvation is Jesus. Jesus saved us by dying on the cross for our sins. That should make us want to sing and shout loudly to him.

Talk about It

:: What does this psalm tell us we should do? *(We should make a joyful noise to Jesus, which means we should sing and shout to him.)*

:: How could a song like this have cheered King Saul? *(It could help him think about God instead of thinking about himself.)*

:: How can a song like this one cheer us up? *(Like Saul, this song can help us to look at God, not ourselves. We can be thankful and encouraged to read that we have a rock of salvation in God. And when we remember that the rock of our salvation is Jesus, we can celebrate all that Jesus did on the cross. When we realize that our sins are taken away, we experience true joy.)*

Pray about It

Praise God for Jesus, the rock of our salvation. If you know a song that talks about Jesus as the rock, sing it at the end of your Bible study.

Week 57

David and Goliath

Find a few pea-sized rocks and one larger rock. At the beginning of Bible study, hold up the larger rock and ask your children if they would be afraid if someone came after them with a large rock like the one you are holding. Then hold up a pea-sized rock and ask them if they would be afraid if someone came after them with a rock like that. They will likely think the smaller rock is nothing to be afraid of.

Ask for a volunteer to go and get a pair of their shoes. Place a few of the small rocks in their shoes and have them walk around. Even the smallest of rocks, if perfectly placed, can really hurt.

Say, "This week you will learn how the giant Goliath laughed at young David's small rocks. But he didn't laugh for long."

DAY ONE

Picture It

There was once a young boy who loved to go fishing in the stream down the hill from his home. Each day in the spring, when he finished his school work, he would run for his fishing pole and head out through the backyard. The stream flowed on the other side of a cow pasture behind his house. Crossing the cow pasture saved a lot of time since the farmer's land ran along the river for a mile. The cows never seemed to mind.

But one day the farmer replaced the cows in the river pasture with his prized riding bull. That day, when the boy walked up to the fence whistling away, the bull came charging to the sound. He stood in front of the boy, stomping his feet and snorting, as though looking for a fight.

The bull stood a good foot taller than the boy and weighed over 1,200 pounds. His legs were like iron and his head was hard like a rock. The boy had heard of the farmer's bull: he had bucked off the last thirty men who had tried to ride him. The only thing the boy could do was to take the long walk around the fence. Day after day the bull met the boy and refused to allow him to pass.

Today we will read about a Philistine man named Goliath, who stood against God's people and, like the bull in the story, dared them to come out to fight.

 Read 1 Samuel 17:1–10.

Think about It Some More

Goliath was over nine feet tall. That means he could dunk a basketball without jumping. The chainmail he wore on his chest was made of small steel rings linked together, so even if you got close enough to cut him with a sword, it would protect him. It weighed over one hundred pounds. The head of his spear weighed fifteen pounds. (If you want to see how heavy that is, make a stack of books on a bathroom scale until you reach 15 pounds, then lift the stack to see how heavy the head of his spear was.)

Like the bull confronted the boy in our story, Goliath confronted the Israelite army. Goliath dared any man to come forward and fight in the place of all Israel. If that one man lost, then all Israel would be defeated. If that one man won, then Israel would be saved and the Philistines would become their servants.

Talk about It

:: What was Goliath's challenge to the Israelite army? (*Goliath challenged Israel to send out one man to fight him.*)

:: What would happen if a man came out to fight Goliath and lost? (*The Israelite soldier who fought Goliath would fight as their representative. If he lost, all of Israel would lose with him. Parents, this is a great story to show how one man can stand in the place of a whole group of men. That is what Jesus did when he died on the cross for us. If he could defeat sin, then everyone who trusts in him would share in the victory.*)

:: Why did God allow Goliath to challenge his people? (*God wanted to show his people that if they trusted him, he would save them.*)

:: God brings all of us challenges to help us to learn to trust in him. What are some of the challenges you are facing? (*Parents, help your children see that doing their school work, obeying parents, and even keeping their rooms clean are all challenges in their lives that they need God's help to conquer.*)

 Pray about It

Thank God for bringing us challenges to teach us to trust in him.

DAY TWO

Remember It

What do you remember about yesterday's story? What do you think is going to happen today?

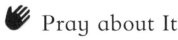 Read 1 Samuel 17:11–27.

Think about It Some More

You may remember learning in Week 54 that Israel originally wanted a king so he could fight their battles for them (1 Samuel 8:19–20). But here in our story, King Saul is just as afraid to confront Goliath as the rest of the men. Now that God's Spirit was removed from Saul, instead of fighting Goliath or leading the battle against the Philistines, he is back at his camp helpless to do anything.

But when David heard Goliath defy the army of Israel, he became angry and spoke against the giant.

Talk about It

:: What did the men do when Goliath came out to challenge them? *(They ran away in fear.)*

:: What about King Saul—what did he do when he heard Goliath? *(Saul was afraid too.)*

:: What do you think Saul should have done about Goliath? *(Saul should have prayed to the Lord and asked him to help him and his men fight Goliath. Saul should have led his men into battle.)*

:: What did David do when he heard the Philistine giant challenging Israel and making fun of them? *(David did not run, but spoke up for God and Israel.)*

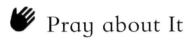 Pray about It

Ask God to help you trust him like David did.

DAY THREE

Connect It to Jesus

Can anyone guess how our story this week is about or points forward to Jesus?

 Read 1 Samuel 17:28–37.

Think about It Some More

Who are you most like in this story: Goliath, Saul and the men of Israel, or David? We all would like to think we are like David, but when trials come to us we can struggle to trust God—like the men of Israel did.

The truth is that we are more like the men of Israel than we realize. We all have a giant in our lives—sin. We can't conquer that giant by ourselves. Like Israel, we need a Savior who will fight and conquer our giant for us. David was the man God sent to save Israel from their enemy, Goliath; and Jesus is the man God sent to save us from our enemy, sin.

David offered to take up Goliath's challenge to come forward and represent Israel. If he won, Israel would win; if he lost, all of Israel would become servants of the Philistines. Like David, Jesus stood in our place. Now everyone who trusts in him shares in his victory over sin.

Talk about It

:: What did David say he would do about Goliath? *(He said that he would fight Goliath.)*

:: When Saul questioned David, who did David say would help him fight Goliath? *(David said that God would help him fight Goliath.)*

:: In this story, how is David like Jesus? *(David brought salvation to God's people, who were too weak to conquer their enemy on their own. That is exactly our condition. Jesus came to conquer our enemies, sin and death, because we cannot conquer them ourselves.)*

 ## Pray about It

Thank Jesus for winning the battle over sin and death for us by dying on the cross and rising again from the dead.

DAY FOUR

Remember It

What has God been teaching you this week through our Bible story?

 Read 1 Samuel 17:38–58.

Think about It Some More

If you remember, God corrected Samuel when he chose Jesse's oldest son as the next king. God told Samuel that man looks at the outward appearance, but God looks at the heart. Then God chose David, the youngest of Jesse's sons.

Goliath made the same mistake Samuel made when he saw David. He looked at the outward appearance. All he saw was a young boy with no armor and no sword, coming out to fight. What Goliath didn't know was that David had a heart for God and was trusting the all-powerful God of the universe to go with him. So, filled with faith, David rushed Goliath and brought down the giant with one small stone.

Talk about It

> ● ● KIDS, ask your parents if they can remember a time when they
> ● ● trusted God to help them.

(Parents, think of a time when you were facing a challenge and God helped you.)

:: Why wasn't Goliath afraid of David? *(He didn't believe in the God of Israel and didn't realize that God was helping David.)*

:: What did the Philistines do when they saw David defeat Goliath with his sling and a stone? *(They all ran in fear.)*

:: What does this story teach us about how God saves? *(God saves us even though we are weak and sinful.)*

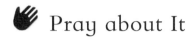 Pray about It

Thank God for all the ways he protects you from danger—try to be specific.

DAY FIVE

Discover It

Today we look at a passage from a psalm or one of the prophets to see what we can learn from it about Jesus.

 Read Psalm 95:3–8.

Think about It Some More

It is easy to read the psalms and miss all the connections there are to Jesus. But if you think about what Jesus did and remember some of what he said, you will begin to see little clues that point to Jesus all throughout the psalms.

For example, Colossians 1:16 says that Christ is the maker of the heavens and the earth, which helps us understand Psalm 95:5. Also, John 10:11 tells us that Jesus is our shepherd, and this makes Psalm 95:7 more meaningful.

Talk about It

:: How does Psalm 95:3–8 remind you of Jesus? *(Jesus is the creator of all things. He is our shepherd and takes good care of us when we hear his voice.)*

:: After telling us what God did, what does this psalm say we should do? *(It says we should worship the Lord.)*

:: What does this psalm say we should *not* do? *(We should not harden our hearts like the Israelites did. Recall the story of Meribah [Exodus 17:2–7] when Israel complained because they had no water. You can reread that story to remind the children what happened there.)*

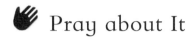 Pray about It

Ask God to help you remember that he is a great God and praise him for all that he has made.

Week 58

The Ark of God

Bring a skillet and a potholder to Bible study, using the potholder as if the skillet were very hot. Ask your children what potholders are used for. (They protect us from injury.)

Ask what would happen if you were cooking and accidentally touched the hot part of a pot or pan. (You would get burned.) What if you're the president of the United States—would you still get burned? What about a millionaire? The answer is always the same. Anyone, no matter how rich or important, would be burned. If the pan is hot, it cannot be touched safely without the protection of the potholder.

This week you will learn what happened when Uzzah put his sinful hands on the holy ark of God. Because God is holy, no sinner may touch his ark and live.

DAY ONE

Picture It

Nuclear submarines are not powered by gasoline or oil, but by a metal called uranium, a radioactive element. Uranium is so powerful that submarines that use it may never need to stop to refuel. Can you imagine not having to refill a car's gas tank for ten years?

But uranium has a drawback: it is very dangerous. You can't touch it without special protective clothing or it could kill you. It doesn't *look* dangerous but the radiation coming off of it, which is invisible, could cause you to get very sick and die. That is why people who handle it must be very, very careful.

In a similar way, God told Israel to be very, very careful with his ark because the presence of God rested upon it. Today we will see what happened when a man disobeyed God and touched the ark.

 Read 2 Samuel 6:1–10.

Think about It Some More

We have now skipped far ahead in our story beyond the day when David killed Goliath. Saul has died and David is now king of Israel. After becoming king, David wants to move the ark of God into the city of Jerusalem.

But the people who move the ark don't follow God's directions. Instead of slipping the carrying poles through the rings in the ark for the priests to carry (1 Chronicles 15:12–15), they put the ark on a cart. They forget that the holy presence of God is on the ark and that anyone who touches it will die (Numbers 4:15). So even though Uzzah was only trying to help when he reached out to steady the ark, he was immediately killed.

Think of it this way: if your shoes were muddy from playing outdoors and you ran into the house across white carpet, you would ruin it. That is why your mom tells you to take off your shoes at the door. Just as your mom protects the carpet from your muddy shoes, so God protects his holiness by judging sin. Sinners were not allowed to touch the ark where the holy, sinless presence of God rested.

Talk about It

:: How did God say the Israelites should carry the ark? *(The ark was to be carried by men who lifted the ark using two poles. These poles went through rings attached to the sides of ark.)*

:: Why couldn't anyone touch the ark? *(The ark was holy because God's presence rested on it. "Holy" is a word that describes God's purity and sinlessness. Because the men of Israel were sinful they could not touch God's ark.)*

:: What did King David do when he saw what happened to Uzzah? *(King David became afraid of God. David's fear was not a bad kind of fear, but a good kind of fear that helped him to obey God's Word.)*

 Pray about It

Praise God that he is holy, sinless, and all-powerful. God is an awesome God!

DAY TWO

Remember It

What do you remember about yesterday's story? What do you think is going to happen today?

 Read 2 Samuel 6:11–15.

Think about It Some More

When they captured the ark of God, the Philistines broke out with tumors and became very sick. When the ark stayed at Obed-edom's, his family obeyed God and did not touch the ark, and God blessed them.

When David heard of God's blessing he came back for the ark—only this time men carried the ark properly. When David saw that God was allowing him to move the ark to Jerusalem where God's people lived, he became very excited. God's presence was going to live with his people again.

Notice that as long as Israel obeyed the word of the Lord there was no need to fear God's judgment. It is only when we disobey God that we need to be afraid of God and his holiness.

Talk about It

:: What did David do after having the ark moved six steps? *(David offered a sacrifice to the Lord. He was glad that God was blessing their journey.)*

:: What did David do with all his might? *(David danced before the Lord with all his might.)*

:: Why was everyone so joyful? *(The ark of God was finally going to be with God's people in the city of Jerusalem. The arrival of the ark was like the blessing of God coming to them.)*

 Pray about It

We can joyfully praise God for sending Jesus just as David and Israel did. Jump and sing and shout praises to God for all that Jesus has done to save us.

DAY THREE

Connect It to Jesus

Can anyone guess how our story this week is about or points forward to Jesus?

 Read Leviticus 16:1–9.

Think about It Some More

The passage reveals God's instructions for what the priest of God was to do around the ark. Notice that when David came for the ark, he was wearing linen clothes and he offered a sacrifice to God as a sin offering.

The sacrifice David offered, like the sacrifices described in this passage, point forward to the sacrifice of Jesus. When animals were killed, they reminded God of his plan to save sinners by giving up his only Son to die on the cross for our sin.

Talk about It

:: Why did God have the priest kill animals when he came into the room where the ark was? *(God had the priest kill animals to cover his sinfulness.)*

:: Why did King David kill animals when those carrying the ark had taken six steps? *(They were killed as an offering or gift to God to follow his instructions for what to do when anyone went near the ark.)*

:: How do these sacrifices point us to Jesus? *(Animals could not really take their sins away. The animals only pointed forward to the sacrifice of Jesus on the cross. Only the sacrifice of Jesus on the cross could take their sins away.)*

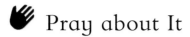 Pray about It

Thank God that we don't have to sacrifice animals for our sin. Jesus paid the price for our sin, once and for all. Praise God that no more sacrifice is needed.

DAY FOUR

Remember It

What has God been teaching you this week through our Bible story?

 Read 2 Samuel 6:16–23.

Think about It Some More

Sin always separates us from God. In our story today, David dances before the Lord as the ark of God is brought inside its tent. Then David joyfully offers sacrifices to the Lord, obeying the commands God had given Israel for how they should behave around the ark.

Michal, David's wife (Saul's daughter), despises him. That is a very strong word to say that she was not happy at all. Maybe she doesn't love the Lord like David does and thinks he looks foolish. Sadly, her sin blinds her to the joy of God's ark returning. Instead of rejoicing and drawing near to God, she angrily pulls away.

That is also what happens when we sin today.

Talk about It

> ● ● KIDS, ask your parents if they can remember a time when they had a
> ● ● sinful attitude that kept them from worshiping God.

(Parents, think of a time you were angry with your spouse or children. Since we are to worship God with joy in all we do, anytime we are angry with someone, we are sinning in the same way Michal did. Perhaps there was a time recently when, on the way to church, you became angry in the car. Instead of being excited to worship God, you were angry with a person.)

:: Why was Michal upset with David? *(It could be that she didn't love God like David did and thought he looked foolish while dancing before the Lord.)*

:: How did Michal's sinful attitude blind her to the joy all of Israel had? *(She didn't seem to even notice the return of the ark and what that meant for Israel.)*

:: Does God want us to worship him with excitement today? *(Yes! God is just as wonderful today as he was back in David's time. If David jumped and danced before the Lord at the arrival of the ark to Jerusalem, how much more should we get excited about the arrival of our salvation and the presence of our God?)*

Pray about It

Ask God to help you worship him with joy in all you do.

DAY FIVE

Discover It

Today we look at a passage from a psalm or one of the prophets to see what we can learn from it about Jesus.

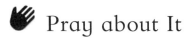 Read Psalm 132:1–14.

Think about It Some More

Psalm 132 was written as a song about David's plan to make a house for the Lord in Jerusalem and to bring the ark into the city with great rejoicing.

But hidden in the middle of this song is a secret promise: God swore an oath to David that his sons would sit on his throne forever. This promise is secret because Jesus was the way God planned to keep that promise to David. Jesus was the far-off grandson of King David. Jesus became King and sits on the throne forever.

The ark of God is also meant to be a picture of Jesus. When the ark was brought into the city, God's presence came along with it, and in this way God lived among his people. Jesus is God, and when he came into the city, God's presence walked as a man among his people. Remember, the people waved palm branches and called out "Hosanna! Blessed is he who comes in the name of the Lord, even the King of Israel!" (John 12:13). Knowing that the ark points to Jesus, we should all rejoice when we read this psalm.

Talk about It

:: How is this psalm connected to our Bible story this week? *(This psalm talks about finding a place for God to live with his people, and our story was about David bringing the ark back to Jerusalem and providing a tent for God so he could live with his people again.)*

:: Who is the king who would sit on the throne of David forever? *(Jesus is the king who would remain on the throne of David forever.)*

:: What should the saints do when God comes to live with his people? *(We should shout for joy.)*

 Pray about It

Celebrate with joy that God still lives with his people. He lives in the heart of every Christian.

Week 59

David the Psalmist

Ask your children the following questions. (The correct answer in each case is "King David the psalmist.")

    :: *"Who is the best known songwriter in world history?"*

    :: *"Which songwriter has had songs translated into more than 350 languages?"*

    :: *"Which songwriter has had the lyrics of more than 70 songs reproduced in the Bible?"*

Say, "This week you will learn about David, the writer of many psalms."

DAY ONE

Picture It

If you were going to write a song, what would it be about? Many songwriters write songs about things that happen in their lives.

For instance, the words to "The Star Spangled Banner" tell the story of the battle of Fort McHenry during the War of 1812. When the battle was over, the American flag was still flying over the fort, indicating the fort had not been captured. One of the lines to the song says, "Gave proof thro' the night that our flag was still there."

In our lesson today, we are going to read the words of a song that David wrote. Let's see if we can recognize what it was about.

 Read Psalm 23:1–3.

Think about It Some More

Psalms contains the words to songs that God's people sang a long time ago. King David was the greatest of the psalm writers. If you read about David in the Bible, you can sometimes figure out how the psalms fit his story.

For instance, our psalm today talks about God as our shepherd. As a young boy, David was a shepherd who watched over his father's flocks. He knew that shepherds carefully watched over the sheep to protect them. When a shepherd is present, the sheep have no fear of wolves or other enemies. The shepherd also leads the sheep to the best pastures and streams.

In this psalm, David compares God to a shepherd. David's peace came from God's shepherd-like protection. Throughout David's life, God always provided for him.

Talk about It

:: If God is a shepherd, who are his sheep? *(Everyone who believes in God becomes a part of his family. God calls all of his children his sheep.)*

:: How did God take care of King David? *(Parents, help your children think of stories about King David. For instance, you could ask them how God protected David when the lions and bears attacked, or how God cared for David when Goliath stood against Israel.)*

:: When a shepherd leads his sheep to green pastures or still waters, he is providing food and drink for them. How has God provided for you or your family? *(Help your children think of ways God has provided for them. Every good thing we have comes ultimately from the kindness of God. But most of all, God has given us his Word so we can learn about him.)*

 Pray about It

Praise God for the way he leads us to green pastures (gives us everything we need to serve him).

DAY TWO

Remember It

What do you remember about yesterday's story? What do you think is going to happen today?

 Read Psalm 23:4.

Think about It Some More

In these verses, David describes a time when God provided for him when his enemies were really close. Although David doesn't tell us when this happened, there was a time when King Saul was jealous of David and tried to hunt him down (1 Samuel 23:15). It could be that David was thinking about one of those times when he wrote this part of the psalm. David's words can help us to trust God when we feel like our enemies are closing in on us. We might not have someone trying to kill us, but sometimes things like sickness or having a lot of bills and expenses can feel like we have enemies closing in.

Talk about It

:: Do you remember how God protected David from Saul? *(God allowed the Philistines to attack God's people so King Saul had to halt the search for David and use his army to defend Israel.)*

:: How do you think God's protection encouraged David? *(David learned to trust God through his difficult trials.)*

:: Can you think of ways the Lord has protected you? *(Help your children see that even their good health shows that God has protected them from disease, and having a home shows that God has protected them from the weather.)*

:: God's rod, mentioned in this psalm, refers to how God corrects and disciplines us. How can that be comforting? *(God only corrects and disciplines us to keep us away from evil and sin. God's correction can be painful at times, but it helps us live in the safety and blessing of obedience to God.)*

 ## Pray about It

Thank God for the way he protects and corrects us for our good.

DAY THREE

Connect It to Jesus

Can anyone guess how our story this week is about or points forward to Jesus?

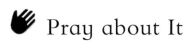 Read Psalm 23:6.

Think about It Some More

We are jumping over verse 5 to verse 6 today because of how this verse points to Jesus. David said that mercy followed him all his life and that, when he dies, he knows he will live in God's house forever.

There is only one way any of us could enjoy God's mercy and live in heaven with him forever. God sent Jesus, his only Son, to die on the cross for our sin. Now all those who trust in Jesus are forgiven and get to live in the house of God (heaven) forever. Jesus is the way God kept the promises David sang about. If we trust in Jesus we can live forever in heaven.

One day, everyone who goes to heaven will meet David, the man who wrote Psalm 23.

Talk about It

:: What did David say would follow him all the days of his life? *(Parents, if your children are too young to read and look for the answer, reread the verse and have them raise their hands when they hear the answer. Then have them repeat the answer, goodness and mercy, back to you.)*

:: What is God's mercy? *(God's shows us mercy when he does not punish us for the sinful things that we do against him. God can show us mercy because Jesus took our punishment when he died on the cross.)*

:: How long does David say he will live with God? *(David says he will live with God in his house forever.)*

:: Will we live with God forever too? *(If we trust in Jesus and his death on the cross for our sins, then we will live with God forever.)*

 Pray about It

Thank God for creating a wonderful place like heaven where we will live forever with him. Remember, we won't have any sin, sickness, death, or pain; and we will see all kinds of wonderful things and precious loved ones, including the best of all—Jesus!

DAY FOUR

Remember It

What has God been teaching you this week through our Bible story?

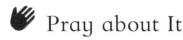 Read Psalm 23:5.

Think about It Some More

Today we are going back to verse 5 to see if it might point to a story in David's life.

Remember, Samuel invited Jesse, David's father, to a feast. Samuel had come to town to anoint one of Jesse's sons as the next king of Israel. Even though David, the youngest, had been left in the field, he was the one God chose. After passing by all of Jesse's sons, Samuel had David brought from the field and anointed him the next king over Israel. From that day on, God provided and cared for David even though he had many enemies.

God also provided for us. Even though our enemies—sin and death—threaten to destroy us, Jesus died for us. Jesus described himself as the bread of life. If we eat of this bread we will live forever (John 6:48–51). That was Jesus' way of saying that if we trust in him he will save us, and we will get to live with him for all time.

Talk about It

> ●● KIDS, when David says his cup overflows he means God gave him
> ●● more than he needed. Ask your parents if they can remember a time
> when God gave them more than they needed.

(Parents, think of a time when God gave you more of something than you needed. Perhaps your house is bigger than you actually need to survive and represents the abundant blessing of God. Then talk about how the greatest gift God has given you is your salvation in Jesus. Our hearts cannot contain all the blessings of God and what he has done on the cross.)

:: How has God provided more than you need? *(Parents, now help your children answer the same question for their lives.)*

:: When was David anointed? *(Samuel anointed David when he chose him to be the new king. This was also when the Holy Spirit came on David.)*

 Pray about It

Thank God for the ways he gives your family more than you need.

DAY FIVE

Discover It

Today we look at a passage from a psalm or one of the prophets to see what we can learn from it about Jesus.

 Read 2 Samuel 7:1–17.

Think about It Some More

What would it be like if God sent a prophet to tell you all about your future?

God told David that he was going to make him a great king, he was going to win all his battles, and then his son Solomon would build God a house. God also told David that his throne would last forever and David's son Solomon would be God's son too.

Both of these parts of the story point to Jesus. God planned through Jesus to keep his promise to place a son of David on the throne forever.

Talk about It

:: If you could find out one thing about your future, what would you like to know? *(Parents, you can draw your children out here but in the end, share the gospel with them and tell them that if they trust the Lord then they can know one important thing about their future. They can know that they will live with God in heaven after they die.)*

:: How did God say David would be different from Saul? *(God took the throne away from Saul and his children. God was going to allow David and his family to keep the throne forever.)*

:: If God promised that David would always have a son to sit on his throne, who sits on David's throne today? *(Jesus is a great far-off grandson of David and he is the one who now sits on David's throne as king.)*

 Pray about It

Tell God that you trust him with your future, even though you don't know how your life will turn out.

Week 60

Solomon and the Temple of God

Bring your children together and tell them that for the building of God's temple, King David provided one hundred thousand talents of gold and one million talents of silver. Ask the children to guess how much that amount of gold and silver would be worth today.

It is thought that a talent of gold or silver weighed at least 50 pounds. Assuming 50 pounds for each talent of gold at a price of $900 per ounce, each talent of gold would be worth $720,000. Each talent of silver at $16 per ounce would be worth $12,800. This means that the gold and silver used to construct the temple would be worth almost $84 billion. On top of that was the cost of the wood, stone, iron, bronze, and labor!

This week you will learn about the amazing temple Solomon built for the Lord.

DAY ONE

Picture It

Imagine you were a builder hired to design and build a palace for a king. Right from the start you would plan to use the best of everything. You wouldn't want to use anything cheap like plastic or fake wood. Only the best quality building materials would work. As for size, the palace should be large and grand to show the importance of the person living there.

Now imagine you were asked to build a palace for God. Only the finest materials like gold and silver should be used in the construction. Building a palace for God out of the materials found here on earth would be a tough assignment, but that is exactly what David told his son Solomon to do: build a house for God. What an amazing thing that God wanted to live with his people.

 Read 1 Chronicles 22:7–10.

Think about It Some More

If we read these stories too quickly we can miss how amazing they are. For instance, in our passage today the writer tells us that God was going to give David a son, he would name him Solomon, and God would bring peace to Israel so Solomon could build a house for God. And it all happened just as God said.

God knows the future, God controls peace and war, and God knew that Solomon, not David, would be the one to build him a temple. So, when Solomon grew up and God brought peace to the land, it was time for David to charge his son with the task of building a house for God.

We can easily forget that the same God rules over our lives. He knows our future and is directing our lives to work out his plan.

Talk about It

:: What did David tell his son to build? *(David told his son to build a house for God among the people so God didn't have to live in a tent anymore.)*

:: What did David do to help his son? *(David gathered the things Solomon would need to build the temple.)*

:: Why did God want Solomon to build his house (temple) in Jerusalem? *(God wanted to live among the people he loved. That is ultimately why God sent his Son Jesus to live among his people. One day everyone who believes will get to live with God in heaven forever.)*

 Pray about It

Praise God for his mighty power and ask God to help you in all you do.

DAY TWO_____

Remember It

What do you remember about yesterday's story? What do you think is going to happen today?

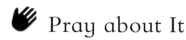 Read 1 Chronicles 22:11–19.

Think about It Some More

If you take a careful look at what David told his son Solomon, you will notice how much David loved God and talked about God. He prayed that the Lord would be with Solomon and that the Lord would give Solomon discretion and understanding. He also told Solomon to keep God's laws, and promised that God would bless him. Then David talked to the leaders to tell them about God too, and said they needed to seek God as well.

Talk about It

:: What can we learn about David's life from what he told his son Solomon? *(We learn that David is a man who loves God and trusts the Lord to help his son build the temple.)*

:: How is David an example for us? *(We need to trust God for the things we have to do. Even though we are not building a temple for the Lord, we still need God's help to do all that we have to do.)*

:: Can you think of an area in your life where you need God's help? *(Parents, help your children to see that we need God's help in every area of life. We need his protection from illness and his grace to say no to sin. We need to remember that everything we eat and drink is provided by God.)*

 ## Pray about It

Ask God to help you love and trust him like David did.

DAY THREE

Connect It to Jesus

Can anyone guess how our story this week is about or points forward to Jesus?

 Read 1 Chronicles 28:1–19.

Think about It Some More

In the middle of David's speech to the officials of Jerusalem, he said something to connect our story to Jesus: David repeated God's promise to make him king over Israel forever.

Before all the officials, David passed that promise on to his son Solomon and to Solomon's children. David said that God would leave his kingdom as an inheritance (gift) to his children forever. God kept all those promises by sending his Son Jesus from the tribe of Judah and the family of David and Solomon to be king forever.

Talk about It

:: What did David tell the leaders of Israel he had gathered together? *(David told them God's plan for his son Solomon to build God a house and take over as king after him. That way, they would all know it was a part of God's plan, and they would support Solomon.)*

:: *Read 1 Chronicles 28:9 again.* How is this verse true for us today? *(God is still a searcher of hearts and knows everything, and he desires that we come to him. It is also fearfully true that anyone who rejects God will be cast off forever.)*

:: Why did God give specific plans for the temple instead of letting Solomon make a design of his own? *(The temple and its furnishings were to be holy, set apart for the Lord. When men are left to themselves, sin can lead them astray, like Aaron and the golden calf.)*

 Pray about It

Thank God for giving us the Bible as our instruction manual, which teaches us how we should live. Ask God to help us follow his Word in all we do.

DAY FOUR

Remember It

What has God been teaching you this week through our Bible story?

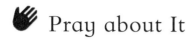 Read 2 Chronicles 7:1–18.

Think about It Some More

Every day thousands of homes remain empty with no one to live in them. Some of them are too expensive for people to buy. It doesn't matter how beautiful a house is if no one lives in it to enjoy it.

It took Solomon seven years to build a temple for the Lord, and it was magnificent! But no matter how beautiful it was, all the work would have been for nothing if God had not filled the temple and come there to live.

But God *did* fill the temple, and all the people bowed down when they saw fire from heaven consume the burnt offering. On that day Solomon sacrificed thousands of animals—but no number of offerings could take away sin.

All those sacrificed animals pointed to Jesus. If Jesus had never come, all those sacrifices would have been for nothing. But Jesus *did* come and die on the cross for our sins so God's presence, which filled the temple, can now live inside everyone who trusts in Jesus.

Talk about It

> ● ● KIDS, ask your parents to describe the most magnificent building they
> ● ● have ever seen.

:: What makes that building different from the temple of Solomon? *(God's presence fell upon Solomon's temple.)*

:: In Solomon's day God came down to live in the temple. Where does God come down to live today? *(God sends his Holy Spirit to live inside our hearts, and all of us who believe become the new temple of God.)*

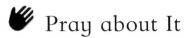 Pray about It

Thank God for filling the temple with his glory, and ask God to help you believe so you can be filled with his Spirit too.

DAY FIVE

Discover It

Today we look at a passage from a psalm or one of the prophets to see what we can learn from it about Jesus.

 Read Isaiah 60:16–20.

Think about It Some More

These words from Isaiah sound a little confusing, but there are several clues that tell us the prophet Isaiah is speaking about Jesus. He uses names like "Savior" and "Redeemer," which are names that were given to Jesus. Isaiah was trying to encourage Israel by telling them that a day was coming when God would make everything better.

Isaiah also talked about a day when the sun and moon would be gone and God himself would provide the light. In the last book of the Bible we read that this is exactly what is going to happen in heaven. Jesus is going to be our light (Revelation 21:23)!

Isaiah went on to say that in that day our mourning and crying will be no more. That also matches up with the words in the book of Revelation that say, when Jesus returns for his children, God will wipe every tear from our eyes and there will be no mourning.

Talk about It

:: How does this part of the Bible point to Jesus? *(Parents, see if your children can remember some of the names for Jesus you just read. If you have small children, reread the passage and ask them to raise their hands when they hear something that points to Jesus.)*

:: Why is the sun no longer needed in heaven? *(Jesus is the light of heaven!)*

:: Will there be night in heaven? *(No. There will be no night. The light of Christ will shine all day, every day, forever! [Revelation 22:5])*

:: How could Isaiah know what was going to happen at the end of the world when Jesus was not even born yet? *(God spoke to his prophets and gave them the words to speak and write down.)*

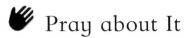 Pray about It

Thank God for the way he has planned our salvation from beginning to end.

Week 61

The Kingdom Is Divided

Find a penny, a quarter, and a stone and call in your children to talk about them. Show the penny to your children and ask if they have ever found one outside on the ground. Ask them why people leave their pennies on the ground when they drop them. Pennies are not worth much, so even if people know they have dropped one, sometimes they do not bother to pick it up.

Show your children the quarter and ask if they ever found one outside on the ground. Because quarters are more valuable, people normally will pick them up if they drop them. Now show your children the stone. Would they pick up a stone if they saw one on the ground?

The Bible tells us that Solomon made silver as common as the stones. During Solomon's rule there was so much silver it became almost worthless. Say, "This week you will learn how the riches and pleasures of the world turned Solomon's heart away from God."

DAY ONE

Picture It

Although Mary had known her friend Beth since first grade, she had never been to her house. Now she was going to visit her for the very first time. Beth was one of the smartest kids in the class when they were younger, but ever since third grade last year she started talking more and more about television.

When Mary reached her friend's house she finally understood why Beth talked so much about television. On the living room wall was a giant flat screen TV surrounded by a dozen smaller flat screens. Each one played a different channel. As Beth gave Mary a quick tour of the house, Mary noticed that every room had at least ten televisions along the walls and furniture, and some of the rooms even had televisions on the ceiling.

There were TVs in the bathroom, garage, kitchen, and patio and they all looked brand new. The older models, Beth explained, were replaced with the newest and latest and then sent to the outside storage shed. All together, Beth says her family had about 300 televisions on, each with a different program to watch, with about 200 in storage.

Mary enjoyed watching television at home, but she couldn't imagine having so many TV's on all the time. She asked Beth how she could possibly do her quiet time with so much noise.

Beth admitted that it had been hard to read her Bible in the morning with so many different programs to watch.

Today in our story, we will see what distracted Solomon away from living for God.

 Read 1 Kings 11:1–8.

Think about It Some More

Having over 300 televisions in one house is a crazy idea. However, Solomon had more than twice that number of wives. His palace was large, but where would he put 700 wives? He would need 700 beds and 700 closets for their clothes. What if only half of them wanted to say good morning? He would have to say good morning 350 times!

But the worst part about Solomon's wives was that many of them worshiped idols. They brought their false gods into Solomon's life. God had warned Solomon not to take many wives (Deuteronomy 17:17), and God had warned all Israel not to marry women from other nations. But Solomon did not obey God.

Solomon started well as king by building an awesome temple for God, but because of his idol-worshiping wives, he ended up building temples to their false gods too.

Talk about It

:: How are the televisions from our funny story a lot like Solomon's wives? *(Parents, draw your children out on this one. As crazy as the TV illustration was, Solomon's life was worse. Talk about how televisions can distract you from doing what God wants you to do, just as Solomon's wives did.)*

:: Why didn't God want Solomon to take a wife from the other nations? *(They were all idol-worshipers who would lead Solomon away from God.)*

:: What lessons can we learn from this story about obeying God? *(Disobeying God brings bad consequences. Things, even God's good gifts to us, can become idols. An idol in our lives is anything that we love more than God.)*

 Pray about It

Ask God to help you obey his Word and not allow anything to become more important to you than him.

DAY TWO

Remember It

What do you remember about yesterday's story? What do you think is going to happen today?

 Read 1 Kings 11:9–12.

Think about It Some More

When Solomon first became king, God invited him to ask for anything he wanted. Solomon prayed and asked God for wisdom (2 Chronicles 1:10). God was pleased with Solomon's choice and gave him amazing wisdom to rule over Israel.

But even the wisest man in the world is nothing but a fool if he does not obey God's Word. Although Solomon was wise, he became a fool when he started to worship the false gods of his foreign wives. The great King Solomon, who had once judged Israel with great wisdom, now stood in God's courtroom to have the judge of the whole earth take away his kingdom.

Talk about It

:: What is wisdom? *(Wisdom is a word that means the ability to make right choices.)*

:: What is a fool? *(A fool is a person who turns away from wisdom and truth to do what she wants instead of what is right. The worst example is the man who turns away from God and does not obey his commands.)*

:: How did Solomon become a fool? *(Solomon turned away from God's Word.)*

:: Can you think of wise and foolish things you have done in your life? *(Parents, help your children. You might make a list of five things they have done recently, three wise and two foolish. As you tell them each one, have them identify it as wise or foolish. Any time we disobey we are breaking God's commands and acting foolishly.)*

 Pray about It

Ask God for wisdom to help you follow him all your life.

DAY THREE

Connect It to Jesus

Can anyone guess how our story this week is about or points forward to Jesus?

 Read 1 Kings 11:13–40.

Think about It Some More

Even though God judged Solomon for worshiping false gods, there was hope in God's punishment. God gave Solomon good news mixed with the bad news. The bad news was that God took the kingdom away from Solomon, but the good news was that he promised not to do it until Solomon's son was king. And even then God promised not to take all of Israel away, but to allow Solomon's son to be king over one tribe.

The math seems wrong here. Ten tribes were torn away, leaving two—but God said he would spare one tribe for the sake of Jerusalem. Commentators believe the tribe of Benjamin was not mentioned because it was assumed that it came with its city, Jerusalem. So God was giving one more tribe to be with Jerusalem while ten tribes were pulled away.

God did this for the sake of David and for the sake of Jerusalem. You see, God had promised David that he would have a son on the throne forever. So even though Solomon disobeyed God, he remained on the throne so God could keep his promise to David.

Jesus, one of Solomon's far-off grandchildren, is the ultimate way God kept that promise. By saving the tribe of Judah (the tribe Jesus came from) and allowing Solomon to remain on the throne, God kept his promise to David and opened the way for the good news of the gospel to come to all of us.

Talk about It

:: Why didn't God take all the tribes away from Solomon and remove him as king? *(God promised Solomon's father, David, that he would always have a son on the throne. God allowed Solomon to remain as king to keep his promise to David.)*

:: What was so special about Jerusalem and the tribe of Judah that God didn't want them to be taken away from Solomon's son? *(God promised David he would always have a son on the throne.)*

:: What is the good news God gave Solomon? *(Instead of judging Solomon by taking his entire kingdom away, God promised to give Solomon's son one tribe to rule.)*

:: What is the good news God gives us? *(Instead of judging us, God judged Jesus in our place, and if we believe and trust in Jesus we can live with God in heaven.)*

 Pray about It

Thank God for the good news of the gospel: Jesus died on the cross for our sin and then rose again so we can live forever in heaven with him.

DAY FOUR

Remember It

What has God been teaching you this week through our Bible story?

 Read 1 Kings 11:41—12:20.

Think about It Some More

Rehoboam, Solomon's son, made a foolish choice. Instead of listening to the older, wiser men of Jerusalem, he listened to his younger friends whom he grew up with. Because these prideful younger men had no experience running a kingdom, they gave Rehoboam bad advice.

Children today can make the same mistake. Instead of listening to what their parents say, they listen to the advice of their friends. As in Rehoboam's case, that usually leads to trouble. It led to big trouble for Rehoboam—he was rejected by all of Israel except for his own tribe, the tribe of Judah. You might wonder why it was Rehoboam's fault that Israel split up when God had already said it was going to happen. Even so, Rehoboam rejected the wise advice of the elders and followed the foolish counsel of his friends to treat the people unkindly and burden them with higher taxes.

Talk about It

> ● ● KIDS, ask your parents if they ever made the same mistake that
> ● ● Rehoboam did by listening to bad advice from their friends.

(Parents, think of a time when you did something foolish because your friends dared you to do it, or a time when they suggested something sinful or foolish and you followed along.)

:: What was Rehoboam's foolish mistake? *(He listened to his friends instead of the older, wiser men.)*

:: Why do you think Rehoboam didn't listen to the older, wiser men? *(Parents, help your children to guess why Rehoboam didn't listen to the wiser men. Youthful pride and independence and wanting to do things on your own might have been the cause.)*

:: Did you ever try to do something on your own when you should have asked for help? *(Sometimes when young children get new toys that need to be put together they try to do it by themselves. They can even break a new toy by not handling it carefully. Sometimes children get angry when their parents tell them how to do something.)*

 ## Pray about It

Ask God to help you to be wise and to listen to your parents.

DAY FIVE

Discover It

Today we look at a passage from a psalm or one of the prophets to see what we can learn from it about Jesus.

 Read Psalm 132:8–14.

Think about It Some More

This psalm is about God's promise to bless David and keep one of his sons or grandsons on the throne of Israel. It even repeats the words God spoke to Solomon: "For the sake of your servant David." It also says that God plans to live with his people forever.

The only way God could live with his sinful people forever is if he took our sins away. That is why he sent Jesus. Jesus came as a son of David and took up his throne. Jesus died on the cross to take away our sins so we could live with God forever in heaven.

God gave all kinds of hints through the Psalms and the books of the prophets to tell his people how he was planning to save them.

Talk about It

:: Why didn't God replace Solomon with a king from another family like he did with Saul? *(God had promised David that he would always have a son on the throne.)*

:: Who is the son that God put on David's throne as king forever? *(Jesus is the Son that God put on the throne of David.)*

:: What did God do for us so we could live as his people in heaven forever? *(God provided a way to make us righteous. When we believe and trust in Jesus and his death on the cross, God takes our sins away so we can live with him in heaven.)*

 ## Pray about It

Thank God for taking our sins away. Thank him that if we believe in his Son's work on the cross, we can live with him forever in heaven.

Week 62

God Provides for Elijah in Miraculous Ways

Collect ingredients for making a small batch of pancakes that may be similar to "the little cake" the widow made for Elijah in this week's story.

In a bowl, mix together the following:

1/2 cup flour

1 1/2 teaspoons baking powder

1/4 teaspoon salt

2 tablespoons of oil

1/3 cup of milk

(Normally pancakes have egg and sugar in them, so these will taste plain.) Heat a lightly oiled skillet on the stove. Pour a tablespoon of the batter onto the hot skillet and cook until brown on both sides.

Say, "In tomorrow's story we will read about a widow who had no money and only enough food for her and her child to each eat one small pancake. No wonder she was discouraged. But we will also see this week how, through Elijah, God provided miraculously for the widow and for others."

DAY ONE

Picture It

What would happen if the water company that provides your family's water got mixed up and put your parents' payments on someone else's account? It would look like you were not paying your bill. If the problem wasn't corrected, your water would be shut off.

Imagine getting up one morning and having no water to shower or wash or make oatmeal. When we call the water company we find out that the person in charge of turning the water back on is away on vacation for two weeks! How could we live without water for two weeks?

In our story today, God stopped the rain from falling on Israel because of their sins against God. Then God sent his prophet Elijah away on a vacation so King Ahab couldn't talk to God and ask for rain even if he wanted to.

 Read 1 Kings 16:29—17:7.

Think about It Some More

We have now jumped more than 50 years ahead in the story about God's people. The ten tribes of Israel that followed Jereboam are now being led by wicked King Ahab. Instead of worshiping the true God in Jerusalem, they worship the false god Baal.

Those who worship Baal believe that he controls the weather. God declares that he will stop both rain and dew to show his people that Baal is powerless. With Elijah gone, Ahab has no way to call out to the true God. He is forced to call out to Baal, who cannot help him.

Talk about It

:: Elijah told King Ahab who really controls the rain. Who was it? *(Elijah told Ahab that God controls the rain. Unless God gave the word through his prophet, no rain would fall on Israel.)*

:: Who does Ahab trust instead of the God of Israel? *(Ahab trusts the idol Baal, a made-up god who has no power.)*

:: What happens when there is no rain for a long time? *(Without water, everything dies.)*

:: What happens to Elijah during the drought? *(God provides for Elijah by sending ravens with food for him to eat and by giving him a brook that still has water for him to drink.)*

 Pray about It

Thank God for the amazing way he is in control of all things.

DAY TWO

Remember It

What do you remember about yesterday's story? What do you think is going to happen today?

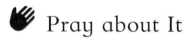 Read 1 Kings 17:8–16.

Think about It Some More

It is easy to read the story about the widow and not understand how bad things were for her. By the time God sent Elijah to the widow, the lack of rain was so bad that streams and brooks had dried up. Without water, crops like wheat and barley, which provided food for the people, shriveled up and died. The little grain that was left became very expensive.

The poor widow was down to her last meal. She didn't have a husband to provide for her. With food prices high, people wouldn't be giving food away and she couldn't afford to buy any. Then Elijah arrived and asked for her last meal.

Sometimes we can get annoyed if someone asks for our last piece of gum or candy. But this woman believed that God would provide for her, so she prepared the last food she had for Elijah.

Talk about It

:: How did Elijah and the woman both trust God? *(Elijah trusted the Lord's word enough to eat the last meal of a widow. The widow trusted God enough to give it to him.)*

:: How can their example help us to trust God for what we need? *(Parents, draw out your children here. If the widow could trust God enough to give away her last meal in a terrible drought, then we should have faith enough to share what we have and trust the Lord for the things we need.)*

:: What did God do for the widow? *(Because she trusted God, what Elijah said came true: God provided flour and oil for her and her son all through the drought.)*

 Pray about It

Thank God for the way he cared for the widow and ask God to help you to trust his Word.

DAY THREE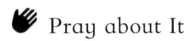

Connect It to Jesus

Can anyone guess how our story this week is about or points forward to Jesus?

Read Luke 4:16–30.

Think about It Some More

After Jesus read from the book of Isaiah in the synagogue in Nazareth, his hometown, the people were amazed at his teaching. But Jesus knew that soon those same people would reject his message, just as Ahab had rejected God. So Jesus reminded them of the story of the widow. He said that God sent Elijah to a foreign widow instead of one from Israel because Israel rejected God and his prophet Elijah, and followed the false god Baal.

Those in the synagogue didn't like what Jesus said, and they tried to kill him. They thought God's salvation was for the people of Israel only, but even in Elijah's day God saved a widow who was not from Israel.

Talk about It

:: In this story, where was Jesus teaching? *(Jesus was teaching in a synagogue in his hometown of Nazareth where he had probably been a carpenter with his dad Joseph.)*

:: Did the people recognize him? *(Yes, they figured out that he was Joseph the carpenter's son who was teaching them, and they were amazed at Jesus' teaching.)*

:: What happened to the people when Jesus told them the story of the widow? *(They became angry and wanted to kill him because, by using the story of the widow, Jesus was comparing them to evil King Ahab and himself to the prophet Elijah.)*

 Pray about It

Thank God that his plan of salvation is for people from every nation.

DAY FOUR

Remember It

What has God been teaching you this week through our Bible story?

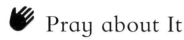 Read 1 Kings 17:17–24.

Think about It Some More

The whole time Elijah lived in Zarephath at the widow's house, no rain fell in Israel. No matter how loud or how long Ahab called out, Baal could not help him, and the drought continued. But in Zarephath, God was doing miracles to show that his power was great. Not only could the Lord make the widow's flour and oil multiply, God also had power over life and death!

Talk about It

> ● ● KIDS, ask your parents how this story reminds them of stories in the
> ● ● New Testament about Jesus.

(Elijah called out to God who enabled him to perform miracles; Jesus was God and could heal and raise people back to life all by himself.)

:: Why couldn't Elijah raise the widow's son all by himself like Jesus raised people? *(Elijah was only a man; Jesus is God.)*

:: What happened to the widow's son after Elijah prayed? *(God raised him from the dead.)*

 Pray about It

Ask God to heal people who are sick.

DAY FIVE

Discover It

Today we look at a passage from a psalm or one of the prophets to see what we can learn from it about Jesus.

 Read Psalm 78:23–39.

Think about It Some More

Psalm 78 tells the story of how Israel turned away from God again and again, and how each time God punished them, they returned to him, only to fall away again. Like Ahab in our story this week, Israel deserved to be destroyed but God kept forgiving them.

Sometimes people wonder why God didn't destroy Israel for their sin. This psalm gives us the answer in verse 38: God was compassionate, meaning God loved and cared about his people.

This psalm also says that God atoned for their sin. That means God took their sin away and forgave them. God did that by sending his only Son Jesus to die on the cross and take their punishment upon himself. God could have destroyed Israel for disobeying, but he didn't because he knew that one day Jesus would take their sin away. And, of course, Jesus took the punishment for our sins too.

Talk about It

:: Why didn't God destroy Israel for their sin? *(God didn't destroy them because he had a plan to save them by sending his Son to die on the cross for their sins.)*

:: Why doesn't God destroy us when we sin? *(God wants us to trust in Jesus. If we believe in Jesus and what he did on the cross, we can have our sins paid for too.)*

:: How can God's example of forgiving us help us to forgive others? *(If God forgives us for our sin against him, then we should forgive others for their smaller sins against us.)*

 Pray about It

Thank God for his amazing compassion that keeps him from treating us as our sins deserve. We deserve to be punished, but God loves us instead and sent Jesus to die for us. Praise God for the way he showed us his love.

Week 63

Elijah and the Prophets of Baal

Water is made up of two gases that burn very easily: hydrogen and oxygen. But water itself doesn't burn! Here is a fun exercise to help your children understand how wet things don't burn well. You will need a glass of water, a sheet of newspaper, and a lighter. You should plan to do this exercise outside.

Call your children together. Roll the newspaper up loosely and ask what would happen if you put a flame to the end of the newspaper. To demonstrate, light one end of the newspaper. Allow it to burn for a few seconds, then step on the paper to put it out. Ask the children to guess what will happen if you dip the paper in water first and then try to light it. Dip the paper in the water and keep it there for about five seconds. Then try to light the paper. You will be able to hold the flame on the wet paper without it igniting.

Say, "This week you will learn how God consumed Elijah's offering with fire, even though his offering was soaking wet!"

DAY ONE

Picture It

Only rarely can we get a good look at a bald eagle. If you told your friends that you saw an owl or a bright red cardinal in your front yard, they might believe you. But if you told them that a bald eagle landed in your front yard, they would find it hard to believe. The next time they visited they might even ask, "So where is your bald eagle?" A photo might be the only way you would be able to prove your claim.

In our story today, Obadiah, a servant of King Ahab, could have used a camera. He found Elijah, whom King Ahab had been looking for desperately. Obadiah, however, was hesitant to report his find to the king because Elijah had the habit of disappearing unexpectedly. Without a photo, Obadiah would have no way to prove to the king that he really had seen Elijah. Elijah promised that he would stay put until he spoke with the king.

 Read 1 Kings 18:1–19.

Think about It Some More

While Elijah was living in the widow's house eating bread made from the flour that did not run out, Ahab was back in Israel enduring devastating drought (no rain) and famine (no food). After three dry years, there was no grass to feed the horses and mules. It is likely that many of the other animals, like the sheep and goats, had long since been eaten.

When the king finally meets up with Elijah, he blames him for Israel's trouble. But the real trouble is that Ahab worships the idol Baal. Baal has no power to make it rain. This is why Ahab is searching so desperately for Elijah, a prophet of the true God of Israel.

Talk about It

:: What happens when it stops raining for a long time? *(Plants die and then animals, which have no food, also die. Unless food is stored away—remember Joseph during the drought in Egypt—people start to die as well.)*

:: Why was Obadiah afraid to tell the king he had found Elijah? *(Obadiah was afraid that Elijah would disappear before the king could see him. If the king thought Obadiah was lying, he would kill Obadiah.)*

:: Why do you think God is going to send rain again on Israel (verse 1)? *(God is going to show Ahab and the rest of Israel that he can do what their false god Baal is powerless to do.)*

 Pray about It

Thank God for providing us with food.

DAY TWO

Remember It

What do you remember about yesterday's story? What do you think is going to happen today?

 Read 1 Kings 18:20–35.

Think about It Some More

Before God sent rain to Israel he was going to prove, once and for all, that Baal was a false god. If the Lord sent rain right away, the people might think that Baal was the one who had sent it. So the Lord instructed Elijah to challenge the priests of Baal to a contest, to see which god could send fire from heaven to burn up an offering.

In the contest, the priests of Baal tried everything they could to get an answer from their god. But because Baal was just an idol made of wood or stone, he didn't answer. Elijah mocked the false prophets because he knew their god was powerless.

Remember: anything we love more than God can be an idol for us.

Talk about It

:: Why did Elijah set up the contest using the bulls? *(He set up the contest to prove that Baal was a false god.)*

:: What happened when the prophets of Baal called out to their god? *(Nothing at all happened.)*

:: Why do you think Elijah had water poured all over his offering? *(Elijah wanted everyone to know that he wasn't using some cheap trick to ignite his offering. By pouring water onto the offering, there was no way it would naturally catch fire.)*

 Pray about It

Ask God to show you what you love more than him. Ask him to help you turn from your false gods and trust in him alone like Elijah did.

DAY THREE

Connect It to Jesus

Can anyone guess how our story this week is about or points forward to Jesus?

 Read 1 Kings 18:36–38.

Think about It Some More

Even though Israel turned away from the Lord to worship the false god Baal, God did not give up on them. When Elijah prayed, God heard and answered by burning up the whole sacrifice with fire. That meant that God accepted Elijah's offering.

The contest of the offering soaked with water was God's idea. One day in the future, God would accept another offering—the offering of his Son Jesus on the cross. The offering of the bull on the altar pointed to the day when God would offer up his own Son for our sins.

Talk about It

:: Whose idea was it to have a contest between the priests of Baal and God and his prophet Elijah? *(The whole thing was God's idea. Elijah prayed, "I have done all these things at your word" [verse 36].)*

:: Did Elijah have any power in himself to bring fire down from heaven? *(Elijah had no power himself. But Elijah knew the God of power!)*

:: How can reading the stories of the Old Testament build our faith? *(God does not change [Malachi 3:6]. The same God who answered Elijah's prayers hears our prayers. It was*

Jesus who said that if we had faith as small as a mustard seed we could move a mountain [Matthew 17:20].)

 Pray about It

Take time to lift up your prayer requests to the Lord. *(Parents, help your children come up with a list.)*

DAY FOUR

Remember It

What has God been teaching you this week through our Bible story?

 Read 1 Kings 18:39–45.

Think about It Some More

If God tells you that he is going to send rain, you can be assured that you are going to need your umbrella. After praying on top of the mountain, Elijah told his servant to go look for rain clouds. When the servant came back and said there were no rain clouds, Elijah wasn't concerned—he just kept on praying. If God told him there was going to be rain, there was going to be rain. Sure enough, after sending the servant to look seven times, clouds began to form and the rain began to fall. Elijah trusted God's word.

Talk about It

> ● ● KIDS, ask your parents to tell you a story of how they trusted God's
> ● ● Word even when it was difficult.

(Parents, try to think of a time when perhaps you tithed or gave an offering, trusting that the Lord would provide, even though it was difficult.)

:: Why wasn't Elijah afraid when his servant kept coming back to tell him there was no sign of rain? *(Elijah trusted the Lord to do what he said he would do.)*

:: What did Elijah tell Ahab to do? *(Elijah told Ahab that he had better get into his chariot and go where he wanted to go because the coming rain might interfere with his travel plans.)*

:: How do we know Ahab finally believed Elijah? *(Ahab got in his chariot just like Elijah told him to and was traveling when the rains came.)*

 Pray about It

Praise God for the way he controls everything, including the rain.

DAY FIVE

Discover It

Today we look at a passage from a psalm or one of the prophets to see what we can learn from it about Jesus.

 Read Psalm 98:1–9.

Think about It Some More

If you had been watching the contest between the priests of Baal and Elijah, you may have laughed when Elijah made fun of Baal by suggesting he'd fallen asleep. And if you had been there when God won the contest by burning up the offering, you would have jumped and shouted and made a joyful noise to the Lord to celebrate.

That is just what Psalm 98 tells us to do. Psalm 98 is not celebrating God's victory on the mountain, however, it is celebrating what Jesus did on the cross. Though the psalmist did not know about Jesus who hadn't been born yet, the Holy Spirit inspired (gave the words to) him. We can find clues about Jesus in most of the psalms. For instance, when a psalmist says that the earth sees the salvation of the Lord, he might be thinking of a time when God saved Israel from their enemies. But today, as we look back, we can see how these songs also point to the salvation that comes through Jesus. Look over Psalm 98 again and see if you can find clues that tell us that this song is about Jesus.

Talk about It

:: What are the words that give us a clue that this song is about Jesus? *(Verses 1–2 tell us that God has made known his salvation to all the nations. The sacrifice of Jesus on the cross made salvation for the nations possible. This psalm also tells us that we should celebrate before the king—King Jesus.)*

:: What does this psalm say we should do? *(We should sing praises and play instruments to the Lord.)*

:: When are we supposed to sing and shout? *(We can sing and shout praises to God all the time. We sing and praise God when we gather for church on Sunday, but we should praise God the whole week through.)*

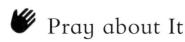 Pray about It

Sing your favorite praise song or hymn to the Lord.

Week 64

Elijah Is Taken Up to Heaven

Lay out one pile of candy for each of your children. All the piles should have the same amount—except one, which should have twice as much as the others. Then call in your children.

Ask them which pile they would like to have and why. They will say they want the larger pile because it has more. Tell them the larger pile actually has twice as much as the others. Then explain that, among the Israelites, the oldest son was promised a double portion of his father's estate when his father died.

Say, "In our story this week, Elisha asks Elijah for a double portion of his spiritual power." Ask your children who would like the double portion of the treat. Double the portion for each one who asks to help them understand what the term "double portion" means.

DAY ONE

Picture It

Imagine that you overheard Mom talking on the phone, saying that the family was going to fly in an airplane, taking a two-week vacation and visiting a giant amusement park. When Mom finished her call, you asked her if it was really true. But Mom explained that it was supposed to be a surprise and urged you not to tell anyone.

How hard would it be to keep a secret like that? Every time you saw one of your brothers or sisters you would want to say, "I know something you don't know." Or you might want to ask a question like, "What do you think it's like to fly in an airplane?"

In today's story, Elisha knew that God was going to take his master, Elijah, up to heaven, but he wanted other people who found out about it to keep it a secret.

 Read 2 Kings 2:1–6.

Think about It Some More

In this week's lesson, Elijah is going to be taken up to heaven in a whirlwind. People don't get taken up to heaven in a whirlwind every day. In fact, as far as we know, Elijah is the only person to ever experience this.

The Bible doesn't tell us if Elisha knew all the details of how God was going to take his master, Elijah, but he did know God was going to do it. That is why there was no way Elisha was going to leave his master's side. He wanted to be there when God took Elijah, no matter how much he was told to stay back.

Talk about It

:: Tell about a time when you had to keep a secret. *(Parents, this is a fun question. Perhaps they knew what you were getting your spouse or one of their siblings for a birthday or Christmas, and they had to keep it quiet.)*

:: Why didn't Elisha want to leave Elijah? *(Elisha knew that God was going to take Elijah up to heaven and he wanted to be there when that happened. This doesn't mean that disobeying is okay. Think of it more this way: if Mom were going to the store and you asked to go along but she said no, it would not be disobeying if you made a respectful appeal and said, "Mom, I'll miss you. I've got to go along.")*

:: Why do you think Elisha wanted the sons of the prophets to keep Elijah's departure secret? *(Parents, the Bible doesn't say why Elisha wanted to keep this a secret, so let your children try to imagine why. The sons of the prophets were likely a group of young men who were training as prophets.)*

 Pray about It

Thank God for his Word and all the stories he preserved for us to read.

DAY TWO

Remember It

What do you remember about yesterday's story? What do you think is going to happen today?

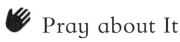 Read 2 Kings 2:7–14.

Think about It Some More

When we read these Old Testament Bible stories, sometimes we forget how amazing they really are. Elijah was a real person who really did get taken up to heaven.

What would it have been like if, when Elisha got back home, one of his neighbors had asked, "So how was your day?" Imagine his reply, "Oh, you know, a typical day for a prophet. First we parted the Jordan and walked across it on dry ground, then the Lord sent a chariot and horses of fire to separate me from my master, Elijah, and took him up in a whirlwind to heaven. Lucky for me I got to see him go, so I got a double portion of his spirit. So by the grace of God I was able to divide the Jordan River and return again from that place on dry ground. So what about you? How was your day?"

What if you told this story to one of your non-Christian neighbors—would she believe you?

Talk about It

:: What happened when Elijah struck the Jordan River with his cloak? *(The river parted, allowing them to walk across on dry ground.)*

:: What is another Bible story where God parted a river? *(When Joshua first went into the Promised Land, God told him to send the ark of God ahead and the river parted. Also, God parted the Red Sea for Israel as they escaped from Egypt and Pharaoh's army.)*

:: Was the cloak Elijah used magic? *(No, the cloak was not magic. God parted the river. Notice in verse 14 what Elisha prayed to the Lord as he struck the river.)*

 ## Pray about It

Praise God for the amazing way he shows his power.

DAY THREE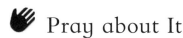

Connect It to Jesus

Can anyone guess how our story this week is about or points forward to Jesus?

Read Mark 9:2–9.

Think about It Some More

Eight hundred years after Elijah left earth in the whirlwind, he appeared again on earth with Moses. This happened when Jesus changed from a normal looking man and showed his disciples the bright white of his glory—when Jesus was transfigured. This showed the disciples who were present that Jesus was the one these men's lives were pointing to.

Elijah's life pointed forward to Jesus as a prophet who would bring God's Word to his people. The life of Moses pointed forward to Jesus as a mediator who would stand in the middle for us, pleading with God. Jesus traded his perfect life for our sinful one that we might be saved. To be sure the disciples understood who was most important, God the Father spoke out saying that Jesus was his Son. Jesus remained while Moses and Elijah disappeared.

Talk about It

:: Who were the two men who appeared on the mountain with Jesus? *(Moses and Elijah were the two men who appeared with Jesus on the mountain.)*

:: How did Moses' life point to Jesus? *(Moses often stood in the middle between God and his people, pleading for their salvation. His life pointed forward to the day when Jesus died on the cross. Now Jesus stands in the middle between God the Father and his children and asks for our salvation. Unlike Moses, Jesus offers his death on the cross as payment for our sins.)*

:: How did Elijah's life point to Jesus? *(Elijah did miracles like Jesus, but most importantly Elijah brought God's word to his people so they could be saved. Jesus not only brought God's word of salvation; the Bible tells us that Jesus is the Word.)*

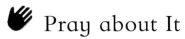 Pray about It

Thank God for the way he used people like Moses and Elijah to point the way to Jesus.

DAY FOUR

Remember It

What has God been teaching you this week through our Bible story?

 Read 2 Kings 2:15–22.

Think about It Some More

A little boy accidentally let go of his helium balloon and it disappeared into the sky. The next day he wanted to go searching for it in his backyard, but his dad told him that he would not find it. Still he urged his father to allow him to look. But after searching his backyard and then his whole neighborhood, he did not find the balloon.

Elijah was the hero of the sons of the prophets. He had probably taught them about God and how to listen for his voice. That is why they insisted they search for him. They didn't understand that God had taken Elijah and he was never coming back.

Talk about It

> ● ● KIDS, ask your parents if they can remember a time when they
> ● ● searched for something that was lost.

(Parents, share a time when you lost something valuable and went on a search for it. Perhaps you lost your keys at the beach or a ring in a lake. Even though you thought you would not find it, you searched anyway.)

:: What did Elisha do in our story today that tells us that he became Elijah's replacement as a prophet? *(First, he told the sons of the prophets not to look for Elijah because he knew they would not find him. Second, he spoke a word of prophecy over the water, and what he said came true.)*

:: Who do the prophets of the Old Testament point forward to? *(The prophets of the Old Testament point forward to Jesus.)*

:: Since we don't have prophets who speak the word of God to us like Elijah and Elisha, how do we hear God's voice? *(We have God's Word written down for us as the Bible. God still speaks through his Word to tell us about his salvation and teach us how to live.)*

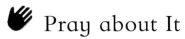 Pray about It

Ask God to speak to you through the Bible.

DAY FIVE

Discover It

Today we look at a passage from a psalm or one of the prophets to see what we can learn from it about Jesus.

 Read Malachi 4:4–6.

Think about It Some More

Years after Elijah was caught up in the whirlwind, God raised up another prophet: Malachi. Malachi prophesied that God was going to bring back Elijah before the Lord returned to save his people. Because of what Malachi said and then wrote down, the people of Israel began to look and hope that Elijah would return one day. They believed that, once Elijah returned, God would send them a deliverer or a savior to lead them to victory.

What they didn't know was that God wasn't going to send the real Elijah back; he was going to send them another prophet who acted like Elijah. John the Baptist was the prophet God sent, and Jesus is the one he came to announce. Jesus said, "For all the Prophets and the Law prophesied until John, and if you are willing to accept it, he is Elijah who is to come" (Matthew 11:13–14).

Talk about It

:: Who did Jesus say was the second Elijah—the one Malachi said was going to come? *(Jesus said John the Baptist was the person Malachi wrote about.)*

:: Read Luke 1:13–17 and then ask your children how the angel's words to Zechariah, John the Baptist's father, fit into our story today. *(The angel told Zechariah that his son would be the Elijah who Malachi wrote about.)*

:: Why do you think God gave his people clues about Jesus, like the one he gave Malachi? *(Parents, use this answer to help draw out ideas from your children. Feel free to give them clues. God wanted his people to be looking forward to Jesus. And, when Jesus finally came, God's people could look back at all that he said through the prophets and see how God worked out his wonderful plan.)*

 Pray about It

Thank God for the way he worked out his plan of salvation from the days of Elijah all the way to today.

Week 65

Elisha's Ministry

Ask each of your children to think of the person who is most like him or her—someone who likes or does the same things as he or she does. Perhaps your son is left-handed and plays basketball and has a friend who is left-handed and plays basketball too. See if you can come up with the person most like each member of your family.

Say, "This week you will hear more about the prophet Elisha, whose ministry was very similar to that of his master, Elijah, and very similar to the prophet of prophets: Jesus Christ."

DAY ONE

Picture It

Imagine that Mom says she's giving you a miracle cookie jar. She says that no matter how many cookies you take out of the jar there will always be more. Each day when you go to bed you look in the cookie jar and count the cookies that are left. Then when you get up in the morning and open the jar, it is full again.

When your friends come over, one of the first things you do is tell them about the miracle cookie jar. And for three months the cookie jar never runs out of cookies. Then, one day when you are having trouble falling asleep, you decide to get a drink of milk. But when you go into the kitchen, you discover the secret of the miracle cookie jar: your mom is hard at work baking cookies. She has been the one filling the miracle jar all along.

In today's story, you will read about a widow's jug of oil that pours and pours and pours out more oil. See if you can figure out who was working to make that miracle happen.

 Read 2 Kings 4:1–7.

Think about It Some More

This story reminds us of the earlier one about Elijah and the widow whose flour and oil didn't run out during the drought. We shouldn't be surprised that Elisha is doing similar miracles as his former teacher. After all, he did ask God for a double portion of Elijah's spirit. Elisha is not a magician, and the jug of oil in the widow's house is not a trick jug. Elisha did not sneak into the widow's house and hide a small pipe, through which he could secretly pump oil from a barrel behind her house. God, working through Elisha, created oil inside the jar and it kept pouring out.

In order to pay her debts off and have money left over, the widow must have had to collect many jars. Her neighbors must have wondered why she needed all those containers. They may have thought that the poor widow, who owed a lot of money, was losing her mind.

But in spite of Elisha's strange instructions, the widow obeyed them exactly. The woman had faith in Elisha's instructions—she believed that Elisha's plan would save her.

Talk about It

:: Elisha gave the widow the instructions, but who really multiplied the oil? *(God is the one who multiplied the oil.)*

:: How did God make the oil pour and pour? *(Parents, this is a trick question that leads the children to look for a logical explanation when there is none. You can have some fun and ask them follow-up questions like, "Are you sure Elisha didn't have a large barrel of oil hidden in her roof where the oil leaked into the jars?" Then help your children understand that there was no trick to what happened. God by his power multiplied the oil!)*

:: How did the widow trust God in this story? *(The widow did what Elisha told her to do. Her husband had also been a prophet. Therefore we can assume she believed in God and went to Elisha, God's main prophet, to ask him for help. She knew help would come, not just from Elisha, but from God whom Elisha represented.)*

 ## Pray about It

Ask God to help you to have a strong faith like the widow and trust and obey his Word.

DAY TWO

Remember It

What do you remember about yesterday's story? What do you think is going to happen today?

 Read 2 Kings 4:8–17.

Think about It Some More

Did you ever notice that when someone gives you a gift it makes you want to give them something back? For instance, if a friend from school sends you a birthday card you might want to send a card to them when it is their birthday. Or if a friend gives you a present for your birthday, something would stir inside you to bless them on their birthday as well.

One of the reasons we like to give gifts is because God is like that. He says that if we give a gift to God, or even to another person, God will reward us (Luke 6:38).

That is what happened in our story today. A woman was serving Elisha to bless him. But really, the woman and her husband were serving God. She was not looking for any payment in return, but God knew that she wanted a son—exactly what Elisha promised God would give to her. We can't outgive God.

Talk about It

:: What did Elisha promise to the woman? *(Elisha promised her that in one year she would have a son.)*

:: Although Elisha was the one to tell the woman she would have a baby, who really gave the woman a son? *(God was the one who gave the woman her son.)*

:: Can you remember other stories where God gave children to women who were not able to have children for some reason? *(Sarah had Isaac. Rebekah had Jacob and Esau. Rachel had Joseph. Hannah had Samuel. Elizabeth had John the Baptist.)*

:: What was the most miraculous birth of all? *(God gave Mary the baby Jesus, who was completely human, yet completely God.)*

 Pray about It

Think of ways that God has been kind to your family. Thank God for his kindness.

DAY THREE

Connect It to Jesus

Can anyone guess how our story this week is about or points forward to Jesus?

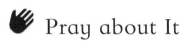 Read 2 Kings 4:18–37.

Think about It Some More

God used Elisha to multiply a widow's oil, to give a wealthy woman a son, and then to raise the son back to life after he dies. The miracles that Elisha performs illustrate God's power and point to the day when God would send another prophet even greater than Elisha.

When Jesus comes, he also does miracles. He turns water into wine and multiplies a few fishes and loaves of bread to feed a crowd of five thousand. Jesus heals the sick and even raises the dead. But Jesus goes further than Elisha: he dies on the cross for our sin and then rises again from the dead.

Because Jesus was a man, he could take our punishment; because he was God, death had no power over him. Every time we read about God raising a person from the dead, like in this story, it should remind us of Jesus' resurrection and his power over death. Through the raising of the Shunammite woman's son from the dead, God was showing us his power over death.

God uses that same power to save all of us who believe in Jesus. Jesus said, "I am the resurrection and the life. Whoever believes in me, though he die, yet shall he live" (John 11:25).

Talk about It

:: How did the Shunammite woman show that she had faith in God? *(When her son died, she knew that Elisha could help her.)*

:: How do we know from this story that God was the one who raised the boy from the dead? *(Elisha prayed to God to raise the boy.)*

:: What does this story teach us about God's power over death? *(This story teaches us that even though a person dies, God can raise him from the dead. That should give us hope that even though we die, God can raise us from the dead.)*

:: If you had been the Shunammite woman, what would you have done when you saw God raise your son? *(Help your children see that she would have been excited and would have praised and thanked God for what he did.)*

 ## Pray about It

Praise God for his power over death.

DAY FOUR

Remember It

What has God been teaching you this week through our Bible story?

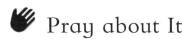 Read 2 Kings 4:38–41.

Think about It Some More

If someone put poisoned mushrooms in your stew, you would have to throw the whole pot away or risk dying.

That is pretty much what happened to the men in our story today. They went out into the field looking for wild plants to make some stew. Someone found some gourds and added them to the stew, unaware that they were poisonous. As soon as the others tasted the stew, they realized it was no good and called out to Elisha. When they followed Elisha's command to bring some flour and he added a little to the stew, it was fine to eat.

Before their fall, God told Adam and Eve they could eat of all the fruit in the garden. It was only after they sinned that some of God's creation became poisonous. Our story today gives us a sneak peek into God's plan to take away the curse and remove poison from the earth.

Talk about It

 KIDS, ask your parents what food they like the least.

(Parents, this is a fun question you can then turn around and ask your children.)

:: How did one man ruin the stew? *(He picked poisoned plants and added them to the stew.)*

:: What would have happened if the poisonous plants tasted good? *(All the men would have eaten the stew and would have become sick and possibly died.)*

:: Who had the power to make the stew tasty and safe to eat? *(Although it was Elisha who added the flour to the stew, it was God who prevented the poison from hurting the men.)*

Pray about It

Thank God for his power over all creation.

DAY FIVE

Discover It

Today we look at a passage from a psalm or one of the prophets to see what we can learn from it about Jesus.

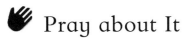 Read Habakkuk 1:5–12 and Acts 13:38–48.

Think about It Some More

The Chaldeans had a terrifying army. They attacked quickly like a leopard because they were on horses. They were also compared to an eagle that attacks its prey without warning. Because an eagle attacks by diving down through the air, you can't hear him coming.

But hidden in Habakkuk's description of the terrible Chaldean army is a promise that God was going to do a work so amazing, that even Israel would not believe it if God told them what he was going to do.

In the book of Acts, Paul teaches that Jesus' death on the cross was the amazing thing that God was planning to do. Paul uses Habakkuk's words about the Chaldean army to warn the people he speaks to. He says that anyone who does not believe in Jesus will one day find that a swift enemy will come in and attack them without warning, just as Habakkuk had described.

Talk about It

:: What made the Chaldean army so terrifying? *(They attacked quickly on horseback, without warning.)*

:: What did Paul explain was the amazing thing that God planned to do? *(Paul told them about the gospel—Jesus' death and resurrection.)*

:: How did Paul use Habakkuk's words to warn the people he was speaking to? *(Parents, if your children don't get the answer reread Acts 13:40–41. Paul was warning that if they did not believe, they would face an enemy like the Chaldeans that Habakkuk described.)*

:: What is the enemy that comes to us swiftly like the Chaldeans? *(God warns that death and God's judgment can come upon a man or woman swiftly and without warning. If we die without trusting Jesus, we will face God's judgment for our sin.)*

 Pray about It

Ask God to help each person you know to believe and put his or her trust in Jesus so they do not need to be afraid of death.

Week 66

Naaman Is Cured

Use the following description of leprosy to teach your children about the disease. This will prove to be helpful later in the week. If you have access to a microscope, focus in on a drop of pond water to give them a glimpse of God's microscopic world. Or explain to them that if your house were the size of a grain of rice, the little ants that run around in the backyard would be like the bacteria.

Gerhard Hansen was a doctor who worked among leprosy patients in Norway in the late 1800s. After caring for many patients, he guessed that the disease was caused by a very small bacterium, so to prove his theory he began to look for these tiny organisms through a microscope. In 1873, Hansen discovered the bacterium that causes this terrible disease. Everyone laughed at him at first, but his discovery led to medicines that can cure leprosy, which is now called Hansen's disease.

Today, people with Hansen's disease can be cured, but they have to take pills for six months or even a year. This week we will learn how God healed Naaman of this terrible disease in a single instant.

DAY ONE

Picture It

Imagine that you lived in California and came down with a terrible disease like cancer. When you went to the doctor he told you that the local hospital would not be able to help you, but that there was a hospital in Philadelphia, Pennsylvania, that could cure your disease. Even though you would have to travel far, and it would be expensive to fly across the country and pay for a place to stay in Philadelphia, you would do whatever it took to get there.

In our story today, that is what happened to Naaman. He thought his leprosy was incurable, but one servant girl knew differently. She told him where he could go to be healed.

 Read 2 Kings 5:1–7.

Think about It Some More

God makes all things work together for good to accomplish his plans. For instance, God used the Syrians to attack Israel in a time when the kings of Israel were wicked and leading the people in idol worship.

During one of those raids, God allowed a little girl to be taken away from her family. Even though that sounds bad, God had a plan. He placed the little girl in the home of a man he wanted to heal. Perhaps in heaven we will meet this little girl who trusted in God. She didn't tell Naaman to pray to Baal or one of his false gods; she pointed Naaman to Elisha, a prophet of the living God. She also believed strongly that Naaman would be healed.

Talk about It

:: Why was a little Israelite girl living in Syria serving Naaman's wife? *(The little girl had been captured in a raid and taken to Syria as a slave.)*

:: When the servant girl learned about Naaman's sickness what did she say? *(She told him to go to the prophet Elisha and he could be healed.)*

:: Why would Naaman believe the servant girl and travel all that way? *(Parents, it does not tell us why, but we can assume two things. First, the girl's faith was strong and did not waver. Secondly, Naaman was desperate. His leprosy must have been in the early stages, as he still had contact with people. But Naaman would have known how terrible the disease was. Soon he would have to leave his wife and king and become an outcast with the other lepers.)*

 Pray about It

Ask God to give you a strong faith in the power of God like the little girl in the story had.

DAY TWO

Remember It

What do you remember about yesterday's story? What do you think is going to happen today?

 Read 2 Kings 5:8–14.

Think about It Some More

Naaman left Syria with 750 pounds of silver and 150 pounds of gold. That meant he needed about ten camels or mules along with servants to lead them. He needed food for his journey and feed for the animals, and the king gave Naaman ten changes of clothes to take.

Naaman traveled all the way to Israel and finally found Elisha, the prophet the little girl had told him about. But when he got to Elisha's house, the prophet didn't even come out to greet him. Thankfully for Naaman his servants convinced him to obey the word of the prophet and wash in the river. As soon as he did the leprosy was gone!

It is always good to listen to the people God has put in our lives to help us.

Talk about It

:: What did Naaman take along on his journey? *(Naaman took silver, gold, servants, changes of clothes, etc. Parents, have your children guess other things that he needed as well, like a pillow or blanket and food.)*

:: Why did Naaman get angry once he reached the prophet? *(Elisha would not even come out of his house, but only sent Naaman instructions to wash in the river. Naaman felt he could have washed in the rivers back home and not made such a long journey, but his servants encouraged him to obey the prophet's word and when he did he was healed.)*

:: How does the healing of Naaman, a Syrian, remind us of God's promise to Abraham to reach all the nations? *(Naaman's healing reminds us that God's love extends to all people on earth.)*

:: Who has God placed in your life to help you when you get angry? *(Parents, help your children see that God has placed you in their lives to help them when they get angry, and to point them back to trusting God.)*

 Pray about It

Ask God to heal the people you know who are sick.

DAY THREE

Connect It to Jesus

Can anyone guess how our story this week is about or points forward to Jesus?

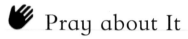 Read 2 Kings 5:15–19.

Think about It Some More

Jesus said, "There were many lepers in Israel in the time of the prophet Elisha, and none of them was cleansed, but only Naaman the Syrian" (Luke 4:27). Naaman had no idea that Jesus would use his story to show the stubborn people of Israel that God's salvation was going to reach out to all people.

Just as the people of Israel in Elisha's day rejected God and followed idols, the people of Israel rejected Jesus and refused to believe in him. But God's plan was bigger than the nation of Israel—God planned to reach all the nations. That is why he healed Naaman, who was not from Israel; that is why everyone, no matter what nation they come from, can be saved today. God's salvation through Jesus is for everyone.

Talk about It

:: What did Naaman do when he came out of the water and saw that his disease was gone? *(Naaman was excited and went back to Elisha to give him a gift.)*

:: What did Naaman think about the God of Israel after he was healed? *(Naaman realized that the God of Israel was the only true God.)*

:: How are we like Naaman? *(Although we don't have leprosy, we all need God to heal us from our sin; and most of us don't come from Israel. Naaman's healing was a sign that pointed to the day when God would reach out to people from every language and country to heal them of their sin and grant them forgiveness.)*

Pray about It

Thank God for healing us of our sin.

DAY FOUR

Remember It

What has God been teaching you this week through our Bible story?

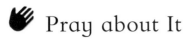 Read 2 Kings 5:20–27.

Think about It Some More

Gehazi couldn't believe Elisha would let Naaman go without taking some of the treasure he offered to him. So without talking to Elisha, Gehazi decided to catch up to Naaman and ask him for a gift. Instead of telling Naaman the truth, Gehazi lied. Then when he returned to Elisha, he told a second lie to hide his first one. But since God knows everything, Gehazi could not hide his sin from the Lord, who told Elisha what he had done.

Talk about It

> ● ● KIDS, ask your parents if they remember a time when they told a lie
> ● ● and to cover their first lie, they had to keep on lying.

(Parents, try to think of an example and humble yourselves in front of your children. Our example in confessing our weaknesses before them gives them courage to do the same.)

:: Why did Gehazi lie to Naaman? *(Gehazi wanted a gift and thought up a story that would make Naaman want to give it to him. Gehazi lied to hide his sin.)*

:: Can you remember a time when you lied to get something or a time when you lied to hide your sin? *(Parents, encourage your children to try to think of a time when they didn't tell the truth.)*

Pray about It

Ask God to forgive you for not telling the truth and help you to obey the Lord.

DAY FIVE

Discover It

Today we look at a passage from a psalm or one of the prophets to see what we can learn from it about Jesus.

 Read Psalm 111.

Think about It Some More

The words of Psalm 111 make up a song that praises God for who he is and all he has done. Once you understand that, you can try to think of Bible stories that match the different lines of the psalm.

For instance, verse 2 tells us, "great are the works of the LORD." This reminds us that God has done all kinds of great things starting with the world that he created. Verse 5 says the Lord "provides food for those who fear him." This reminds us of how God sent ravens with food for Elijah during the drought.

The most important verse is verse 9, which says, "He sent redemption to his people; he has commanded his covenant forever." This verse points to Jesus. "Redemption" means to buy back something. God sent his only Son Jesus to buy back his people from the curse of death. The price Jesus paid to buy us back (redeem us) was his life. Jesus died on the cross to take our punishment and set us free. Anyone who trusts in him gets to live with God in heaven forever.

Talk about It

:: Take a look at verse 6 and see if you can remember a story where God showed his people the "power of his works." *(Your children should be able to come up with several stories like the crossing of the Red Sea, healing the sick, or sending the plagues to Pharaoh.)*

:: How could the psalm writer know to include a line about redemption long before Jesus came to earth? *(The simple answer is that God told him to. Many of the psalms are prophetic. That means they speak things that God revealed to the psalmist that he wanted his people to know. Since God knew exactly what he was going to do in sending his Son, God directed the psalm writer to include some words about his redemption.)*

:: There is a line in this psalm that tells us that God tells the truth and can be trusted. Which one is it? *(Verses 7–8 describe God as faithful and trustworthy. Unlike Gehazi in our story this week, God does not lie.)*

:: Which is your favorite line from this psalm? *(Parents, if your children are too young to read, coach them along by giving them a few choices to pick from.)*

Pray about It

Instead of making up a prayer, simply pray the words of this psalm out loud. Most of the psalms work as great prayers to God.

Week 67

The Fall of Israel

One of the reasons God judged Israel was because they set up wooden poles and statues of the goddess Asherah on every high hill and under every green tree. The Scriptures tell us they did this secretly.

To demonstrate this, take wooden blocks, clothespins, or dominoes, and set them up all over the room where you have your Bible study. Place them on top of picture frames, furniture, and door frames, and under tables, chairs, and lamps.

When the children come in and notice the objects and ask why they are there, pretend you don't know anything about it. After playing along for a bit, explain that the objects represent the idols Israel set up in the land, thinking God would not see them. Leave them up as you do this week's lesson, which considers the consequences God brought to Israel for their disobedience.

DAY ONE

Picture It

Imagine that as you are leaving home for school one day, Mom reminds you to be sure to take your coat. But since you don't feel like carrying a coat, you deliberately disobey her instructions.

As you walk down the road, a cold wind begins to blow and it starts to rain. Instead of running home to get your coat, you stubbornly continue on. By the time you get to school, you are soaking wet, you're sneezing, and your throat is beginning to hurt. Only then do you realize you were wrong for disobeying Mom's instructions.

Sometimes God allows bad consequences in order to teach us not to disobey. Let's see what bad consequences God brings to Hoshea.

 Read 2 Kings 17:1–5.

Think about It Some More

Hoshea disobeyed God. Because of this, God brought Shalmaneser to attack Israel. But even then, Hoshea did not call upon God. He was stubborn and looked to So, the king of Egypt, to save him instead. But when Shalmaneser found out Hoshea was calling to Egypt for help, he put Hoshea in prison.

Hoshea thought he could live his life without God, but he was wrong. God used Shalmaneser to discipline Hoshea. The Bible says that when we disobey God we get bad consequences.

Talk about It

:: What bad consequences did Hoshea get because he didn't obey the Lord? *(God didn't rescue him when Shalmaneser attacked him. Then he was thrown into prison.)*

:: Did you ever get bad consequences when you disobeyed? *(Parents, help your children remember a time when, because of their disobedience, they received bad consequences.)*

:: Who did Hoshea send messengers to for help? *(Hoshea sent messengers to So, king of Egypt, hoping that he would side with Hoshea against Shalmaneser.)*

:: Whom should Hoshea have called out to? *(He should have called out to the Lord.)*

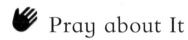 Pray about It

Ask God to help you obey the Lord, and call out to him for help in times of trouble.

DAY TWO

Remember It

What do you remember about yesterday's story? What do you think is going to happen today?

 Read 2 Kings 17:6–14.

Think about It Some More

Warnings are meant to help us. If you see a sign on a park bench that says, "Warning, wet paint" and you sit down on the bench anyway, you can't blame anyone but yourself when you get paint all over your pants.

God sent prophet after prophet to warn his people not to worship idols. But in the end they would not listen to God's prophets. So God used the king of Assyria to punish them. He captured their cities and carried the people of Israel away as his slaves.

Talk about It

:: How did the people of Israel disobey God? *(They built "high places" and altars to false gods and worshiped them instead of the Lord.)*

:: Whom did God send to warn them to turn away from their idol worship? *(God sent his prophets to ask them to turn away from their idol worship.)*

:: God sent his prophets to warn Israel. How does God warn us today? *(God warns us through his Word, the Bible. God also gives us wise parents and friends who love God. Like Israel, we make a choice to follow God or turn away from him.)*

 Pray about It

Ask God to help you follow him and obey his Word.

DAY THREE

Connect It to Jesus

Can anyone guess how our story this week is about or points forward to Jesus?

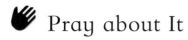 Read 2 Kings 17:15–17.

Think about It Some More

When you look at Israel's history, you can see the consequences that came to them when they turned away from the Lord. Their sin got so bad that in the end they were killing their children as sacrifices to their false gods.

God could have completely destroyed all of Israel because of their sin, but he didn't because God had a plan to save his people. One day he would send his only Son Jesus to die for their sins. No matter how bad Israel's sin became, the Lord did not abandon his people because he loved them. Even though he allowed them to be defeated, captured, and taken to Babylon, their captivity would last for only seventy years.

Talk about It

:: How many of God's commands did Israel break? *(They broke all of God's commands.)*

:: Why didn't God destroy Israel for their sin? *(God made a promise to Abraham to bless all the nations of the world through his children. That promise was to come through Abraham's far-off grandson Jesus.)*

:: Why doesn't God destroy us when we sin? *(God wants to give all of us a chance to become a part of his promise to Abraham. If we trust in Jesus all our sin is taken away. Instead of punishing us, God punished his Son Jesus in our place.)*

 Pray about It

Thank Jesus for not punishing us as soon as we sin, but for giving us a chance to believe and trust in his Son, Jesus.

DAY FOUR

Remember It

What has God been teaching you this week through our Bible story?

 Read 2 Kings 17:18–20.

Think about It Some More

Hoshea and the other kings who led northern Israel were all very wicked. That's why God used the nation of Assyria to attack and defeat them. But God protected the tribe of Judah in the south because many of their kings worshiped him and obeyed his commands. (We are going to learn the story about the kings of Judah next week.) But in the end, even the kings of Judah disobeyed the Lord and would not listen to God's prophets.

Talk about It

> ● ●   KIDS, ask your parents if they can remember a person who disobeyed
> ● ●   God's commands and, as a result, received bad consequences.

(Parents, think of a person whom you can remember who did something foolish or, if you don't have any personal stories, you can even look in the daily newspaper to find a story about a person who went to jail because of something he did.)

:: Why does God allow bad consequences to come when we sin? *(God uses bad consequences to teach us that sin is bad.)*

:: What happened to the people of Judah in the south? *(Even though God spared them at first, in the end they fell away like the ten tribes in the north. In the end all of Israel and Judah left God to follow idols.)*

:: The last thing verse 20 says is that the Lord cast his people out of his sight. What did God do to save them? *(God sent his Son Jesus to die for them. Even though Israel and Judah sinned badly, God always had a few people left who loved and obeyed him. Some in Judah rejected idols and trusted that the Lord had a plan to deliver them. Since God's plan was to send Jesus to take away their sin, anyone who was trusting in God's plan was trusting in Jesus. That is how people who lived before Jesus was born were saved.)*

 Pray about It

Thank God for allowing bad consequences to come when we sin to help us stay away from sin and follow him.

DAY FIVE

Discover It

Today we look at a passage from a psalm or one of the prophets to see what we can learn from it about Jesus.

 Read Psalm 78:1–8.

Think about It Some More

Hidden in the first four verses of this psalm is a secret message that points to Jesus. If Jesus had not pointed it out, we might have missed it. Jesus said that when Asaph wrote this psalm he was talking about how Jesus was going to teach in parables.

Isn't it amazing that long before Jesus was born God gave his prophets hints about how he was going to save them? Even while God's people were unfaithful, he was speaking to them about the way he would one day save them.

Talk about It

:: What are the ways God's people were stubborn and rebellious? *(God's people often turned away from him to serve the false gods of the people around them.)*

:: Verse 2 says that God is going to open his mouth and tell parables. Who is that verse speaking about? *(Verse 2 is speaking about Jesus.)*

:: Do you remember any of the parables Jesus taught? *(Parents, if your children can't remember any, give them a few hints. Luke 15 contains parables about a coin, a sheep, and a son who ran away.)*

Pray about It

Thank God for never giving up on us—even though we sin.

Week 68

Good King, Bad King

To demonstrate how the kings of Judah went back and forth from good to bad and bad to good, read the following names aloud in numbered order and see if your children can guess if they were good or bad kings.

Bad king	Somewhat good king	Really good king
1. Rehoboam		
2. Abijam		3. Asa
		4. Jehoshaphat
5. Jehoram		
6. Ahaziah		
7. Athaliah	8. Joash	
	9 Amaziah	
	10. Uzziah (Azariah)	
	11. Jotham	
12. Ahaz		13. Hezekiah
14. Manasseh		
15. Amon		16. Josiah
17. Jehoahaz		
18. Jehoiakim		
19. Jehoiachin		
20. Zedekiah		

    Going through this list should help your children realize how many of the kings of Judah did not do what was right in the eyes of the Lord. (During the divided kingdom there were also 19 kings of Israel, and only one was somewhat good.) This week we will begin to learn about some of the good and bad kings of Judah.

DAY ONE

Picture It

When water from a flood breaks into a home, it creates a terrible mess. As water rushes over the riverbank, it picks up loose soil, clay, and any trash that is left on the ground. Then as it rages downriver and enters the house, it brings with it a slurry of mud and garbage. When the flood is over, the water returns to the river or dries up, but it leaves behind a thick coating of stinky mud on everything.

The mess left behind in the flood-damaged house can be over an inch thick and may smell like dead fish! The only way to save a house that has been flooded is to strip it down to the wood skeleton. All the muddy carpet and drywall must be thrown away, and the bare wood walls dried out. Only then can rebuilding begin.

Our story today isn't about a flood of water, but a flood of sin. Sin brought a lot of bad things into Israel, like idols, that had to be cleaned up by the new king.

 Read 2 Chronicles 29:1–30.

Think about It Some More

Hezekiah became king of Judah not long after the Kingdom of Israel was conquered by Assyria. (We read about that in last week's lesson.) For 160 years before Hezekiah took the throne, the kings of Judah were not following God. During that long time the temple was neglected and false idols were brought into it.

When Hezekiah became king, he cleansed the temple and destroyed the idols. Then he restored worship of God there. The sin of the kings and people before him was like a flood, leaving behind a big mess. But Hezekiah did a great job clearing out the idols and turning the hearts of the people back to God.

Talk about It

:: Why did the temple need to be cleaned out and repaired? *(The wicked kings had brought their idols into the temple. They also were careless, so there were parts of the temple that needed to be repaired.)*

:: What else did Hezekiah do after he cleaned up the temple? *(He offered sacrifices for the sin of Israel and worshiped God.)*

:: Why did the priests throw or sprinkle blood on the altar and other parts of the temple after they had just cleaned it up? *(You can't sweep out sin like you can dirt. Sin needs to be covered. The blood of the animals represented the blood of Jesus that covers our sin.)*

:: What was Hezekiah talking about when he said in verse 9 that "our fathers have fallen by the sword"? *(The ten tribes in the north had been taken captive by force as a judgment from God against their sin. However, because of the grace of God working through Hezekiah, the Kingdom of Judah was spared.)*

 Pray about It

Ask God to help you obey him as Hezekiah did.

DAY TWO

Remember It

What do you remember about yesterday's story? What do you think is going to happen today?

 Read 2 Chronicles 32:32—33:13.

Think about It Some More

Instead of obeying God like his father, Hezekiah, Manasseh rebelled against all that his father had done and rejected the God of Israel to follow pagan gods. The list of his sins goes from bad to worse.

First, he rebuilt the high places around Jerusalem. If that wasn't bad enough, he built idols to Baal and even brought them back into the temple, God's house. This was very sad because his father was the one who had cleaned up the temple and taken the idols out. Then the worst thing of all happened: Manasseh sacrificed his sons to a false god.

Instead of destroying Manasseh on the spot, God was kind to Manasseh and allowed him to be captured instead of killed. God wanted to give Manasseh a chance to turn away from his sin. When the king of Assyria defeated Manasseh and captured him, Manasseh realized that none of his false gods could save him. Then he remembered the God of his father and called out for help. God showed kindness and mercy to Manasseh by restoring his kingship.

Talk about It

:: How was Manasseh different from his father? *(Manasseh rebelled against his father, Hezekiah. Even more, he rebelled against God and served idols.)*

:: Why can't a parent's faith automatically save her children and guarantee they will follow God? *(There are no guarantees that you will follow God just because you were raised in a Christian home. Each person has to choose to follow God for herself. Our parents' faith in God cannot save us; we need to have our own faith in God.)*

:: What can children do to make sure they follow God like their mom and dad? *(You can read your Bible to learn about God; you can pray and ask God to help you believe and trust in him; and you can recognize that you are a sinner who needs God to save you.)*

 Pray about It

Parents lead your children in a prayer to ask God to help them follow him.

DAY THREE

Connect It to Jesus

Can anyone guess how our story this week is about or points forward to Jesus?

 Read 2 Chronicles 30:1–26.

Think about It Some More

In today's story, we return to Manasseh's father, King Hezekiah, to learn about something that he did after he took down the idols in the land.

Hezekiah called the people to obey the Lord by celebrating the Passover. Then, after the Passover lamb was sacrificed, thousands of bulls were also killed. All of these animals that were sacrificed pointed forward to Jesus. In the end, when Hezekiah's son Manasseh sinned against God, God did not kill him. The only way God could allow Manasseh to be forgiven was because of what Jesus did.

Likewise, there is only one way God can forgive our sin. He did that by giving up his Son to die in our place. That's what the Passover celebration pointed to.

Talk about It

:: What did God want his people to remember by celebrating the Passover? *(God wanted them to remember the day he sent the last plague through Egypt, and how each Israelite family killed a lamb in the place of their firstborn son and smeared the blood on the doorpost. When the angel of death came through, he passed over the homes with the blood on the doorframes.)*

:: Who did the Passover lamb point forward to? *(The Passover lamb pointed to Jesus. God sent his Son to die in our place so death would pass over everyone who trusts in Jesus for the forgiveness of their sins.)*

:: Why don't we worship God by killing bulls and goats and lambs anymore? *(When Jesus died on the cross his sacrifice took away the sins of all men for all time. Jesus becomes the once forever Passover lamb offering for everyone who believes and trusts in him.)*

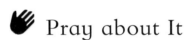 Pray about It

Ask God to help you trust in Jesus as your Passover Lamb.

DAY FOUR

Remember It

What has God been teaching you this week through our Bible story?

 Read 2 Chronicles 33:14–23.

Think about It Some More

If a puppy is allowed to climb all over the furniture as it grows up, you are going to have a difficult time retraining him to stay off a new couch when he gets older. Although you might want to keep him off, his old habits of climbing up on the couch will not go away so easily.

That is what happened to Israel. For years Manasseh worshiped idols at the high places in and around Jerusalem. Although Manasseh turned away from his sin, the people had been trained to worship idols at the high places. Even though they joined him in worshiping the Lord, they did it at the high places, not at the temple. Then, sadly, after Manasseh died his son Amon led the people back to idol worship again.

Talk about It

> KIDS, ask your parents if they ever had a dog that they trained to do something they regretted.

(Parents, this is a fun question. If you never had a dog, perhaps you can remember a friend who had a dog that was trained to do something that the owner later regretted.)

:: Why didn't the people worship the Lord in the temple? *(They had been trained to worship at the high places and continued worshiping the Lord there even after Manasseh turned away from his sin.)*

:: Why do you think Manasseh's son Amon turned away from the Lord? *(Amon probably grew up watching his father worship idols. When his father died he returned to the idol worship he learned as a boy.)*

 ## Pray about It

Ask God to help you worship him only.

DAY FIVE

Discover It

Today we look at a passage from a psalm or one of the prophets to see what we can learn from it about Jesus.

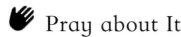 Read 2 Kings 19.

Think about It Some More

In this story, the king of Assyria attacked God's people around Jerusalem and demanded that King Hezekiah surrender. But what the king of Assyria didn't know was that God had special plans for the tribe of Judah. Hezekiah called upon God's prophet Isaiah who told the king not to worry, that God had plans for the tribe of Judah. Not an arrow would fall in the city of Jerusalem because God was preserving a remnant. (A remnant is a portion of something left over.) In this case, God promised that a portion of the tribe of Judah would always survive because one day a very special king would be born into that tribe. That king, of course, was Jesus.

Talk about It

:: What is a remnant? *(A remnant is a part left over. Even though God judged Israel by allowing enemies to attack them, he promised they would always have survivors. He called the people that were left over the remnant of Israel.)*

:: Why was it important for God to make sure there were always survivors from the tribe of Judah? *(God had promised that the Savior would come from Judah, and God always keeps his word. When God promised to bless all the nations of the world through Abraham's offspring, he meant it. So God preserved a remnant of Israel as part of his promise to bring the world a Savior, Jesus.)*

:: When the king of Assyria was about to attack, what did Hezekiah do? *(He prayed to the Lord [see verses 16–19].)*

 ## Pray about It

Thank God for always keeping his word, and for protecting Judah so one day Jesus could be born from that tribe.

Week 69

Jonah and Nineveh

Gather your children and play a game of charades with scenes from the life of Jonah. Here are a few scenes you can act out to see if the others can guess who and what is being represented:

    :: *Jonah runs away from Nineveh and boards a ship that sails into a great storm.*

    :: *Jonah is thrown overboard and swallowed by a great fish.*

    :: *Jonah prays to the Lord, and the fish spits him out onto dry land.*

    :: *Jonah goes to Nineveh and proclaims God's word.*

Say, "This week, you will read the story of Jonah and how he tried to run away from God."

DAY ONE

Picture It

Imagine that you were in your room and you heard Mom announce that it was time to do homework. You could hide under the bed or behind some clothes in your closet, but if you didn't come out in a few minutes, Mom would call again and soon come looking for you. In a situation like this, there is no way to get out of doing your homework.

    If you know you can't hide from Mom when she asks you to do something, you can be sure that you can't hide from God when *he* asks you to do something. But in our story, Jonah tried to do just that.

 Read Jonah 1:1–6.

Think about It Some More

This is one of the most amazing adventures in the Old Testament. In it we learn that we can't run away from God and his plan for our lives, and that when God wants us to do something, he can use his power over creation to lead us to obey.

    Jonah was a prophet in the Kingdom of Israel about 65 years before King Hezekiah took the throne. God told Jonah to go to the city of Nineveh and tell the people to repent of their sin. Later in the book of Jonah, we will learn that Jonah did not want to obey because he didn't want the people of Nineveh to repent. He didn't want God to forgive them. That is why he ran away—he wanted God to wipe them out! But God didn't have to come looking for Jonah because God sees everything all the time. Not a minute goes by that God doesn't know exactly where we are and what we are doing.

Talk about It

:: Where can you go to hide from God? *(There isn't any place you can go to hide from God. God knows everything and always knows where you are and what you are doing.)*

:: Where did Jonah go to try to get away from God? *(Jonah boarded a ship going in the opposite direction from Nineveh.)*

:: What did God do to stop Jonah from running away? *(God brought a great wind upon the sea that threatened to destroy the boat Jonah was on.)*

:: Why didn't Jonah want to obey God? *(Nineveh was one of Israel's enemies, so Jonah wanted God to destroy them. He was afraid that if he warned the people of Nineveh, they would turn from their sin and God would forgive them.)*

 Pray about It

Praise God that he knows where we are all the time and that we can't run away from God.

DAY TWO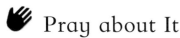

Remember It

What do you remember about yesterday's story? What do you think is going to happen today?

Read Jonah 1:7—2:10.

Think about It Some More

When you run away from God, watch out! It is like playing tag with a thousand kids who are all trying to catch you. There is no possible way to run away and hide.

Since every plant and animal and all the land and ocean are under God's command, he can use any of them to chase you down. God didn't allow Jonah to get away. He used the storm, the sailors, and even a giant fish to capture Jonah. Imagine what that day was like!

Did you ever wonder what it was like for Jonah to stay in the belly of that fish? It might have been like sitting in a dark and slimy roller coaster seat, as the fish rose to the top of the water then dove deep, back into the ocean again and again.

Talk about It

:: What would have happened to Jonah if God had not sent the fish to save him? *(We don't know for sure, but he could have drowned.)*

:: How did God show his mercy toward Jonah? *(God was patient with Jonah and allowed him to live, even though he was disobedient. He could have killed Jonah, but instead God put him through a storm and into the belly of a great fish to teach Jonah an important lesson.)*

:: What did Jonah do that shows us that he turned away from his sin? *(Jonah prayed and thanked God for saving him.)*

 Pray about It

Thank God for saving Jonah, even though he disobeyed.

DAY THREE

Connect It to Jesus

Can anyone guess how our story this week is about or points forward to Jesus?

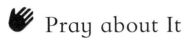 Read Matthew 12:39–41.

Think about It Some More

It might seem like Jonah's running away could have ruined God's plan. After all, God told him to go to Nineveh and Jonah ran the other way. But our sin can never stop God's plan.

God knew that Jonah was going to try to run away. God knew he would get on a ship. God even planned that Jonah would be swallowed by a great fish. God also knew that one day Jesus was going to use Jonah's story in talking to the religious rulers who didn't believe in him. Isn't it amazing how God can plan all of history from beginning to end? Jesus said that Jonah's time in the fish was just like his time in the grave before his resurrection. God rescued Jonah from the fish and God rescued us by the death and resurrection of his Son Jesus. Everything that happens is a part of God's plan. In this case, Jonah's story became a small part of the gospel story.

Talk about It

:: How do we know that Jesus believed the story of Jonah was true? *(Jesus talked about Jonah and the fish as an historic fact and used it as an example.)*

:: How did Jesus compare his life to the life of Jonah? *(Jesus compared Jonah's time in the fish to his time in the tomb following his death.)*

:: God saved Jonah by having a fish swallow him and then spit him back up onto the shore. How did God save us? *(God sent his only Son Jesus to die on the cross for our sins.)*

 Pray about It

Thank God for the way he plans all of history from beginning to end.

DAY FOUR

Remember It

What has God been teaching you this week through our Bible story?

 Read Jonah 3:1—4:11.

Think about It Some More

Instead of punishing Nineveh for all the bad things they did, God heard their prayers and did not destroy them. That made Jonah mad. He thought Nineveh deserved to be punished, and he knew that God was kind and forgiving. That was why he didn't want to go in the first place.

But what Jonah didn't understand was that we are all sinners and we all deserve to be punished. If God had been fair and destroyed all the people who sinned, he would have had to destroy Israel too. Jonah didn't realize that God's plan to save people included not only Nineveh, but people from every tribe and every nation.

When the people of Nineveh heard Jonah's warning, they realized they needed God to save them and forgive them. When God heard that, he thought of his Son Jesus and turned his fierce anger away.

Talk about It

 KIDS, ask your parents if they ever struggled to forgive someone.

(Parents, see if you can relate to Jonah's struggle by recalling a time when you forgave someone instead of punishing them. For example, perhaps someone scratched or dented your car. In your heart you may have wanted them to pay for it, but you decided it would honor God to forgive them.)

:: Why was Jonah angry? *(He wanted God to punish Nineveh and wasn't happy when God forgave them.)*

:: Why didn't God punish Nineveh? *(There are a few different ways to answer this question. You could say that Nineveh turned away from their sin, but you could also talk about how God was compassionate and loved the people of Nineveh.)*

:: How are we like the people of Nineveh? *(We all have sinned against God and deserve to be punished, but God who is full of mercy and love sent his Son Jesus to die on the cross for us so we could be forgiven.)*

 Pray about It

Ask God to help you turn away from your sin.

DAY FIVE

Discover It

Today we look at a passage from a psalm or one of the prophets to see what we can learn from it about Jesus.

 Read Isaiah 2:1–4.

Think about It Some More

Isaiah the prophet is speaking of a day when all kinds of people will worship God. People from all different nations will stop fighting and will turn their weapons into tools for farming. Can you imagine a world without war? Something would have to happen to change the hearts of sinful people. There is only one way people will stop fighting forever, and that is if their sins are taken away by trusting in Jesus.

One day God will separate all those who don't believe in Jesus from those who do believe. Then he will change everyone who believes and give them new bodies that cannot sin. On that day there will be no more fighting and no more wars.

Until that day, God is calling all believers to reach out in love. Jesus said that we should love even our enemies. When people see how our lives are changed by following the Lord, they will want to know more about Jesus.

Talk about It

:: Can you think of a place where we won't need our swords and spears anymore? *(We won't need them in heaven because there won't be fighting or war in heaven.)*

:: What did Jesus say we should do to our enemies? *(Jesus said we should love our enemies [Matthew 5:44].)*

:: What did Jesus do for his enemies? *(Jesus died on the cross for us while we were his enemies [Romans 5:8–10] so if we place our trust in Jesus we can be forgiven.)*

Pray about It

Since Jesus died on the cross when we were his enemies in sin, ask God to help you love the people around you who might treat you like an enemy at times. *(Parents, help your children think about times when even their own brothers or sisters can act like enemies in anger.)*

Week 70

Josiah, the Eight-Year-Old King

Make a simple crown out of paper. Decorate it if you like. Then call your children together and tell them you have decided to make one of them king (or queen). Place the crown on his head and ask him to think of one wise judgment or command he would give the family if he were king for the day. Take turns placing the crown on each child to find out what each would do. Try to keep them focused on wise judgments, not silly or selfish ones.

Say, "This week you will learn about Josiah, the boy who became king of Judah when he was just eight years old!"

DAY ONE

Picture It

Imagine that you became king overnight and suddenly were in charge of a whole country. As king you could pretty much do anything you wanted. For instance, you could tell all the people in your kingdom that you are making your first day as king National Ice-Cream Day and give everyone in your country free ice cream. As king you could build a great castle for yourself, or you could tell your servants to bring all the king's treasures into your throne room so you could look at all your gold. You could also tell your people to give you more gold.

Because a king can do what he wants, you can learn a lot about what kind of a man he is by watching what he does. Our story today is about what Josiah did after he became king of Judah. Let's see what kind of man he was.

 Read 2 Chronicles 34:1–7.

Think about It Some More

Josiah's grandfather, Manasseh, was a wicked king who, for most of his life, put idols everywhere—all over Jerusalem and the surrounding land. He even put idols in God's temple. When God punished him, Manasseh turned back to God and took the idols out of the temple. But there were still a lot of idols in the land.

When Manasseh died, his son Amon became king and went right back to worshiping idols. By the time Amon's son Josiah became king, there were idols everywhere, even inside God's temple.

Talk about It

:: How old was Josiah when he became king? *(Josiah was eight years old when he became king. Parents, you can point out one of your children or your children's friends who is eight years old and help them marvel over what it would be like for an eight-year-old to become king.)*

:: What did King Josiah start to do while he was still a boy? *(He tore down the idols his father had put up.)*

:: Why did Josiah break the idols into pieces and scatter them on people's graves? *(Josiah wanted to make sure no one would ever be able to use those idols again.)*

 Pray about It

Ask God to help you to love him more than all the other things in your life—more than games, toys, sleep, relaxation, or even friends.

DAY TWO

Remember It

What do you remember about yesterday's story? What do you think is going to happen today?

 Read 2 Chronicles 34:8–31.

Think about It Some More

When he was 26 years old, King Josiah commanded his servants to clean up and repair God's temple. While they were working in the temple, the servants found the Book of the Law, which was a part of the Bible. It was probably the books of Leviticus and Deuteronomy and perhaps a few more as well. The Book of the Law had been cast aside when Josiah's father and grandfather had worshiped idols.

Even though Josiah had done a lot of good things up until then—like tearing down idols and cleaning up the temple—when he heard what the book of the law said, he tore his clothes. He realized that he and all of his people had been sinning against God. Josiah's only hope was to call out to God.

Huldah, a woman prophet who spoke for God, told Josiah that God was watching when he tore his clothes and God was not going to punish Josiah. Josiah was grateful and promised to obey God's Word all his life.

Talk about It

:: How do you think the Book of the Law got lost? *(Josiah's father and grandfather worshiped false gods and did not use or follow God's law. During their lives the book was cast aside and forgotten.)*

:: Why was Josiah so upset after the book was read? *(God's people still had idols in the land and God's Word was very clear; there was only one God and idol worship was wrong. The Book of the Law also talked about celebrating the Passover, which had also been forgotten during that same time.)*

:: Who did Josiah call upon once he realized he was a sinner and needed to be saved? *(Josiah called upon God through Huldah.)*

:: What did God promise Josiah? *(Because Josiah had called out to God and repented for the sins of his people, God said he would not punish him. God also promised to give Josiah peace. Parents, if necessary, reread verses 27–28 to help your children pick up the answers.)*

 Pray about It

Thank God for his mercy and forgiveness.

DAY THREE

Connect It to Jesus

Can anyone guess how our story this week is about or points forward to Jesus?

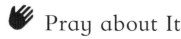 Read 2 Chronicles 34:32—35:19.

Think about It Some More

Josiah commanded that the Book of the Law be read to all the people in Jerusalem. He also took away their idols and prepared to celebrate the Passover. As offerings for that celebration, more than 40,000 animals were killed—enough animals to fill a baseball stadium with one animal in every seat!

The Passover reminded the people of how God had delivered their far-off grandfathers from slavery in Egypt. If you remember, the angel of death passed over every house that had the blood of the Passover lamb painted on the door frame. The Passover lambs, sacrificed for the firstborn sons, pointed forward to Jesus, God's only Son, who would later die on the cross as our Passover Lamb and take the punishment for our sins.

Talk about It

:: Why was the Passover so important? *(The Passover pointed to the way God was going to save his people through his Son Jesus.)*

:: Why did they need so many lambs? *(Each family needed their own animal to celebrate the Passover.)*

:: Who did the Passover lambs point forward to? *(The Passover lambs pointed forward to Jesus. Jesus was sacrificed on the cross in our place so the judgment of God would pass over us.)*

:: Were the thousands of animals sacrificed able to take away the sins of God's people? *(No. The sacrifice of animals could never take away sin. They only reminded God of another sacrifice, Jesus, who was able to pay the debt for sin and make a way for God to forgive his people.)*

 Pray about It

Thank God that the Book of the Law was not lost.

DAY FOUR

Remember It

What has God been teaching you this week through our Bible story?

 Read 2 Chronicles 35:20–27.

Think about It Some More

You may remember, God spoke through the prophetess Huldah and promised Josiah that he would give him peace all his life. For some reason, later in his life, Josiah didn't remember those words. When he heard the army of Egypt was passing by Jerusalem, he decided to go out and fight them.

It could be that Josiah thought he was doing a good thing by attacking the king of Egypt, who was considered an enemy of Israel. But Josiah must have been very surprised to hear the Egyptian king's messenger say that God was leading King Neco of Egypt. Clearly, Josiah didn't believe that God was with the king of Egypt. But Josiah made a big mistake: he didn't ask for God's help, and in the end he was killed.

Talk about It

> ● ● KIDS, ask your parents if they can remember a time when they tried
> ● ● to do something on their own without help or permission.

(Parents, perhaps you can remember a time when you tried to put something together without the instructions; or, as a child, you did something without your parents' permission that ended up badly.)

:: Why do you think Josiah went out to attack the king of Egypt? *(Egypt was Israel's enemy. Josiah had learned from the story of the Exodus that Egypt enslaved God's people and God brought the plagues against them. Josiah probably assumed God would help him fight the Egyptians.)*

:: What should Josiah have done before going out to attack the king of Egypt? *(Josiah should have prayed to God or asked God's prophet what he should do before going out on his own without God's help.)*

:: If you were Josiah and received a message from the king of Egypt that said God was on his side, what would you think? *(The message King Neco sent sounded like a trick. There was no reason for Josiah to believe that God was speaking through the Egyptian king. But, because Josiah did not ask God first, he had no way to know that the king was telling the truth.)*

:: Is there any area of your life that you could ask God to help you with? *(Parents, help your children think about the day-to-day issues they face.)*

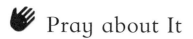 Pray about It

Ask God to help you with the areas of your life you mentioned above.

DAY FIVE

Discover It

Today we look at a passage from a psalm or one of the prophets to see what we can learn from it about Jesus.

 Read Daniel 7:9–14.

Think about It Some More

Daniel was a great prophet whom God spoke to about a time when the world as we know it would end. That was when God was going to bring his judgment. In this part of the Bible, Daniel writes about someone called "the Son of Man" whom God the Father ("the Ancient of Days") made king over all the earth.

Ever since Daniel gave Israel these words, the people of Israel wondered who this Son of Man would be. When Jesus started his ministry he called himself the Son of Man. One of the first times Jesus said he was "the Son of Man" was when the paralyzed man was lowered from the roof to Jesus so he could be healed. Jesus said, "But that you may know that the Son of Man has authority on earth to forgive sins." He said to the man who was paralyzed, "I say to you, rise, pick up your bed and go home" (Luke 5:24). The religious rulers were amazed because they knew about Daniel's words and saw Jesus' power.

Talk about It

:: Who is the Son of Man that Daniel is talking about? (*Jesus is the Son of Man that Daniel is talking about.*)

:: Why couldn't this passage be about any other man? (*No other man comes from the clouds or has dominion, glory, or a kingdom that is everlasting.*)

:: Daniel says that the Son of Man will have everlasting dominion. What does this mean? (*Everlasting means that something will last forever. When someone has dominion they are the one in charge. So Jesus is the one who is in charge of the whole world forever. Another way to say it is, Jesus is the boss of the whole earth. He has the authority to do what he wants. In the Scripture we read that Jesus had the authority to forgive sins and the authority to heal the crippled man.*)

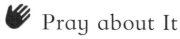 Pray about It

Thank God that Jesus, the Son of Man, has the authority to forgive our sins.

Week 71

The Fall of Jerusalem

Gather some wooden blocks or dominoes—something that will stack to form a tower. Show your children that if you stack one block directly on top of another you can build a tall tower that will stand. But if each block is just a little off center, soon the tower will tilt and eventually collapse.

Explain that the tower is like God's people. Place one block directly on top of another and say, "God commanded his people to obey him. Obeying God is like a block directly on top of the one below. But God's people did not obey, and that is like a block that is crooked." Stack a block off center. Continue the dialogue and when the tower starts to tilt, but before it falls, say, "God sent the prophet Jeremiah to warn the people of Judah to stop their crooked ways or they would fall. The kings and the people of Judah did not listen." Continue the warnings with each block until the tower falls.

Say, "This week you will learn how Jerusalem fell because they didn't obey the Lord."

DAY ONE

Picture It

When you go to a cemetery, you'll notice that each gravestone tells you the name of the person who is buried there and the date he or she died. Some gravestones also have a few words to describe what that person did or what kind of person she was while she was alive.

For instance, Thomas Jefferson's gravestone reads, "Author of the Declaration of American Independence." Most people hope that one day they will be remembered with words like, "A loving husband and a caring father," or "She loved God with all of her heart." Nobody wants to be remembered by the words, "He did what was evil in the sight of the Lord."

Although they are not on a gravestone, those are the last words God used to describe the lives of the four kings that ruled Jerusalem before it was captured. See if you can find each time they are mentioned as you read the story.

 Read 2 Kings 23:31—24:20.

Think about It Some More

Even though King Manasseh turned away from his sin at the very end, his sinful life left a bad impression on his son Amon. Once Amon became king, he led the people of Judah straight back into idolatry.

God had warned that he would punish Judah for following other gods, but Amon, like his father before him, did not care about what God said. The only reason the Lord did not punish his people during King Josiah's reign was because he obeyed God and removed the idols of his father Amon and grandfather Manasseh. But after Josiah died, his son Jehoahaz returned to idol worship. Thus, God used the pharaoh of Egypt to attack and capture King Jehoahaz.

Instead of turning back to God, the next three kings did the same kind of evil. The Bible describes each of them with the same words: "He did what was evil in the sight of the LORD." So God judged each of them. Jehoiakim was attacked; Jehoiachin was taken prisoner by Nebuchadnezzar; and Zedekiah, whom we will read more about tomorrow, was captured and led away to Babylon.

Talk about It

:: What words did God use to describe each of the four wicked kings we read about today? *("He did what was evil in the sight of the LORD.")*

:: If God were going to write something about you after you died, what would you want it to say? *(Parents, help your children here by giving some examples to pick from like: He obeyed his mom and dad and served God; she was a servant who loved the Lord; he did what he wanted and ran away from God.)*

:: What can we do to make sure our lives count for good, not evil? *(We are all sinners. Apart from following God and asking for his help we would all turn away. The exciting thing is that if we trust in Jesus, God promises that even though we sin, one very important word will be written about our lives: forgiven.)*

 Pray about It

Ask God to help you trust in Jesus and live for him.

DAY TWO

Remember It

What do you remember about yesterday's story? What do you think is going to happen today?

 Read Jeremiah 25:1–11 and 2 Chronicles 36:1–21.
(The book of 2 Chronicles tells the same story that we read yesterday from the book of 2 Kings.)

Think about It Some More

Have you ever disobeyed and received a warning instead of immediate punishment? Perhaps you can remember a time when you refused to come when called, but instead of being disciplined Mom said, "If you don't come, you are going to regret it." Anytime we get a warning instead of punishment it is an act of mercy, a special kindness.

In our story today, God caught Israel in their sin and sent Jeremiah to give them a warning to stop worshiping false gods. For twenty-three years Jeremiah repeated God's warning over and over. But in the end, when the people of Judah and their kings refused to turn away from their idolatry, God sent the Babylonian armies to capture them and take them away into exile for seventy years.

Talk about It

:: Whom did God send to the kings of Judah to warn them? *(God sent the prophet Jeremiah to the kings of Judah to warn them.)*

:: What did God promise to do if the people listened and turned away from their idol worship? *(God promised that they could stay in the Promised Land if they would turn away from their idols and worship him only.)*

:: Can you remember a time when you were punished for continuing to disobey in spite of being warned? *(Parents, help your children to remember how they disobey and need to be disciplined. Help them identify with the kings and people of Judah who did not listen and obey.)*

 Pray about It

Ask God to help you obey your parents and listen to their warnings.

DAY THREE

Connect It to Jesus

Can anyone guess how our story this week is about or points forward to Jesus?

 Read Jeremiah 23:1–8.

Think about It Some More

We learned yesterday that God sent his prophet Jeremiah to warn the kings of Judah. Yet year after year the kings did not listen to Jeremiah. Finally the Bible records this frightening statement about God's people: "But they kept mocking the messengers of God, despising his words and scoffing at his prophets, until the wrath of the LORD rose against his people, until there was no remedy" (2 Chronicles 36:16).

Because of the people's disobedience to God, Jerusalem was ransacked and its people were taken into captivity. But in the midst of God's judgment there was also a message of hope.

God was not finished speaking through Jeremiah. God said he would bring his people back out of captivity and give them a new king from the line of David. This king would be a good king who would rule wisely and bring peace and righteousness to God's people. Jesus was the king Jeremiah was talking about.

Talk about It

:: What punishment did Jeremiah say God was going to give his people? *(They were going to be captured and led away into the foreign kingdom of Babylon.)*

:: The news Jeremiah brought wasn't all bad. What good things did Jeremiah say God would do? *(Jeremiah said God was going to rescue his people and bring them back home.)*

:: What kind of new king was God going to give his people? *(The new king would be a good king who would bring peace and righteousness and would save his people.)*

:: Who was the king that God promised to send? *(Jesus was the king God promised to send.)*

 Pray about It

Thank God for promising to rescue his people even when they were disobeying him.

DAY FOUR

Remember It

What has God been teaching you this week through our Bible story?

 Read 2 Kings 25:1–15 and Lamentations 1:1–3.

Think about It Some More

Jerusalem had a high wall all around it to protect it from attack. When the king of Babylon came to fight Jerusalem, the wall stopped him from getting in. So instead of fighting, the King of Babylon surrounded the city and laid siege to it.

A siege is when you don't allow any food, water, or supplies to be brought into a city. Unless the people have a way to get food and water, they will starve and have to give up. Also, while blocking any supplies from getting in, the enemy army works to take apart the wall, stone by stone. Eventually a breach or hole is created in the wall.

That is what happened to Jerusalem. When the army of Babylon finally broke through the wall, the king of Judah and his army tried to sneak out of one of the back gates, but they were stopped. Then the army of Babylon came into the city, burned the temple, broke down the walls around the city, and carried the people back to Babylon as prisoners. The book of Lamentations is made up of five sad poems written to describe the sorrow the people felt over the fall of their great city.

Talk about It

> KIDS, ask your parents to tell you about a war they lived through.

(Parents, you may have never been in a battle, but perhaps you have a family member who was. Or, simply talk about a war you remember watching scenes from on television. Talk about how terrible war is.)

:: What did the army of Babylon do to God's temple? *(The army of Babylon emptied the temple of its treasures and set it on fire.)*

:: What did the enemy do to the people who lived in Jerusalem? *(The enemy carried them off to Babylon as prisoners.)*

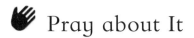 Pray about It

Ask God to help you obey his Word and follow him.

DAY FIVE

Discover It

Today we look at a passage from a psalm or one of the prophets to see what we can learn from it about Jesus.

 Read Jeremiah 32:37–41.

Think about It Some More

During the very time that Jerusalem was under siege by Nebuchadnezzar, Jeremiah brought an encouraging word from God. Not only did God have a plan to return his people to Jerusalem, he also promised to give them a new heart so they could follow him forever.

The covenant (agreement) God promised them was the covenant Jesus spoke to his disciples about at the Last Supper, the meal they shared before he died. Jesus held out a loaf of bread and said that it represented his body, which was given up for them. The cup represented his blood shed for them.

In the end, instead of God punishing the people for their sin, he punished his Son Jesus. Now, if we trust in Jesus, our sins are taken away as well. That is what the new covenant is all about. Once our sins are forgiven, we too can live in peace with God forever.

Talk about It

:: How do you think these words would have encouraged the people who were captured and taken away to Babylon? *(Jeremiah promised that God would deliver his people from captivity and bring them back to Jerusalem. That would have given them hope that God did not forget them.)*

:: Jeremiah said God's new covenant would be everlasting. What does that mean? *(Everlasting means it will last forever.)*

:: Make a list of all the things God said he would do. *(Parents, if your children are younger, reread the passage and have them clap each time you read something that God said he would do for his people. Then help your children to see that even in the things God requires us to do, it is God who will help us to do them.)*

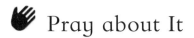 Pray about It

Thank God for his wonderful promises. *(You can use this passage of Scripture to name God's promises in your prayers, such as, "God, thank you for promising to give us a new heart.")*

Week 72

Nebuchadnezzar's Dream

Write the letters of the alphabet on individual note cards or slips of paper. Tell your children you want to play a simple game. Pick a card at random, show the letter, and ask each child to think of something that starts with that letter. Do a couple of rounds.

Then, tell them you think you have made it too easy. Explain that you are going to do it again—only a little differently. This time, once you pick the card, they have to guess the correct letter and then think of something that starts with that letter, without ever seeing the card. They will probably object, saying it is impossible.

Say, "This week, you will learn how King Nebuchadnezzar asked his wise men to interpret a dream, but first they had to tell what the dream was."

DAY ONE

Picture It

Taking a test in school can make you nervous, even if you did a good job studying for it. But think how nervous you would be if your teacher told you that there was going to be only one question on the test. If you didn't answer it correctly you would fail. That might make you more nervous, especially if you knew the question was going to be very difficult.

Then, imagine that your teacher hands you a blank paper and explains that you are going to have to first write the correct test question and then the correct answer.

That is the kind of test that King Nebuchadnezzar gives his wise men in our story today.

 Read Daniel 2:1–16.

Think about It Some More

This story takes place while God's people are held captive in Babylon under King Nebuchadnezzar. Nebuchadnezzar is not too happy with his wise men. It seems they have been lying to him and giving him poor advice. So, to test if they were truly wise, the king commands them to tell him his dream and what it means.

Since the king is the only one who knows his own dream, it seems like an impossible request. The wise men can't make up anything because the king would know immediately whether they were telling the truth. The magicians and enchanters know they are only normal men, not gods. They don't know what the king dreamed and they have no way of finding out. They are fakes who have no power. So the king orders that all the wise men in the land be killed.

But one man, Daniel, knows where to get the answer for the king. Daniel sends word to the king that he can give the king the answer. Although Daniel is an ordinary man who doesn't know the answer himself, he does know where to get the answer—from God who knows all things.

Talk about It

:: Why did the king demand that his wise men tell him his dream? *(The king thought his wise men were lying to him. He wanted to test them to see if they were truly wise or if they were fakes.)*

:: Did you ever get bad consequences for lying? *(Parents, help your children remember times when they were disciplined for lying or their lies caused other trouble for them.)*

:: Who was the wise man who asked if he could tell the king his dream? *(Daniel asked for permission to tell the king his dream.)*

:: How did Daniel, one of God's people from the tribe of Judah, get into Babylon? *(Daniel was one of the men whom Nebuchadnezzar captured when Jerusalem was conquered.)*

 Pray about It

Thank God for giving Daniel courage to speak up and say that he could interpret the dream.

DAY TWO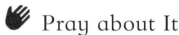

Remember It

What do you remember about yesterday's story? What do you think is going to happen today?

Read Daniel 2:17–30.

Think about It Some More

Daniel didn't know the king's dream, but he knew who did. That is why he called the other men to pray to the true God who knows all things. Later, after God answered Daniel's prayer, Daniel paid a visit to the king.

When the king asked Daniel if he could tell him his dream, Daniel didn't take credit for what God had shown him. Daniel told the king that no one could know another's dreams, but there was a God in heaven who had revealed the answer. Daniel never thought about himself or boasted in himself. Instead, he gave God the glory, and even asked for the other wise men to be freed.

Talk about It

:: What did Daniel do differently from the king's other wise men? *(Daniel asked the true God of the universe for the interpretation, and never considered trying to come up with the dream on his own. Daniel knew that only God could give him the dream and its interpretation.)*

:: How did Daniel's behavior honor God? *(Daniel did not take credit for what had been revealed to him. Daniel pointed to God as the source of the revelation.)*

:: What can we learn about God from all that Daniel said to the king? *(Parents, if you have younger children who cannot read back through the passage to find the answer, reread the passage yourself and have them raise their hands when they hear something that we learn about God from what Daniel said. You can even substitute "God" for the pronoun "he" in verses 21–22 to help them out.)*

 Pray about It

Use the list of things Daniel spoke about God to praise and thank him.

DAY THREE

Connect It to Jesus

Can anyone guess how our story this week is about or points forward to Jesus?

 Read Daniel 2:31–45.

Think about It Some More

The most important part of Nebuchadnezzar's dream was the part about a great rock from God that destroyed the statue and grew into a mountain and filled the whole earth.

The rock was a picture of Jesus Christ and the mountain a picture of God's kingdom. Throughout the Bible, God often uses a rock or stone to represent his work on the earth. Another example is when water came out from a rock in the desert so the children of Israel could drink from it.

Later, in the New Testament, we are told that the rock in the desert represents Christ (1 Corinthians 10:4). Jesus compared a life lived for God to a house that was strong and sturdy because it was built on the rock of God's truth (Matthew 7:24). The apostle Paul said that the rock of God's truth is Jesus (Romans 9:33).

Talk about It

:: What did the statue in the king's dream stand for or represent? *(The statue represented the kingdoms that would come after Nebuchadnezzar and Babylon. Today, Bible scholars believe the head of gold represents King Nebuchadnezzar of Babylon; the arms and chest of silver represent the Medo-Persian Empire; the belly and thighs of bronze represent the Greek Empire; and the legs of iron represent the Roman Empire.)*

:: Who did the stone stand for or represent? *(The stone represents Jesus and God's kingdom coming to earth.)*

:: What did the rock do to the statue? *(The rock crushed the statue and broke it into pieces so when the wind blew, nothing was left.)*

:: What did Jesus do to crush the worldly kingdoms and make a way for God's kingdom to grow? *(Jesus died on the cross and took the penalty for our sin. Everyone who believes in Jesus becomes a part of God's kingdom.)*

 Pray about It

Thank Jesus for crushing our enemies—sin and death—when he died on the cross. Now we can trust the Lord and be free from the power of sin and live forever in heaven with God.

DAY FOUR

Remember It

What has God been teaching you this week through our Bible story?

 Read Daniel 2:46–49.

Think about It Some More

When Daniel finished telling the king his dream and what it meant, the king fell on his face amazed.

But the king was confused, because instead of worshiping God, Nebuchadnezzar paid homage to Daniel and offered incense up to Daniel. Although Nebuchadnezzar did praise Daniel's God, he made God seem like a servant who helped Daniel.

God was going to have to do more work in Nebuchadnezzar's life to show him that man was supposed to serve God, not the other way around.

Talk about It

> ● ● KIDS, ask your parents what God used in their lives to show them he
> ● ● was real.

(We all have a story of how we came to believe that God is real and all-powerful. Some people read about it in the Bible and believe, while others fall into sin and are almost ruined before they call out to God. Tell your children what God used to reach you.)

:: How was the king affected by Daniel's knowledge and interpretation of the dream? *(The king understood that Daniel's God was the God of gods and the King of kings. Nebuchadnezzar saw that Daniel's God was all-powerful.)*

:: What did the king do for Daniel? *(He promoted Daniel, giving him high honors and many gifts, making him a ruler in Babylon.)*

:: What was the king's mistake? *(The king gave more praise to Daniel than he did to God.)*

 Pray about It

Give God all the praise for helping Daniel with the king's dream.

DAY FIVE

Discover It

Today we look at a passage from a psalm or one of the prophets to see what we can learn from it about Jesus.

 Read Isaiah 12:1–2.

Think about It Some More

Isaiah speaks about a day when God's anger against the sins of man would be taken away. Today we know that there is only one way that the anger of God can be taken away from us. God's anger was taken away when he turned his anger toward Jesus, his Son, and punished him for our sin.

Jesus stood in our place and took the penalty we deserved. When Jesus was dying on the cross, he said, "It is finished." This meant that God's anger had been poured out on him and it was all gone. So when Isaiah speaks of a day of salvation when God would no longer be angry, he is referring to Jesus' taking on himself God's anger over our sin and the punishment we deserve. That's why Isaiah says that God has become our salvation.

Talk about It

:: If God is love, why was he angry with us? *(God was angry because we have sinned against him.)*

:: Since God is good, what does he have to do to people who do evil and sin against him? *(God must punish sin.)*

:: How did God take away his anger for our sin? *(Instead of punishing us, God sent his only Son Jesus to be punished in our place.)*

 Pray about It

Thank God for becoming our salvation by taking our sins upon himself.

Week 73

Four Men in the Furnace

For this exercise you will need an empty plastic bottle with an opening big enough to fit a penny through. Roll up a small piece of masking tape, sticky side out, and tape a penny to the inside of the lid of the bottle. There needs to be enough tape to hold the penny in place until you shake the bottle, but not so much as to keep it stuck to the lid when you shake the bottle hard. Adjust the size of the tape if needed.

Distribute three pennies to your children. Give one of them the bottle and ask if the bottle is empty. When he has confirmed the bottle is empty, have him drop the three pennies into the bottle, making sure everyone knows exactly how many were dropped in. Carefully place the lid on the bottle and give the bottle a hard shake to dislodge the penny you've hidden in the lid.

Let the children hold the bottle, and remind them how many pennies they put in: three. Then open the lid and dump out the pennies. Have the children count the pennies. They will be amazed that there are four, when they only put in three. Don't tell them your secret.

Say, "This week you will learn that Nebuchadnezzar was even more amazed when, after throwing three men into the furnace, he saw four men walking in the fire."

DAY ONE

Picture It

Many people visit the Statue of Liberty each year to admire her beauty and think about how she represents freedom and liberty. But what would you do if you were visiting the Statue of Liberty and the park ranger on duty ordered you to bow down and worship the statue, saying that you would be arrested if you didn't?

As a Christian, you would have a big problem because God tells us in the Bible that we must worship only him. It is fine to admire a great statue, but if we are to obey God's Word we must refuse to worship anything but God.

In today's story, we will see what happened when Nebuchadnezzar commanded everyone to bow down to a statue of himself.

 Read Daniel 3:1–12.

Think about It Some More

King Nebuchadnezzar made a gold statue ninety feet tall (about as tall as two telephone poles standing one on top of the other). Then he commanded everyone to bow down and worship it. The people of Babylon didn't mind obeying because they already worshiped many other gods. But the young Israelites Shadrach, Meshach, and Abednego refused to bow down because God had said they should worship only him.

Talk about It

:: Do you know which of the Ten Commandments tells us not to bow down to idols? *(The very first commandment tells us that we should not have any other gods besides the Lord, the true God.)*

:: What was the punishment the king threatened to give for refusing to bow down to the golden idol? *(The king said that anyone who refused to bow down would be thrown into a fiery furnace.)*

:: What are the idols that we have today? *(An idol is anything we love more than we love God. Parents, draw out your children by discussing some of the idols in your own life first. Possessions, money, and popularity are three things that can easily become more important to us than God. For children, video games, sports teams, a favorite toy, wanting attention from others, or wanting their own way can all steal affections away from God.)*

:: How do we know if something is an idol? *(Anything we love more than God is an idol. We can tell if we love something too much by how we respond when it is taken away. If we become angry and sin, we know it held too strong a place in our hearts.)*

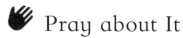 Pray about It

Ask God to help you love him more than you love the things of the world.

DAY TWO

Remember It

What do you remember about yesterday's story? What do you think is going to happen today?

 Read Daniel 3:13–18.

Think about It Some More

It is easy to say that you believe in something, but it is a lot harder to trust your whole life to it. For instance, you might say you believe that a parachute can save your life if you jump out of an airplane with one, but only if you decide to skydive wearing one would you really be trusting that parachute to save you.

That's what Shadrach, Meshach, and Abednego did with the fiery furnace. They trusted God with their lives. They believed God could save them; but even if God did not, they were not going to bow down to the golden statue. In that case, they were willing to die and go to heaven. That is really trusting God!

Talk about It

:: What was the only way the king said Shadrach, Meshach, and Abednego could escape the fiery furnace? *(They had to bow down and worship the image he made.)*

:: How do we know Shadrach, Meshach, and Abednego trusted God? *(They refused to bow down to the king's statue, even when he threatened to throw them into the fire.)*

:: What did Nebuchadnezzar forget about the God of the people of Judah? *(After Daniel interpreted his dream, King Nebuchadnezzar said that Daniel's God was the "God of gods and Lord of kings" [Daniel 2:47]. But now it seems that Nebuchadnezzar has forgotten the power of Daniel's God.)*

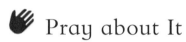 Pray about It

Thank God for his power, which is able to deliver us from all harm.

DAY THREE

Connect It to Jesus

Can anyone guess how our story this week is about or points forward to Jesus?

 Read Daniel 3:19–27.

Think about It Some More

When King Nebuchadnezzar ordered the three men thrown into the fire, he expected them to burn up instantly. But instead of burning up, they started walking around! Then God came down and walked right along with them as a fourth man in the fire.

What a wonderful picture of how God reaches out to help us. We are all sinners who deserve the fires of hell as our punishment, but God came down to rescue us. By going into the fire and saving Shadrach, Meshach, and Abednego, God was showing us that even though we are sinners, he will not allow us to die in the flames if we trust in him.

We are not facing Nebuchadnezzar's anger, but we are all facing God the Father's anger for the bad things we have done in our lives. But if we trust in God's plan through Jesus, we will be saved from God's punishment and will live forever in heaven with him.

Talk about It

:: How many men did the king have thrown into the fire? *(The king had three men thrown into the fire.)*

:: How many men did the king see walking around in the fire? *(The king saw four men walking around in the fire.)*

:: Who was the fourth man? *(God came down as a man into the fire to be with the other three.)*

 Pray about It

Praise God for saving Shadrach, Meshach, and Abednego and praise him for the people in your family whom he has saved from their sins.

DAY FOUR

Remember It

What has God been teaching you this week through our Bible story?

 Read Daniel 3:28–30.

Think about It Some More

King Nebuchadnezzar was amazed by what he saw in the fiery furnace. When Shadrach, Meshach, and Abednego came out of the fire unharmed, the king knew their God had protected them.

A few moments earlier, Nebuchadnezzar had demanded that everyone in his kingdom bow down to the statue he had made. But after seeing the power of God to save, Nebuchadnezzar issued a proclamation to honor the God of Judah.

The faith of Shadrach, Meshach, and Abednego didn't just save them from death; it opened the way for all the Jews to worship God freely!

Talk about It

:: How did God work the events of this story for the good of all his people? *(The king was so impressed that he issued a decree protecting all of God's people in Babylon.)*

:: What did the king think about God after the three men came out of the fire unharmed? *(The king said there is no other God that could do what Shadrach, Meshach, and Abednego's God did.)*

:: How does this story encourage your faith? *(Parents, draw out your children to help them to see that we can have the same response as the king—that there is no other God like our God.)*

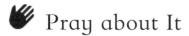 Pray about It

Praise God for the way he came down to be with Shadrach, Meshach, and Abednego in the fire.

DAY FIVE

Discover It

Today we look at a passage from a psalm or one of the prophets to see what we can learn from it about Jesus.

 Read Isaiah 12:3–6.

Think about It Some More

Last week we learned that the first two verses of Isaiah 12 are about Jesus and how he took God's anger so we could be saved. The part we read today tells us what we are supposed to do after God saves us.

First, we are to give thanks. Then, we should tell others about Jesus so the whole world can know. And finally, we should shout and sing for joy because of the Holy One of Israel, which is just another name for Jesus.

Talk about It

:: What does Isaiah say we should do? *(Parents, if your children are younger, reread the passage and have them raise their hands when they hear something we are supposed to do, like give thanks, sing, and shout.)*

:: What did Jesus do that should make us want to give thanks, sing, and shout? *(Jesus died on the cross for our sins to take our punishment away.)*

:: Why does God want us to tell people all over the earth about Jesus? *(God wants us to tell everyone so they can believe in Jesus too.)*

 Pray about It

Thank the Lord for dying on the cross. Sing a song of praise to God, and offer up a family shout—have all your children shout out "Praise the Lord!" together.

Week 74

The Glory Belongs to God Alone

Pick a few blades of grass from your lawn, one for each of your children. (Use grass that has not been treated with chemicals. Perhaps you will want to wash it anyway, just to be safe.) Pass out the grass and invite your children to taste it.

Grass contains some vitamins that provide a bit of nutritional value, but people cannot digest the cellulose fiber in grass. Bacteria that break down the cellulose fiber live in animals that eat grass to help them digest it. Your children can get the flavor of grass without swallowing it by biting down on a blade of grass, releasing some of its flavor.

Say, "This week you will learn how God humbled King Nebuchadnezzar and had him eat grass like the cattle of the field."

DAY ONE

Picture It

There once was a zookeeper who worked with the snakes in the snake house. Most of the snakes in the zoo were harmless, but the large king cobra that was about ten feet long was very dangerous. At first the zookeeper took special care around the large snake; but because the snake's cage was large and the snake liked to stay hidden under a log, the keeper became careless over time.

One day the snake pretended to be asleep, but when the keeper opened the cage and reached in to change the cobra's water, the snake lunged out to bite his hand. Luckily for the keeper, the snake's fangs hit the keeper's wristwatch. With lightning speed the keeper pulled his hand back before the snake could strike again.

Now what do you think the keeper will do the next time he needs to change the king cobra's water? Our story today is not about a king cobra, but it is about a king. The last time King Nebuchadnezzar had called together his wise men to interpret his dream, they had almost been killed. Let's see how careful they are this time with the king's dream.

 Read Daniel 4:1–18.

Think about It Some More

When King Nebuchadnezzar called his wise men together to interpret his dream, none of them dared to try and guess. Remember the last time the king demanded they give him both the interpretation and the dream? When they could not, the king struck out against them and issued a decree that they all be killed. (Happily for them, Daniel asked that they be spared.) That's probably why none of them would even try to give the king an interpretation this time: they were all afraid!

When Daniel arrived, the king was sure that he would be able to interpret the dream. But if you look closely to what Nebuchadnezzar said to Daniel, you can see that the king was still worshiping false gods. Even though he saw how Daniel's God had protected the three men in the furnace and how Daniel had been able to give him both his dream and the interpretation, Nebuchadnezzar still worshiped his false gods. He even changed Daniel's name to Belteshazzar, after his favorite false god.

Talk about It

:: Why didn't the king's wise men try to guess what his dream was about? *(They had gotten into trouble for lying to the king before. They would rather admit they couldn't interpret the dream than give a fake interpretation. It seems like they had learned their lesson.)*

:: Nebuchadnezzar called Daniel "chief of the magicians." What kind of magic did Daniel use to interpret the king's dreams? *(Daniel didn't use magic. The king had forgotten that Daniel said, "There is a God in heaven who reveals mysteries" [Daniel 2:28].)*

:: What is wrong with what Nebuchadnezzar said to Daniel in verse 18? *(Parents, if your children can't read verse 18, reread it yourself and emphasize the word "gods" to see if your children can pick up that Daniel only worshiped one God. Nebuchadnezzar was lumping Daniel's God in with all the false gods.)*

 Pray about It

Ask God to help you trust in the Lord and not be slow to believe like Nebuchadnezzar.

DAY TWO

Remember It

What do you remember about yesterday's story? What do you think is going to happen today?

 Read Daniel 4:19–26.

Think about It Some More

When God gave him the interpretation of the king's dream, Daniel was concerned because it was bad news for the king. The tree in the dream represented the king whom God was going to cut down. He would drive the king away from men to live with the beasts of the field, to eat grass like an ox. That is not exactly an easy message to give to a king who had recently thrown people into a blazing hot furnace.

Talk about It

:: If you were Daniel, why would you be afraid to tell the king the meaning of his dream? *(The king had the power to kill Daniel. It took courage for Daniel to tell the king the truth.)*

:: Why do you think God was going to punish the king? *(One thing we know is that in spite of all God had done to show his power, the king was still following false gods.)*

:: What was God trying to teach Nebuchadnezzar? *(If your children can't come up with the answer, reread verse 25. God wanted to teach Nebuchadnezzar that he, not the king, was the ruler over all.)*

Pray about It

Praise God for how he rules over everyone and everything.

DAY THREE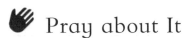

Connect It to Jesus

Can anyone guess how our story this week is about or points forward to Jesus?

Read Daniel 4:27–33.

Think about It Some More

Daniel told the king to obey God's commands—to stop sinning and practice righteousness. But even if the king wanted to stop sinning, he would not be able to. And if he could stop sinning, he would still be guilty of all the bad things he had already done, and would still need to be punished for his sin. What the king really needed was to give up and call out to God for mercy.

We are all sinners. We continue to sin no matter how hard we try not to. Plus, all the good things we do cannot cover up the bad things we have already done. Our only hope is to call out to God to save us. God has provided a way for us to be forgiven by sending his Son Jesus to die on the cross for our sins. It is only when we trust in the good work of Jesus on the cross that we can be saved.

Talk about It

:: What can we do on our own to take away our sin? *(There is nothing we can do ourselves to take our sins away.)*

:: What did God do to take our sins away? *(God sent his only Son to die on the cross and take our punishment so our sins could be forgiven.)*

:: What does God want us to do? *(God wants us to believe in Jesus and place our hope and trust in him.)*

 ## Pray about It

Ask God to help you put your trust in Jesus.

DAY FOUR

Remember It

What has God been teaching you this week through our Bible story?

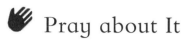 Read Daniel 4:34–37.

Think about It Some More

Everything happened to Nebuchadnezzar just as his dream predicted. Nebuchadnezzar was driven away to eat grass like the cattle in the field. It took a while, but Nebuchadnezzar finally realized that nothing was going to change unless he admitted that God was greater than he was.

Finally, Nebuchadnezzar admitted that God was in charge, not him. Once Nebuchadnezzar turned from his sin and called out to God with faith to believe, God restored his kingdom. Then Nebuchadnezzar worshiped Daniel's God, calling the Lord the "King of heaven."

Talk about It

> ● ● KIDS, ask your parents if they can remember a time when God humbled them.

(Parents, we all have stories of how God humbled us. Perhaps you thought you were a shoe-in for a particular job and boasted as though it was yours for the taking, only to find out the job was given to someone else. Or maybe you boasted about how you could beat someone in a game, but in the end you lost. It is helpful for us to share the stories of our failures with our children and how God used them to help us.)

:: Read James 4:6 and describe how it fits our story this week. *(When Nebuchadnezzar was proud God opposed him, but once he humbled himself and called out to God, God gave him grace and returned him to power.)*

:: What can we learn about God from Nebuchadnezzar's prayer? *(Parents, reread Nebuchadnezzar's prayer in verses 34 and 35. Have your children raise their hands when they hear something we can learn from the king's prayer.)*

:: What will God do to us if we become proud? *(Read 1 Peter 5:5 to help your children see that God requires that we live humble lives, doing what God wants us to do, not what we want to do.)*

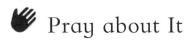 Pray about It

Ask God to help you live a humble life.

DAY FIVE

Discover It

Today we look at a passage from a psalm or one of the prophets to see what we can learn from it about Jesus.

 Read Psalm 118:19–24 and Acts 4:11–12.

Think about It Some More

To erect a stone building, first a large pile of stones must be gathered and then the stones individually checked to see how they might fit together. Every now and then a stone that is cracked, or stained, or too small cannot be used. That stone is then thrown away—rejected.

This psalm tells of a rejected stone that God used as the most important stone of all, the cornerstone. Peter told the Jews that Jesus was the stone that they rejected, but God used him as the cornerstone. Peter went on to say that Jesus is the only way any of us can be saved. Once again, like the stone from Nebuchadnezzar's dream, Jesus is compared to a stone.

Talk about It

:: Who is the stone mentioned in Psalm 118:22? *(Jesus is the stone mentioned in Psalm 118:22.)*

:: What is a cornerstone? *(A cornerstone is the first stone that is laid when constructing a building. The entire foundation of the building must line up to the cornerstone in order for the building to be strong and solid.)*

:: Look back at Psalm 118:19–24. What other words do you see that remind you of Jesus? *(Parents, you can reread the passage for smaller children and have them raise their hands if they hear a word like "righteousness" and "salvation.")*

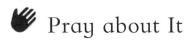 Pray about It

Do what Psalm 118:24 tells us to do: rejoice because Jesus, our cornerstone, has become our salvation. Praise him for rising from the dead so we could be saved.

Week 75

Daniel in the Lions' Den

Bring a picture of a lion to Bible study. Showing the picture to your children, tell them some facts about lions:

:: *The African lion is the largest carnivore (meat eater) in Africa.*

:: *Male lions can grow eight feet long—not counting the tail!—and stand four feet high. (Show your children how that compares to the size of your living room couch.)*

:: *A mature male lion can weigh more than 500 pounds.*

:: *His roar can be heard five miles away. (Give your children an idea of how far this would be from your home.)*

:: *Their needle-sharp claws are an inch-and-a-half long.*

:: *Their longest pointed front teeth are more than an inch long and their jaws are very strong.*

:: *They can run thirty miles an hour in short bursts.*

:: *They can knock down a zebra with one swipe of their paw.*

Say, "You would not want to be put in a den with hungry lions! This week you will learn how God protected Daniel in the lions' den."

DAY ONE

Picture It

Once there were two sisters who lived in a small house in the center of town. The older sister enjoyed baking. People loved to walk past their home because of the wonderful smell of fresh cookies and pastries flowing from the kitchen. Everyone agreed that she made the best cookies in the world.

Because of this, the younger sister became jealous. "No one ever said my cookies were the best in the world," she said to herself. Then she set out to trick her older sister. She mixed plaster in the flour so when the cookies were baked, they would be as hard as rocks.

But what she didn't remember was that the next Monday was her own birthday. She didn't know that her sister planned to make the next batch of cookies to celebrate. So instead of enjoying her sister's usual delicious cookies, her birthday cookies were so hard she almost broke her teeth trying to get a bite.

Envy will often lead us to do cruel things. We have to be careful because sometimes the things we do out of envy will come back to bite us. Let's see how envy is at work in our story today.

 Read Daniel 6:1–9.

Think about It Some More

By this time, King Nebuchadnezzar is gone and his once great empire, Babylon, has been conquered by a country called Persia. Daniel is still an important man, but now he's serving Darius, the new king.

Daniel is doing such a good job that the other leaders of Persia (some Bible versions call them presidents while others translate different titles) are envious. They plan a way to ruin Daniel by convincing King Darius to make a new law to trap him. To get Darius to approve the law, they lie by saying that all the officials agree it is a good law. But they never even asked Daniel!

Talk about It

:: Why did the leaders want to set a trap for Daniel? *(They were envious of Daniel. Parents, take time to explain envy to your children. Envy is when we get angry with a person who can do something better than we can.)*

:: How did the wicked leaders get Darius to sign their law? *(They told him that all the leaders agreed to the law, which was a lie. They never asked Daniel about it.)*

:: Have you ever been envious of someone who did things better than you? *(Parents, help your children remember situations in games or school where they may have envied the accomplishments of others.)*

:: What can we do if we become envious of someone? *(The best thing to do is tell your parents what is going on in your heart and ask them to pray for you. Then, encourage the person you envy instead of tearing her down.)*

 Pray about It

Ask God to help you to not be envious of others.

DAY TWO_____

Remember It

What do you remember about yesterday's story? What do you think is going to happen today?

 Read Daniel 6:10–18.

Think about It Some More

Even though Daniel found out about the new law against praying, he was not afraid. He knew that God could protect him. Daniel surely remembered that God had protected Shadrach, Meshach, and Abednego in the furnace. That was a story the satraps had not been around for. They didn't consider that Daniel might get help from God, but Daniel did. So, even though it was against the law, Daniel continued to pray with courage at his open window.

When the wicked leaders reported Daniel to the king, he was very upset and tried to help, but there was nothing he could do. All he could do was hope that Daniel's God could save him.

Talk about It

:: How did the king know about Daniel's God? *(Even the king had seen Daniel serving God all the time, which meant Daniel didn't hide his faith [verse 16].)*

:: How could remembering the story of Shadrach, Meshach, and Abednego encourage Daniel? *(If God could deliver them from the flames of Nebuchadnezzar's fiery furnace, then God could deliver Daniel from the lions.)*

:: While the king was sad and fasting, what do you think the satraps were doing? *(Parents, the Bible doesn't tell us what they were doing, but it is likely they were celebrating that their evil scheme had worked just like they planned.)*

 Pray about It

Ask God to help you to trust him like Daniel trusted God.

DAY THREE

Connect It to Jesus

Can anyone guess how our story this week is about or points forward to Jesus?

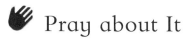 Read Daniel 6:19–23.

Think about It Some More

When we trust in the Lord to save us we will be saved. That is the message this story teaches us. Daniel didn't trust his own strength and try to fight the lions off by himself. Daniel trusted the Lord to save him.

That is the same thing God wants us to do. We all have broken God's law and deserve to be punished. God's law, like the law in Daniel's day, cannot be changed. Instead of a lions' den, our punishment is a terrible place called hell. Our only hope to escape is if we trust in God who sent his Son Jesus to die in our place.

Jesus took our punishment on the cross so the law of God, which cannot be changed, could be satisfied. There is one big difference: God wanted Daniel to disobey the bad law made by men, but God does not want us to disobey the Bible, which contains God's laws that were written for our good.

Talk about It

:: What name did the king give Daniel's God? *(The king called Daniel's God "the living God" [verse 20]. Our God is much different than an idol that cannot talk or hear or do anything because it is dead.)*

:: Why didn't the lions eat Daniel? *(God sent an angel to shut the mouths of the lions.)*

:: Why was Daniel saved? *(Parents, if your children don't mention that Daniel trusted God, reread verse 23 to them.)*

 Pray about It

Praise God for saving Daniel and for making a way for us to be saved too.

DAY FOUR

Remember It

What has God been teaching you this week through our Bible story?

 Read Daniel 6:24–28.

Think about It Some More

When the wicked leaders first told the king about the law they used to trap Daniel, they lied to him. They said that all the other leaders had agreed to it, but Daniel had not been a part of making the law. When the king saw that the purpose of the law had been to trap Daniel, he punished the other rulers by giving all of them the same punishment they had planned for Daniel: he threw them into the lions' den.

But their false gods could not protect them from the hungry lions, which attacked and killed them. Then the king praised Daniel's God. We don't know if King Darius trusted in God for himself but, given what he said about God, we may one day see King Darius in heaven.

Talk about It

> ● ● KIDS, ask your parents if they remember a story of envy and how it
> ● ● can lead to greater sins.

(Parents, think back to when you were growing up. Envy is a sin that often leads to gossiping, or even destroying the property of others. Help your children to see that envy is a dangerous sin.)

:: What do we learn about God from the king's letter? *(Parents, if your children cannot read, take time to reread the king's letter and have your children raise their hands when you come to something the king said about God.)*

:: What did the king mean when he called Daniel's God "the living God"? *(Daniel's God could do and say things, while the idols and false gods could not do anything because they were made of wood or stone.)*

 ## Pray about It

Use the king's letter to praise God in your prayers.

DAY FIVE

Discover It

Today we look at a passage from a psalm or one of the prophets to see what we can learn from it about Jesus.

 Read Psalm 118:26–29 and Matthew 21:6–9.

Think about It Some More

We learned last week that this psalm is talking about Jesus. In today's reading, we see more connections to Jesus. Jesus is the one who came in the name of the Lord. Jesus is the light God sent to shine upon us, and it is through sending his Son Jesus that God showed us his great love that lasts forever.

Talk about It

:: How is the story in Matthew connected to Psalm 118? *(When Jesus rode into Jerusalem on Palm Sunday those who waved palm branches shouted words from Psalm 118: "Blessed is he who comes in the name of the LORD.")*

:: *Read John 8:12.* How does this verse compare to what we read today? *(Verse 27 tells us that God "made his light shine upon us"; and Jesus told the people that he was "the light of the world.")*

:: How did God show us his steadfast love? *(Read John 3:16 to your children if they don't guess by sending us Jesus.)*

 ## Pray about It

As a family, try to come up with reasons for thanking God. Make sure to include the most important reason: our salvation.

Week 76

The Exiles Return

Make a batch of muffins and set a timer for when you should take them out of the oven. Call your children into the kitchen about three to five minutes before the timer goes off. Explain that you are the maker of the muffins and by your own strength you placed them in the oven. Also, you have determined that they will remain in the oven for _____ minutes (however long is left). You have also arranged that a timer will go off at the proper time.

When the timer goes off, take the muffins out and invite each of them to have one. While they are enjoying the treat, explain that we do have control—in a limited way—over some things like the muffins, but God controls all things.

Say, "This week we will learn that God planned the captivity of Israel, decided how long his people would remain in Babylon, and moved the heart of a king to allow his people to return home and rebuild Jerusalem."

DAY ONE

Picture It

Imagine that Mom or Dad came home from work on Friday and told you to go to bed early because, before dawn the next morning, you were leaving for a surprise: a three-day vacation!

If we told you that, would you believe us? If you are like most kids, you would trust and not doubt at all. The moment we announced the vacation you would start to celebrate. Then the next morning, when you woke up, you would excitedly try to guess where you were going. You would never think that we may be lying to you because we have always treated you honestly and kept our word and promises.

In our Bible story today, we see that God always keeps his promises. First, we'll read a promise God made to his people through the prophet Jeremiah, and then we'll see how God kept his promise. Did you know God is even more trustworthy than our parents? He has never ever broken a promise. So if he says in the Bible that he will do something, we can trust that he will keep his promise.

 Read Jeremiah 29:7–14 and Ezra 1.

Think about It Some More

God used King Nebuchadnezzar to teach his people a lesson. When they refused to listen to the warnings he gave then through the prophets, he used Nebuchadnezzar to swoop in, defeat

Jerusalem, and take his people away as captives to Babylon. But the whole time God's people were captives in Babylon, God protected them.

In our first Bible passage today, we learned that God planned to rescue his people from Babylon after 70 years. Remember back when God rescued his people from slavery in Egypt, how he hardened Pharaoh's heart and used Moses to deliver them? In this story, he did the opposite with the king's heart: he softened the heart of Cyrus, King of Persia, to allow the Jews to return to Jerusalem and rebuild God's temple. Cyrus even gave the people of Israel all the money they needed to rebuild the temple, and returned all the things from the temple that king Nebuchadnezzar had taken when he attacked Jerusalem.

Talk about It

:: Who moved the heart of King Cyrus to rebuild the temple? *(God moved the heart of King Cyrus to rebuild the temple.)*

:: What did King Cyrus tell the people of Babylon to give the Jews as they left? *(Cyrus told them to give the Jews silver and gold, animals for the journey, and money to rebuild the temple. Parents, remind your children of the similarity in this story to when the people of God left Egypt and received gifts of silver and gold. Notice that it seems the people of Babylon gave gladly [verse 6].)*

:: What can we learn from these two Bible passages about God? *(We can clearly see that God is in control of kings and even all the people under them. We also learn that, in spite of our sin, God cares for us. Finally, we learn that God keeps his promises.)*

 ## Pray about It

Praise God for always keeping his promises.

DAY TWO

Remember It

What do you remember about yesterday's story? What do you think is going to happen today?

 Read Ezra 3:1–7.

Think about It Some More

Once the people of Israel had settled back in their homes, they gathered in Jerusalem and rebuilt the altar there. You may remember, the reason they were captured by Babylon is because they were following the false idols of the people around them. But now, it seems they have learned their lesson. They didn't rebuild the high places around Jerusalem, nor did they make an altar to Baal. They rebuilt God's altar in the place where it was supposed to be and offered sacrifices to the Lord according to the directions God gave to them through Moses.

Talk about It

:: What lesson did God's people learn by getting captured and held in Babylon for 70 years? *(The people learned that it is wrong to worship idols and idols can't help you. When they returned to Jerusalem they didn't rebuild the high places or altars to false gods.)*

:: What were the people of God afraid of? *(The people of God were afraid of the other people in the land. They still had enemies who would not like them to rebuild their temple.)*

:: Why wasn't it safe in Jerusalem? *(All the walls had been broken down by Nebuchadnezzar. If someone wanted to attack God's people, they would be in danger with no protection from the walls. But God protected them.)*

 Pray about It

Ask God to protect your family from any danger you might face.

DAY THREE

Connect It to Jesus

Can anyone guess how our story this week is about or points forward to Jesus?

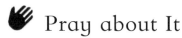 Read Ezra 3:8–13.

Think about It Some More

Some of the people of God who returned to Jerusalem from Babylon were very old. If a boy had been a ten-year-old when he was first captured, he would be an eighty-year-old now, after the 70 years of captivity in Babylon.

Those older men remembered how beautiful Solomon's temple was before it was destroyed. That's why they were sad and crying. But their children, who had grown up in Babylon, had never seen Solomon's temple, so they rejoiced when the foundation was laid.

Even though the new temple was not as big and beautiful, something very special would one day happen there. Jesus would visit this new temple. He would walk across the very foundation they were laying. The older men had good reason to be sad, but if they had only known that Jesus was going to teach in the rebuilt temple, heal the sick there, and teach about the gospel, they would have rejoiced instead of cried.

Talk about It

:: Why did the young men rejoice when the temple foundation was finished? *(They rejoiced because they could build the walls and have a temple again. The temple was where the presence of God lived on earth.)*

:: Why did the older men cry? *(The older men remembered Solomon's temple and knew the new temple would not be as large or as beautiful, so they were sad.)*

:: What made the temple more special than any other building? *(God's presence living in the temple is what made it special. It wasn't just a building; it was where God came down to be with his people.)*

:: What would have cheered the older men up? *(If the older men had known that one day Jesus, God's Son, was going to come down to their temple and live and teach there, they would have been very excited.)*

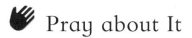 Pray about It

Thank God for bringing his people out of Babylon and helping them rebuild the temple.

DAY FOUR

Remember It

What has God been teaching you this week through our Bible story?

 Read Ezra 4:1–5 and 17–24.

Think about It Some More

Before Nebuchadnezzar attacked Jerusalem, it was a strong city with high walls all around it. But after the battle, Nebuchadnezzar broke down the walls, burned the temple, and destroyed the homes inside the city.

Without its high walls, and with all the strong young men captured, Israel's enemies were happy. They knew that without the walls or an army Israel could not attack them. But now, as we see in our story today, thousands of God's people had returned. They were rebuilding the temple and the walls of the city. This made Israel's enemies afraid again.

Israel's enemies offered to help them so they could see what was going on. But Zerubbabel refused. So Israel's enemies complained to the king, who then ordered the work to be stopped. That discouraged God's people. But they obeyed the king's order and stopped working on the temple and the wall and started rebuilding their homes instead.

Talk about It

> ● ● KIDS, ask your parents if anyone ever tried to stop them from doing
> ● ● something.

(Parents, try to remember a time when a neighbor didn't want you to put up a fence, or a boss didn't want to put up a picture at work; or perhaps you can remember a story from when you were a child and a fellow student tried to stop you from doing something. Even if you don't have a story, help your children identify with the people of God who were afraid.)

:: Why didn't Israel's enemies want them to rebuild Jerusalem? *(Israel's enemies knew that once the walls of the city were finished, Israel would grow strong again. As long as the walls were down, the people of Jerusalem were weak and could not easily fight off an attack.)*

:: What mistake did the people of Jerusalem make? *(They became afraid and stopped the work on the city. They should have known that God is more powerful than their enemies.)*

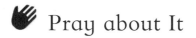 Pray about It

Thank God for his great strength and promise to trust in God when you are afraid.

DAY FIVE

Discover It

Today we look at a passage from a psalm or one of the prophets to see what we can learn from it about Jesus.

 Read Haggai 2:6–9 and John 2:19–22.

Think about It Some More

This Bible story took place when God's people were rebuilding Solomon's temple. Those who were old enough to remember the old temple were sad because the new one was not as nice. But Haggai, one of God's prophets, told them that one day the glory of God's temple would be even greater than it was in Solomon's day. That gave the people of Israel hope that one day a great temple would be built again.

But what they didn't know was that Haggai wasn't talking about building a bigger building or one with more decorations. He was talking about Jesus. When Jesus came, he said his body was the true temple of God. And when we become a Christian, God's Spirit comes to live inside of us so we become a part of God's temple too. Having God's Spirit live in our hearts is way better than having him live in a building.

So you see, Haggai was right: the latter glory of God's temple is much greater than its former glory.

Talk about It

:: Who was Haggai talking about when he said that God's temple would be even greater than it was in Solomon's day? *(Haggai was talking about when God would send his Son to earth to be born as Jesus.)*

:: Why did Jesus say he was God's temple? *(Since Jesus was God, anywhere he went God was living with his people.)*

:: Where does God live today? *(God lives in the heart of every person who believes; together we make up the church where God lives among all his people.)*

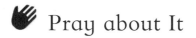 Pray about It

Ask God to save each member of your family so they can become a part of God's temple too.

Week 77

The Temple Is Completed

Gather a few baby photos of each of your children and call them together to show them the pictures. Kids always get a charge out of seeing themselves as babies. After showing them the photos, ask them why we keep photos at all. Explain that we do this to help us remember the special events of our lives so we never forget.

Ask your children if they know how God helped the Israelites to remember the days when Moses led them out of Egypt. The answer is that God commanded them to celebrate the Passover every year. God's directions for the Passover were recorded in the book of Moses (the first five books of the Bible).

Say, "This week you will learn how the Passover tradition was preserved, even through the captivity of the Israelites in Babylon."

DAY ONE

Picture It

Two brothers, Bob and Eric Smith, decided to build a tree house with a few scraps of lumber, in a tree at the back of their yard. But when Sam Jones, the boy who lived behind them, saw it, he complained. He said he was going to report them to his father. He claimed the tree they were building in belonged to his family. But Bob and Eric didn't stop building; they were certain the tree was in their own yard. They had no fence between the yards, so it wasn't always clear where one ended and the other began.

When Mr. Smith came home he assured Bob and Eric that the tree was on their property and encouraged them to keep building their tree house. He phoned Mr. Jones, who then scolded Sam for causing trouble and warned him not to bother Bob and Eric again. Then Mr. Jones directed Sam to collect all their scrap lumber and give it to Bob and Eric for their tree house.

Today we will read how the governor in the land tried to stop Israel from completing the temple, but the people didn't listen. They trusted God and continued to build.

 Read Haggai 1:1–15 and Ezra 5:1–5.

Think about It Some More

When King Ahasuerus had ordered the people of Jerusalem to stop rebuilding the temple and the city, they had become afraid and stopped working. Instead of rebuilding God's house, the people worked on their own homes and gardens. But God didn't bless their crops so, at harvest time, they didn't collect very much grain.

God then sent the prophet Haggai to give them a message. Haggai told God's people to stop work on their own homes and return to working on God's house, the temple. The people obeyed God's word through the prophet and went back to building God's house.

When Tattenai, the local governor, saw them rebuilding he tried to stop them. But God's people didn't stop. This time they trusted God and kept on building.

Talk about It

:: Why were God's people working on their own houses instead of rebuilding God's house? *(They had grown afraid when their enemies opposed them and had stopped working on the temple.)*

:: What did God do to get them to start building his house again? *(The Lord withheld rain so their crops did not grow well. Then he sent the prophet Haggai to tell them to start building God's house again.)*

:: After the people obeyed God and returned to working on the temple, God sent the prophet Haggai to give them another message. What did he tell them? *(Parents, if your children can't read yet, reread Haggai 1:12–13 and have them raise their hands when they have the answer.)*

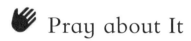 Pray about It

Thank God for patiently helping Israel rebuild the temple.

DAY TWO

Remember It

What do you remember about yesterday's story? What do you think is going to happen today?

 Read Ezra 6:1–12.

Think about It Some More

Governor Tattenai sent word to King Darius that the Jews were rebuilding the temple. He asked the king to investigate to see if the former king, Cyrus, really had given them permission to rebuild. Tattenai probably thought the Jews were making up that story.

King Darius ordered his servants to investigate to see if it was true. They searched the records of the former king. Sure enough, they found the decree from King Cyrus and read it out loud to Darius. Not only had King Cyrus ordered that the temple in Jerusalem be rebuilt, he had also ordered that the royal treasury pay for it.

King Darius ordered Tattenai to allow construction to continue. And, much to Tattenai's surprise, the king ordered him to pay for everything the Jews needed to finish the job. Tattenai must have been shocked. Instead of getting permission to stop the Jews from rebuilding, the king ordered him to help them.

Talk about It

:: What prompted King Cyrus to tell the Jews to rebuild the temple to begin with? *(See if your children can remember that God told King Cyrus to rebuild the temple. To jog their memory, read 2 Chronicles 36:22–23.)*

:: What was the punishment the new king, Darius, said would come upon anyone trying to stop Jews from constructing the temple? *(They would pull a support beam out of that person's house, kill them with it, and turn their home into a dung pile—parents you can explain to your children what a dung pile is. It is safe to say that Tattenai didn't want that to happen to him.)*

:: What do we learn about God from this story? *(We learn that no man can stop God's plan. God can even move the heart of a king to do what God wants him to do. If you notice, Darius includes in his decree a prayer to God, which you can find in verse 12.)*

:: Read Proverbs 21:1 and ask your children how it fits into our story. *(God was able to steer the heart of Cyrus and Darius to help his people finish the temple.)*

 Pray about It

Praise God for the way he can turn the heart of a ruler to do God's will.

DAY THREE

Connect It to Jesus

Can anyone guess how our story this week is about or points forward to Jesus?

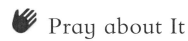 Read Ezra 6:13–22.

Think about It Some More

When the new temple was completed, over 700 animals were sacrificed as an offering to God for the sins of the people. By killing animals for their sins, they were saying that they knew they were sinners who needed to be saved from their sins.

These sacrifices pointed to the day God would send his Son Jesus to die on the cross. God's people also celebrated the Passover by killing a lamb for each family. They didn't realize it at the time, but the Passover lamb also pointed to Jesus, the Lamb of God, who would one day come to take away their sins.

Talk about It

:: Why were the people so happy to see the temple rebuilt? *(The temple was God's house where he lived among his people. God's people were happy because they believed God was going to live among them. He could protect them and bless them like in the days of David.)*

:: Why did God's people kill animals when they finished the temple? *(The way God taught his people to worship him was by sacrificing animals. They also killed animals as sin offerings. By killing those animals, they were confessing their sin before God and asking him to forgive them.)*

:: Who does the Passover lamb point forward to? *(The Passover lamb pointed forward to Jesus, who died on the cross for our sins.)*

 ## Pray about It

Thank God we don't have to kill any animals for our sins. Jesus paid the price for our sin once and for all.

DAY FOUR

Remember It

What has God been teaching you this week through our Bible story?

 Read Ezra 7.

Think about It Some More

Once again we see how God was working in the hearts of kings to help his people. King Artaxerxes gave Ezra permission to return to Jerusalem with anyone who wanted to go. On top of that, the king ordered that gold and silver and special gifts be given for use in the temple. When Ezra heard all that the king had ordered to help God's people, he knew that God was behind it all.

Talk about It

> ● ● KIDS, ask your parents which president or ruler of a foreign country
> ● ● they would be most surprised to see God use to bless his people today.

(Parents, think of a ruler of a foreign country who is not serving God that would surprise you if he changed and started serving God. Tell your children why you would be so surprised.)

:: What surprised you the most about what the king said to Ezra? *(If you have younger children, reread the king's letter and have them raise their hands when they come across the part that surprised them the most.)*

:: Why was Ezra the right person to teach God's people? *(Ezra knew the law of God.)*

Pray about It

Thank God for the way he used foreign kings to accomplish his plan.

DAY FIVE

Discover It

Today we look at a passage from a psalm or one of the prophets to see what we can learn from it about Jesus.

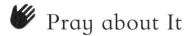 Read Zechariah 3:1–5.

Think about It Some More

In this prophecy Zechariah is describing a courtroom. There are three people in the courtroom: Satan, the Angel of the Lord (another name for God), and Joshua (who represents all of God's people).

In the prophecy Joshua stands, dressed in filthy clothes, before the king. His dirty clothes represent his and all of our sins. When Satan sees the dirty clothes, he begins to accuse him (he tells Joshua he is a bad person). But God stops Satan and tells him that Joshua has been rescued out of the fire. Then God gives Joshua bright, white, pure, clean clothes to wear.

This vision is a picture of what God does for everyone who trusts in Jesus. When we trust the Lord, our sins (our dirty clothes) are taken away and God gives us clean clothes to wear (the sinlessness or righteousness of Jesus).

Talk about It

:: Why did Satan accuse Joshua? *(Joshua was standing before the king in dirty clothes.)*

:: What do the dirty clothes stand for? *(The dirty clothes stand for sin.)*

:: What do the clean clothes stand for? *(The clean clothes stand for the sinlessness of Jesus.)*

:: Who does Joshua represent or stand for in the story? *(Joshua represents all believers, everyone who trusts in Jesus.)*

 Pray about It

Thank God for taking away our sin and giving the sinlessness of Jesus to everyone who trusts in the Lord.

Week 78

Nehemiah

Take your children to your front door and show them how thick and hard the door is and how the lock works. Then ask them the following questions to stimulate a discussion:

    :: *Why do we build houses with strong front doors? (One reason is that they keep out animals and bad weather.)*

    :: *Why do we have locks on our doors? (To keep out people we don't want to come into our homes.)*

    :: *Why do some people put up fences around their yards? (To give privacy, and sometimes to keep pets in and unwanted animals and people out.)*

    :: *Why were walls built around the city of Jerusalem? (For all the same reasons we have locks and doors and fences. The walls protected the city from attack and intrusion.)*

    Say, "This week you will learn how God moved Nehemiah to rebuild Jerusalem's walls."

DAY ONE

Picture It

Imagine how sad you would be if you heard that your grandparents' house was burned to the ground, and they were living in a tent until it could be rebuilt. Wouldn't you and your family be sad when you heard the news and want to pray for them and go to help them?

In our story today, a man named Nehemiah heard that the walls of Jerusalem were broken down and the gates had been burned by fire. He became very sad at the news and prayed to God for help.

 Read Nehemiah 1.

Think about It Some More

Nehemiah was the cupbearer to King Artaxerxes. Artaxerxes was the same king who gave permission to Ezra to return to his people in Jerusalem, and he gave all the gold and silver and other gifts to help rebuild the temple. When Nehemiah heard that the walls of Jerusalem were still broken down, he was very sad because that meant that God's people and the temple of the Lord were open to attack. But instead of becoming afraid, Nehemiah prayed to the Lord for help.

Talk about It

:: Why was Nehemiah sad? *(The walls of Jerusalem were broken down and the gates were burned.)*

:: Why were the walls of Jerusalem so important? *(The walls protected the people who lived inside from robbers and attack. Parents, remind your children of how your front door locks to keep people out who don't belong in your home.)*

:: What was the most special thing inside the walls of Jerusalem? *(God's rebuilt temple was inside the walls.)*

Pray about It

Read Nehemiah's prayer in verse 5 and use it to praise God like Nehemiah did.

DAY TWO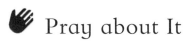

Remember It

What do you remember about yesterday's story? What do you think is going to happen today?

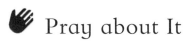 Read Nehemiah 2.

Think about It Some More

Nehemiah was a courageous man. He was not afraid to ask the king to send him to Jerusalem to repair the walls. He wasn't afraid to stand up and challenge the people of Jerusalem to start the work. And he wasn't afraid of Sanballat, who accused him of rebelling against the king. The reason Nehemiah could be so courageous and brave was that he trusted the Lord.

Talk about It

:: Who gave Nehemiah the idea to fix the walls of Jerusalem? *(In verse 12 Nehemiah said that God put it on his heart to fix the walls. Parents, if your children don't know the answer, have them look up verse 12. If they can't read, read that verse and have them raise their hands when they have the answer.)*

:: What did Nehemiah do at night? *(Nehemiah inspected the walls of the city.)*

:: When Nehemiah answered Sanballat, whom did he say was going to help them rebuild the walls? *(Nehemiah said that God was going to help them rebuild the walls.)*

 Pray about It

Ask God to give you courage to live for him like Nehemiah did.

DAY THREE

Connect It to Jesus

Can anyone guess how our story this week is about or points forward to Jesus?

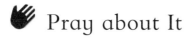 Read Nehemiah 3.

(Parents, this is a long section of Scripture. If you have younger children, read Nehemiah 3:1–15. Reading the whole list of repairs helps to give a picture of how all the families worked together to finish the job.)

Think about It Some More

God gave Nehemiah a great plan: all the families of Jerusalem would work together to rebuild the wall. With everybody helping, the job of rebuilding the huge walls of Jerusalem could be completed quickly.

Nehemiah assigned each family to work on the wall near their own house. The people were glad to rebuild the walls where they lived because the walls protected their homes from attack. All around Jerusalem the families were working to complete the project.

While they were working, there was something special happening that they didn't know about. One day, about 400 years later, Jesus would walk along the very walls they were rebuilding, and he would walk through the gates of Jerusalem they were repairing. They didn't know it, but their work to rebuild the walls of Jerusalem was a part of God's plan to save his people from their sin.

One day Jesus would teach at the temple they rebuilt and be arrested within the walls they were rebuilding. Then, when Jesus was found guilty, he would once again walk through one of the gates in the wall to be crucified just outside the city.

Talk about It

:: What was Nehemiah's plan on how to get the large wall around Jerusalem rebuilt? *(Nehemiah assigned each family to rebuild the wall near their own house.)*

:: If you lived in Jerusalem why would you want to rebuild the wall near your house? *(The wall protected Israel from attack. If you didn't repair the wall near your house, and enemies attacked, guess where they would try to come? That's right—in the very spot where you lived.)*

:: What do you think Sanballat thought when he saw the whole wall going up in front of him? *(We will learn about Sanballat tomorrow, but he wasn't too happy.)*

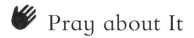 Pray about It

Thank God for the wisdom he gave Nehemiah in rebuilding the walls of Jerusalem.

DAY FOUR

Remember It

What has God been teaching you this week through our Bible story?

 Read Nehemiah 4 and 6:15–16.

Think about It Some More

At first Sanballat made fun of the people of Jerusalem who were working to rebuild the huge walls of Jerusalem. But when he heard the breaches (holes) in the wall were being closed up, he stopped laughing. He knew that when the openings were closed and the wall rebuilt, he would have a hard time attacking Jerusalem if he wanted. Israel would grow strong again. Then they could attack Sanballat!

That's why Sanballat gathered together the other leaders in the area to form an army. They wanted to plan a surprise attack to defeat God's people before the wall was finished.

But God made sure their plan was discovered by Nehemiah. When he found out, he gathered the people of God to pray and then ordered them to guard the lowest parts of the wall with weapons. When Sanballat heard the workers were armed with swords and spears, he realized his plan to attack by surprise wouldn't work. Every day the workers took their weapons with them. If Sanballat tried to attack, the people of God were ready for him. With each passing day the openings of the wall were closing up, and the wall grew taller until attack was impossible and the wall was finished.

The sad part is that, even though the walls of Jerusalem were rebuilt, and the people confessed their sin and promised to follow God (Nehemiah 9), God's people still sinned against him. Rebuilding Jerusalem and the temple was not enough. God needed to send Jesus, his only Son, to die on the cross to take away our sin.

Talk about It

> ● ● KIDS, ask your parents if they can remember a **time when they**
> ● ● worked together with a bunch of folks to get a **big job done.**

(Parents, try to remember a big job that was made easier by a large group of people. Perhaps a group of your friends helped a person move or build a house on a mission trip.)

:: Who did Nehemiah say frustrated Sanballat's plan to attack? *(If your children don't remember the answer, have them look at 4:15 or read it to your younger children and have them raise their hands as soon as they know the answer. God frustrated Sanballat's plan.)*

:: What did the people inside the city do while they worked to discourage anyone from attacking them? *(They brought their swords and spears and bow and arrows to use to fight. That way if an enemy spy came to see what was going on, he would see they were not only working—they were also armed.)*

:: How long did they work each day? *(They worked all day long, from the time the sun rose at dawn, until the stars shone in the sky at night.)*

 ## Pray about It

Thank God for helping his people finish the walls of Jerusalem.

DAY FIVE

Discover It

Today we look at a passage from a psalm or one of the prophets to see what we can learn from it about Jesus.

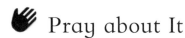 Read Zechariah 3:8–10.

Think about It Some More

Several times in these lessons we have seen where the prophets of old use the code word "branch" to refer to Jesus. (For example, see Isaiah 4:2; 11:1–2; and Jeremiah 23:5; 33:15–16.) Here in our last lesson of the Old Testament, Zechariah said something amazing. He said that this Branch will remove the iniquity (take away the sins) of God's people in a single day.

That is exactly what Jesus did when he died on the cross and took the punishment we deserved. On the cross when Jesus said, "It is finished" (John 19:30), he meant that the punishment God poured out on him (instead of us) was finished and taken away. In a single day, the Branch had taken away the sins of the world.

Talk about It

:: Who is the Branch that Zechariah is talking about? *(The Branch is Jesus.)*

:: What did Zechariah say the Branch would do in a single day? *(Zechariah said that he would remove the iniquity [the sins] of God's people in a single day.)*

:: What did Jesus do to take all our sins away in a single day? *(Jesus died on the cross and took the punishment we deserved upon himself.)*

 ## Pray about It

Thank Jesus for taking all our sins away by his death and resurrection from the dead.